# THE COMPACT HISTORY OF THE CIVIL WAR

COL. R. ERNEST DUPUY and
COL. TREVOR N. DUPUY, U.S. ARMY (RET.)

MJF BOOKS

NEW YORK

Published by MJF Books
Fine Communications
Two Lincoln Square
60 West 66th Street
New York, NY 10023

*The Compact History of the Civil War*
ISBN 1-56731-393-0

Manufactured in the United States of America on acid-free paper

MJF Books and the MJF colophon are trademarks of Fine Creative Media, Inc.

10  9  8  7  6  5  4  3  2  1

*To little Laura*

# ACKNOWLEDGMENTS

To Laura Nevitt Dupuy the authors owe much. As usual, her clarity of vision has kept us from deviating from our intended purpose, and her constructive criticism has vastly improved the quality of our work.

Christine G. Dupuy's meticulous assistance in the preparation of the maps has been most valuable.

To N. J. Anthony, associate editor of *Army*, whose encyclopedic knowledge of Civil War operations has on a number of occasions assisted in resolving questions of places and names, goes our sincere appreciation.

# CONTENTS

☆ **ix** ☆

# LIST OF MAPS

☆ **xi** ☆

# CONVENTIONAL MAP SYMBOLS

*Frequently Used*

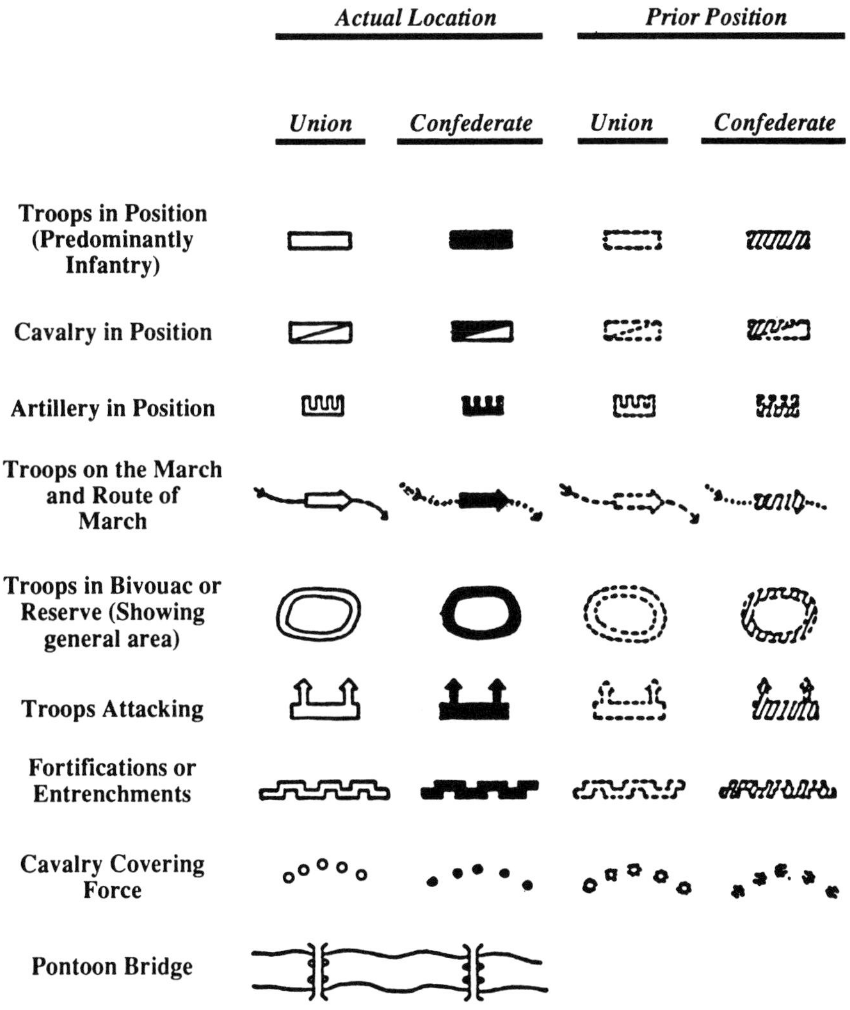

Actual Location
Prior Position
Union
Confederate
Union
Confederate
Troops in Position (Predominantly Infantry)
Cavalry in Position
Artillery in Position
Troops on the March and Route of March
Troops in Bivouac or Reserve (Showing general area)
Troops Attacking
Fortifications or Entrenchments
Cavalry Covering Force
Pontoon Bridge

# AUTHOR'S NOTE

Why does the American Civil War continue to hold such great fascination for so many Americans? The old debates continue, as vigorously north of the Mason and Dixon Line as to the south. Providing fuel for the debates, every year there is a flood of new books about the war and about some of its many, many aspects. And also many old classics are republished, demonstrating that the issues of the numerous debates change little as time goes on.

Apparently, a book that my father and I wrote a little more than thirty years ago, *The Compact History of the Civil War*, has achieved status as such a classic, and is being republished. I am sorry that my father cannot join me in writing this note for the very slightly revised, republished version. But, were he here, I think he would agree that a suitable theme is those continuing debates, even though most of them are no more likely to be settled a century and a third from now than they were a century and a third ago.

But a recent experience leads me to a slightly different

theme. I shall still focus on the debates, but in such a way as to challenge the reader to try quantified analysis to resolve some of the debate issues. Let's begin by listing ten of several hundred potential debate topics:

1. Which side won the Battle of Antietam?
2. Was the outcome at Antietam affected by Lee's lost order?
3. Could Lee have won at Gettysburg?
4. Why didn't Lee win at Gettysburg?
5. Did Johnson outgeneral Sherman from Chattanooga to Atlanta in 1864?
6. Did Lee outgeneral Grant in Virginia in 1864?
7. Was Grant a "butcher"?
8. Was Lee at Malvern Hill and Gettysburg as much a "butcher" as Grant was at Cold Harbor?
9. Were Southern generals better than Northern generals?
10. Were Southern soldiers better fighters than Northern soldiers?

This list can be continued almost indefinitely. But for the moment let's look only at the first two debate topics listed above: Who won Antietam? Was the Antietam outcome influenced by the "lost order"? The experience that led to the challenge I am throwing out to you, dear reader, is that, quite by chance, I recently used Antietam data to check the utility for historical analysis of a computer model or simulation I have designed: the Tactical Numerical Deterministic Model (TNDM). Most of the key data will be found in Chapter 12.

Analysis with the TNDM showed that the engaged forces of the two armies fought themselves to a bloody standstill. On the defensive, the Confederates had the benefit of some simple, numerical multiplying factors, described in a book I wrote several years ago (*Numbers, Predictions, and War*): defensive posture, worth 1.3; defensible terrain, a factor of 1.2; and an all-out defense effort, a factor of 1.1, influenced by an unfordable river behind the Confederates. Lee's 38,566 men and 219 guns held their positions—barely—at Sharpsburg against 65,820 Union troops with 293 guns. (The Union numerical advantage of 1.7:1.0 was exactly offset by the three listed multiplying factors.) The fighting capability of the Northerners almost exactly matched that of the Southerners. (Which, incidentally, gives an answer to debate topic 10, above.)

However, the Southerners accomplished their mission, which was to maintain their defensive positions near Sharpsburg and to repel the Union attack. The Northerners failed to accomplish their mission, which was to drive the Confederates from Sharpsburg and back into the Potomac River. (The Civil War would have been decided that afternoon had the Union troops accomplished their mission.) Thus, the tactical victory was unarguably with the Confederates—even though the matter is sometimes argued.

Equally unarguable is the fact that—aided by the information received from Lee's "lost order"—McClellan had blocked the Confederate invasion of the North. The outcome of the Antietam Campaign was a strategic victory for the North.

But what does the quantitative analysis, summarized very simplistically above, tell us about the generalship of the two commanders? Quite a bit! Since McClellan had available another 23,000 men, who never got into the battle, his numerical preponderance was 2.28:1:00. With total multiplying factors of 1.7 for Confederate defensive advantage, McClellan had a 1.34 combat power advantage—and he didn't use it! Manipulating the figures one way, and rating Lee's generalship at 100 percent, then McClellan's was 74 percent. Manipulating another way, McClellan's generalship can be calculated at 56 percent, against Lee's 100 percent. In either event, whatever was the difference in generalship, it meant that the war continued for two and a half years, instead of ending in 1862, as it should have under competent Union generalship at Antietam.

However, for you, dear reader, what I have shown suggests

a method of using data in this book, and elsewhere, to seek a quantified approach to resolving at least some of the hoary debate topics of the Civil War. How about Gettysburg?

T. N. Dupuy
McLean, Virginia
November, 1992

# PREFACE

The Civil War was the greatest emotional experience of our nation. Hence its unceasing attraction for Americans. It gripped the physical existence of an entire generation and embraced the total economy of the country.

Not alone were those affected who heeded the call to arms. Remote from the battlefields, the farmer and the planter, the banker and the blacksmith, the artisan and the artist, in both North and South, were enmeshed in the gears of their respective war machines. They became cogs often as vital to the prosecution of the war as the lean soldiers and sailors who, every so often, shot at one another in anger and—in between times—swapped tobacco, coffee, newspapers and wit.

The Civil War brought about important changes in America's social and economic way of life, and in the role our government could and would play in international affairs. No other period in our history has so broadly affected our national outlook, so influenced the growth of the United States, and so enriched our literature.

The military lessons learned and paid for in blood, tears and treasure would, of course, be utilized overseas by the grandsons and great grandsons of the men who wore the Blue and the Gray. The Civil War was the first conflict of the technological age, pointing the way to subsequent developments affecting the art and drudgery of war throughout the world.

It would be ridiculous to suggest that the Civil War, with its terrible toll of lives, was a good thing for the United States. A peaceful solution of the differences which split the country asunder would have been infinitely better, for all wars are intrinsically evil. But a peaceful solution of these differences was probably impossible. Unlike most wars, this one settled the issues for which it was fought, and the solution was accepted as fully by the vanquished as by the victors. For this reason the Civil War has become an inspiration not only to Americans, but also to the world.

The saga of 1861–1865 must be indelibly preserved in our national memory as a symbol of American determination, courage and ingenuity, and as the springboard from which America leaped from insignificance to world importance.

The end product of the Civil War was a nation undivided, and a government of the people, by the people, and for the people. Its history, therefore, has become a monument to our national rebirth.

The patina of one hundred years glosses over the tragedy of the war. And this patina has partly obscured the salient features of the war. The causes and effects of the military operations have, to a large degree, merged into patterns created by a century of wishful thinking and partisan apologiæ. Consequently, the achievements and failures of leadership have been distorted in popular legend. The unfortunate result is that truth has suffered.

The average American pictures the Civil War as having been fought and won in Northern Virginia and nearby regions of the

Potomac Valley, while a number of unrelated and relatively minor operations were also being conducted further west in the Mississippi River basin. Actually the war was decided in the West, while the great armies defending Washington and Richmond were locked in a bloody stalemate. The passage of time has also obscured the significance of naval operations to the war strategies of the opposing nations, and has almost blotted out, from our image of the war, the decisive contributions of both Northern and Southern seamen.

Perhaps the clearest popular war image is that portraying Abraham Lincoln as the noble war President of the United States. Yet, it seems that the remarkable growth of his stature, and of his understanding of military strategy and tactics as the war progressed, has become obscured.

The image of Lincoln's misunderstood opposite number, Confederate Jefferson Davis, is really befogged.

The all-important roles of both these men must be clarified. As commanders-in-chief of the opposing armed forces, they were responsible for the military as well as the political strategies of their nations. What these two men and their civilian advisers did or did not do, and how they reacted to the sentiments and passions of their respective electorates, significantly affected the fortunes of their armed forces on the battlefield.

The balanced story of the Civil War is one of land and sea power in combination and opposition; of economic and political pressures; and of the interplay between civil and military power in this total war.

This is the story we have attempted to put on paper, in an effort to present the "big picture," so seldom visible amidst fantastic wealth of factual detail and cherished legend.

# 1

# Dawn's Early Light

At 4:30 A.M., on April 12, 1861, a 10-inch mortar shell screamed in a high arc halfway across Charleston Harbor, South Carolina. It struck and burst inside red-bricked Fort Sumter, squatting on the Middle Ground shoal that splits the harbor mouth.

Major General Pierre Gustave Toutant Beauregard, Confederate States Army, commanding secessionist forces at Charleston, had opened formal hostilities in the Civil War. Incidentally, he had also set a pattern for the four-year struggle. For West Pointer Beauregard, erstwhile brevet Major, United States Army, was attacking a post defended by Major Robert Anderson, USA, also a graduate of the U.S. Military Academy at West Point. Not only was the nation split asunder, but the Army was to be divided against itself, with former comrades-in-arms leading opposing forces in battle.

Beauregard followed his opening shot with cross-cannonading from heavy batteries emplaced on both sides of the harbor.

As dawn broke the Stars and Stripes went fluttering up on Fort Sumter's staff and the Union fortress spoke in counter-battery. But Anderson had been virtually besieged for almost four months; his rations were exhausted and he was forced to capitulate on the 14th, after thirty-four hours of intense though bloodless bombardment. The garrison, marching out with the honors of war after a final salute to their flag, embarked for the North on board the vessels of a U.S. Navy flotilla which had been just offshore observing the engagement—silent because its commander had taken his orders literally to await the arrival of an additional warship.

In such a fashion was a political upheaval referred to the arbitration of war.

But the Civil War didn't really begin with the shelling of Fort Sumter. It had begun many years before, when the Industrial Revolution and the western expansion of the United States brought the divergent economies of the industrial North and the agricultural South into collision.

The Negro was the focal point of this clash. Without his slave labor, on which the economic structure of the South was based, the Southern economy would crumble. The institution of slavery was abhorrent to many Northerners, who hoped to abolish it through potent political and propaganda pressure on the Federal government. A Northern preponderance in Congress would result in the destruction of slavery and with it the Southern economy. Hence, any deviation from the political balance of 1819, when free and slaveholding states were equal in number—eleven each—was resented and actively opposed by the South.

The trouble began slowly, with wars of words and legal actions. The Missouri Compromise of 1820 was followed in 1850 by the clash on the Senate floor of those giants of debate, Webster, Calhoun, and Clay. As the Kansas Territory approached statehood in 1856, emotions rose to fever pitch in the established states as well as on the frontier. Violence flared. Northern and Southern tempers were further inflamed by news of the bloodthirsty sacking and burning of the abolitionist settlement at Lawrence, Kansas, by a lawless mob of border ruffians, and of John Brown's retaliation in the equally grisly massacre of pro-slavery adherents at nearby Pottawatomie. Even more shocking evidence of the state of America's emotions at this time was the brutal, and almost fatal, bludgeoning of Massachusetts' Senator Charles Sumner by North Carolina's Representative Preston S. Brooks on the very floor of the Senate itself. The famous Dred Scott case in 1857, and the Lincoln-Douglas debates of 1858 heightened the tension and the hatreds.

Then the grim figure of John Brown once again stalked briefly across the national stage. In October, 1859, hoping to spark a slave uprising, Brown and a small group of fellow fanatics tried to seize the U.S. arsenal at Harper's Ferry, Virginia. Here he hoped to get the arms with which to equip the slaves whom he expected would flock to his banner. Quickly subdued by a mixed Army-Marine force, under the command of Colonel Robert E. Lee, USA, Brown's effort failed utterly. A few weeks later he was hanged for treason. Southern extremists now had all the evidence they needed to prove that abolitionists would not only defy law in order to destroy slavery, but that they would also incite the slaves to riot and to massacre the white population of the South in order to accomplish this purpose. If any one event made war inevitable, it was John Brown's raid.

In the North abolitionists were whipped to frenzy by 1,200,000 copies of Harriet Beecher Stowe's *Uncle Tom's Cabin*, first published in 1852. In the South the emotional escape reaction centered on "States' rights," the concept that the United States was a voluntary confederacy of independent nations, any of whom were free to break away at will if they disagreed with Federal interference.

Lost in the darkening turmoil were two inherent contradictions. Only a small minority of Southerners owned slaves at all. On the other hand, not a few of the smug, self-righteous New

Englanders and New Yorkers who prated of the black man's rights to liberty were still amassing fortunes in the old, abominable but lucrative trade in "black ivory"; shipment of unfortunate captives for sale as slaves in the Western Hemisphere.

Political impasse was reached at the polls November 6, 1860, when Republican Abraham Lincoln was swept into the Presidency over a Democratic party split three ways; between support of States' rights, of the Constitution, and of slavery. The Republican platform specifically condemned attempts to reopen the African slave trade, and denied the authority of Congress or of a territorial legislature to give legal status to slavery in the territories.

South Carolina's reaction to the election was quick and violent. A state convention was hurriedly called at Columbia; and without one dissenting voice voted on December 20 to secede from the Union. The landslide had started. On January 9, Mississippi followed South Carolina's lead; Florida the next day and Alabama the day after that. On January 19, Georgia broke away, followed by Louisiana on the twenty-sixth and Texas on February 1.

Authorities and militia of the seceding states began seizing Government property—Army posts and Navy yards—forcing their Federal garrisons to capitulate. In Texas, septuagenarian Major General David E. Twiggs traitorously surrendered his entire department to local authorities on February 18.

The United States was splitting at the seams, yet few Northern people realized the danger or knew what to do about it. Lieutenant General Winfield Scott, commanding the Army, as early as October had urged reinforcement of the garrisons of all southern coastal forts. But Scott was old; Secretary of War John B. Floyd was violently pro-Southern; and President James Buchanan, with elections only a month away, procrastinated. As their world crumbled about them, a few men in uniform attempted to preserve the property, prestige and authority of their Government in the seceding states. Receiving from Washington only admonitions for appeasement and conciliation, some were bold enough to seize the initiative.

At Charleston, hotbed of secession, the harbor defense garrison was, as we have noted, commanded by Kentucky-born Major Anderson. When South Carolina seceded on December 20, 1860, Anderson's command was stationed in crumbling Fort Moultrie, its weak defenses inviting land attack from the threatening South Carolina militia. On December 26, Anderson secretly and efficiently moved his entire force—seven officers and seventy-six enlisted men—into the most defensible post in the harbor; partly-completed Fort Sumter, on its tiny island at the harbor mouth.

On January 9, 1861, a futile attempt was made by the Government to reinforce and supply the Sumter garrison by means of an unarmed steamer, *Star of the West*. South Carolinian shore batteries opened fire on her—the first shots of the Civil War. The transport turned and stood out to sea.

At the same time that Anderson occupied Fort Sumter, similar action by Regular Army officers at three other army posts in the South also took place. Fort Pickens, guarding the mouth of Pensacola harbor, Florida; Fort Taylor, Key West; and Fort Jefferson, Dry Tortugas—all of them key locations—were saved for the Union.

Events now marched rapidly. On February 4, delegates from the seceding states convened at Montgomery, Alabama, to frame a constitution, establish a provisional government, provide for armed forces, and elect as President Jefferson Davis of Mississippi; West Pointer, Mexican War hero and former U.S. Senator as well as U.S. Secretary of War.

Two days after Lincoln was inaugurated as President of a sluggish and seemingly disintegrating United States, Jefferson Davis, on authorization from the Confederate Congress, issued a call for 100,000 volunteers for one year's military service. The Confederate States Army had been born. By mid-April 1861, 35,000 men were under arms; a force twice as large as the then-existing U.S. Army.

\* \* \*

By attacking and capturing Fort Sumter, the South had now thrown its gauntlet down in earnest. Abraham Lincoln picked it up. On April 15, proclaiming that ''insurrection'' existed, the President called upon the states to provide 75,000 militia for three months' service.

Virginia, declaring that Lincoln's call to arms constituted an invasion of the Southland, seceded April 17. Arkansas, North Carolina and Tennessee soon followed suit. By May 20, eleven states were in armed, open rebellion; a rebellion which could be quelled only by force, which, at the time, did not exist.

The U.S. Army strength in early 1861 was 16,367 officers and men. The 198 line companies were so scattered as to preclude any mobilization in force; 183 of them on the wide Western frontier or en route to various distant points, and the 15 remaining distributed along the Canadian border and Atlantic coast.

The militia, 3,000,000 strong on paper, was in fact a huge unorganized mob. The President could call it to duty with Federal troops provided the respective state governors acquiesced—but this service was limited to three months by a law unchanged since 1795.

A few units of volunteer militia in both north and south were uniformed, and had some semblance of training, but the military élan of most of the militia was restricted to an annual one-day muster, more of a whisky-flavored picnic than a military gathering. When Lincoln's call did come, the militia of the states seceding or about to secede were lost to the United States.

The United States Navy in 1861 consisted of a mere ninety wooden craft of various categories; many of them were sailing vessels, the others combining both sail and steam. The Navy was scattered all over the world, with part of its ships laid up for repairs. Only forty-two vessels were actually in commission. There were a dozen comparatively new steam cruisers; five frigates and seven sloops of war. But of armor-clad vessels, to which European navies were already turning, there were none. In the home squadron of thirteen vessels, only four lay in Northern waters ready for immediate use. Naval personnel consisted of 1,300 officers and 6,700 enlisted men.

Both Regular Army and Navy were, like the rest of the nation, divided by secession. Commissioned personnel only were affected; enlisted men, who had contracted to serve for a stated period of time, had no choice but to stay or desert. Less than fifty soldiers and sailors in all fled the United States colors. But officers, by long-established custom of the services, were at liberty to resign their commissions at will, and a number did so.

Of 1,036 Army officers on active service, 286 resigned and went south; 322 of the 1,300 Navy officers did likewise. With the flagrant exception of General Twiggs' treasonable surrender in Texas, these officers honored their oath of allegiance to the United States until their actual departure from their posts. The great majority were most meticulous in turning over their commands and accounts in strict conformity to regulations.

Among these officers were a few Northerners, impelled by ties of marriage or of association. Notable among them were Pennsylvanian John C. Pemberton and New Yorker Samuel Cooper. The former, quitting his captaincy of artillery, became a Lieutenant General; the latter, a Colonel Adjutant-General, became Adjutant General of the Confederate Army and its senior general officer. A number of Southerners held unwaveringly to the old flag; men like George H. Thomas, soldier from Virginia; and the Navy's David Glasgow Farragut, born in Tennessee. In civil life there were men like Texan hero Sam Houston, who was deposed as Governor when he refused to swear allegiance to the Confederacy. But foremost in the ranks of men of Southern birth who spurned secession was the Army's General-in-Chief, doughty old General Scott, Virginian through and through.

Once the attack on Sumter made war a certainty, Scott, his brilliant mind unimpaired by his seventy-four years, made a thoughtful and objective estimate of the situation. As immediate measures, he urged naval blockade of Southern ports and the raising of a tremendous army—300,000 men or more. As soon as that army was equipped and trained, he would launch an invasion of the South down the Mississippi River. Once the river was held, down to the Gulf, the Confederacy would be in a vise, between Union army and navy, isolated from the world and from all possibility of obtaining the supplies needed for carrying on a war. Constant and increasing pressure would be maintained until, after months or even years, the rebellious states would be overwhelmed and forcibly brought back to the Union.

But the thought of a long, expensive and probably bloody war was not palatable in Washington in the spring of 1861. Quick, cheap victory was demanded by the politicians. Scott's concept of squeezing the South into submission, as a snake might crush its prey, was half-derisively dubbed the "Anaconda Plan" by those who counted on the early collapse of Southern resistance. President Lincoln adopted the blockade suggestion immediately after the fall of Fort Sumter. Scott's other major strategic suggestions were generally ignored or forgotten. Yet the old general was probably the only man in the United States capable of evaluating the complex strategic problems facing the two governments.

Geographically, the Confederacy was a territorial entity bounded on the north by the Union, on the east by the Atlantic Ocean, on the south by the Gulf of Mexico and the Mexican Rio Grande border, and on the west by the Rocky Mountains. Its most prominent and important terrain feature was the Mississippi River, splitting the area from the north to the south. The population of the eleven seceding states consisted of 5,500,000 whites and 3,500,000 negro slaves. There were 22,000,000 inhabitants in the twenty-two Northern states (including three border states with divided loyalties).

These population figures would indicate a gross superiority in Union manpower. However, the slaves in the South performed labor which in the North had to be done by free white men. Actually, the ratio of available combat manpower was about five to two in favor of the North. The North, in both manufacture and agriculture, was an economic entity capable of supporting a protracted war. The South was an agricultural area; its principal crops, cotton, tobacco and sugar, were valuable mainly on the foreign market. The Confederacy's capability for united economic effort, insofar as manufacture was concerned, was small. In a nutshell, the North was self-sufficient; the South depended on its ability to market its produce abroad and import war matériel. There was its Achilles heel.

Yet this Northern economic superiority can be overestimated. The industrial and mobilization capability was, of course, there—a capability which in the end would prove to be decisive. But in 1861 this was only a potential capability for war support; the North was entirely unprepared for its transition to wartime needs, and there was considerable resistance to any such change.

There was also an important psychological factor. While the Southern white population was almost uniformly determined in its objective, the North was far from being united in its opposition both to States' rights and to slavery. Many of the most fervent abolitionists and patriotic unionists were hesitant when their objective could be attained only by war.

The South, having set up a *de facto* government, would be successful so long as that government and its armed forces remained intact on Confederate soil. The Federal government could compel the seceding states to return to the Union only by invasion, establishing an unchallenged control over the entire region, and eliminating all armed resistance. A stalemate, or anything short of total Federal triumph, would, *ipso facto,* be a Confederate victory.

The Southern leaders were fully aware of the greater war potential of the North, and were never under any illusions that they might be able to invade and conquer the loyal states. Yet they thought—and not without valid reason—that their strength in manpower and other resources were adequate, in a defensive strategy, to offset the greater potential of the North.

Of particular strategic significance, in the eyes of Confederate leaders, was the political and economic importance of cotton. The bulk of the world's raw cotton came from Southern fields, and was manufactured into cloth by the great mills of England's Midlands.

Jefferson Davis' assertion that "cotton is king!" was a reflection of his confidence that internal economic pressures would force Britain to take whatever action was necessary to assure the flow of Southern raw cotton to her mills. Thus, Davis expected, as a minimum, British economic support and, if necessary, outright military intervention.

The weakening of the United States, by its division into two sovereign nations, would also be favorable to the ambitions of France's Napoleon III, already planning the re-establishment of French power in the western hemisphere through adventures in Mexico. From the outset, this possibility of foreign aid was a major consideration in the political and military strategy of the Confederacy.

Barring such aid, the result of a protracted war, waged by a determined, united Northern people, would be inevitable. But the Union could be held firm to the grim, painful, costly task of fighting such a war only under the most capable political and military leadership. As one historian has aptly written: "The South merely had to make the North so tired of the war that it would give up the conquest and let the Confederates have their own government in peace." It came very close to working out that way.

As we have noted, the North's manpower advantage was approximately five to two. Given the military rule of thumb that, all other things being equal, successful offensive requires a three to one superiority, while a successful defense can be fought with a one to two inferiority, it is apparent that the differing strategical missions of the two opponents cancelled out the apparent Northern manpower superiority. Once the issue was joined, furthermore, the South had the advantage of interior lines. In addition, Northern generals, invading a hostile, united and determined nation, would be forced to use a great percentage of their available military strength merely to protect lines of communication.

From the broad strategic point of view, this was initially a war between two relatively evenly-matched antagonists. In fact, so long as either political disunity or military incompetence persisted in the North, it is fair to state that a slight strategic advantage rested with the South.

The Confederate Government enhanced this advantage by a wiser military policy. As we have noted, by April the Confederacy had twice as many men under arms as the United States. When Lincoln called for 75,000 militia volunteers after Fort Sumter, under the law he could request these only for a three-month period. On the other hand, the first 100,000 men of the Confederate Army, who began to flock to the colors early in March, were enlisted for twelve months.

The skilful utilization of the experienced officers of the "Old Army" was another example of Southern military wisdom. They were spread as an effective leavening throughout the entire new army. Thus the South—unlike the North, as we shall see—was able to take maximum advantage of its slender resources of trained military leadership, and the results were soon demonstrated by the Confederate Army.

The Confederate Navy was something else again. Having no warships in commission, it would have to start from scratch. Its personnel, headed by former U.S. Navy officers of experience, would not lack in ability. The Secretary of the Confederate Navy, Stephen R. Mallory of Florida, was a driver of ingenuity, administrative ability and experience. He had been chairman of the U.S. Senate Committee on Naval Affairs. He would remain at the head of the Confederate Navy till the end of the war.

The first Confederate Secretary of War (there would be five in all) was Leroy P. Walker of Alabama, a man of little ability. This incompetency in civilian control of the Confederate Army was largely compensated for by President Davis' experience as a professional soldier and as United States Secretary of War. As commander-in-chief of the Confederate forces, he possessed military knowledge and experience completely lacking in President Lincoln.

To direct and administer his inadequate military and naval array, Mr. Lincoln had, at the outset, as Secretary of War a fumbling political "boss," Simon Cameron of Pennsylvania; as Secretary of the Navy there was strong-hearted and competent Gideon Welles, newspaper publisher from Connecticut. It was a curious coincidence that both sides entered the fray with incompetent war secretaries, but with able civilian administrators of their respective navies.

Cameron, physically and mentally incapable of handling his job, speedily became so bogged down that the early operation and enlargement of the War Department were directed by Salmon P. Chase, Secretary of the Treasury.

Welles was the antithesis to Cameron. Between him and his assistant, brilliant Gustavus Vasa Fox of Massachusetts, a former naval officer, a remarkable job of building a navy would be accomplished.

A grievous handicap to the U.S. Navy at first was the seizure of all its Southern yards and installations; the Norfolk Navy Yard being the most serious loss. Here the fine steam frigate *Merrimack* and a large quantity of naval stores and armament—including fifty-two modern 9-inch Dahlgren guns—were seized by Virginia militia on April 20. The incompetent Navy Yard commander had failed to take measures to protect the installation, and a hasty attempt by loyal officers to destroy it by fire had failed. The *Merrimack*, although scuttled and partly burned, was still readily repairable.

But the North did have the advantage of a strong, healthy mercantile marine—ships and seamen, shipyards and chandlers, dry docks and salt water "know-how"—as a potential naval reserve to draw upon. This, however, was for the future.

In matters of general military policy President Lincoln, once the die was cast, did act with remarkable vigor—in fact, he assumed dictatorial powers. In the absence of Congress, on May 3, he arbitrarily increased the regular Army and Navy and called for 42,000 volunteers. By July, when Congress validated the President's actions, a quarter-million men had rushed to the colors.

But the valor of ignorance governed both in organization and in choice of Union leaders. The little Regular Army was held intact and separate from the new elements, whose composition was left to the discretion of state governors, without any direction as to type of troops or appointment of officers. In consequence, a rabble in arms was gathering; unbalanced in proportion of horse, foot and artillery, and commanded by political appointees or elected officers, most of whom were ignorant of the military art.

Thanks to the conscientious efforts of a few governors, there were some exceptions. Men like Ulysses S. Grant, George B. McClellan, Ambrose E. Burnside, William S. Rosecrans, and many other West Pointers in civil life, flocked back to uniform at the onset of war, and were given Volunteer commissions and important positions of command. William T. Sherman, another West Pointer who had resigned during the years of peace, came back to the Regular Army as a colonel, thanks to his Senator brother's influence. Some of these men would fulfill the promise; others would fail. But at least they were professional soldiers.

But for each such case, there were dozens of other West Pointers, in the Army when the war began, frozen in their Regular Army units by misguided policy. Most of them would remain in these units throughout the war without any opportunity to display talents that might have outshone those of their more fortunate classmates. This sad waste of trained officers—the nation's scarcest resource—would be costly indeed in terms of human life and would jeopardize the national future; but the amateur warmakers in Washington took little thought of that. Of the five major generals of volunteers appointed by September, 1861, four were prominent politicians: Robert Patterson, Benjamin F. Butler, Nathaniel P. Banks, and John A. Dix. Banks and Butler were important figures in Massachusetts politics; neither had had any prior military experience. Patterson, now sixty-nine years old, was a power in Pennsylvania politics. He had had some experience in the War of 1812, and had been a Major General of Volunteers during the Mexican War. Dix had served as a Regular infantry officer from 1813 to 1828, and then had gone into politics in New York. He served as Secretary of the Treasury in Buchanan's cabinet from January to March in 1861.

The provision of weapons for the rising tides of soldiery on both sides proved to be an immediate problem. The North, with its technological resources, would solve it in time, but the South would always be in straits. There would never be enough weapons for Confederate troops and too many diverse weapon types required different kinds of ammunition—all usually in short supply.*

The North, with its vast manufacturing and agricultural resources, would have little trouble in supplying clothing, equipment and food to its armed forces. Again the South was not so fortunately situated. The major supply source of the Confederate armies, particularly in the East, would be by capture from the Union armies.

Although none of its supporters suspected it in the beginning, the Confederacy, through the very nature of its political structure, contained a major flaw further affecting its limited ability to support its armies in the field. Under the principle of States' rights, each state governor controlled the spigots both of manpower and supply in his domain. Consequently, selfish parochial vagaries would from time to time deprive field commanders of much needed assistance.

Such was the status of the opposing armed forces when war

*See Appendix, pp. 461–467.

began. South of the Mason-Dixon line—save for the stronghold of Fortress Monroe at the tip of Virginia's peninsula, guarding the mouth of Chesapeake Bay; and for Fort Pickens at Pensacola, Fort Taylor at Key West and Fort Jefferson off the tip of the Florida Keys—a new flag waved and a new nation stood.

# 2

# The Preliminaries

In the weeks after Sumter, the strategic dimensions of the Northern task seemed to grow, rather than to diminish. The capital of the Confederacy was flauntingly transferred from Montgomery, Alabama, to Richmond, a mere one hundred miles from Washington. The Federal capital, meanwhile, was threatened with isolation from the North by the wavering of Maryland. The situation was critical for a short time. On April 19 in Baltimore, pro-Southern mobs attacked a Massachusetts militia regiment rushing to the defense of Washington. Prompt action by President Lincoln and General Scott brought more Union troops into Maryland, establishing unquestioned Federal authority.

Delaware, though a slave state, had loyally responded to the President's call for volunteers, and so—with Maryland now held firmly in the Union—the northeastern limit of the Confederacy had been held to the Potomac River.

Further west the situation was not so clear. Missouri and

Kentucky both had pro-Southern governors, while a majority of both state legislatures were loyal to the Union. In the mountain regions of eastern Tennessee and western Virginia—where there were very few slaves—violence flared as the furiously pro-Union populations protested their respective states' secession.

In Missouri, pro-Southern Governor Claiborne Jackson had called out the militia; nearly 1,000 of them encamped on the outskirts of St. Louis, a strongly pro-Northern city and the site of an important Federal arsenal. An impetuous young Regular Army officer, Captain Nathaniel P. Lyon, fearing for the safety of the arsenal, and supported by Francis P. Blair, Republican leader in Missouri and brother to Lincoln's Postmaster General, on his own initiative called into Federal service German-American home-guard units in St. Louis. With them, he surrounded the militia encampment on May 10, 1861, and forced its surrender. The Washington administration at once legalized Lyon's action and Scott promoted him to brigadier general.

When Governor Jackson refused to submit to Federal authority, Lyon at once steamed with his troops up-river to Jefferson City and, after a brief clash at Booneville, June 17, drove the governor and his pro-Southern militia down toward Arkansas.

Meanwhile, another bright Union star was rising further east. George Brinton McClellan, of the West Point class of 1846, had made a reputation for himself as a young engineer officer under Robert E. Lee in Scott's army in the Mexican War. After further distinguishing himself as an official observer of the Crimean War, McClellan had resigned from the Army in 1857 to become within two years the president of the Ohio and Mississippi Railroad. When President Lincoln called for volunteers, McClellan promptly offered his services to the state of Ohio, and soon found himself a major general of Volunteers, commanding all Federal forces in southern Ohio. He was directed by General Scott to cross the Ohio River and to seize western Virginia for the Union.

Aided by the pro-Union inhabitants, McClellan and his subordinates drove quickly into the Greenbriar Mountains, pushing unready and confused Virginia Confederates before them. At Philippi, June 3, with 3,000 men, he crushed a small force of 800 men under Colonel George A. Porterfield. At Rich Mountain–Carrick's Ford, June 11–13, McClellan's troops, 8,000 strong, under Brigadier General William S. Rosecrans, swept away 4,000 Virginia volunteers under Brigadier General Robert S. Garnett, who had graduated from West Point one year ahead of Rosecrans. Garnett was killed in the battle. By mid-July, McClellan had gained control of most of northwestern Virginia. President Jefferson Davis was so concerned by this development that he sent his most trusted military adviser, General Robert E. Lee, McClellan's Mexican War commander, to assume personal direction of affairs in the region west of the Allegheny Mountains.

When his native Virginia seceded, Colonel Lee had one of the finest military reputations in the United States Army. There is ample evidence that in April the Federal Government had unofficially offered Lee a position of high command in the Federal Army. General Scott himself tried earnestly to persuade his favorite subordinate to follow his example and put loyalty to Union ahead of loyalty to state. But Lee's ties to the Old Dominion were stronger than his adherence to the United States, and so Lee—personally opposed to both secession and slavery—reluctantly resigned his Federal commission on April 20, three days after Virginia had joined the Confederacy. He had been placed in command of all Confederate troops in Virginia, and had, in effect, become the Chief of Staff to his fellow West Pointer, President Jefferson Davis. Lee's personal drive and military knowledge made possible the really remarkable mobilization in his native state.

Lee, who arrived in the area July 28, was unable to retrieve the situation west of the Alleghenies. Hampered by the hostility of the natives, by jealousy among his subordinates, and by poor lines of communications from eastern Virginia, Lee was forced to concede the loss of most of the western portion of the state. His former subordinate, young General McClellan, quite properly received credit for this first major Union success, though he had been called to greater tasks and challenges by the time Lee reached the scene.

Between Missouri and western Virginia lay the key state of Kentucky, almost equally torn between Unionist and secessionist sentiments. Pro-Confederate Governor Beriah Magoffin and the barely pro-Unionist legislature reached an uneasy compromise by a declaration of Kentucky's neutrality on May 24. Both Presidents Lincoln and Davis realized the decisive strategic significance of the state in the coming struggle and, each, exercising the utmost caution, tacitly—but only temporarily—accepted this declaration of neutrality.

Kentucky's population of more than 1,155,000 (plus some 225,000 slaves) would have augmented the South's military manpower by about 20 percent. Geographically, Kentucky lay like a great wedge thrusting into the heart of the North. If the state were to secede, the United States would be squeezed to a width of less than 200 miles between the Ohio River and Lake Erie. Second only to the Mississippi as an artery of commerce, and a potential avenue of war, the Ohio River rolled for more than 400 miles along Kentucky's northern boundary. And just above the great river—bordering it in places—lay the vital east-west railroads connecting the Northwestern states and their rich resources with the industrial Northeast. With Kentucky in the Confederacy, a bold strategy might conceivably nip the United States in two at the outset of the war, discouraging the diverse elements in the North from undertaking the massive, coordinated efforts absolutely essential to Union victory.

Small wonder that President Lincoln remarked: ''I hope I have God on my side, but I must have Kentucky.'' While both sides, then, warily waited for the opportunity to bring tortured Kentucky into their respective folds, all eyes now focused on

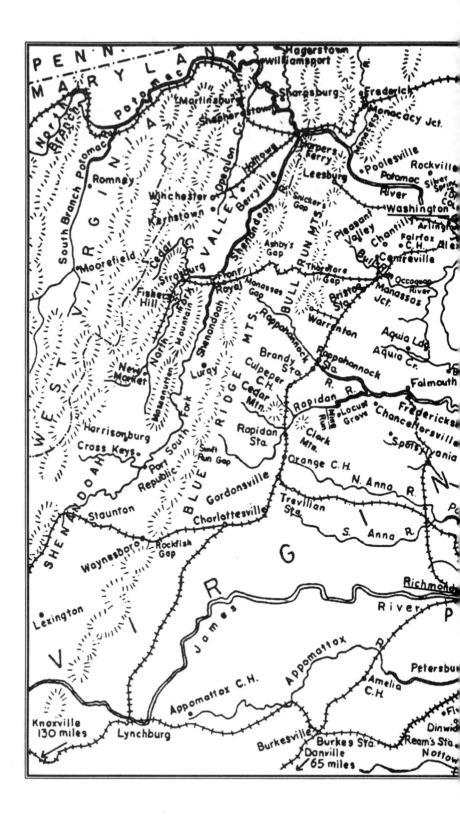

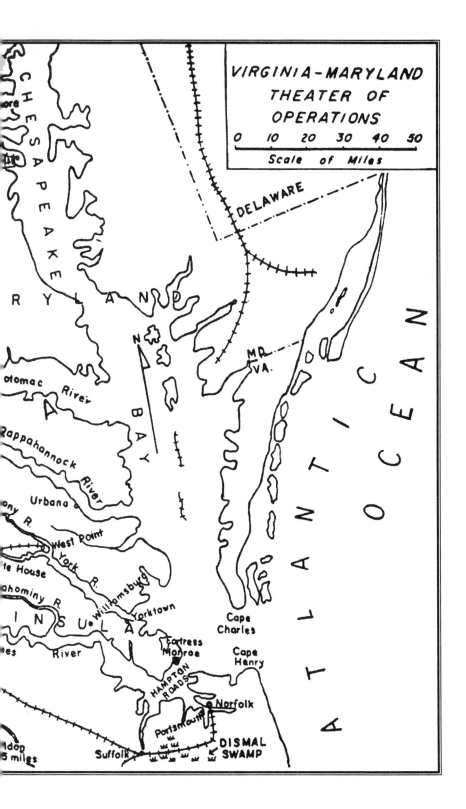

VIRGINIA-MARYLAND
THEATER OF
OPERATIONS

0    10    20    30    40    50
Scale   of   Miles

northeastern Virginia, rapidly becoming a crucial theater of operations.

The first move in the East came on May 24, the day after the Virginia electorate overwhelmingly ratified the state's secession. Federal troops crossed the Potomac and seized Alexandria and General Lee's mansion at Arlington, on the heights overlooking the river and the city of Washington. But Virginia militia held the rolling hills west and north of Alexandria—in sight of the unfinished dome of the national Capitol itself—and Confederate artillery batteries controlled the river approaches to Washington. The Federal Government was literally in the front lines.

On May 28, Brevet Major General Irvin McDowell was placed in command of the newly created Department of Northeastern Virginia, which included the city of Washington and its environs. By early July he had an army of some 35,000 men, mostly composed of green three-months volunteers who had responded to President Lincoln's original call on April 15. McDowell, who a few weeks earlier had been a major in the Regular Army, was now responsible for the largest force which had yet been commanded by an American. He was well aware, however, that this untrained army, with little or no idea of the harsh realities of war, would soon have to be disbanded. The three months' period of service of most of its men would expire shortly after July 15.

Two other small strips of northeastern Virginia were also held precariously by Federal troops. Old Major General Patterson had about 18,000 short-term men in and around Harper's Ferry. General Ben Butler commanded some 15,000 men based at Fortress Monroe, at the tip of the "Virginia Peninsula" between the York and James Rivers. Butler, who had acted with commendable efficiency and vigor in re-establishing Federal authority in riot-torn Baltimore in May, had been promoted to major general of Volunteers.

By July the Confederate Government had been able to mobilize close to 60,000 men in Virginia. About 5,000 held the mountain passes across the Alleghenies against the threat of

McClellan's victorious army. General Joseph E. Johnston, who had abandoned exposed Harper's Ferry to Union General Patterson, now sat with 12,000 men at the northern end of the Shenandoah Valley north of Winchester. Johnston had been a brigadier general in the Regular Army before the secession of his native Virginia; much of the Southern disappointment about General Scott's failure to resign from the Union army had been alleviated when able, respected Johnston offered his sword to the Confederacy.

The largest Confederate force was located near Centreville and Manassas Junction, only 25 miles from the Federal capital. Here were about 22,000 men, commanded by General Beauregard, whose bloodless Sumter victory had made him the military hero of the South. An additional force of 3,000 men, part of Beauregard's command, was at the mouth of Aquia Creek near Fredericksburg, to guard against a possible Federal movement around his right flank, down the Potomac.

As we have noted, General Lee was in overall command of the Confederate forces in Virginia, and held most of his remaining troops in the vicinity of Richmond. To contain Butler's command at Fortress Monroe, Lee had detachments in eastern Virginia; at Yorktown, under General John B. Magruder and at Norfolk, under General Benjamin Huger. Each commander had about 10,000 men.

The stage was set. But were the principal actors really prepared for their roles? Save for a few of the elderly veterans of the Mexican War, none of these men had commanded units larger than companies, battalions or regiments. And the forces that were assembling were far larger than any ever before seen in the Western Hemisphere.

The answer, generally accepted by most authorities, is summed up by Douglas S. Freeman in his splendid study* of the Confederate high command:

---

*Freeman, Douglas S., *Lee's Lieutenants*, III, xvii. New York: *Scribner's*, 1959.

Professional training in arms for men who would exercise command was vindicated throughout the history of the Army of Northern Virginia. Precisely as training in medicine saves lives, so does careful instruction in the art of war. . . . The Army of Northern Virginia could not have been organized or commanded successfully without West Point.

Unquestionably, with very few exceptions, the men who would excel on both sides, had come, directly or indirectly, from the tiny Regular Army; their high professional standards resulting from small army combat experience under Scott or Taylor in the Mexican War, or from their training at West Point, or both. Military Academy graduates would command the forces on one side or the other, if not on both sides, in practically every important battle.

Out of this matrix would come some of the greatest prodigies of leadership in the annals of war. Yet military professionalism alone cannot explain why the standards of combat leadership in the Civil War became so far superior to those displayed five years earlier by the professional officers of Europe's leading armies during the Crimean War.

The fact was that all these West Point graduates had been influenced directly or indirectly by America's one-man war college—Dennis Hart Mahan, Professor of the Art of War at West Point since 1832. Colonel Mahan, from his studious analysis of the campaigns of great generals—particularly those of Napoleon—had imbued his pupils with the concept of fire and movement. He stressed, above all, the importance of speed. "Celerity is the secret of success," was axiomatic in his works on strategy, tactics and military engineering—works which were pirated in Richmond and New Orleans when his publishers in New York refused to sell them to Confederate outlets.

Mahan was indeed a prophet of modern war. As it turned out, the land operations of the Civil War became the testing ground of his system, as the outstanding leaders on both sides utilized his principles against one another.

But in the beginning, as untried men and leaders found out from bitter experience, the path to victory was thorny indeed. The first big lesson was Bull Run.

# 3

# Bull Run

It was sunny and hot, that Sunday morning of July 21, 1861, and fashionable Washington, it seemed, had gone picnicking across to Virginia heedless of the church bells. Fine ladies in barouches, their parasols mushrooming above them; smart gentlemen tooling gigs or astride horses, packed the dusty Warrenton Turnpike. They were bound for Centreville to see Union General McDowell trounce his West Point classmate General Beauregard, commanding the Confederates at Manassas. Hampers and saddlebags were packed with goodies—solid and liquid—and everyone was in holiday spirit, despite the heat and the dust and the delays incident to threading their way through a straggling column of men in blue uniform, bound in the opposite direction. These were militiamen hurrying homeward, their three-months' service completed, oblivious of the rumble of cannonading behind them. The merrymakers' only worry, on the other hand, was that they might miss something of the splendid opportunity to see a real battle. As it turned out, their curiosity was more than satisfied. It was also the last picnic that Washingtonians would indulge in for a long time.

Three months of patriotic fervor had come to its frothing climax. Since President Lincoln issued his first call for militia the response of the Northern states had been overwhelming. Uniformed hordes in variegated costumes poured into Washington, bedded down in public buildings, huddled in tented camps, roistered in the streets. Two things they all had in common: determination to crush rebellion; and, with the exception of a few regiments, an almost complete ignorance of soldiering. There had been some difficulty in getting there; the 6th Massachusetts—first to answer the call—had had to fight its way through a secessionist mob in Baltimore, at a cost of four men killed and thirty-one wounded. New York's "silk stocking" 7th Regiment, next to arrive, had been detoured around Baltimore, taking steamboats at Perryville for Annapolis.

The match was soon applied to this collective powder-keg. The Northern public and press, enraged by the fall of Fort Sumter, and united for victory, clamored for an immediate advance. Here were the men; there, at Manassas, was the enemy. What were we waiting for?

Further Union irritation was caused by a clash on June 10, at Big Bethel Church near Yorktown. The Southerners were commanded by General John B. Magruder, holding the Peninsula against the threat of Butler's Union forces assembled at Fortress Monroe. Butler had attempted a surprise move toward Yorktown, but the green Federal troops collided with one another and the clumsy assault was handily thrown back by a small number of Confederate troops. The Southerners, equally green, were led by Colonel D. H. Hill, West Pointer and ex-Regular.

Physically nothing more than a skirmish—the Federals lost seventy-six men and the Confederates eleven—psychologically this clash brought exultation to Southern adherents, the *Richmond Dispatch* hailing it as one of the most extraordinary victories in the annals of war. To the North, Big Bethel was just another infuriation. The pressure on the administration became overwhelming.

McDowell had been wrestling with the Augean task of trying to create soldiers overnight. Under the pressure for action, he reluctantly brought out a plan. He would move on the Manassas Confederate concentration, turn its position by a wide flanking envelopment, and eject his enemy "by threatening or seizing his communications." Approved June 24, the plan was ordered into execution July 8. Vital to success would be the Federal government's ability to keep Confederate concentrations in the lower Shenandoah Valley from reinforcing Beauregard at Manassas. General Scott sent urgent orders to General Patterson to keep Johnston pinned down near Winchester.

Not until July 16 was McDowell able to begin his move, for not until that very day had he been able to organize his so-called army into brigades or divisions. The long, ungainly column marched bravely out from Alexandria, banners streaming, to inchworm through Fairfax Courthouse and on to Centreville. In all that mass of 38,000 men there were not 2,000 professionals.

It took the Union army the better part of two days to concentrate about Centreville, and McDowell wasted two more days in determining how best to tackle his enemy. The Confederates, he knew, lay behind the steep tree-lined banks of Bull Run, which meandered generally southeast across the Warrenton Pike about four miles west of Centreville. Their line apparently ran seven miles, from the Stone Bridge carrying the Pike, down to the Orange and Alexandria Railroad trestle across Bull Run at Union Mills.

On the eighteenth, a Federal reconnaissance, moving in force against the approximate center of the Confederate position, directly south of Centreville, met with bloody repulse in front of Mitchell's and Blackburn's Fords. To turn the Confederate right presented difficulties; neither the terrain nor the water courses favored such approach. But McDowell's engineers, reconnoitering to the northwest, found favorable ground. Believing he had more men than Beauregard, McDowell decided he would turn the Southern left flank. Starting in the morning hours of darkness on July 21, two divisions—McDowell would lead them in person—were to make a twelve-mile circuitous march west from Centreville, cross Bull Run at Sudley Springs ford well beyond Beauregard's left—then strike due south down the Manassas-Sudley road. Another division would drive directly west along the Turnpike and across the Stone Bridge. A detached brigade would make a feint against the fords directly south of Centreville where the Union fingers had been burned on the eighteenth. Back at Centreville another division would lie in reserve. The remaining Union division was scattered along the line of communications all the way back to Washington; it would take no part in the battle. The total combat force available for battle was 32,000 men.

The plan was ambitious, with success dependent upon the coordination of the movements of three widely separated forces. Given competent commanders, an efficient staff and highly-trained troops, it might well have worked. But it was far beyond the capability of a poorly-trained, just-organized team, running out on the field for its first tussle. What McDowell didn't know, when he issued his order on the evening of July 20, was that his offensive plans were known to the enemy high command even before he left Washington; that Beauregard had expected to be attacked on the seventeenth; and that Johnston, deftly screening his move from doddering Patterson's Winchester front, had left the Shenandoah Valley for Manassas. Actually Johnston and the bulk of his troops, moving by rail—the first time the railroad played a strategic role in war—had joined Beaureagard. Johnston's last element, Edmund Kirby Smith's brigade, would be rattling down the Manassas Gap R.R. from Strasburg next morning. In addition, Holmes' brigade from Aquia Creek had also arrived.

Two strikes, then, had been called on McDowell before he came up to the plate. Confederate intelligence had diagnosed the Union intentions and strength. The railroad had furnished the

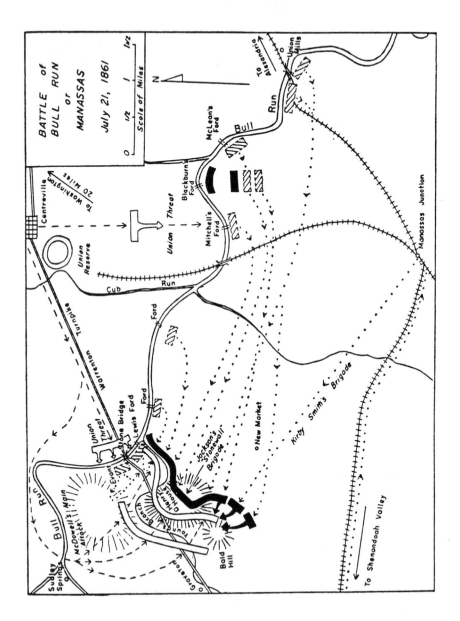

BATTLE of
BULL RUN
or
MANASSAS
July 21, 1861

Confederacy the strategic mobility with which to concentrate on interior lines. As a result, McDowell's available 32,000 strength would be pitted in an offensive against 35,000 men who lay in a defensive position on very favorable terrain. Beauregard's elements covered all the Bull Run crossings. The bulk of his strength, including Johnston's newly-arrived troops, lay opposite Centreville for a very good reason. Beauregard intended to take the offensive himself, driving between Centreville and Fairfax Courthouse and cutting McDowell's exposed communications. Johnston, who was senior to Beauregard, assumed command on arrival, but approved Beauregard's dispositions for the battle and, for all practical purposes, left the immediate tactical control to him.

On the Union side, things went wrong from the first, that Sunday morning. The feint against the fords never materialized. The main effort, 12,000 strong, was delayed in getting away. It didn't reach the Sudley Spring ford until after nine o'clock. The secondary attack, against Beauregard's extreme left at the Stone Bridge, was pushed so half-heartedly that the local Confederate commander, wily Brigadier General Nathan G. ("Shanks") Evans suspected that it was not the main attack. A courier from a Confederate picket at Sudley Springs brought word of Federal troops moving south on the Manassas-Sudley road, and this was confirmed by flag signals. So Evans shifted the major part of his command—a little more than one regiment—to the left rear onto high ground not far north of the turnpike, just in time to meet the main Union advance.

Evans' action changed the entire complexion of the battle. His small force, far out on the Confederate left, was at once involved in hot engagement as McDowell attacked and the Federal artillery came into action. Beauregard, who early that morning had become convinced that the Union commander was committing himself to an attack along the Warrenton Pike in the Stone Bridge area, had begun, with Johnston's approval, to shift his reserves—Johnston's troops from Winchester—to back up that sector. At the same time, also with Johnston's approval, he ordered his own attack. His right center would cross Bull Run on its front and hit the Federal left and rear at Centreville.

But it was now the Confederates' turn to stumble. The attack order, because of faulty staff work, never reached the brigade commander who was to lead it. Since he didn't move, neither did the others. By 10:30 A.M., when Beauregard discovered that his plan had miscarried, the sound of battle on his left indicated a serious engagement, although the point of impact and the Union objective were still both nebulous.

Johnston and Beauregard, galloping to the sound of the guns, found that Evans, together with two reinforcing brigades, was being driven back eastward upon the Henry House Hill—a flattish ridge pointing into the southeastern angle between the Turnpike and the Manassas-Sudley road. In overwhelming force, the Federal attack was overlapping the Confederate left on this new battlefront, while Brigadier General William T. Sherman's Union brigade, fording Bull Run west of the Stone Bridge, was threatening its right. The sole remaining Confederate local reserve was Brigadier General Thomas J. Jackson's Virginia brigade, just arrived on the Henry House Hill.

Johnston, putting Beauregard in charge of the combat area, established his command post further behind the line and busied himself with withdrawing the remaining Southern forces originally lining Bull Run and disposing them to meet the new situation.

Meanwhile, Jackson, picking his terrain carefully, formed his brigade on the northeastern side of the Henry House Hill, to cover the disorganized retreat of the Southern troops recoiling from McDowell's assault. The immovable Virginians checked the Union advance and the retreating troops reformed behind them. "There stands Jackson like a stone wall!" cried Confederate General Barnard E. Bee as he rallied the fugitives.

But McDowell still had twice the strength of the Confederates at Henry House Hill, and his men had plenty of fight left in them. He pressed on.

The Federals gained the northwestern edge of the ridge, their lines lapping around the Henry House Hill. Two Union artillery batteries came slashing into action in close support of the infantry, but they dropped trails within musket-shot of woods on their right, from which Confederate sharpshooters began picking off horses and cannoneers. A squadron of Southern cavalry— J. E. B. Stuart's—scattered the Union infantry near the guns and overran the batteries. Immediately, additional Union infantry moved in to regain them.

Three times the silent guns were taken and retaken as the fighting surged back and forth. Then McDowell's rear guard brigade, his last reserve south of the stream, arrived on the field, extending the Union line to the right. Victory, it seemed, was almost in the Federal general's hands; Beauregard's left was again outflanked.

But up from the railroad at Manassas Junction came Kirby Smith's brigade, just in from Winchester. Johnston threw it against the Federal right. Hot on its heels, ordered from its position at the lower fords on the original Confederate right, came Early's brigade. McDowell's offensive collapsed; the Northern soldiers who had now been marching and fighting for twelve hours could do no more against these fresh troops. The blue lines melted, soldiers simply leaving their ranks and starting back the way they had come, heedless of their officers. By 4:30 P.M., not a Union soldier remained on the battlefield, except for the dead and the wounded.

Protected by the Regulars—Sikes' infantry battalion and Palmer's cavalry—who never broke formation, the Federal horde went trudging back to the turnpike west of Bull Run. Most of the Confederates on the field were themselves too tired and too disorganized to make any great effort. Stuart's cavalry made a few passes but the dogged Regulars easily beat them off. Federal losses were 481 killed, 1,011 wounded and 1,216 missing (many of these prisoners). The Confederates lost 387 men killed, 1,582 wounded and 13 missing.

For a while the steady tide of Federal defeat flowed eastward, with the Washington picnickers and their transport scattered amidst the men, guns and wagons crowding the road. Then across the field from the lower fords of Bull Run came R. C. W. Radford's squadron of Confederate cavalry, with a four-gun battery, to make a tentative jab at the pike. The fugitives hurried their pace. Two miles east of the Stone Bridge, a lucky Southern shell smashed a wagon and momentarily blocked passage. That did it. Panic flared and the entire mob stampeded. Except for the little clump of Regulars, protecting the rear, McDowell's army evaporated in the dusk.

The Union's bright bubble of enthusiasm had been pricked. The last of the tattered refugees were still crossing the Long Bridge into Washington next morning. It took another twenty-four hours to pick up the wounded from the battlefield. In the Southern Confederacy hopes soared high. Its combat superiority had been proven on a stricken field, for all the world to see. Virginia in particular was justly proud of herself; Virginia troops had made up a good twenty-five percent of the victorious army.

While Confederate pickets roamed the Potomac heights within sight of a dazed capital, President Lincoln now began wrestling with the problem to plague him for three more years to come: he had to find a general. Out of the ruck and frustration a meteoric personality was to soar into view.

# 4

# New Brooms on Land and Sea

Thirty-five-year-old George B. McClellan, hurriedly appointed to command all troops in the vicinity of Washington, arrived six days after the Bull Run battle, to be hailed by the press and public as the savior of the nation. His problem was simple in objective, but stupendous in fact: to fortify the nation's capital and, at the same time, to build a field army.

He found a disorganized rabble of discouraged pseudo-soldiers; a rabble augmented by daily arrivals of volunteer recruits. All vestiges of discipline were vanishing; grog shops and bawdy houses replaced drill grounds.

But McClellan knew what to do and he did it. His provost guards swept the city clean, sparing neither the hellholes nor the gas-lit glittering bars of the fashionable hotels where officers were drowning their sorrow. He shook out existing units as one would shake a dusty jacket, and droves of ignorant and inefficient officers were swept into the dustbin.

He gathered about him an efficient staff. His engineers laid out a ring of forts about the capital. His regimental, brigade, division and corps commanders set about their reorganization and training. New volunteers, answering the call for 500,000 three-year enlistments—the call had gone out the very day Bull Run was fought—were corralled on arrival into training camps apart from the older troops. Not until these green formations had learned military fundamentals would they join the cadres already formed.

The discipline was rigid, the training grueling. The dashing new general seemed to be everywhere at once. His soldierly figure on a galloping black horse, with his glittering staff and smart cavalry escort pounding behind, all impinged on the eyes of every man in the ranks: here was a leader!

The Army of the Potomac was being born; an army which would retain the cachet "Made by McClellan" long after he had passed from its command. "Little Mac" was their general; they would be forever "Little Mac's" men.

Meanwhile, in the Manassas-Centreville entrenchments, Johnston was having his own troubles. The Confederate forces had been almost as disorganized by victory as their opponents had been in defeat. In addition, food and supply were both short. But Johnston well knew the effort being made to revamp the Union army. To permit the North sufficient time to mobilize and train a force overwhelming in number, he reasoned, would be fatal to the Confederate cause.

Accordingly, at a conference on September 30, Johnston recommended to President Davis that his 40,000 men in the Manassas area be reinforced by "seasoned soldiers" to 60,000 strength. This force then should be given sufficient supplies and ammunition and invade the North. Generals Beauregard and Gustavus W. Smith, his two corps commanders, concurred. But Davis turned the proposition down; he could not furnish reinforcements without "total disregard for the safety of other threatened positions.'' With Mr. Davis' decision went much of the fruits of victory won at Bull Run. In fact there is some ground for argument that this timidity on the part of the Confederate President, which the historian Ropes terms a ''serious, probably a very serious error,'' was the turning point in the war; a surrender of the initiative which would have been even more costly had McClellan taken advantage of it.

But the heady wine of adulation had gone to McClelland's head. He produced a grandiose scheme for the conquest of the South, with the Atlantic seaboard of the Confederacy the target. He envisioned—under his command—a great joint Army-Navy operation to occupy all its coastal cities. Operations along the Mississippi line would be subordinate, and the essential destruction of the South's armed forces forgotten. His plan, which ignored the realities of means and of available trained manpower, was in radical opposition to Scott's sound ''Anaconda Plan.'' Only on one point did both men agree: the necessity for methodical raising and training of the troops before any movement began.

Ruffled by Scott's opposition, McClellan became insolent to his boss. He even snubbed President Lincoln. Time ticked on and the fickle public and press began deserting the ''young Napoleon,'' as he had, at first, been nicknamed. Impatient of all delay, the ''on to Richmond'' slogan was resurrected from the ashes of Bull Run. When Confederate batteries were permitted to rise along the lower Potomac, practically closing water navigation to the national capital, the mutterings became violent. Yet McClellan took no action, claiming that future major operations would force the elimination of the nuisance without loss of life or risk of failure.

On October 21, at Ball's Bluff near Leesburg, Virginia, an incautious reconnaissance by Union troops crossing from the Maryland shore of the Potomac resulted in a minor disaster which would have major repercussions. Colonel Edward D. Baker, just resigned as U.S. Senator from Oregon, was in command. Filled with the valor of ignorance, Baker led his brigade across the river, engaged it piecemeal against a superior Confederate force under the command of canny "Shanks" Evans—who had done such brilliant work at the opening of the Bull Run battle—and was disastrously defeated. The Union troops were penned on the edge of the precipitous river bank and most of those not killed in action, or drowned in attempting to recross the Potomac, were captured. Union losses were 237 killed and wounded and 714 captured or missing. Among the dead was Baker himself.

Reaction in Washington was violent. On December 20 Congress established a Joint Committee on the Conduct of the War, with Senator Benjamin F. Wade of Massachusetts as its chairman. Wade, a violent abolitionist, savagely led the hunt for a scapegoat. Brigadier General Charles P. Stone, who had ordered the reconnaissance, was removed from command and for eight months imprisoned in Fort Lafayette, New York, without any charges ever having been brought against him. Popular clamor against McClellan himself also rose higher. Most important was the fact that this Wade committee would, from that time on, exert a malign influence on all facets of the Union war effort.

But patient Lincoln still placed confidence in "Little Mac." When old General Scott resigned as General-in-Chief on November 1 and retired, McClellan was appointed to his post and attempted to personally direct nationwide military operations from Washington.

All this time Johnston, with his main army concentrated at Manassas, and maintaining a long line of observation from Winchester on the north to Fredericksburg on the south, continued to have troubles. Beauregard—who would soon be transferred to Kentucky—was bickering jealously with Johnston, and Johnston himself was feuding with President Davis on the matter of his own seniority. Winter closed in. The Virginia roads became utterly impracticable for any large-scale movement and both sides settled down to enforced inaction.

There was another side to the war, however; a side extremely important but obscured to some extent by the dramatic developments on land in Virginia and elsewhere.

# ANCHORS AWEIGH!

When Abraham Lincoln called, on April 15, 1861, for 75,000 volunteers to serve for three months, Jefferson Davis in quick riposte offered letters of marque to all mariners wishing to prey on Union commerce. On Scott's advice, Lincoln thereupon proclaimed a formal naval blockade of the Confederacy; a shoreline more than 3,500 miles long, including 180 harbors and navigable inlets. Southern privateers, Lincoln announced, would be considered as pirates.

Gideon Welles, Secretary of the Navy, finding he had but a handful of naval vessels immediately available, issued orders to the commandants of the New York, Philadelphia and Boston Navy Yards to charter or purchase at once twenty steamers capable of mounting naval ordnance for convoying troops and supplies.

Then began an amazing program of naval procurement—by extemporization and construction—with concurrent recruitment and training of personnel. Civilian concerns and public utilities, dockyards and transportation facilities, all rallied to the goadings of Welles the driver. Their response was, perhaps, more spontaneous than was that of the over-aged and conservative senior Navy officers who would long resist revolutionary changes. It was a program which by 1865 would have 670 vessels in commission, a personnel aggregate of 6,700 officers and 51,500 men, and a budget of $123,000,000.

Partly replacing the 322 Regular officers who had left the Navy to go South, a handful of ex-officers returned from civil life. From the merchant marine came many volunteers. By the end of 1861, 993 temporary commissioned officers, selected by examination from the merchant marine, were in Navy uniform and on board the now rapidly expanding fleet of regular and extemporized warships.

But Welles' most important decision had been made on May 8. Gustavus V. Fox, who had resigned from the Navy in 1856, after eighteen years of service, was selected for the new post of Assistant Secretary of the Navy. Fox's past experience, both in the Navy and in business, gained him the confidence of both Navy folk and civilians. He and Welles made a perfect team.

Welles' first preoccupation was of course with the blockade. Actually, had Mr. Lincoln simply closed the southern ports by proclamation, making all violators of his order subject to capture, he would have made things easier. As it was, his announcement of a formal blockade conceded, in effect, belligerent rights to the Confederacy, as well as neutral rights to foreigners, with all the complicated formality of the rules of international law.

The blockade would have to be established piecemeal, as vessels became available from the fantastic conglomeration being acquired by purchase or charter. These ranged from ocean-going steamers to double-ended paddle-wheel New York City ferryboats—anything which would float and upon which guns could be mounted. Seaworthiness was no consideration.

First to be established was the Potomac flotilla, an oddly-matched assortment of two warships and five converted river steamers which patrolled the Potomac from Washington to Chesapeake Bay, assisting in the transport of troops and blocking the river to Confederate craft. However, Confederate batteries soon rose at Aquia Creek, definitely closing, for some time, the Potomac to passage of Union vessels and blockading in turn Washington itself.

Charleston, S.C., was the most important point in the blockade in the early part of the war. But the Atlantic Blockading Squadron, operating from Hampton Roads, with but fourteen vessels, was also attempting to cover the rest of the coast down to Key West. The task was almost impossible. Many Southern ships were captured, but as many slipped through, and three

Confederate privateers, *Jefferson Davis*, *Dixie* and *Savannah*, eluding the blockade, began playing hob with Union coastwise commerce all the way up to New England.

By June the blockade had operationally extended from Key West to the mouth of the Mississippi delta. But the big clumsy deep-draft ships—never intended for chasing fleeter merchantmen—had to keep well offshore, while the comparatively few available shallow-draft craft spent half their time shuttling between Hampton Roads and their posts for re-coaling. The situation was far from satisfactory, although there was no doubt that the Confederacy's sea gates were slowly closing.

Meanwhile, down South, Mallory, the Confederate Secretary of the Navy, was evolving a plan of aggressive defense. Commerce raiders built explicitly for speed, "able to engage or avoid an enemy at will," armed with long-range batteries and capable of extended sea service would, he believed, devastate Northern commerce and compel pursuit by Union vessels which would have to be removed from blockade duty.

He also had something more fearsome in mind: the construction of powerful iron-clads which would crush the wooden-hulled Union navy, sweep the blockaders from the seas, open Chesapeake Bay and its network of waterways, and even threaten Washington.

Despite the inadequate industrial resources of the South, the construction of iron-clads was begun. Also, on June 30, the CSS *Sumter* came flying out of the Mississippi through Pass a l'Outre into the Gulf of Mexico to usher in a new chapter of the naval warfare—commerce destruction.

*Sumter*'s skipper, Captain Raphael Semmes, erstwhile Commander, USN, had under his feet a 500-ton fast screw steamer formerly engaged in passenger traffic between New Orleans and Havana. Her frame had been strengthened, her spar deck cleared away, and she mounted an 8-inch pivot gun and four 24-pounders in broadside.

Showing her heels to the slower Union vessels on station,

the *Sumter* began a commerce destroying career in the Caribbean and the Atlantic which would not end until the following January. In all, she captured seventeen prizes. Finally trapped in Gibraltar, with no hope of eluding Union warships awaiting her outside, *Sumter* was abandoned. Semmes' further tempestuous career we shall take up later.

What interests us now is a by-product of *Sumter*'s cruise; an incident which almost brought war between the United States and England. Among the ships detached to hunt down the raider as she swept the Caribbean was the USS *San Jacinto*, steam screw sloop, commanded by Captain Charles Wilkes, a crusty sea dog of the old naval school, accustomed to making and carrying out his own decisions afloat.

Wilkes, putting into Havana October 31, found *Sumter* had eluded him, but also discovered what he considered might be a greater prize. In the city were James M. Mason and John Slidell, Confederate commissioners on their way to England to represent President Jefferson Davis. They had slipped over in a blockade runner and had booked passage on board the British mail steamer *Trent*. The *San Jacinto* put to sea at once, to lay in wait in the Bahama Channel, through which the *Trent* came bowling on November 8. The British vessel hove to after Wilkes put a shot across her bow. Sending an officer and an armed boarding party to the *Trent*, the Confederate commissioners and their two secretaries were forcibly removed and brought to the United States. They were locked up in Fort Warren, Boston. For a few days the North cheered and feted Wilkes. Navy Secretary Welles congratulated him on his initiative, and Congress presented him with its thanks.

Then came the repercussions. There was in fact no justification in international law for this high-handed act, and Britain boiled. A British expeditionary force was immediately embarked for Canada; an embargo laid on shipment of war matériel to the United States. Fortunately, through the quick change of face of

Secretary of State William H. Seward, the adroit diplomacy of our ambassador to the Court of St. James, Charles Francis Adams, and the personal intervention of Albert, Queen Victoria's Prince Consort, the matter was composed. Lord Palmerston's blunt demand for release of the prisoners and an apology was toned down, while Wilkes' action was disavowed by the United States. Mason and Slidell on December 26 were quietly slipped away on a tugboat and put on board HMS *Rinaldo*, off Provincetown, Mass.

Settlement of the crisis ended the Confederate hope for an immediate military alliance with Britain. A month later the British embargo on munitions was removed. As epilogue to this reestablishment of cordial relations, the British expeditionary force of 8,000 men, having arrived at the mouth of the St. Lawrence to find the river ice-blocked, was given permission to march across American territory on its way to Quebec!

Meanwhile the Confederates had found a way to bypass the Chesapeake Bay blockade of Richmond and Norfolk. Hatteras Inlet, opening into Pamlico and Albemarle Sounds and the Dismal Swamp Canal, was the back door to these cities. At the Inlet the Confederates had erected fortifications mounting some of the ordnance captured from the Norfolk Navy Yard. Under this protection small craft were already moving freely in and out, despite the blockade of Chesapeake Bay, the front door.

Flag Officer Silas H. Stringham, commanding the North Atlantic Blockading Squadron, on August 26, led a flotilla from Hampton Roads to reduce the forts and block the entrance to Hatteras Inlet. On board his squadron was an army contingent of 800 men from Fortress Monroe commanded by General Butler, who was authorized by General Scott to act under Stringham's orders. Rounding Cape Hatteras, the expedition stood inshore. Under the fire of the warships, Butler's men landed with some difficulty through heavy surf and occupied the Confederate fortifications. It was later decided to leave a permanent army garrison there and the Inlet became a blockade base.

The next amphibious operation was even more important. Port Royal sound and harbor, in South Carolina, a beautiful anchorage, lay athwart the important protected inland waterway connecting Savannah and Charleston. Its seizure by the North would not only be of advantage in the blockade but would also threaten the Confederate land flank. President Lincoln and Secretaries Stanton and Welles had long been in agreement that capture of Port Royal was essential from every point of view.

So on October 10, Flag Officer Samuel F. Du Pont in the steam frigate *Wabash* led out of Hampton Roads the largest amphibious force the United States had ever yet assembled—its mission known only to its commander and to the Army commander on board. Nine warships escorted more than sixty colliers, supply ships and transports, with 17,000 army troops aboard, under Brigadier General Thomas W. Sherman. There was no doubt that the Navy was in charge, but this was also to be a joint operation.

Nature was uncooperative. Off Cape Hatteras a violent storm spread Du Pont's armada to the four winds. Two transports were wrecked on the North Carolina coast. One of the converted merchantmen sprang leaks and had to dump her guns overboard; still another, a chartered old sidewheeler from Boston, carrying Marines, began to break up. The USS *Sabine*, a sailing frigate, rescued all but six of the men aboard the foundering craft.

Fortunately, each vessel in the squadron carried sealed orders giving a rendezvous, to be opened in case they were separated. So on November 4 most of Du Pont's scattered vessels regathered off the bar outside Port Royal harbor. Several additional vessels of the South Atlantic Blockading Squadron also arrived, under orders to report to Du Pont.

After his light craft had reconnoitered the estuary, Du Pont brought his entire expedition across the bar and anchored about five miles out from Port Royal. At the mouth of the harbor were Forts Walker and Beauregard; the former on the left, the latter, opposite it on the right, nearly three miles away. These fortifications mounted eighty pieces of heavy ordnance.

On November 7, Du Pont, leaving his transports huddled at their anchorage, stood in to attack the Confederate fortifications. Fort Walker, to his left, was the initial target. Against it the heavier warships—frigates and sloops—moved in single column, led by *Wabash* and closed by the sailing sloop *Vandalia*, which was towed by a steamer. At the same time, on the right, five gunboats in another column had the primary mission of preventing the few armed Confederate river craft present from sneaking out to attack the transports.

In faultless precision the main Union column of tall ships made for Fort Walker, opening fire at 600-yard range as they passed it in classic run-by. Turning in an elliptic course, they passed again, their gunnery—at first too high—damaging the masonry emplacement, dismounting some guns and spreading fear among the green defenders.

On the second run-by, USS *Pocahontas*, late for the rendezvous, came churning up under forced draft to join the column. Her blazing guns underlined in fire the irony of fate; Commander Percival D. Drayton, skipper of the Federal sloop, was the brother of Brigadier General Thomas F. Drayton, CSA, commanding the shore defenses.

Meanwhile Confederate Flag Officer Josiah Tattnall, ex-USN, with his tiny Confederate flotilla, had stood boldly out in the channel as the Union squadron first approached. At the first shot fired in his direction, Tattnall, recognizing the overwhelming odds, dipped his blue command flag in salute to his former comrades-in-arms, and sent his Confederate gunboats scurrying for the shelter of Skull Creek, where the deeper-draft Federal vessels could not follow.

On the turn for a third run-by it became evident that the defenders had abandoned Fort Walker. Du Pont sent ashore a landing party from *Wabash*, the transports were signalled up and

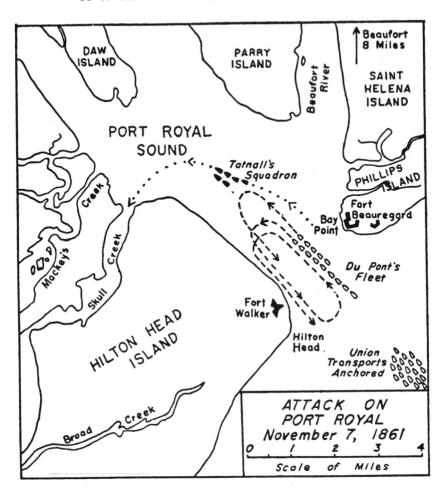

ATTACK ON PORT ROYAL
November 7, 1861

that afternoon General Sherman's troops formally occupied the place. Fort Beauregard across the harbor mouth, also abandoned, was later taken over and Port Royal harbor was in Union hands.

Sherman's troops later cleared out the vicinity of the harbor, being assisted in remarkably close cooperation by the navy gunboats. For the remainder of the war Port Royal became one of the most important navy bases for the blockading squadrons. This clear-cut naval victory was received with joy throughout the Union, which had been frustrated by the other events of the year.

For the South it meant a tightening of the strangling pressure of Union sea power.

The first year of the war ended in the east with an irritating stalemate evident on the Virginia front and portents not yet clearly visible on the Atlantic coast. But in the Mississippi Valley the thunderheads of war were rolling up in the sky.

# 5

# Rivers Shape the War in the West

T he Battle of Bull Run had little impact on the war in the West, where military and political maneuvering on both sides centered on gaining control of the border states of Missouri and Kentucky.

Major General Albert Sidney Johnston commanded the Confederate Department of the West, which was the area along the Mississippi River. This included all of Tennessee and the western part of Mississippi on the east bank, and Missouri, Arkansas and the Indian country on the west.

The Union picture, on the other hand, was one of divided command responsibility. From the Alleghenies on the east to the Rocky Mountains on the west, military jurisdiction was split; not by the Mississippi River, the principal terrain feature, but by the Indiana-Illinois boundary, a stretch of the Ohio River, and the Cumberland River up to the southern boundary of Kentucky.

For the Union, Major General John C. Frémont, with his headquarters at St. Louis, commanded the huge Department of the West, reaching from the Mississippi to the Rocky Mountains and—on the east side of the river—southern Illinois and all that part of Kentucky west of the Cumberland River. Major General Robert Anderson of Fort Sumter fame commanded the Federal Department of the Cumberland, with central and eastern Kentucky and all of Tennessee as its potential maneuvering area. This violation of the fundamental principle of unity of command would continually plague Union efforts in the Mississippi Valley.

Frémont, "The Pathfinder," was well known as an explorer. At one time an officer in the U.S. Army Corps of Engineers, and a controversial figure in the conquest of California and the Mexican War, he later became a politician, and in 1856 the first presidential candidate of the Republican Party. He owed his rank and command not to his sketchy military experience, but to this political influence.

Johnston, on the other hand, was a West Pointer from Kentucky, who had distinguished himself as a leader in Texas' War for Independence, and later with Taylor in the Mexican War. He had also had experience as an Indian fighter, and had commanded the U.S. Army expedition of 1857–58 against the rebellious Mormons in Utah. Johnston was, at the onset of the war, one of the ablest commanders on either side.

In the southwest corner of Missouri, Confederate Brigadier General Sterling Price's Missouri militia, routed by Union General Lyon at Boonville, had rallied with Brigadier General Ben McCullough's Arkansas Confederates. Together they moved north—12,000 strong—to regain control of the state. On the night of August 9, this force was bivouacked beside Wilson's Creek. Watchful Lyon, who had followed closely on Price's heels, characteristically resolved to carry the fight to his opponents, although he had only 5,400 men.

At dawn on August 10, Lyon mounted a two-pronged surprise attack. He led the main body while Colonel Franz Sigel led an enveloping force which struck the Confederate right rear.

Although almost overwhelmed by the initial shock, McCullough and Price rallied their men and took prompt advantage of the lack of coordination between the two Union assaults. Lyon, twice wounded, led a desperate charge, in a supreme bid for victory. The attack, close to success, came to an abrupt halt when Lyon fell with a bullet through his heart. After several more hours of inconclusive action, Major Samuel D. Sturgis, who assumed command after Lyon's death, withdrew the Union troops, leaving the field to the battered, disorganized Confederates.

Although tactically a Confederate victory—there were only 1,235 Federal losses compared to 2,084 Confederate losses— Wilson Creek's bloody field came too late to be of strategic value to the South. Lyon's three months of fierce, aggressive action which culminated there had prevented the otherwise irrevocable fall of Missouri into the Confederate grasp. For the duration of the war its southern and western portions would become a No Man's Land, but Missouri as a state would remain in the Union.

Meanwhile both North and South were massing large forces of militia and volunteers on the borders of "neutral" Kentucky. By the end of August, 1861, some 65,000 Federal troops lined the Ohio River in Illinois, Indiana and Ohio, while Johnston's 45,000 Confederates were concentrated in northern Tennessee.

Newly-promoted Brigadier General Ulysses S. Grant was appointed on August 30 to command Federal forces in southern Illinois and southeastern Missouri; a part of Frémont's jurisdiction. Grant, a graduate of West Point in 1843, had distinguished himself for heroism in the Mexican War, and had then resigned from the army in 1854. His subsequent civilian career had not been outstanding; though he was not down-and-out as so often represented by popular legend. A relatively obscure, but respected merchant in Galena, Illinois, when the war broke out, he had immediately offered his services to the state, and was soon assigned command of a regiment, with the rank of Colonel of Volunteers. He had been busy assisting in the re-establishment of firm Federal authority in central Missouri before he was promoted and assigned to his new command.

Grant arrived at his headquarters at Cairo, Illinois, on September 3, the same day that General Johnston ordered his subordinate, Major General Leonidas Polk, to seize key points in western Kentucky. Polk, another West Pointer, had resigned immediately after his graduation in 1827 to become a clergyman, and was Protestant Episcopal Bishop of Louisiana when his conscience led him to offer his military talents and training to the Confederate cause.

On September 4, Grant learned of the movement of Polk's troops into Columbus, Kentucky. Like Johnston and Polk, Grant well realized that control of the Mississippi must be a major objective of the strategy of both North and South.

The critical point was Cairo, at the southern tip of Illinois; junction of the Ohio and Mississippi Rivers, and meeting place of Illinois with the key border states of Missouri and Kentucky. Cairo was probably the most strategically important spot in the United States in September, 1861. And its significance as a base for future operations along the rivers, or in either of the border states, was enhanced by two major geographical features nearby.

Less than forty miles upriver, east of Cairo, the Tennessee River flows into the Ohio at Paducah, Kentucky. The Tennessee, rising far to the east in the mountains of southwestern Virginia, sweeps some 860 miles on a wide arc through the heart of the Confederacy. With the railroad complex which paralleled it and complemented it, the river provided a highway for war between the vitals of the South, and the great western agricultural region of the North.

Hardly less important was the Cumberland River, also flowing into the Ohio, and forming an inner, roughly concentric arc within that of the Tennessee, flowing through Nashville. At Dover in western Tennessee the two rivers are only ten miles apart. From that point to the Ohio they flow in parallel, never less than three nor more than ten miles separating them.

It was obvious to Grant that with the Confederates in Kentucky at Columbus it would not be long—perhaps a number of hours—before they could reach Paducah and Smithland on the Ohio to gain control of the mouths of the strategic Tennessee and Cumberland. Johnston's abrupt move had placed the onus for violation of Kentucky "neutrality," on the Confederacy, but it had also given the Southerners a practical military advantage.

It was equally obvious to Grant that prompt action was required. He telegraphed General Frémont that he was planning to seize Paducah at once, unless he received orders to the contrary. He also warned the Kentucky legislature of the Confederate invasion. Less than twenty-four hours later, without waiting for a reply from Frémont, Grant and every available man of his command were on steamboats heading up the Ohio. Early on the morning of August 6, less than seventy-two hours after he had assumed command at Cairo, Grant's force landed at Paducah. At that very moment Polk, with his subordinate, Brigadier General Lloyd Tilghman, was on the outskirts of Paducah, completing a reconnaissance preparatory to occupying it. Grant promptly threw up entrenchments around the town.

Johnston, informed of this unexpected Federal movement, decided that his strength would not permit a full scale assault on Grant's position. He undertook, therefore, to establish a line across southern Kentucky which would block the Mississippi, Tennessee, and Cumberland river avenues into the South. He intended this as a base for further offensive action toward the line of the Ohio if he could obtain additional troops. Columbus, on the east bank of the Mississippi, became the western anchor of this line, and was heavily fortified by Polk with 12,000 men. An outpost was established on the opposite bank, at Belmont, Missouri, to facilitate liaison with the Confederate irregular units of southern Missouri and to help block the waterway. The great river was now closed to Union commerce and troop movements; no Federal gunboat could pass without being subjected to crossfire from the heavy guns at Columbus and at Belmont.

Further east, where the Tennessee and Cumberland crossed the Tennessee-Kentucky line, two strong Confederate forts were built—Fort Henry on the Tennessee and, 10 miles across the mucky lowlands to the east, Fort Donelson on the Cumberland. Some 5,000 men under General Tilghman held these posts. At Bowling Green, Kentucky, Johnston placed his main body of 22,000 effectives in another strongly entrenched camp, commanded by General William J. Hardee, also a West Pointer, well known as the author of the then standard U.S. Army text on infantry tactics.

Another 5,000 Confederates, under General Felix K. Zollicoffer, held the eastern end of Johnston's extended line, protecting the Cumberland Gap against any possible Federal move to reach the pro-Unionists of east Tennessee. Scattered groups of irregulars provided a tenuous link between Hardee's and Zolicoffer's commands. So long as it was not ruptured, Johnston's cordon now not only blocked the rivers to any Union advance southward, it also shielded the vital rail network linking Tennessee with the East and with other Confederate states of the South and the Southeast.

A general Union move across the Ohio River followed Grant's seizure of Paducah. Federal troops quickly gained control of northern Kentucky, and General Anderson had outposts south of Louisville and the state capital at Frankfort. Neither side as yet felt strong enough to mount a major offensive, but skirmishes and minor bickerings continued in Kentucky through September and October. An important command change occurred when Union General Anderson fell sick and was replaced by his senior subordinate, highstrung Brigadier General William Tecumseh Sherman, whose excellent leadership of a brigade at Bull Run had led to his promotion. He had been sent to join Anderson shortly afterward.

Meanwhile, in Missouri, Frémont's shortcomings were becoming apparent. Evidence of fraud and corruption in his subordinates' supply contracts, as well as his inability to handle field command, greatly concerned Lincoln. Confederate General Price was rampaging unchecked in western Missouri, while in the southeast, Southern raiders from Arkansas, in conjunction with Polk's command at Columbus and Belmont, stirred up more trouble. Frémont, after Price had captured the Federal garrison at Lexington, September 20, took the field in person in a vain effort to repair his sagging fortunes.

In Frémont's absence, his headquarters in St. Louis ordered Grant to undertake counter-demonstrations in southeastern Missouri, without "attacking the enemy," and also to assist other forces in southern Missouri in driving the raiders back into Arkansas.

Grant at once dispatched a force under Colonel Richard J. Oglesby to move against the raiders. Brigadier General Charles F. Smith, an elderly but extremely capable combat soldier commanding at Paducah, cooperated by taking a column southward towards Polk at Columbus. Grant himself, with 3,000 men, moving by steamboat, planned to threaten Polk's fortifications from the riverside at the same time. Convoying Grant's expedition were three matchbox gunboats commanded by Commander Henry Walke, USN.

En route, Grant learned by courier that Polk had already taken the steps that he and Smith had hoped to forestall. Confederate reinforcements had been ferried over to Belmont, raising its garrison to nearly 4,000 men, considerably stronger than Oglesby's command, then but a few miles to the northwest of Belmont. Oglesby was to be trapped between this force and the Arkansas raiders.

Grant, first warning Oglesby of the situation, and ordering reinforcements to him, immediately attacked Belmont. His little force, debarking near the town early on the morning of November 7, routed the garrison after a sharp fight, capturing both Belmont itself and the Confederate camp. Simultaneously Walke's gunboats engaged the Columbus fortifications in order to prevent interference from the Southern garrison across the river.

Polk, however, was neither deceived nor daunted by this diversion. While heavy guns of his river batteries held off the Federal gunboats, he personally led a strong body of reinforcements across the Mississippi to cut Grant off from his transports. The Federal troops, somewhat disorganized in their looting of the Southern camp, were at first thrown into confusion by this unexpected counter-attack.

Grant, demonstrating the cool courage that had won him renown in the Mexican War, was able to rally his shaken men. Exposing himself recklessly—one horse was shot from under him—he fought his way back to the transports. Assisted by fire from Walke's gunboats, he embarked with a number of captured guns, equipment, and prisoners. The General was the last man to leave the shore, actually riding his mount up a narrow gangplank to his steamer. Both Grant and Polk acquitted themselves well in this somewhat inconclusive combat. The Federal attackers numbered slightly more than 3,000 men; the Confederates, initially about the same strength, were reinforced to 5,000 or 6,000 by Polk's prompt reaction. The raid, planned by Grant as a hit-and-run affair, was a tactical success, but the Federal troops suffered heavy punishment in the closing phase of the battle, and were only too happy to escape to the safety of their boats. Federal losses in killed, wounded and missing were 498 men; Confederate casualties were probably 900—though Polk reported 641.

But Grant had accomplished his mission. While he kept Belmont busy, Oglesby, protected from surprise attack, and reinforced, was able to drive the raiders from Grant's district in Missouri. And Polk was careful in the future never to allow his troops to become involved in costly adventures on the west bank of the Mississippi.

Meanwhile, Confederate General Johnston's cordon defense, from Columbus on the Mississippi River to the Cumberland Gap in the Appalachians, remained inviolate. However, Federal command changes in the West during the next two months foreshadowed more activity. Lincoln, having lost all patience with

Frémont, relieved him of command November 2, shifting him to the Eastern front. Old Brigadier General David Hunter, his senior subordinate, temporarily took his place. On November 9, a sweeping directive from Washington split the Western Department into the Departments of the Missouri and of Kansas. Major General Henry W. Halleck was put in command of the former, which included Grant's command at Cairo and Smith's at Paducah; General Hunter commanded the latter. At the same time the former Departments of the Cumberland, and of the Ohio, north of it, were combined into a new Department of the Ohio under Brigadier General Don Carlos Buell, who would be responsible for operations in central and eastern Kentucky. These shifts, be it noted, left unchanged the faulty Union concept of two independent commanders in the same theater of operations.

Halleck arrived in St. Louis to assume his new command on November 18, and proceeded to clean up the administrative mess left by Frémont. West Pointer Halleck's deserved reputation as the most knowledgeable military theorist in the Army was reflected in his nickname, "Old Brains." He had resigned from the Army in 1854 at thirty-nine and had become a successful lawyer in California, while still a major general in the California militia. Now called back as a major general in the Regular Army, he was second only to McClellan in rank and in promise as a leader in the North.

Like McClellan, Halleck would never quite live up to the promise. Nevertheless, after the incompetent Frémont, he was a breath of fresh air in the West during the fall and winter and 1861. In justice, he must receive a share of the credit for the successes which were to take place in his Department early the following year.

Buell, another West Pointer, was also a commander who would never quite live up to expectations. He superseded Sherman, whose farseeing statement that 200,000 Union troops would be needed to clear the Mississippi Valley had enraged incompetent War Secretary Cameron. Cameron held Sherman up to public ridicule and branded him as a ''crazy man.'' Largely because of this, Sherman was at this time near a nervous breakdown.

The only break in the calm of the closing weeks of 1861 was a surprise but unsuccessful bombardment of Cairo on November 27 by Confederate gunboats based on Columbus. Lack of action in the West distressed Lincoln almost as much as did McClellan's inactivity in and around Washington. He was concerned about the plight of the pro-Union inhabitants of eastern Tennessee, and also aware of the strategic significance of the East Tennessee and Virginia R.R., the only direct link between Virginia and the western regions of the Confederacy.

The President, therefore, kept prodding Buell—directly and by way of General-in-Chief McClellan—to push through Kentucky to eastern Tennessee as rapidly as possible. Buell felt that he did not yet have sufficient strength to undertake such a major offensive, and he was not satisfied with the state of training of the forces he did have. While perhaps he overrated the numbers and quality of the available Confederate opposition, his caution at this time was probably justified.

Finally, Buell began tentative movements toward Cumberland Gap, in early January, 1862. At the same time he requested Halleck to carry out diversions in western Kentucky. In response, Generals Grant and C. F. Smith were busy from January 13 to 20, making demonstrations to occupy the attentions of the garrisons of Columbus, Fort Henry and Fort Donelson, while Brigadier General George H. Thomas of Buell's command was advancing with about 6,000 men against the defenders of southeastern Kentucky. Confederate General G. B. Crittenden had just assumed the command of this region from energetic General Zollicoffer. With about 5,000 men, Crittendon and Zollicoffer moved to meet Thomas' challenge.

Early on the morning of January 19, Crittenden moved north from the vicinity of Mill Springs, Kentucky, to attack Thomas, then encamped at Logan's Crossroads. Though surprised by the Confederate assault, Thomas calmly organized his units defensively, then, in the face of the strong Confederate pressure, counterattacked, and drove the Southerners from the field. General Zollicoffer was killed; total Confederate casualties were 533, opposed to a Union loss of 262. Crittenden, after a commendable beginning, apparently lost control of his command and Zollicoffer's death brought the complete collapse of Confederate leadership.

East of the Mississippi, Johnston's cordon barrier still barred the Union way. The roads in Kentucky were abominable, and Buell had an excellent excuse for being unable now to press forward to reap the full fruits of Thomas' victory at Mill Springs. In their demonstration and reconnaissances further west, Generals Grant and C. F. Smith had encountered similar trouble with the roads, but reached the conclusion that if the roads were difficult for Federal movements, they were undoubtedly just as bad for the Confederates.

And there were always the rivers. Grant went into consultation with Flag Officer Andrew H. Foote, USN, commanding the flotilla of river gunboats in General Halleck's Department of the Missouri. As a result, on January 28, Halleck received similar telegraph messages from Grant and Foote. Grant's merely said: "With permission, I will take Fort Henry on the Tennessee, and establish and hold a large camp there." In scarcely more words, Foote endorsed Grant's proposal and expressed his readiness to support the move.

On the twenty-ninth, while Halleck was still pondering these messages, he received a telegram from Washington, informing him that Beauregard was reportedly leaving Manassas for Kentucky and taking fifteen regiments with him. Obviously a blow should be struck before these Confederate reinforcements arrived. Actually the information later turned out to be false, but "Old Brains" made one of the few emphatic decisions of his career. On January 30 he telegraphed Grant to prepare "to take and hold Fort Henry." He immediately began to scour his department for reinforcements to send to Grant, and he asked Buell to make demonstrations and diversions to keep General Johnston from reinforcing western Kentucky.

Grant promptly informed Halleck of plans he and Foote had already jointly prepared for movement up the Ohio, Tennessee and Cumberland Rivers by steamboat. On February 3 he was ready, and reported, "Will be off up the Tennessee at six o'clock." Early next morning his troops were disembarking on both sides of the river, just out of range of the guns of Fort Henry.

A bastioned work, Fort Henry swept the river with its guns, but it was on such low ground that it was an easy target for the Union gunboats. Partly because of this, partly because heavy rains had caused the river to overflow into part of the fort, and mostly because of the slow but steady encirclement of Grant's troops, Confederate General Tilghman despaired of being able to hold the place. He sent most of the garrison of 2,500 men eastward to stronger Fort Donelson, while he remained in the fort with seventy men to cover the evacuation and to shoot it out with the gunboats. Grant's troops, floundering in the mud, were unable to prevent the evacuation.

On the morning of the sixth, the seven gunboats began their bombardment. After two hours of naval attack and before the Army became engaged, the Confederate flag was hauled down. One gunboat, its boiler pierced by a Confederate shell, had been put out of action; another was badly mauled. Grant, not begrudging the Navy the honor of winning Fort Henry, immediately reported the capture to Halleck, adding "I shall take and destroy Fort Donelson on the eighth."

The unexpected loss of Fort Henry was a shattering blow to General Johnston. He considered counterattacking to repair his shattered line. But the condition of the roads, his shortage of troops and lack of suitable river transports, caused him to reject such a move. The only alternative was to withdraw from the now-breached cordon defense in Kentucky, and to establish a new defensive line in northern Tennessee. To cover the withdrawal until the new line could be established, Johnston, as he evacuated

Bowling Green, sent 12,000 men to Fort Donelson under the command of General John Buchanan Floyd, erstwhile U.S. Secretary of War, and one of the Confederacy's most incompetent political generals.

Continuing rains thwarted Grant's plans to move against Donelson on the eighth. Not until late on the twelfth was he able to begin the attack. By this time Floyd and his reinforcements had arrived, bringing the garrison to a total of 20,000 men. Fort Donelson frowned over the Cumberland, on a 100-foot height, armed with powerful batteries, while the land approaches, well entrenched and protected by abatis, were accessible only over one narrow ridge.

Grant began his operation with the mere 15,000 men in the two divisions with which he had marched overland. But another division, sent around from the Tennessee by water, with Foote's flotilla, arrived the next day, February 13. Additional reinforcements, scraped up by General Halleck from all over the Missouri Department, also began to stream in.

Grant hoped that, as at Henry, naval gunfire would force Confederate surrender. In any event, on the twelfth and thirteenth, he did not wish to chance an assault against a numerically superior foe behind powerful fortifications. But despite Grant's orders not to engage, McClernand's division on the Union right attempted on February 13, to charge some troublesome Confederate batteries. The attackers were repulsed with heavy loss.

Contentious John A. McClernand, Brigadier General, U.S. Volunteers, was a military ignoramus bolstered to his rank through political influence. He was one of the leading Democrats in Illinois and a forthright foe to secession. His disobedience of Grant's orders on this occasion was only the first of many similar incidents brought about by his overweening ambition and jealousy.

Next day the gunboats began a bombardment. The ease with which he had overwhelmed Fort Henry caused Foote to underestimate the power of Confederate artillery and the determination of Southern gunners. Instead of standing off at long range, he closed to within 200 yards of the defending batteries—with four ironclads (his injured vessels had been replaced) and two wooden gunboats. He caused considerable damage to the fort, but his own vessels suffered so seriously that some of them began to float down the stream, out of control. Foote himself was wounded, and he had to call off the attack.

Grant, without wavering, tightened his lines and prepared for the siege that now appeared necessary.

Unfortunately for the Confederate cause, Southern leadership within Donelson was neither so philosophical nor so tough as the Union leadership outside. It was, in fact, unnecessarily taking the counsel of its own fears. The three Confederate officers—Generals Floyd, Gideon J. Pillow, and Simon B. Buckner—held a council of war that evening of February 14. They pictured themselves surrounded by an army whose strength they greatly exaggerated, as well as threatened by a fleet of ironclads whose limitations should have been evident from the results of the day's gunnery duel. So instead of holding on for several more days, as Johnston was expecting, they decided to fight their way out of Donelson, and to abandon it to the enemy. Pillow's division on the left, supported by the cavalry of Colonel Nathan B. Forrest, would make the initial breakout to the south. Buckner, after making a demonstration to pin down the Federals opposite the right flank, would follow quickly behind Pillow.

The Confederate assault, early on the fifteenth, was initially successful. Five Confederate brigades, under Pillow, came smashing out of the eastern side of the position through heavy timber and underbrush. They struck McClernand's division, thin-spread on the Federal right, and punched through, with Forrest's cavalry on their outer flank. A battery was overrun, some 300 infantrymen captured and McClernand's troops, their ammunition shot away, were in almost complete confusion. Behind the attacking force Buckner's fresh division was now forming for an additional punch. The road to Nashville was open. The entire

Confederate strength could now have been hurled into battle for a complete victory over the surprised Northerners.

At this moment Pillow, seeing some movement in the trenches on the other flank, from which Buckner's men had come, lost his nerve. He ordered Buckner back to defend his trenches. Buckner, a professional soldier, who could assess the success already gained, naturally demurred. With Floyd as a referee, the two generals argued while the minutes ticked by. The argument was ended by Floyd's final decision to recall his entire force back into the fortifications.

Meanwhile Grant, who had gone on board Foote's flagship for a conference with the wounded Navy man, had heard the noise of battle. Dashing off to the scene, he found his left and center untouched, but his right shattered. He rushed a note to Foote: "If all the gunboats that can come will immediately make their appearance . . . it may secure us a victory. Otherwise, all may be defeated . . . A terrible conflict . . . has demoralized a portion of my command . . . I must make a charge to save appearances. . . ."

He did just that, in his own quiet way, ordering reliable General C. F. Smith, commanding the left division, to assault the area into which Buckner's men were now returning. Tough old Smith, cap lifted high on the point of his saber, personally led the charge, sweeping the off-balance Confederates back into the walls of the fort itself. At the same time Wallace's division, in the center, was shifted by Grant to face the now halted Confederate threat on the right and cover McClernand's shattered troops. By early afternoon the entire Union situation had been re-established. The Confederates, so close to success that morning, knew now that escape was impossible and the outer defenses of the fort untenable.

Once more the unhappy trio of Southern generals huddled in a council of war. There seemed no course but surrender. But Floyd was under indictment in Washington, accused of having deliberately and traitorously weakened the nation's defenses in

1860 and 1861, while he was President Buchanan's Secretary of War. Pillow, too, feared that he might be tried for treason if he fell into Union hands. So these two political generals, abandoning their men to save their own hides, slipped up the river in boats, leaving the conscientious Regular, Simon Bolivar Buckner, to surrender.

One man would have nothing to do with this. Nathan Bedford Forrest, hard-riding, hard-fighting cavalryman, led his regiment through the swamps between the Union right flank and the river. He got safely away, taking with him a few infantrymen who, too, wished to fight again another day.

Late that night Buckner sent a message to Grant proposing an armistice to discuss capitulation terms. Grant made the immortal reply ever afterwards linked to his name:

"No terms except an unconditional and immediate surrender can be accepted. I propose to move immediately upon your works."

Henceforth, he would be known to his countrymen as "Unconditional Surrender" Grant.

Buckner had apparently hoped to be able to negotiate terms permitting him to give up the fortress with the honors of war—the garrison marching out unmolested with flags flying, drums beating, weapons in hand, to rejoin the main Confederate army to the south. But Buckner knew Grant; they had been old friends in Regular Army days and he knew that Grant meant what he said. Buckner surrendered.

It was a touching meeting for these former comrades-in-arms. They had last seen each other in New York, more than seven years earlier, when Captain Grant, just resigned from the Army, was penniless and unable to pay his transportation from New York to his home. Captain Buckner, knowing that Grant's situation was caused by his loan of a large sum of money to a sick, discharged soldier, had pressed funds on his old friend. Presumably Grant had long ago repaid Buckner, but a colorful legend suggests there had been no opportunity to repay the debt, and that when he met Buckner after Donelson's surrender, he pressed his purse on the disconsolate Confederate. In any event, the old friends discussed the recent fighting, with Buckner saying that had he been in command at the outset, Grant would not have gotten Donelson so easily. Grant, thinking of the risks he had deliberately taken against the incompetent Floyd, replied: "If you had been in command I should not have tried in the way I did."

In belated response to Halleck's appeal for assistance, Buell now sent one of his divisions by boat to join Grant at Donelson. Grant immediately returned the force to Buell, but in a rather unorthodox manner. He simply ordered the division to proceed up the Cumberland to rejoin Buell at Nashville, now evacuated by the Confederates. Buell was chagrined to arrive in the city on February 25 and find his division already there, waiting for him.

Four days later the Confederate fortress at Columbus was evacuated. Grant's two-week campaign against Forts Henry and Donelson had driven the Confederates from Kentucky, and deep into Tennessee. Union gunboats were raiding up the Tennessee River into Mississippi and Alabama. The rivers were apparently the highroads to Union victory.

# Some Generals Fight

**M**eanwhile, events on the western side of the Mississippi River must be examined. In western Missouri Major General Samuel R. Curtis, with about 12,000 men, had been pushing Confederate Generals Price and McCulloch back down to where southwestern Missouri meets northwestern Arkansas. The Southerners were now joined by Major General Earl Van Dorn, who on March 3, 1862, assumed command of the combined Confederate forces just south of the Missouri-Arkansas border. Van Dorn's total strength was about 16,000 men.

The Confederate general immediately assumed the offensive. On March 5, he attempted a surprise blow against a portion of Curtis' command at Bentonville, Arkansas, but the Union commander was able to pull his exposed units back, and next day took up a strong defensive position in front of Pea Ridge, an elevation some thirty miles northeast of Fayetteville, Arkansas. Van Dorn decided to avoid a frontal attack against the awaiting

Federals. That night he moved around Curtis' right flank, placing his entire command on the Union line of communications.

Curtis discovered the movement, so when Van Dorn attacked from the north on March 7, the Federal army was ready. In the intense fighting which followed, Southern General Ben McCulloch was killed. By nightfall neither side had been able to gain any advantage, and the battle was resumed early on March 8. The Southerners were almost out of ammunition, however, and when Van Dorn found himself still unable to displace the stubborn Federals, he acknowledged failure and withdrew in good order. There was no pursuit by the Federals; their casualties had been heavy, about 1,300 men, while Confederate losses were upwards of 800.

Tactically the Battle of Pea Ridge was a draw, but its strategic results were considerable. Curtis, by his stubborn defense against a larger force, had established the western anchor of a battle line that was now stretching across half a continent.

Before we look into this, however, we must cast our eyes a good 900 miles west into New Mexico, where for a while a briskly-burning Confederate brush-fire threatened Union control of the Southwest.

In July, 1861, Confederate Brigadier General Henry Hopkins Sibley, West Pointer and former Regular Army cavalryman, had been sent to Fort Bliss, Texas, near the site of modern El Paso, to organize an invasion of California. Gathering some 4,000 Texan volunteers, Sibley advanced up the Rio Grande. On February 21, 1862, at Valverde, New Mexico, about 170 miles upriver, he met and defeated a Union force under Colonel Edward R. S. Canby—another West Pointer—who commanded the newly-created Union Department of New Mexico.

Canby's force, of almost equal strength, consisted of some fragments of Regular troops gathered from frontier garrisons, and New Mexico Volunteers. Kit Carson, noted scout, led one of the volunteer regiments.

Sibley now occupied Albuquerque and Santa Fe in turn. Canby, however, had devastated the countryside, after gathering ample supplies in Forts Craig and Union, which were too strong for Sibley to attack. After some inconclusive skirmishing near Santa Fe, lack of food forced the Confederates to withdraw southward early in April. On the fifteenth, Canby, reinforced by Colorado Volunteers, fell on Sibley at Peralta, twenty miles south of Albuquerque. In a series of running fights the starving Confederates were driven clear back to Fort Bliss, where Sibley's little army disintegrated, having lost approximately half its strength in killed, wounded and missing. With it evaporated Southern dreams of a conquest of California. From that time on, New Mexico was held firmly in the Union.

Meanwhile another operation was getting under way in southeastern Missouri. Immediately after the capture of Fort Donelson, Halleck decided to drive the Southerners from the fortified area in the vicinity of New Madrid, on the Mississippi River. Brigadier General John Pope, with 10,000 men, was given this task.

On February 28, Pope's command started southward from Commerce, Missouri. That same day Southern General Polk evacuated Columbus, Kentucky, as he moved south to form the left wing of Johnston's new line across Tennessee. But before leaving, Polk reinforced the units holding the New Madrid area to about 10,000 men.

Some twenty-five miles below Columbus, where Missouri, Kentucky and Tennessee meet, the Mississippi turns sharply northwest for five miles, then south again, in a perfect S turn. At the first, or southeastern, bend of the river an island almost two miles long and over half a mile wide lay in the channel. Island No. 10, as it had been called by the U.S. Engineers, had been heavily fortified by the Confederates, completely blocking the river to traffic. Swamps along the banks of the river made it inaccessible to overland approach. (The island today has

NEW MEXICO
CAMPAIGN
Feb.- Apr., 1862

0   50   100        200

Scale  of  Miles

completely disappeared; swallowed by the restless Mississippi floods.)

On the Missouri (right) bank of the river, at the northwestern bend of the S turn, lay the fortified town of New Madrid. The guns of the two fortresses complemented each other in blocking the approach of Federal gunboats. In addition a flotilla of Confederate gunboats augmented the defenses.

Arriving before New Madrid on March 3, Pope—now reinforced to 23,000 men—soon discovered the magnitude of his task. He had hoped to make an assault, assisted by Flag Officer Foote's gunboats. But the vessels could not pass the two Confederate fortresses, so Pope, deciding to take New Madrid, established heavy guns on the river below the town, completely cutting its communications with the south. On March 13, the Confederate forts around New Madrid were subjected to an intensive bombardment. This was more than the inexperienced defenders could

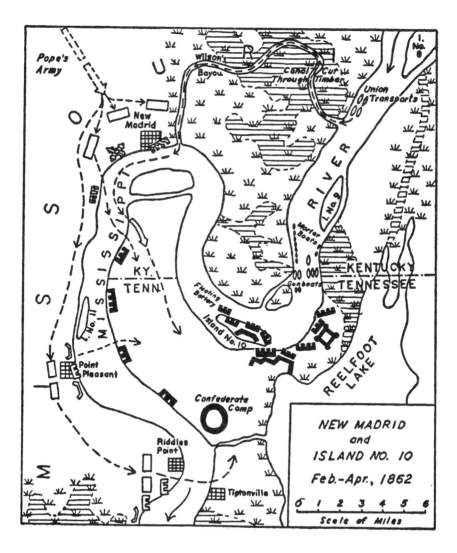

stand. That night they evacuated the town, the entire garrison moving to Island No. 10. Here, apparently invulnerable to attack, and well provisioned, the Southerners still effectively blocked the river.

Pope now discovered that within the encircling swamps there was a long stretch of solid ground on the left (east) bank of the river below the fort. But his own troops were on the right bank, and it was impossible to cross under fire without naval assistance. He called on Foote for help.

During a thunderstorm on the night of April 4, Commander Walke successfully took the gunboat *Carondelet* on a daring ride past the powerful Confederate batteries of the island. Foote sent a second vessel down through another storm, before dawn on the seventh. Later that day under cover of heavy fire from the two boats, Pope's troops began to cross, and to approach the fort along the nearby stretch of solid ground.

The defenders now realized that they could not hold out much longer, and shortly after dark the main garrison attempted to escape. But now the island's inaccessibility was against them. They were completely cut off, and by dawn of April 8 the entire fortress and its garrison were in Pope's hands. Almost 7,000 officers and men, as well as great quantities of guns, ammunition, and supplies were captured. The Mississippi bottleneck had been unstopped and the new Southern defensive line was now open to harassment and possible turning from the river.

But other events had affected that defensive line, and the career of Albert Sidney Johnston, even more significantly.

Almost immediately after his victory at Fort Donelson, Grant, realizing the opportunity now offered aggressive Northern leadership, took action to pursue Johnston, now retiring from Nashville to Murfreesboro, Tennessee. He telegraphed to General Halleck at St. Louis that unless he received orders to the contrary he would take Clarksville on February 21 and Nashville about March 1. Receiving no answer, Grant sent General C. F. Smith up the Cumberland River. Smith arrived at Clarksville on schedule, to find it evacuated.

Again Grant wired Halleck that he was himself going up to Nashville, where he knew Buell was now bound, and again receiving no answer, started up-river. Finding Buell sitting opposite Nashville, Grant urged him to pursue Johnston. Buell, however, fearing a counterattack, declined to move.

Orders now came from Halleck for Grant to concentrate all his troops back at Fort Henry, on the Tennessee River. All chance for the unremitting pressure on Johnston which might have shortened the war had been tossed aside. Worse yet, that same day, March 4, by Halleck's order, Grant was relieved of command. The ostensible reason was a vague charge that Grant had failed to answer Halleck's messages during his Donelson campaign, and that he had left his command without authority when he had visited Buell at Nashville. General C. F. Smith was given command of the Army of the Tennessee.

President Lincoln, however, was beginning to look with some interest at the record of the fighting general of Belmont, Henry and Donelson. He demanded that Halleck produce evidence to substantiate his charges against Grant. Halleck then proclaimed that there had been a misunderstanding, and restored Grant to his command on March 13.

One might sum up the Northern command situation now as being entangled in a web of conflicting self-interests. Halleck had long been urging General-in-Chief McClellan and President Lincoln to combine the forces west of the Appalachians under one commander, and was not delicate in hinting that he, Halleck, was the man for the job. McClellan, however, was afraid Halleck might become a rival if he became the sole commander of the western theater of operations. He hoped his good friend Buell, as an independent commander, would achieve enough of a reputation to balance Halleck's growing prestige.

But on March 11, for reasons we shall note later, McClellan

was relieved of his responsibilities as General-in-Chief in order to devote his full efforts to command of the Army of the Potomac. At the same time Lincoln issued orders placing Halleck in overall command in the West.

On March 17, Grant rejoined the Army of the Tennessee in the vicinity of Savannah and Pittsburg Landing, Tennessee, re-assuming command from his old friend, C. F. Smith, now dying from injuries received in the campaign. Buell had been ordered to march his Army of the Ohio from the vicinity of Nashville to join Grant, who was peremptorily ordered to avoid any possibility of a major engagement until after his arrival. Halleck then intended to come down from St. Louis to assume field command personally, and to lead these combined armies of 80,000 men to a victory which would redound solely to the credit of Henry W. Halleck. But having failed to keep pressure on the Confederates, Halleck, like so many other dilatory generals of history, was to find his foe less than cooperative.

Johnston had been violently berated in the South for his failures in Kentucky and Tennessee. But given this unexpected breathing spell, and with the continued expression of confidence of President Davis—who almost alone still supported him—he now began to collect reinforcements from all over the South and Southwest. His fighting spirit was bolstered also by newly-arrived General P. G. T. Beauregard, flamboyant hero of Manassas, who became Johnston's deputy.

By the end of March Johnston and Beauregard had collected an army of almost 50,000 men at Corinth, Mississippi, a bare twenty miles away from Grant's 42,000 camped by the banks of the Tennessee River below Savannah, Tennessee. There was considerable cavalry action, and maneuvering of small forces, in the area between the two armies, but Grant, told to wait for Buell, was not permitted to probe firmly to determine Confederate dispositions and apparent intentions. But somehow or other Buell just couldn't get his army moving, and April arrived before he did. Meanwhile Grant was still frozen in place by his orders.

Grant would be in command until Halleck's arrival. He assumed that when the armies were combined all limitations against offensive action would be removed. He planned, therefore, that as soon as Buell and his troops joined, he would immediately strike Jackson at Corinth. There lay the logistical solar plexus of the Confederacy in the theater of operations; the junction of vital rail lines running east-west and north-south. Corinth was, as Grant put it—"the great strategic point . . . between the Mississippi and Tennessee Rivers and between Nashville and Vicksburg."

Waiting impatiently now for Buell, who would, as it turned out, take eighteen days to march eighty-five miles, Grant prepared for the advance. The Army of the Tennessee, on April 6, 1862, totalled about 42,000 men. Five divisions—some 35,000 in strength, were concentrated between Pittsburg Landing and Shiloh Church. These were Sherman's, McClernand's, Hurlbut's, W. H. L. Wallace's (not to be confused with Lew Wallace) and Prentiss' divisions. Sherman was the only professional soldier of the five. Most of McClernand's and Wallace's divisions were veterans of Fort Donelson; the other three were composed almost entirely of raw recruits.

At Crump's Landing, five miles north of Pittsburg Landing and two miles west of Savannah, across the river, was Lew Wallace's division, also veterans of Donelson; charged with protecting the army's supply dumps in the area and covering the right flank and line of communications against a possible Confederate turning movement.

During the first week of April, the Confederate cavalry was active, providing much more effective reconnaissance and screening for Johnston than the Federal horsemen did for Grant. There was considerable skirmishing in the heavy underbrush of the forest around the Federal camps, particularly in front of Sherman's division—camped around Shiloh Church—which was furthest west.

Grant kept his headquarters at the little town of Savannah,

to facilitate personal liaison when Buell should appear. He spent each day inspecting his units, supervising training, and observing outpost skirmishing. He returned to Savannah—eight miles by boat from Pittsburg Landing—each night. Late April 4, returning after dark to his boat at the Landing during a storm, Grant's horse fell with him, badly injuring his ankle. He could walk only with the assistance of crutches, and he was confined to his headquarters on the fifth.

Meanwhile, on April 3, Johnston began to move eastward from Corinth with 42,000 men. His army, which had about the same proportion of veterans and recruits as Grant's, was divided into four corps, under Major Generals Hardee, Bragg, Polk, and Breckenridge. The first three of these, like Johnston and his second-in-command Beauregard, were graduates of West Point and former U.S. Regular Army officers. John C. Breckenridge, former Vice President of the United States, was to prove himself in this battle to be one of the few able political generals of the Civil War.

Johnston's plan was to launch a surprise attack on Grant on April 5, before Buell's Army of the Ohio could arrive within supporting distance. But poor roads and the inexperience of his staff and of his soldiers delayed the advance. It was not until late that day that his advance guard arrived within two miles of Shiloh Church. This was about the time that Sherman penned a dispatch to Grant, reporting that "the enemy is saucy, but . . . I do not apprehend anything like an attack on our position." About this same time General Nelson's division of Buell's army arrived at Savannah.

Grant ordered Nelson to move next day down the east bank of the Tennessee in order to be ferried over to Crump's or Pittsburg Landings. Despite his painful injury, the Union general intended to go to Pittsburg Landing the next day, after an early morning meeting with Buell, who was reported to be nearby. (Actually Buell had reached Savannah but had failed to advise Grant of his arrival.)

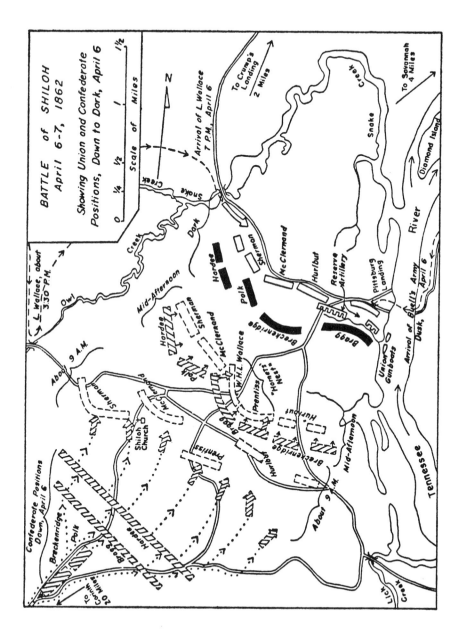

BATTLE of SHILOH
April 6-7, 1862

Showing Union and Confederate
Positions, Dawn to Dark, April 6

Anticipating a long and busy day, Grant was eating breakfast at about 6:00 A.M. on the sixth when he heard the sound of heavy firing up the river toward Pittsburg Landing. He sent orders to Nelson to move his division immediately up the east bank "opposite Pittsburg." He wrote a note to Buell, explaining that he would not be able to meet him as planned, and informing him of the orders just issued to Nelson. He then hobbled to his dispatch boat and headed upstream toward the sound of battle. On the way he pulled into the dock at Crump's Landing where General Lew Wallace was waiting. Pausing only long enough to tell Wallace to be prepared to move his division if ordered, Grant continued upstream, arriving at Pittsburg Landing about 8:00 A.M.

The noise of battle, and information he gathered from officers at the Landing, made Grant certain that the Confederate main body was attacking here, and that Crump's Landing was not threatened. He immediately sent a staff officer to order Lew Wallace to bring his division to Pittsburg Landing. Wallace received this order about 9:00 A.M. Since the distance was about five miles, his division could have been expected well before noon. After checking on the supply of ammunition, Grant mounted his horse and galloped to inspect his hard-pressed divisions near Shiloh Church.

The fury of the Southern attack was still mounting, as fresh units deployed off the Corinth Road. First into action had been Hardee's corps, whose battle line had been moving through the woods toward Shiloh Church when discovered shortly after dawn by Sherman's outposts. Slowed down by the Union defenders in front of the church, Hardee had been joined by Bragg's corps, then Polk's, the regiments swinging off the road into action on both flanks. As the battle line built up in this rather haphazard way, with units becoming more intermingled, Johnston arbitrarily divided the line between Hardee, Polk and Bragg from left to right. Breckenridge's corps, now coming up, was sent to the extreme right flank to try in a vain attempt to get between the Federals and the river.

Noon came and went, and the Confederate attacks continued with unabating fury, driving the Union defenders back further toward the Landing. Both armies were becoming increasingly disorganized. Grant discovered that Prentiss' men, holding a keystone position in the left center of the arc of the battle line, had taken advantage of a sunken road as a ready-made trench. He ordered Prentiss to hold "at all hazards," then went on to revisit and to encourage his other commanders.

Now, for the first time, the Confederates failed to make headway. Attack after attack was repulsed by Prentiss, whose position was called the "Hornets' Nest" by the baffled Southerners. Shortly after 2:00 P.M. General Johnston rode up to find out the cause of the halt. Discovering for himself the strength of the Union position, he ordered renewed attacks against the units on Prentiss' flanks, while he prepared to lead another assault on the "Hornets' Nest" itself. Riding to the front amidst a hail of Federal bullets, Johnson received a mortal wound and died within a few moments. Beauregard now assumed command of the Confederate army.

About this time (2:30 P.M.) Grant, worried about the absence of Lew Wallace, sent several staff officers scouring the countryside. They finally found the missing division approaching the bridge over Owl Creek, just north of Shiloh. Actually it was behind the Confederate army. Whether Wallace's orders had been incomplete, whether he had misunderstood them, or simply got lost in the confusing network of roads and streams in the region, has never been clear. In any event, he now retraced his steps towards Pittsburg Landing.

It was about 4:00 P.M. when Grant received word of Wallace's wanderings. He now knew that the missing division could not arrive before dark. This was extremely serious, since, despite the loss of their commander, the Confederates were pressing forward with apparently undiminished vigor. General W. H. L. Wallace had been mortally wounded, and his division was disintegrating, exposing Prentiss' right flank to envelopment. Grant was visiting the "Hornets' Nest" at about this time, and found Prentiss to be "as cool as if expecting victory." But Grant knew that this line could not be held much longer. Repeating his instructions to hold on as long as possible, he immediately set about establishing a final defensive line just in front of Pittsburg Landing. Shortly after Grant left, Prentiss and his division were cut off completely, but they kept on fighting with grim determination for another hour. Prentiss finally surrendered with 2,000 men between 5:00 and 6:00 P.M.

This gallant defense had given Grant the time he needed to prevent disaster. He had stretched out his cavalry—unable to operate in the underbrush battle—as a straggler line near the Landing, and as individuals and broken units drifted back, they were collected, reorganized and placed in the new defensive position. Sherman and McClernand were holding their own on the right flank, but the danger spot was in the center, where Prentiss and W. H. L. Wallace had been, and on the left where Hurlbut was now being pushed back toward the river. Grant assembled all available artillery along the high ground just above Pittsburg Landing, and here Hurlbut's division, still more or less intact, fell back to be bolstered with the pickup units Grant had created along the straggler line. Two gunboats took position on the river to form a potent extension of Grant's great concentration of artillery. As a result of these measures the exhausted Confederates, all reserves expended, were finally brought to a halt about 6:00 P.M., just short of the landing.

More than once during that terrible Sunday it had seemed that the destruction of the Army of the Tennessee was inevitable. At times there had been as many as 5,000 or more panic-stricken refugees milling near the river bank at Pittsburg Landing. The distinguished British military historian, J. F. C. Fuller, has commented that the scene was "a spectacle of complete defeat, and any ordinary general would have at once planned to retreat, hoping to save some small fraction of his shattered army. But Grant was no ordinary general; for he was one of those rare and strange men who are fortified by disaster in place of being depressed." And now, before dark, having decided that defeat was only a frame of mind, the indomitable general had issued orders based on his confidence that "the next day would bring victory to our arms."

During those dreadful hours one of the great military partnerships of history was forged in fire and blood. Sherman's division of raw recruits, first to be hit, and constantly under heavy pressure in the Confederates' endeavor to turn the right flank, performed magnificently. Sherman was twice wounded, and had several horses shot from under him, yet seemed always present at any threatened spot on the division front. After a couple of visits to the right of the line Grant decided that it was not necessary to "stay long with Sherman." And the fiery, redheaded division commander would never forget the coolness and confidence of Grant under fire, as he issued his orders, made suggestions, or called out words of encouragement to hard-pressed soldiers.

After the Southern drive had been halted, and shortly before darkness settled over the bloody field, Nelson's division of Buell's army crossed the river and took position on the thin left flank of the Army of the Tennessee. During the night two more of Buell's divisions crossed to bolster Grant's left wing. And soon after dark Lew Wallace's division marched up to slip into position between Sherman's right and Snake Creek. Grant ordered Buell and Wallace to join in the counterattack he had planned for the next morning.

There was little rest for weary troops that night as Union and Confederate officers labored in a heavy rainstorm to untangle the confused mixture of units. Despite rain and sleeplessness, Grant launched the attack at dawn.

The Confederates fought as bravely on the defensive as the Federals had the day before. But disorganization, exhaustion, and the numerical superiority of the Union army—almost half of whom were fresh troops—proved too much for Beauregard and his gallant men. Shortly after noon the Southerners were streaming away in complete defeat, and Grant personally organized a charge which drove the last Confederate unit off the field near Shiloh Church.

There should have been a pursuit of the defeated Southerners. But the words of two Union generals provided a human explanation for this failure. Grant wrote: "I wanted to pursue, but had not the heart to order the men who had fought desperately for two days, lying in the mud and rain when they were not fighting, and I did not feel disposed to positively order Buell, or any part of his command to pursue." In a letter to a friend, Sherman candidly explained why the Confederates were not pressed: "I assure you, my dear fellow, that we had quite enough of their society for two whole days, and were only too glad to be rid of them on any terms."

The first of those two days some 42,000 Confederates came within an ace of shattering the 35,000 men Grant had at Pittsburg Landing. With the arrival of Lew Wallace and three of Buell's divisions, Grant had more than 20,000 fresh troops, and the result was inevitable. Union losses were 1,754 killed, 8,508 wounded, and 2,885 missing. Southern losses were 1,723 killed, 8,012 wounded and 959 missing. This was by far the bloodiest battle yet fought in the Civil War.

Tactically both sides were guilty of a combination of glaring errors. Neither Grant nor Johnston had established an adequate field headquarters, so that both armies, once battle was joined, fought without coordinated direction.

Strategically, Grant was surprised. His enemy had concentrated 42,000 men within a few miles of his camps without his knowing about it, and the power and energy of the Confederate attack were totally unexpected. More extensive reconnaissance and an advanced outpost line would have prevented, or at least reduced, the extent of this strategic surprise. It is to his credit that local security measures of his divisions were adequate, and enabled his startled troops to scramble into battle formation barely in time to meet the Southern onslaught. But this can in no way absolve him from his responsibility to take adequate measures to avoid surprise.

The Confederate attack was over-extended, lacked a real main effort, and by noon of the first day all Southern reserves had been sucked into the fight. The Union defense was a patchwork affair with islands of resistance frequently acting in complete isolation from each other. Grant's personal presence was the sole unifying factor on the Union side. Panicky flight on the part of green Federal troops in several instances, was matched by the skulking of some of the equally raw Confederates.

There has been a persistent legend, resulting partly from Buell's misleading official report, that Grant's army was taken by surprise in its tents, and that it was saved only by the timely arrival of the Army of the Ohio. This, as we have seen, is completely wrong. Grant and his army had saved themselves before a single soldier of Buell's Army of the Ohio crossed the river the evening of April 6. But the presence of the fresh troops on April 7 assured a complete Union victory rather than the draw which would have been likely otherwise.

Previous to Shiloh, many Northerners had believed that the Confederacy would collapse when faced with the full military might of an aroused North. An equal proportion of Southerners had been sure that mercenary and effete Northerners would have neither the spirit nor determination to persevere against the gallantry and *élan* of an aroused South. Both sides had to re-evaluate the struggle. Shiloh proved that the war would be a fight to the finish, with (in Grant's words) "Southern dash" pitted against "Northern pluck and endurance."

The casualty toll of the battle, as reported by the newspapers, coupled with rumors that a drunken, beaten Grant had been saved only by the provident arrival of a vigorous, sober Buell, caused an outcry against Grant in the North. Many Republican leaders felt that, regardless of the validity of the criticisms or truth of the rumors, Grant had become a political liability. A group of these politicians came to Lincoln and appealed to him, for the sake of the Republican Party and the Administration, to relieve Grant. Lincoln, listening patiently, ended the interview with a sentence still ringing down the long years:

"I can't spare this man; he fights!"

# 7

# Father of Waters

**N**aval warfare on the Mississippi was characterized by extraordinary extemporization and ingenuity. It was conducted, on both sides, by men of vision and ability, with U.S. Navy background and training, assisted by a handful of brainy civilians. Perhaps the most remarkable point of the programs on both sides was the almost spontaneous recognition of the ironclad and the ram. This is all the more interesting because the consensus of older officers of the U.S. Navy during the 1850's had been a hidebound disbelief in the efficacy of either.

Possession of the Mississippi River was as essential to the South as it was to the North. Hence, early in the war, as we have seen, Confederate batteries were erected at Columbus, Kentucky, barring the upper river, and at Forts Henry and Donelson on the Tennessee and Cumberland Rivers. Additional fortifications arose at Fort Pillow at Chickasaw Bluffs, at Vicksburg, and at Grand Gulf and Port Hudson—taking advantage of strategic high ground along the eastern bank of the river. And below New Orleans the formidable bastions of Forts Jackson and St. Philip defended the vital Southern water gate.

In brief, defense of the Mississippi River was considered to be the responsibility of the Confederate Army; any naval participation merely an adjunct. A handful of river packets and two ocean-going vessels at New Orleans were converted into gunboats. Two massive ironclads went into construction there, and two more at Memphis. But Flag Officer George N. Hollins, formerly USN, the senior Confederate Navy officer in the entire area, found himself subordinated to Army command, and hampered by lack of funds. Major General Mansfield Lovell, a West Pointer, who commanded in the New Orleans area, did make some attempts to obtain further assistance from Richmond, without success.

To augment naval strength locally against any threat from the Union wooden ships lying off the Delta, Lovell also seized fourteen river boats, which were fashioned into rams by strengthening their bows and forward decks with scrap iron. Midship sections were protected by cotton bales and thick pine bulwarks, and one gun was mounted on each vessel. Officered by a group of river captains and pilots, this River Defense Fleet was purely an Army project. In fact the rivermen, commissioned in the Confederate Army, boasted that, if occasion offered, they would show the Confederate Navy how to fight. The final element of this mongrel force consisted of two steamers armed, operated and equipped by the State of Louisiana. Not only was there no unity of command, but by the course of events, the force was shortly split into elements operating in two separate theaters at the respective ends of a 1,100-mile-long river line.

The Northern plan for breaching the Southern defenses envisaged simultaneous drives from the Gulf of Mexico north, and from St. Louis south. By this means the Confederacy would be split longitudinally, and the blockade maintained by actual occupation of all the river ports between.

This, of course, had been the nucleus of General Scott's

"Anaconda Plan." But not until a St. Louis civil engineer importuned the U.S. Navy Department to blockade the upper Mississippi at Cairo, and also the mouths of the Tennessee and Cumberland, had the Federal Administration taken heed.

# THE "INLAND SEA"

It was in April 1861 that James B. Eads, president of a wrecking and salvage company, and widely conversant with Mississippi River conditions, put his finger on the vital upper river area. Eads also offered his 1,000-ton tough snagboat (wrecker) *Benton*, as a floating battery.

Out of that offer grew the U.S. Navy on the upper Mississippi, with the *Benton* the ironclad flagship of the flotilla; about her would be assembled seven other river craft designed by Naval Constructor Samuel M. Pook, and built at St. Louis and Cincinnati by Eads and other contractors. These became a vital factor in the Army operations along the upper Mississippi Valley waterways, beginning with the Henry-Donelson campaign and the later support of Grant at Shiloh.

The "Pook Turtles" were flat-bottomed craft, 75 feet long, with 50-foot beam and 6-foot draft. Each was propelled by a large paddlewheel hung in a mid-ship trunk just forward of the stern, which ended in a wide fantail. A wooden box-like sloping casemate, like a turtle's carapace, covered the hull from stem to stern, giving the type its nickname. The forward end of the casement was covered with iron plates two and one-half inches thick, backed by twenty-four inches of oak. Similar iron plating protected engines, boiler and pilot house. Each mounted thirteen guns, three abreast in the bow and the rest broadside—old-fashioned 8-inch smooth bores and converted Army 42-pounders.

Built essentially for fighting bow-on, the "Turtles" were extremely vulnerable in the stern, a defect which would cost heavily when the craft swung and heaved in the swift Mississippi current as they attempted to face Confederate batteries. Their high-pressure engines sent white plumes of steam skyward as they chugged audibly along, and their boilers, if pierced, would scald their crews. They were indeed an improvisation, but, as they proved, they could do their work.

But the "Pook Turtles" were still a dream when Ead's plan was bucked from the Navy to the Army, and General Frémont was given the task of clearing the Mississippi Valley southward. In an absurd division of authority the Army was given the task of construction, and of controlling operations, while the Navy would be responsible for manning the vessels. So Commander John Rodgers, USN, was detailed to "assist" the Army.

While the "Pook Turtles" were being built, Rodgers energetically scoured the area up to the Great Lakes for men and equipment. As a nucleus for his fleet he converted three Ohio River packets, stripping their gingerbread upperworks, lowering their engines and boilers into their hulls, and shielding them against small arms fire with 5-inch oak bulwarks.

Almost immediately Rodgers found himself plagued by a lack of interest and understanding of the naval problems on the part of responsible army officers. General Frémont half-heartedly adopted some Navy suggestions, then failed to provide guns or equipment. The principal result of Rodgers' persistent and energetic efforts to organize an effective naval squadron was to so annoy Frémont that the "Pathfinder" demanded that he be replaced.

In Rodgers' place came a tougher barnacle; Captain Andrew H. Foote, with thirty-nine years of naval service behind him. Foote, sizing up the anomalous situation, dove into the struggle with all the vigor of his predecessor. He stood up to Frémont and to his successor Halleck, when the "Pathfinder" was toppled from his empire in early November. He scrounged crews and supplies, frequently battling tooth and nail with rank-conscious amateur general officers. Finally, his incessant urgings to the Secretary of the Navy obtained him the rank of flag officer, putting him on equal footing with Army brigadier generals.

Meanwhile, Foote's three original gunboats, the converted river steamers, engaged in several skirmishes. At Belmont, where these gunboats supported Grant's attack, began the friendship of two fighting men—a loyal understanding and mutual respect resulting in truly joint operations.

It was here also that the Confederate Navy first appeared in action on the upper Mississippi. This was a flotilla of eight converted river packets under command of Flag Officer Hollins, detached from the New Orleans force, with mission to cover the river flank of General Johnston's Columbus-Bowling Green cordon defense. These were the gunboats which made the unsuccessful raid on Cairo in December, 1861. Hollins properly avoided further combat with the heavier Union gunboats as his were lightly armed.

By January, 1862, when the Army's river campaign was scheduled to begin, Foote's organizational task was not quite completed. His "Pook Turtles" were in commission, and his mortar scows assembled at Cairo, but their armament had not yet been provided by the Army. Foote appealed to Fox in Washington, and the energetic Assistant Secretary laid the whole matter of inter-service friction before President Lincoln. That brought results. The Army's Chief of Ordnance lost his official head and Foote was directed to send a daily telegraphic progress report to the White House. Things fell into place. And in early February Flag Officer Foote and his gunboats stood out from Cairo, convoying Brigadier General Grant's Army of the Tennessee on the first step of the Union invasion of the western reaches of the Confederacy.

Technically, Foote was under Grant's command. Actually, the operation became a cooperative effort between two commanders acting in harmony.

We have seen in previous chapters how the Navy flotilla

cooperated at Forts Henry and Donelson, at Island No. 10, and at Shiloh. The next Federal step on the river was against Fort Pillow, the principal unit of Confederate fortifications erected on the Chickasaw Bluffs dominating the Mississippi just north of Memphis and sixty miles south of Island No. 10.

Here lay an augmented flotilla of Confederate gunboats. To the original up-river group had come reinforcement; eight of the fourteen River Defense Fleet rams from New Orleans, under Confederate Army Captain J. E. Montgomery, a river pilot. This force had been ordered north in late March, when the seriousness of the situation on the upper river had dawned on the Confederate high command, but arrived too late to help defend Island No. 10.

Foote's Union gunboats and mortar schooners moved down river now to open a systematic bombardment of the Chickasaw Bluffs positions, while Pope's troops, landing above the forts, prepared to assault Fort Pillow from the rear. Initially unsuccessful, Pope was soon ordered away by Halleck, to join the main army in its advance from Shiloh to Corinth. The Union naval bombardment, however, continued.

On May 9, Foote, incapacitated by the wound received at Fort Donelson, was relieved by Captain Charles H. Davis, USN, who next day found himself involved in violent action. At dawn Montgomery hurled his eight rams in a surprise attack on the Federal gunboats lying off Plum Point. Two Union gunboats were badly damaged and had to be beached, but when the remainder got up enough steam to come into action, the lighter armed Confederate vessels withdrew from the fight.

The Union flotilla was now reinforced by another improvisation. This was the Ellet Ram Fleet, seven light, stern- and sidewheel river steamers which had been especially braced and strengthened for their mission. Carrying no guns, they were projectiles in themselves. Charles Ellet, Jr., a civil engineer who for some years had been a strong advocate of the naval ram, had planned and rebuilt them, and commanded them as an Army colonel, independent of Navy control.

In the face of growing Union land and naval strength, the Confederates abandoned Fort Pillow and the Chickasaw Bluffs on June 5. Next day the combined Union flotilla struck the Confederate gunboats off Memphis; the ironclads opened at long range while Ellet's swift rams darted into the melée. In a ten-mile running flight, observed with dismay by the citizens of Memphis, the River Defense Fleet was destroyed; seven Confederate vessels were sunk or captured. One alone, the *General Van Dorn*, escaped and made her way downriver. After the battle Colonel Ellet sent his son, Colonel Charles R. Ellet, ashore to demand and receive the surrender of Memphis.

Leaving Davis and his gunboats moving down the river, now cleared to the mouth of the Yazoo, we pick up events as they had transpired far down the Mississippi—the Southland's vital water gate.

# FROM THE GULF TO
# THE YAZOO MOUTH

During the autumn of 1861, before active operations began upriver, Confederate Flag Officer Hollins at New Orleans had no doubt about his primary mission. The Federal warships standing off the Mississippi delta mouths were throttling commerce, menacing the Confederacy's most important link with the outside world. Like a good sailor, Hollins decided to do something about this, and he used the best available weapon in his scanty arsenal.

This was the ironclad ram *Manassas*, converted from a former Boston tugboat which had been sent to New Orleans before the war, to help clear the Mississippi channel. A sturdy craft of 384 tons, 128 feet long, the newly-christened *Manassas* had been shod with a cast-iron prow extending forward under water, and her hull and upper-works were shielded with railroad iron. From a slot in her armored bow projected a 9-inch rifle. Though her twin-screw engines had not been designed to carry this additional weight, she was a menace to any wooden-hulled warship.

On the night of October 11–12, 1861, *Manassas* came down the river to Head of the Passes, where a Union blockading squadron of four vessels lay at anchor, without even a picket boat out to guard them. Her speed augmented by the current, *Manassas* crashed into the largest Union ship, the *Richmond*, just as some fire rafts were pushed downstream to further threaten the wooden Federal vessels. Though *Richmond* was seriously damaged, *Manassas'* iron prow was also badly wrenched, and the Confederate ram had to limp back upstream. Meanwhile the Union squadron had scattered in the face of the threat of the ram and the fire rafts. Two of them, including the damaged *Richmond*, went temporarily aground.

The dreaded fire rafts, caught by snags and driftwood, never reached their prey; the Union flotilla sheepishly regained some composure as the rafts burned out harmlessly. But the episode held the entire blockading squadron up to ridicule and stirred a hornets' nest in Washington. The Administration's attention focussed on the New Orleans situation, and the necessity for the capture of the port.

In utmost secrecy an assault was planned. Newly-promoted Flag Officer David Glasgow Farragut, now commanding the West Gulf Squadron, was assigned responsibility for the operation. Sixty-year-old Farragut had had fifty years of continuous naval service, including distinguished combat service in the War of 1812 as a teen-age midshipman. His officers and men both loved and stood in awe of the old sea dog, whose natural dignity did not prevent him from fencing or doing calisthenics on deck, or from scrambling up the rigging with the same agility he had displayed a half-century earlier. Disdaining War Department suggestions that he should wait to go up the river until Army troops had captured the defending forts, Farragut determined to force the passage below New Orleans as soon as possible.

Assisting Farragut was Commander David D. Porter, son of

Farragut's first commanding officer. Young Porter, thoroughly familiar with the Mississippi Delta, was authorized to carry out his scheme of organizing a flotilla of twenty schooners, on each of which would be mounted an enormous 13-inch Army mortar. This mortar flotilla would take the river forts under bombardment while Farragut's squadron ran by. An Army contingent, 10,000 men under General Butler, was secretly concentrated at Ship Island in the Mississippi Sound, where a naval blockading base had already been established.

Confederate General Lovell, at New Orleans, got wind of the increased Federal activity. He appealed to Richmond for more men, ships and money. But the Confederate Administration was obsessed by the threat upriver, and remembering the ease with which Andrew Jackson had defended New Orleans in 1815, assumed Lovell could do likewise. So, with inadequate land and naval forces, he was forced to make do with what he had on hand.

The defense of New Orleans centered on Forts Jackson and St. Philip, which frowned at one another across the river at Plaquemine Bend, ninety miles below the city. Jackson, on the right bank, was below St. Philip, whose raking batteries any Union Fleet would have to face bow-on, while still receiving fire broadside from Jackson. Between them, the forts could sweep the river with 115 heavy guns in crossfire; formidable to wooden ships confined to a prescribed channel and without room for maneuver. All in all, these fortifications constituted a major obstacle, particularly since in those days opinion was that ships could not compete with shore batteries. St. Philip, alone, had stopped a British squadron forty-six years previously.

Regular Confederate Navy vessels under Lovell's command in the area were the ram *Manassas* and two armed, converted merchantmen. Almost completed was the ironclad *Louisiana*, mounting sixteen large-caliber guns and, in theory, capable of taking on the entire Union fleet. Two converted merchantmen of the Louisiana State Navy and the remains of the River Defense

Fleet—six gunboats—made up the rest of the available armed craft.

Farragut's ships began to assemble at Ship Island in February 1862, and he proceeded to the meticulous and tiresome preliminaries to his attack. After getting his squadron over the bars at Pass a l'Outre and Southwest Pass—no mean feat since his heavier vessels had to be dragged and tugged across the shallows—he assembled 17 vessels off Pilot Town at Head of the Passes, 18 miles below the river forts. His was a job-lot of warships; 4 screw sloops and 1 sidewheeler, 3 screw corvettes and 9 screw gunboats, mounting a total of 154 guns. His largest and most

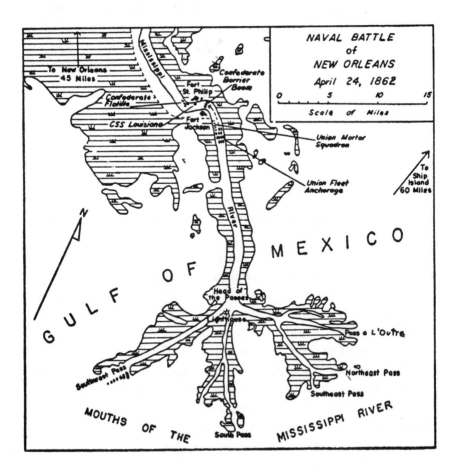

powerful ship, the steam frigate *Colorado*, 44 guns, could not get across the bar and had to be left outside.

The river below the forts had been surveyed—the Coast Survey reconnaissance parties working under fire—and ranges carefully noted. Porter's 20 mortar schooners were towed into positions accurately charted and buoyed. They began pounding the forts April 18, with Fort Jackson the major target, and caused considerable damage. Confederate General Johnson K. Duncan, a West Pointer, commanding both forts, tried vainly to have the ironclad *Louisiana*, at New Orleans, put into action to attack the mortar boats, but her engines were not yet in working order. She was, however, towed down to a position just above St. Philip, to become an immobile floating battery.

From Fort Jackson on the opposite shore the Confederates laid a barrier consisting of hulks and logs chained together. Two Union gunboats made a daring raid on this barrier the night of April 20, trying unsuccessfully to blow it up. Finally Lt. C. H. B. Caldwell, USN, commanding the little *Itasca*, drove his craft full speed ahead against the chain, riding over it and breaking it by the sheer weight of his ship. Thus freed, the hulks on each side were pushed away by the swift current, and a 60-foot-wide channel opened.

Farragut's squadron now cleared for action. Most of the spars and upper masts had been unshipped and dropped at Ship Island. Chain cable was secured up and down the vessels' sides to act as armor; hammocks, sand bags and bags of coal distributed to shield vital points from fore-and-aft fire; mud was rubbed on outside white paint to reduce visibility at night, while inboard, decks and gun carriages were whitewashed to make ammunition and tackle visible without the use of lanterns.

It was 2:00 A.M. April 24, when two red lanterns run up to the mizzen peak of the flagship *Hartford* signaled the attack. In single line ahead (single column) the squadron, divided into three divisions, started upriver. Elderly Captain Theodorus Bailey, whose *Colorado* had been too big to cross the bar, was given the courtesy of commanding the first division and with his flag in the little gunboat *Cayuga* dashed through the barrier at 3:30 A.M.

Bailey's vessels were now subjected to heavy and damaging fire from both forts. Then the little ram *Manassas* steamed out to engage the whole Federal fleet. She hit several vessels, but her weak engines prevented her from maneuvering as quickly as the Federal ships, and most of the blows were glancing ones. Forced into the river bank by one larger Northern ship, *Manassas* freed herself, and continued to carry the fight to the invaders. Finally, after taking terrific punishment, and having created much confusion in the Federal column, she burst into flames and drifted downriver, to blow up just below Fort Jackson.

But now—and while still engaged in a desperate battle with the forts—Farragut's ships were faced with an even more dangerous threat from another intrepid Confederate vessel. The little unarmed tugboat *Mosher* pushed a fire raft downstream. *Hartford*, Farragut's flagship, trying to escape this menace, ran aground close under the guns of Fort St. Philip. The *Mosher* kept pushing the blazing raft against the large vessel until, riddled, the tug went down, with all on board.

*Hartford*, still hard and fast aground, had by now caught fire from the raft. With amazing discipline the crew extinguished the flames while the warship, her engines going full astern, returned the concentrated fire of both forts. Slowly she sucked out of the mud and resumed course.

By daybreak, despite the well-aimed and heavy fire from the forts and from the moored ironclad *Louisiana*, all save three small gunboats of the Union fleet had successfully run the gauntlet, though the cost had been heavy in damage and casualties.

But there was still some hard fighting ahead, where the combined Confederate naval craft had gathered for one desperate assault against staggering odds. The ram *Governor Moore*, gallantly handled by Lieutenant Beverly Kennon, ex-USN, smashed into the screw sloop *Varuna*. Fatally damaged, the Union ship was run into the bank and moored. There she sank, with her battery firing until the water washed up to the gun trucks. Attacked by three other Union vessels, Kennon ran his ram ashore and set her afire. The remainder of the Confederate gunboat flotilla was crushed. Nine in all were put out of action; the remaining two took refuge under the guns of the forts, where the ironclad *Louisiana* still lay.

The way was open to New Orleans. Farragut, halting his ships four miles above the forts, tarried only long enough to make temporary repairs and bury his thirty-six dead. The wounded numbered 135.

On April 25, brushing past two river batteries just below the city, Farragut's ships dropped anchor off New Orleans. The levee had been fired. Alongside it, ships and warehouses were going up in flames. All Confederate troops had been evacuated, and milling mobs of civilians filled the streets. A *New York Herald* correspondent with the fleet, wrote, "Pandemonium was here a living picture."

From *Cayuga*, a ship's boat rowed ashore. Captain Bailey and Lieutenant George H. Perkins stepped out and strode through the howling, threatening mob to hoist the United States flag over the United States Mint building. Then Farragut's Marines took charge.

Meanwhile Porter, assisted by Butler's troops, continued to attack Forts Jackson and St. Philip. On the twenty-seventh they surrendered, while the *Louisiana* was set afire and blown up by her crew.

On May 1, Butler's troops occupied New Orleans. The frog-faced Massachusetts political general did a good job; improving sanitary conditions, feeding the destitute, and establishing law and order. It was unfortunate indeed that his brutal boorishness should overshadow a really efficient demonstration of military administration.

All that the South—and for that matter the North—remembers of Butler's regime in New Orleans is his infamous order No. 28, published May 15, 1862, informing citizens of New Orleans that "Hereafter when any female shall, by word, gesture, or movement, insult or show contempt for any officer or soldier of the United States, she shall be regarded and held liable to be treated as a woman of the town plying her avocation."

Farragut now started north to clear the river and link with the upper arm of the Union pincers. It would be a long and frustrating effort. A division of his lighter craft, moving in advance, accepted the successive surrenders of undefended Baton Rouge and Natchez. But Vicksburg, its batteries on the bluffs manned and ready, contemptuously refused to submit.

The larger vessels of the squadron experienced great difficulty in navigating the tortuous and shallow Mississippi channel. Time and again ships grounded and had to be tugged free. Coal shortages necessitated burning wood, while seasonal epidemics of malaria and dysentery added to the general discomfort. A contingent of 1,400 Army troops, accompanying the expedition, lived in cramped transports under almost unbearably filthy conditions. All in all, it was an irritated force under an exasperated commander which arrived just below Vicksburg on May 23, to find further passage barred.

Vicksburg, on the east bank of the river, stood on a horseshoe bend, its narrow, terraced slopes rising abruptly 250 feet above the water line. Heavy guns had been mounted on those heights. To their plunging fire the Union ships could make no reply, since their guns could not be elevated sufficiently to bear. Farragut, inclined to make a surprise night attack, reconsidered when his captains demurred and the Army commander, Brigadier General Thomas Williams, pointed out that his small force could not possibly land unless the Confederate batteries were first silenced.

In frustrated rage Farragut, two days later, turned and went downriver, leaving his light craft to blockade the southern approaches to the city. When he arrived back at New Orleans he found that Porter, during his absence, had cleared the entire delta and had also occupied Pensacola, which had been abandoned following the successful attack on New Orleans. But he also found peremptory orders from President Lincoln: "Carry out your instruction of January 20 about ascending the Mississippi River, it is of the utmost importance."

Accompanied now by Porter's mortar schooners, for counterbattery against Vicksburg's hill forts, and with its Army contingent doubled in strength, the weary squadron retraced its steps. It was hampered by coal barges and the mortar schooners, all of which had to be towed, and still further slowed down by nightly halts, to minimize damage from grounding or collision. The armada arrived below Vicksburg June 25, one month following the first withdrawal. Farragut's fighting ships were three heavy sloops of war, six gunboats, six steamers of the mortar flotilla and sixteen mortar schooners. The gist of his plan was to run by the city while its hilltop guns were blanketed by mortar fire; join forces with Davis' "Pook Turtle" fleet of river gunboats up above and then, with Army assistance from General Halleck, stage a full-scale joint assault if the city had not already capitulated.

The mortar schooners opened with their 13-inch shells and the ships stood in, June 28. It was a three-mile-long gauntlet, with the shore batteries able to choose their targets, while the ships were confined to firing only when their guns could be brought to bear. The leading gunboat's steering gear jammed and she sheered out of line, causing confusion behind her. Several of Porter's lighter gunboats were badly hit and they added to the mixup. The *Brooklyn*, following the flagship, halted due to misunderstanding of orders, two gunboats following her example. But the main body of the squadron got through, with sixteen men killed and forty wounded, and joined Flag Officer Davis' upriver gunboat flotilla off the mouth of the Yazoo River above Vicksburg on July 1. The Union pincers had closed, but with Vicksburg's defenses still intact,the river was far from being open.

Halleck, who was by this time at Corinth, never answered Farragut's plea for joint action against Vicksburg. And, as Dave Porter put it: "Ships . . . cannot crawl up hills 300 feet high, and it is that part of Vicksburg which must be taken by the Army."

Furthermore the combined Union squadrons were faced by another threat.

Up the Yazoo River lay the Confederate ironclad ram *Arkansas*. Built at Memphis under extraordinary difficulties—western Tennessee had been scoured for railroad iron and scrap to plate her sides—she had been rushed up to Yazoo City, still uncompleted, when the Naval Flotilla first threatened Memphis. Her skipper, Commander Isaac N. Brown, CSN, had antagonized all local authorities in his untiring efforts to get his ship in commission and only by personal application to President Jefferson Davis at Richmond secured her crew.

The 1,000-ton *Arkansas* was a fearsome antagonist; 180 feet long, with a 30-foot beam, and completely covered by strips of railroad iron carefully dovetailed together. From her casemate poked 10 heavy guns. She was driven by twin screws, though, as usual with the Confederate ironclads, the engines were weak and poorly constructed.

On July 15, a Union reconnoitering force of three light ships, poking up the Yazoo, met *Arkansas* headlong as she came rocketing downstream. They turned and ran, followed by the powerful Southern ram. There was no time to warn the Union squadrons, and *Arkansas*, bow and broadside guns blazing, battered her way through the entire Federal fleet. The Union vessels had little or no steam up, and their projectiles bounded harmlessly off the sloping iron sides of the daring Confederate ship. When it was over, *Arkansas* was sheltering snugly under Vicksburg's batteries and Farragut could tote up a loss of eighteen men killed, fifty wounded and ten others missing. This exploit of Isaac Brown, former U.S. Navy officer, constitutes a brilliant example of American naval daring.

Humiliated and angry, Farragut ran down past Vicksburg that same night. He took with him two of Davis' ships, an ironclad gunboat and a light ram, with mission to sink the *Arkansas* as she lay at her mooring, while the squadron covered them. Heavy mortar fire assisted the dash. But *Arkansas* could not be found in the darkness and confusion of crossfire. At dawn on the twenty-second another effort was made to destroy the *Arkansas*, as the "Pook Turtle" *Essex* and ram *Queen of the West* engaged the Confederate craft in desperate battle. *Arkansas* was damaged, but the Union vessels were driven off by heavy fire from her guns and those of the hill forts.

When, a short time later, the Navy Department ordered him to leave Vicksburg and take up again the Gulf blockading chore, Farragut was glad to go. His ships were battered and his men seriously sick. But he would have his revenge on *Arkansas*, after all. In August she was sent down to Baton Rouge to cooperate in a Confederate Army attack upon General Butler's troops there. Her engines broke down just north of the city, and *Essex* found her, helpless. After receiving several hits, *Arkansas* was set afire by her crew and abandoned to blow up.

For the rest of 1862, the Father of Waters, ruled on the north and south by Union flotillas, still remained on Confederate control between Vicksburg and Baton Rouge. In the east, meanwhile, great events had happened.

# 8

# Which Way
# to Richmond?

## DEVELOPING THE PLAN

By the beginning of 1862 General McClellan's honeymoon with
the Northern Government and people had ended. Acclaimed as
the Union's savior in August and September of 1861, he was now
being condemned as a cowardly procrastinator in the press, by
Congress, and in Lincoln's cabinet. The "young Napoleon" of
a few weeks earlier had retained the confidence only of the President and the 170,000 men of the Army of the Potomac.

For this was McClellan's army, which gave to its young
general an adoring loyalty such as few army commanders have
known. They would fight with determination and valor whenever
he committed them to combat, but General and army turned deaf
ears to popular criticism, and to the clamor of "On to Richmond!" They would take the field when they were ready, and
not before.

Furthermore, as McClellan pointed out to President Lincoln,

he did not have enough men to attack Joe Johnston's positions near Manassas. He had learned from his intelligence service that Johnston was being issued 119,000 rations daily. McClellan himself, after deducting troops for the defense of Washington and protecting his line of communications, could not bring more than the same number into battle. And it was a well-known—incontrovertible—military axiom that a substantial superiority of force was necessary in order to attack a well-prepared, entrenched defender.

The chief of McClellan's intelligence service, on whom the general relied implicitly, was Allen Pinkerton, well-known private detective. He reported that his agents had positively "identified" more than 200 Confederate regiments in and around Manassas. The efficiency of his gathering activities is demonstrated by the fact that at the time he was reporting Johnston's strength as 119,000 men, there were actually no more than 50,000 Confederates at Manassas. It is not clear how much of his erroneous reporting was due to ineptness, and how much to his shrewd realization that McClellan liked to picture himself as a hero facing staggering odds. Whatever the reason—and it has never been satisfactorily explained—Pinkerton invariably reported Southern strength as at least double that actually present or available.

But, while Lincoln's own logical mind did not see how the South could provide, or support, armies of the size accepted by McClellan, he had no better source of information. McClellan, after all, was trained and experienced in estimating a military situation; Lincoln was not.

Neither was the new Secretary of War, appointed by Lincoln, on January 13, to replace incompetent Simon Cameron: Edwin M. Stanton, erstwhile bitter critic of President Lincoln, but a man who—unlike Cameron—had proven himself to be honest, energetic, and a capable administrator. Though he tended to be contemptuous of professional military men, he knew nothing of strategy, and he zealously set about learning as much as he could concerning the administration of the War Department.

While Stanton was gaining McClellan's confidence, the President was rapidly losing his faith in the general. After McClellan ignored the President's suggestions to take some action against Johnston, Lincoln, at the end of January, bluntly ordered him to make an advance by Washington's Birthday—February 22. On that date all Federal forces would make a general advance.

Though he had not taken the President into his confidence, McClellan for several weeks had been weighing the relative merits of two possible approaches to Richmond. He could go overland—which would force him to move directly against the Confederate positions at Manassas—or he could bypass Johnston's army by transporting the Army of the Potomac to the lower Rappahannock or to the neighborhood of Fortress Monroe. In either case, the ultimate objective was Richmond, the enemy capital, goal of popular clamor, and of President Lincoln, too. This fatal obsession for a geographical objective, rather than the destruction of the enemy's armed forces, would long continue to obscure Northern vision.

Having decided that the Manassas positions were too strong to attack, McClellan had automatically selected the second of his two alternatives, and had drawn up a tentative plan to move his army by ship to Urbana, at the mouth of the Rappahannock, and thence overland about forty-five miles to Richmond. He felt sure that Johnston could not move from Manassas quickly enough to prevent him from capturing the Confederate capital.

Now faced by Lincoln's order to move against Johnston, McClellan discussed his Urbana plan with Secretary Stanton, and then with the President. Lincoln didn't like the plan very much. He reasoned that if Johnston was as strong as McClellan believed he was, the departure of the Army of the Potomac from the vicinity of Washington would leave the Federal capital in jeopardy. Johnston could march thirty miles to capture Washington far more quickly than McClellan could get to Richmond by way of Urbana. And if Johnston wasn't strong enough to do that, then there was no reason for McClellan to try to avoid him. The

President, in fact, was beginning to understand why the enemy, and not some place on a map, is the proper objective of an army.

But McClellan, the soldier, insisting that his evaluation of Johnston's strength was correct, was able to cite so many military reasons in support of the Urbana plan that the President—who really had a clearer grasp of the strategic situation than did the general—reluctantly gave his approval. But he insisted that McClellan leave adequate strength to defend Washington against a possible Confederate attack. Whether or not he accepted McClellan's military arguments, he evidently reasoned that the general would be likely to procrastinate less in carrying out his own plan than one forced on him. But just to make sure that there was prompt action, on March 8 he ordered the movement to take place by the eighteenth.

The day after Lincoln issued this order, Johnston changed the entire strategic picture by abandoning the Manassas positions, and moving back behind the Rappahannock. The really efficient Confederate spy system had brought him word of McClellan's proposed move; from his new positions Johnston would be as close to Richmond as McClellan would be at Urbana. And a Federal advance towards Richmond from that place would expose McClellan's line of communications to easy attack from the vicinity of Fredericksburg.

The Urbana plan, so painfully developed, so earnestly argued, so reluctantly approved, was out!

While trying to develop a new plan, McClellan occupied the abandoned Confederate positions at Manassas. Though it was obvious from the entrenchments and campsites that no more than 50,000 men had been in these positions, McClellan, despite the evidence of his own eyes, lost faith neither in Pinkerton nor his reports of Southern strength. He still estimated Johnston's strength at the Rappahannock as upwards of 100,000 men. Following the line of reasoning which had produced the Urbana plan, he felt that he should still try to bypass Johnston in his approach to Richmond. He would move his army by boat so as to approach

Richmond from the east, but making his base at Fortress Monroe instead of Urbana. He would then move up Virginia's Peninsula, the finger of land lying between the York and James Rivers, to Richmond at its base.

It is difficult to see how an Engineer officer, trained to appreciate the influence of terrain on military operations, would thus seek to limit his army to an advance up a limited corridor, flanked by unfordable rivers, as an alternative to the wide expanse of maneuverable terrain in northern and central Virginia. It is all the more puzzling in light of the fact that his major concern had been to find a way of bypassing an enemy presumed to be as strong or stronger than his own force. Nothing other than conscious or unconscious fear that he lacked the ability to fight a war of maneuver could have induced such a move.

Nevertheless, when he persuasively presented his plan and his reasoning to a council of war of his corps commanders, they unanimously endorsed it on two conditions. The first of these was that the Navy find some means for neutralizing a Confederate ironclad vessel, formerly the USS *Merrimack*, based at Norfolk; a serious threat to any such Union water-borne operations. The second condition was that which the President had himself made originally: that sufficient force be left to assure the security of Washington from Confederate attack.

Lincoln didn't like this proposal any better than the Urbana plan, but again he reluctantly agreed, provided the conditions established by McClellan's own officers were met. And they *were* met. Let's see how.

# CONDITION ONE: NEUTRALIZING THE MERRIMACK

"Cheese box on a shingle," they dubbed her, and to this day no one has coined a more appropriate phrase. But as she came sloshing westward through the entrance to Chesapeake Bay behind a tug, that chilly March 8, 1862, into the eye of the setting sun—a flattish object almost hidden by the channel chop washing her deck, with a great canvas hood shrouding her turret—she must have resembled a floating haystack at the end of a towline.

No one suspected that within her cramped iron hull this object—USS *Monitor*—carried the wherewithal to quench one of the brightest hopes of the Confederacy: to break the already strangulating blockade. For this was the close of a day when the U.S. Navy had received a blow such as it would not suffer again for seventy-nine years; a day marking for the world the end of wooden warships, and for the Union a disaster bringing flaming panic not only to the capital city of Washington but also to every port in the North.

One armor-clad monster impervious to cannon balls had brought this about. From Norfolk to Richmond the telegraph was already carrying the rousing news of an epoch-making naval victory won by the CSS *Virginia*, formerly the USS *Merrimack*.

Southern hopes had hung on *Virginia* ever since the seizure of the Norfolk Navy Yard. Under the driving impetus of Navy Secretary Mallory the Confederates had raised the scuttled 263-foot-long, 50-gun steam frigate, transformed her into an ironclad ram, and rechristened her. Her masts and upperworks had been stripped away; a heavy cast-iron ram ''shoe'' covered her once-graceful cutwater. Above her hull rose a curious slope-walled oaken structure covered with iron plates four inches thick, and she mounted 10 heavy guns—one each in bow and stern and four more on each side. Two of the broadside guns were fitted for firing red-hot shot (incendiary). She looked like ''a barracks roof submerged to the eaves and surmounted by a large smoking funnel.'' But there had been neither time nor opportunity to change her power plant, so she was still driven by her original engines; underpowered for her greatly increased weight. Her 22-foot-draft would be a serious handicap in shallow inland waters.

*Virginia* came out of her Norfolk berth shortly after noon that momentous day and made for USS *Congress*, 50-gun sailing frigate, and *Cumberland*, 24-gun sailing sloop of war, as they lay at anchor, with sails furled, off the mouth of the James River, waiting for her.

From under the guns of Fortress Monroe across the way, the steam frigate *Minnesota*, 50 guns, sister ship to the *Merrimack*, at once got under way to cut the Confederate craft from her base. She was followed by the tug-towed flagship *Roanoake*, a 40-gun steam frigate, now powerless because of a broken propeller shaft. This Federal move had been long planned; all ships were cleared for action, their batteries manned. In theory, caught between the sailing ships above and the steamers below, the *Virginia* would be trapped and battered to bits.

But Confederate Flag Officer Franklin Buchanan, ex-U.S. Navy, commanding *Virginia*, came plowing straight at *Cumberland*, regardless of intense fire from the Union vessels and from shore batteries at Newport News. For fifteen minutes the Confederate craft, bow gun blazing, moved through a hail of cannon balls. They bounced from her sloping, tallow-greased armor and laced the water with spurts of spray as they ricocheted in all directions like stones skipped across a pond.

Then *Virginia*'s deadly ram crunched loud and deep into *Cumberland*'s starboard bow. The Union sloop reeled, filled as *Virginia* backed away, and in a few moments *Cumberland* sank, "gallantly fighting her guns," as Buchanan admiringly reported, "as long as they were above water." Down with her went the Confederate's iron ram, wrenched away by the force of the collision.

*Virginia* now turned and attacked *Congress*. After a short but terrific pounding, *Congress* made sail and tried to get away, but she went aground. Helpless now under the Confederate's raking fire, *Congress* hauled down her colors. But some of her own gun crews didn't get the word. The Federal shore batteries also kept firing (there was no reason why they shouldn't; *they* had not surrendered). Buchanan, infuriated, opened again on *Congress*, this time with hot-shot, and set her on fire.

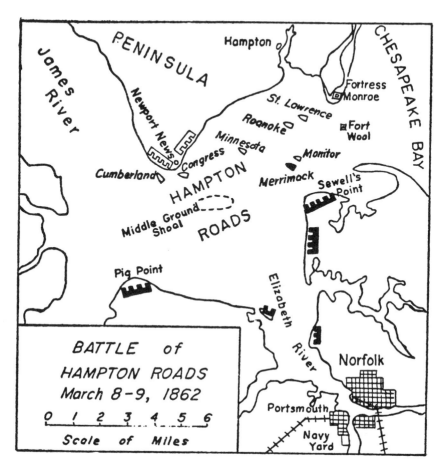

BATTLE of
HAMPTON ROADS
March 8-9, 1862

0   1   2   3   4   5   6

Scale of Miles

*Minnesota*, meanwhile, in her hurry to get into action, had stranded in shoal water, about a mile and a half away. So too did *Roanoake*, far behind her. Neither *Roanoake*, nor *St. Lawrence*, a 50-gun sailing frigate, ever got into action. Buchanan moved to finish her, but feared to close, lest he run his own ship in the mud. It was getting dark, the Elizabeth River channel back to Norfolk was shallow, and the tide about to ebb. Tomorrow would be another day; devoted to destroying the remainder of the Union blockading squadron. Buchanan, wounded but satisfied with the day's work, turned command over to his executive officer, and *Virginia*, leaving the helpless *Minnesota*, steamed homeward.

As she left Hampton Roads that afternoon one Federal war-ship lay sunk, the Stars and Stripes still fluttering from her mast-heads protruding above the surface. Another ship—now a gutted, blazing hulk—was aflame in shoal water. A fine steam frigate was hard and fast aground. More than 100 officers and men of Flag Officer Louis M. Goldsborough's stunned blockading squadron in Chesapeake Bay were dead; perhaps twice that number crowding the hospitals at Fortress Monroe. Only two major vessels remained afloat; a sailing frigate and a steam frigate with a broken main shaft.

Up in Washington War Secretary Stanton, in panic, was preparing to block the Potomac River by sinking stone-laden C. & O. canal boats across the channel; was sending frantic disaster warnings to the governors of the seaboard states of New York, Massachusetts and Maine.

Such was the picture as the *Monitor* arrived.

To realize what happened next; through what seeming mixture of legerdemain and predestination the crescendo of Confederate high naval hopes would be both reached and dashed within a 24-hour bracket, one must look back. By July, 1861, the intentions of Confederate Secretary Mallory, and the progress of work on the *Merrimack*, became common knowledge. Union Navy Secretary Gideon Welles put the problem up to Congress. In August he was authorized to appoint a board of naval officers to investigate ironclads, and $1,500,000 was appropriated to build "one or more armored or iron or steel-clad steamships or floating steam batteries." Bids were invited, and among the plans presented was that of John Ericsson, brilliant Swedish-American inventor and marine engineer. This was so revolutionary in design and concept that it was nicknamed "Ericsson's Folly." However, it was approved, and Welles characteristically authorized the inventor to go into construction even before the contract was formally drawn up.

On October 25, 1861, the keel was laid in a New York

shipyard; on January 30, 1862, the vessel, with engines, armor and armament installed, was launched, and christened by the name Ericsson himself had suggested: *Monitor*.

She was flat-bottomed, built of iron, 172 feet long, with 41-foot beam; in smooth water her deck was but one foot above the surface. Her armor plate varied from five to eight inches in thickness. Midship sat the one turret, carrying two Dahlgren 11-inch smooth bore cannon. The turret, nine feet high and twenty feet across, revolved by means of a donkey engine and gears, and the guns could be fired "on the fly" as the turret rotated slowly. An ingenious recoil system invented by Ericsson brought each piece, after firing, completely inside the turret, whereupon iron flaps dropped over the openings. A little pilot house, completely armored, with eye-slits, poked up in the bow; the flush deck funnel was in the rear of the turret. Her single screw engine was, optimistically, designed to give a speed of seven knots in calm weather.

The *Monitor*—the first warship ever to carry her guns in a revolving turret—was a combination of brilliant inventive genius and of impracticality. In her was the seed of centralized fire control; direct voice connection between the commander in the pilot house and the gunnery officer in the turret. To her enemies she presented a minuscule target for the gunnery of her period; the cylindrical turret, tiny four-foot-high pilot house and the stub of her funnel were the only surfaces appearing above her water-washed deck.

On the other hand, as she immediately showed, *Monitor* was not only useless in an open sea, but dangerous to her crew. With her flat bottom and shallow draft—only ten feet—she was tossed, pounded and battered even in moderate seas, while breaking waves washed down her ventilator and funnel, killing her fires and thus almost asphyxiating her crew. In consequence, she could operate safely under her own power only in the complete calm of inland waters.

John Ericsson had indeed fathered the prototype of conventionally armed warships as we know them today, but, like all prototypes, the *Monitor* was filled with "bugs."

This was the ship which on the morning of March 9, came unexpectedly from behind the still-stranded *Minnesota* to meet *Virginia* as the Confederate vessel came down to sweep a wooden-walled navy from the seas. Rushed from New York to cover McClellan's move to the Peninsula, she had arrived in Chesapeake Bay after a 48-hour sleepless nightmare in heavy seas, to find herself the Navy's forlorn hope in disaster.

Lieutenant John L. Worden, her skipper, navigated *Monitor* from the pilot house; Lieutenant S. D. Greene, the executive, was in the turret. These two men would fight the ship, their only communication a speaking tube.

Lieutenant Catesby R. Jones, CSN, was now commanding *Virginia*, replacing the wounded Buchanan. He brought his ship down toward *Minnesota*, opening on her when a mile distant. Then tiny *Monitor* broke in between, and at close range began pounding the iron sides of her opponent. The surprised Confederate returned the fire, but was hampered in her gunnery by the small size of her target.

Thus began a four-hour battle between a pygmy and a giant, each cloaked in impenetrable armor. Little *Monitor*'s 11-inch projectiles hammered almost fruitlessly on *Virginia*'s sides; the Confederate's 7- and 9-inch cannon balls carromed off the "cheese box" turret. Each ship tried ramming the other, but without success, while their respective crews grew groggier every moment from the clang and clatter and the choking powder fumes in their shut-in compartments.

Twice *Monitor* temporarily broke contact, retiring into shallow water where *Virginia* could not follow. The first time was to replenish ammunition; the turret had to be at rest and centered over a hatchway to get shells and charges up into it. As she was so occupied, *Virginia*, braving the heavy broadside of stranded *Minnesota*, raked that frigate end to end with her big bow gun, setting her momentarily on fire.

Then the ironclads went at it hammer and tongs again, until a Confederate shell burst on *Monitor*'s pilot house, blinding Lieutenant Worden temporarily. *Monitor* swerved into the shallows once more, until Lieutenant Greene could clamber from the turret to take command, leaving Chief Engineer Albert C. Stimer to run the guns.

This time, as *Monitor* returned to the action, *Virginia* was already on her way back to Norfolk. Her skipper, as he later reported, felt that he had driven *Monitor* off and had damaged *Minnesota* irreparably. So, as the tide was ebbing and his ship had suffered some damage, he broke off further action.

This argument does not hold water. Jones' mission was one of destruction, not defense. *Monitor* was the only Union ship in Chesapeake Bay capable of standing up to him. If Jones felt he had put her out of action he should then have proceeded to attack and destroy every other Federal warship in the Bay. The only valid excuse for breaking off action would have been lack of ammunition, and this, it appears, did not worry *Virginia*'s commander.

Be that as it may, there was glory enough for all, that day, as American sailors fought one another to a draw in new and hurriedly thrown together ships. What did matter was that, when the fight ended, little *Monitor* was still shepherding her flock of wooden ships, and that *Virginia* would never again come out in the Bay to give battle.

The *Virginia* had been neutralized. Condition One had been met, and McClellan's Army of the Potomac was able to land at Fortress Monroe without interference.

Two months later, as McClellan's troops began to move up the Peninsula, *Virginia*, drawing too much water to escape from Norfolk up the James River, was blown up by her crew; this was May 11. Little *Monitor*, en route to join in the Union naval attack on Charleston, foundered in a gale off Cape Hatteras December 29. Thus ended the careers of these two vessels which had, overnight, drastically changed naval warfare.

But by this time Northern shipyards were turning out new and improved monitors by the score. If, as a *New York Herald* reporter wrote of the fateful battle, "With that one little vessel-of-war, the *Monitor*, we have broken up all the navies in the world," credit must also go to Stephen R. Mallory, Confederate Navy Secretary, whose wisdom and foresight in developing a *Virginia* made the construction of a *Monitor* necessary.

# CONDITION TWO: ASSURING THE SECURITY OF WASHINGTON

Two days after the *Monitor-Virginia* battle, while McClellan was still pondering the alternative to his ruined Urbana plan, President Lincoln made some sweeping changes in the command organization of the Union army. He felt that one reason for McClellan's unsatisfactory performance as commander of the Army of the Potomac was that, as General-in-Chief, he was also responsible for supervising the operations of all other Federal forces from New Mexico to the Carolinas. Since the general was unable to devote his complete attention to either of these full-time responsibilities, the President correctly believed that both were suffering. McClellan, therefore, was relieved of his broader responsibilities as General-in-Chief in order to devote all of his time to commanding the Army of the Potomac. At the same time Lincoln corrected the faulty command organization west of the Alleghenies by combining Halleck's and Buell's departments under Halleck.

After an initial shock of disappointment, McClellan accepted the President's careful explanation of the reasons for the change, and his assurance that this was not a demotion. The President apparently intended to reappoint McClellan as General-in-Chief as soon as he took Richmond, and he may have implied this to the general.

Then, after the Fortress Monroe plan had been adopted, and after the first units of the Army of the Potomac had embarked and were on their way, their came another development still further affecting McClellan's command status, and the security of Washington which he was required to assure. This took place more than fifty miles away, in the Shenandoah Valley.

Here Union General Nathaniel P. Banks, with some 23,000 men, had driven 4,300 Southerners, under General T. J. Jackson—''Stonewall'' of Bull Run fame—south of Strasburg. Satisfied that he had accomplished his mission of removing any possible threat to Washington from the northern Valley, Banks now proceeded to undertake the remainder of his mission which was to move east to Manassas to cooperate with McClellan in the coming operations against Richmond. To make sure that the Valley stayed secure, Banks left behind him General James Shields, and his division of 9,000 men.

Jackson, thinking that Shields' force was smaller than his own, promptly moved back north, and, on March 23, attacked the Northerners at Kernstown, near Winchester. The Federals were able to repulse this assault by a force less than half their own strength, but the Confederate attack had been so vigorous that Shields did not realize how weak Jackson's command actually was. Certain that the Southerner would not have taken the offensive unless he had been greatly reinforced, Shields so informed Banks, who stopped his own move to Manassas, and reported the situation to Washington.

Jackson, suffering a tactical defeat at Kernstown, had set in motion a train of events which was to have the utmost strategic significance.

When McClellan had been relieved as General-in-Chief, the responsibility for controlling, supervising and coordinating the activities of the various Departments and field armies had reverted to the President as Commander-in-Chief, exercising his command through stubborn, brilliant, excitable Secretary of War Stanton. When Stanton got word of Jackson's attack at Kernstown, and the report that this was evidence of a build-up of Confederate strength in the Valley, he jumped to the conclusion that the

Southerners planned to attack Washington as soon as McClellan's army had completely departed.

With Lincoln's approval, Stanton ordered Banks back to the Valley, and ordered one of McClellan's divisions—just about to embark—to march immediately through Harper's Ferry to join General Frémont's command in western Virginia. Banks and Frémont were ordered to cooperate to eliminate the supposed threat.

It was about this time that Lincoln received from McClellan, just as the general left for the Peninsula, a report of the forces he had left for the security of Washington—to meet the second condition regarding his plan. McClellan stated that, including Banks' command in the Valley, he had left about 75,000 men. But, during the flurry of activity resulting from Jackson's attack at Kernstown, Lincoln and Stanton discovered that McClellan had left only approximately 50,000 men—less than 20,000 in the immediate vicinity of the city, about 10,000 at Manassas, and Banks' 23,000. Lincoln was rightly angry at McClellan for having failed to discuss with him the arrangements for the security of Washington, and then having made an apparently deliberately misleading report about these arrangements.

Two corps of McClellan's army were still waiting at Alexandria to be transported to Fortress Monroe. At Lincoln's direction, Stanton ordered McDowell's corps of 30,000 men to move to Manassas, from where it could either cover the direct approaches to Washington, or move over to join Banks in the Valley, if necessary. A telegram was sent to McClellan at Fortress Monroe, informing him that McDowell had been detained. McClellan, enraged in his turn over what he considered to be high-handed and unwarranted interference with his command, protested bitterly. But the President, bluntly reminding McClellan that he still had 100,000 men, explained why he had taken this action after McClellan had failed to consult with him about adequate security for Washington.

With the departure of McClellan for the Peninsula, the Department of the Potomac was reorganized. Quite logically
McClellan, a field commander completely detached from any
position in which he could exercise centralized control, was to
retain responsibility only for the operations of his own immediate
command: the Army of the Potomac. McDowell, who had moved
down to Fredericksburg, was given command of the new Department of the Shenandoah. McClellan, now bitter and suspicious
of the motives of his civilian superiors, took this as another move
by Lincoln and Stanton to reduce his authority, to undermine his
prestige, and possibly even an effort to cause his campaign to
fail.

So, though this reorganization was logical, almost essential,
it aggravated a command situation already well-nigh impossible.

Lincoln recognized that he and Stanton were not military
men, and that they were untrained to control military operations.
Yet who else was there? Scott had been too old; McClellan was
obviously too young. Perhaps he would mature with experience,
but there was still a hard war on. The President was sure of his
own basic logic and understood the need to conquer the South.
Until he could find the right military man to do the job, he and
Stanton, though militarily untrained, would have to try to do the
best they could.

In retrospect this line of thought is obviously incorrect. Lincoln himself saw it clearly not many months later. Only individuals with military training and experience could evaluate the
complex factors of training, tactics, logistics and administration
which affected each of the many commands which they were
supervising and which, altogether, made up an even more complex strategic situation. Lincoln and Stanton lacked the technical
skill and ability to coordinate the activities of the ten or more
completely independent military commands over which they exercised direct control. They also had not yet learned that even the
most capable military men could not have exercised sufficient

control over these wide-spread units without an intermediate chain of command and an efficient staff organization.

Yet, for better or for worse, there they were. As civilians, they had taken over the responsibility for the security of Washington, and at the same time, had assumed direct responsibility for the entire military war effort of the United States.

# 9

# The Valley Campaign

When Confederate General Joe Johnston withdrew from the Manassas area to the Rappahannock on March 9, 1862, he left newly-made Major General Thomas Jonathan "Stonewall" Jackson at Winchester in the Shenandoah Valley; with some 7,000 infantry, 600 cavalry and 27 guns.

Lying between the Alleghenies on the West and the Blue Ridge on the East, the Shenandoah Valley was a natural path of invasion into the North. Opposite its mouth, where the Shenandoah and Potomac Rivers join, ran both the Baltimore & Ohio R.R., a vital link between Washington and the West, and the Chesapeake & Ohio Canal. In Confederate hands, the Valley threatened Washington and its communications, and was also an avenue of approach to the entire eastern industrial complex of the United States.

Conversely, the Valley's southwesterly wanderings up to the head waters of the Shenandoah and James Rivers led away from

Richmond, yet its agricultural resources were essential to Southern sustenance. Furthermore, through Salem, in the upper reach of the Valley, ran the all-important Petersburg-Lynchburg-Chattanooga rail line, the only direct route between Virginia and the Mississippi Valley.

The Shenandoah Valley, then, was a strategically important factor in the war-making of both North and South. Jackson's job was to oppose any incursion by Federal General Banks, whose troops, across the Potomac, stretched from Frederick to Cumberland.

Stonewall Jackson, whom we met briefly at Bull Run, graduated from the U.S. Military Academy in 1846, and had distinguished himself for gallantry during the Mexican War. He had resigned from the Army in 1852 to become professor of natural philosophy, and artillery instructor, at the Virginia Military Institute in Lexington. Reticent and austere, Jackson's theory of war—and he gloried in war—was a complete paraphrase of the dicta of his West Point instructor, Dennis Hart Mahan: deception, surprise and lightning movement.

Jackson had just passed a somewhat frustrating winter at Winchester, striving to consolidate and improve the position of Johnston's left flank. Confederate War Secretary Judah P. Benjamin (the second man to fill the post) had personally interfered with Jackson's operations by giving him direct orders over Johnston's head. In explosive retort Jackson obeyed, then tendered his resignation. The fracas was finally composed and Stonewall stayed.

War came to the Valley in early March. Banks, obeying President Lincoln's order for a general advance on February 22, threw a pontoon bridge over the Potomac at Harpers Ferry and pushed southward, arriving at Martinsburg with 15,000 men. Thus menaced, Jackson, on March 12, fell back thirty miles from Winchester to Woodstock, leaving behind him a rear guard and a cavalry screen.

Occupying Winchester, the Union commander now ordered Brigadier General James Shields' division, 9,000 strong, up to

Strasburg. Banks' instructions, as we have learned, were to remove the potential threat to Washington and its communications posed by Jackson's presence in the Valley. Meanwhile General Joe Johnston, retiring from the Rappahannock to the Peninsula to counter McClellan's now developing advance on Richmond, became perturbed over Banks' movements and put Brigadier General Richard S. Ewell's division of 8,000 men, which was stationed at Gordonsville—east of the Blue Ridge and midway between the Valley and Richmond—under Jackson's command. In an emergency, their forces would unite. Banks was to be kept either from joining McClellan or from reaching Staunton and thus threatening Richmond.

As we know, after Jackson's retreat Banks was confident that the Valley could now be controlled. He started to obey further instructions to move eastward to Manassas, to assist or join McClellan, leaving Shields behind, in observation. Colonel Turner Ashby, daredevil commander of Jackson's cavalry, observing Federal troop movements towards Manassas, mistakenly believed the entire Federal force was quitting the Valley, and so informed his chief. The result was the Battle of Kernstown, in which Jackson was tactically repulsed, yet succeeded in altering the entire Union strategy.

After Kernstown, Jackson, falling back on Harrisonburg, had then turned east and concentrated his troops at Swift Run Gap in the Blue Ridge, conveniently flanking any further Union movement up the Valley. To appreciate what was to follow, we must glance at the vital terrain over which Jackson would now operate. The Valley, from Strasburg south to Harrisonburg, is split by a spiny, wooded hill-mass known as the Massanutten Mountain. This hogback had but one practicable crossing area in its 40-mile length—east from New Market, where two eight-mile-long trails link the two main roads running up and down the Valley. The north fork of the Shenandoah River flows on the northwest side of the Massanutten; the south fork on the southeast, through the Luray Valley. The forks join at the northern tip of the

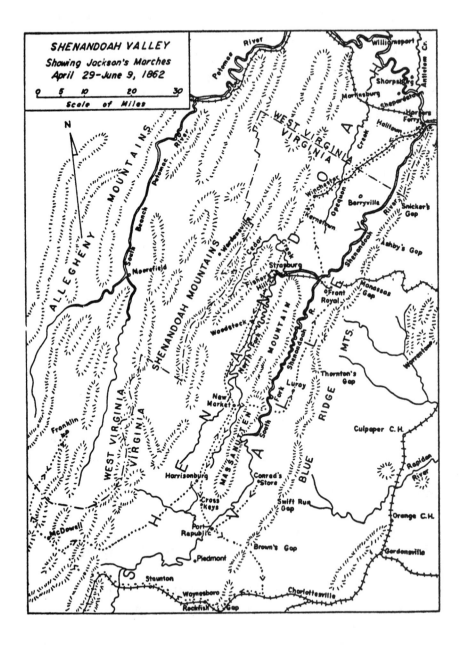

SHENANDOAH VALLEY
Showing Jackson's Marches
April 29-June 9, 1862

hogback, near Front Royal, opposite Strasburg. The Shenandoah chain of the Alleghenies on the west and the Blue Ridge on the east, both heavily forested, frame the sides of this strategical quadrilateral twenty miles wide by sixty long. The Manassas Gap R.R., running east from Strasburg, marks its northern boundary; the Virginia Central R.R., running through Staunton, the southern. Jackson, through the past winter, by careful reconnaissance and mapping, had thoroughly familiarized himself with all of the geography as well as with the road net, down to the smallest detail. He was prepared to make the terrain work for him.

By April 25, as Jackson—still at Swift Run Gap—well knew, Banks from Winchester was coming up the north side of the Massanuttens towards Harrisonburg, his advance elements being but a scant six miles away from the town. Through the Alleghenies, Frémont was moving east; his leading division, commanded by Brigadier General Robert H. Milroy, had reached the vicinity of McDowell, a mountain hamlet some fifty miles by road from Jackson's position. Confronting Milroy was Confederate Brigadier General Edward Johnson, who with an independent command of some 3,000 men had held the Allegheny crest all winter.

Jackson now believed that he must immediately fight either Frémont or Banks, or both, without letting them join, else he would be driven from the Valley by their combined strength. He laid his opinion before General Lee, President Davis' military advisor. Lee concluded that Jackson's situation in the Valley could be fitted into the larger strategic dilemma of the Confederacy. McClellan's army, 100,000 strong, was on the lower Peninsula and would soon be threatening Richmond itself. McDowell, with almost 40,000 men, was at Fredericksburg, and it was expected that he would move south to join McClellan in front of Richmond. To oppose this double threat to the Confederate capital, Joe Johnston had only 60,000 men. And even cautious McClellan would probably dare to attack with a 7 to 3 superiority.

But if McDowell could be kept from joining McClellan,

Johnston could probably save the capital by putting up a bold front in face of the vacillating Federal general. Remembering the effect of Jackson's attack on Kernstown, it seemed to Lee that an effective diversion in the Valley might so alarm the Federal government that they would keep McDowell in Northern Virginia to help meet the supposed threat to Washington. The possibility of such a diversion had been mentioned earlier in Jackson's correspondence with both Lee and Johnston.

So now, in reply to Jackson's latest letter, Lee agreed that he should move against Frémont and Banks. He reaffirmed the assignment of Ewell to Jackson's command, and also placed Edward Johnson's forces under his control. The choice of opponents and all other details were left up to Stonewall.

Jackson now had, in all, 18,000 men. He ordered Ewell to join him at Swift Run Gap. Leaving him there to watch Banks, Jackson, early in May, hurried his own command south to the railroad, leading both friend and foe to believe he was going to move east to join Johnston in the Peninsula. Instead, his trains moved west to Staunton.

On May 8, joining with Edward Johnson, Stonewall unexpectedly struck Milroy's reinforced command at the village of McDowell, and drove the Northerners northwest to Franklin. Frémont was now cut off from direct communication with Banks. Leaving Ashby's horsemen to screen his movements, Jackson and his "foot cavalry" came marching back to Harrisonburg, where he learned that Banks had retired to Strasburg, and was entrenching. Shields' division had been detached from Banks' command to join McDowell at Fredericksburg. Stanton and Lincoln had recovered somewhat from their initial fear of the Valley threat, and in response to McClellan's appeals had agreed to permit McDowell to join the Army of the Potomac in front of Richmond. The addition of Shields' division would make the move south from Fredericksburg less hazardous.

Banks thus had only 8,000 men. His main body was at

Strasburg, with a strong detachment at Front Royal. In theory, the two Valley highways were blocked.

Sending Ewell down the Luray Valley on the east side of the Massanutten, Jackson himself hustled more rapidly down the west side to New Market. But instead of striking directly at the Union position at Strasburg, Stonewall at New Market, turned east, cut through the Massanutten gaps, joined Ewell at Luray, and then moved north. On May 23, he hurled his strength on the Union detachment at Front Royal, smashing it in and driving its remnants down the road towards Winchester.

Actually, Jackson was now threatening Banks' rear. Only the dilatory movement of one of his subordinates prevented an envelopment. Suddenly aware of his danger, Banks came hurrying down the turnpike, clearing the Massanutten tip before Jackson could round it and cut his retreat. Harried every inch of the way by footsore Confederates urged on by Jackson's combat frenzy, Banks, leaving great quantities of stores and matériel behind him, managed to get to Winchester, where he attempted a stand. But on May 25, Jackson's troops, attacking in three columns, drove him pell-mell back to and across the Potomac, the Confederates pursuing to the edge of Harpers Ferry.

More than 3,000 prisoners, 10,000 stands of much-needed small arms, several cannon and a vast quantity of stores were now in Jackson's hands, as his quartermasters scoured the neighborhood for vehicles to transport the windfall. About 1,500 Union soldiers had been killed or wounded. Confederate casualties amounted to 68 killed, 329 wounded and 3 missing.

In Washington, Secretary Stanton erupted in a panicky rage at news of the Union disaster. General McDowell, starting to meet McClellan, was once more halted in the Fredericksburg area and 20,000 men of his command were detached and sent northwest to the Valley. Frémont was told to resume the offensive at once. President Lincoln issued a call for more troops.

On May 29, as Jackson was giving his exhausted men a

breather while he debated whether or not to attack Harpers Ferry, he received word of the approach of converging columns. Next day he ordered a general retirement to Winchester, leaving the Stonewall Brigade as rear guard near Harpers Ferry.

Arriving at Winchester ahead of his men, Jackson learned he was really in a trap. Frémont, with 15,000 men, had reached Wardensville, only 25 miles southwest of Winchester. Shields, commanding 10,000 men of McDowell's corps, had captured Front Royal at the northeast entrance to the Massanutten bottleneck, and 10,000 additional troops were close behind him. Back north across the Potomac, Banks was reviving. He had been reinforced to a strength of 15,000 and might be expected to re-enter the Valley again at any moment. For Jackson there was but one way out: up the turnpike through Strasburg, eighteen miles south of Winchester, and near which Shields was already probing.

One of his staff officers once said of Jackson: "In advance, his trains were left far behind. In retreat, he would fight for a wheelbarrow."

Such, in effect, was Jackson's intention now. His column, forming up on the turnpike, had its head still seven miles north of Winchester, and its rear guard some thirteen miles further back. His combat strength was 15,000, and he was encumbered with more than 2,000 prisoners and a double column of wagons, seven miles long, which contained booty of value immeasurable to the Confederacy.

The indefatigable Ashby was sent galloping off to hold Frémont, while prisoners, wagon train and troops, in that order, started south. By half past two in the afternoon of May 31, the tail of the column had cleared Winchester. By nightfall Strasburg was reached. And still the jaws of the trap were held open by over-caution on the part of both Shields and Frémont, neither of whom knew the other's whereabouts. A Confederate outpost had clashed with Shields' advance details between Front Royal and Strasburg, and Shields, wary of a ruse, had halted. Frémont's advance guard was fencing with Ashby's screening troopers near Cedar Creek instead of plunging through.

Throughout that night Jackson kept his wagon train in motion; the exhausted troops, some of whom had marched thirty miles and more, lay on their arms. But by dawn Ewell's division was marching west to Cedar Creek to delay Frémont while the main column hurried on. The last unit to clear Strasburg was the Stonewall Brigade, which had foot-slogged for thirty-five miles the previous day. The last man out was Stonewall himself. By nightfall Jackson's entire command was safe at Woodstock, bag and baggage, including Ewell's division, which had smartly faded away from Frémont's front. On June 2 Frémont's and Shields' patrols met one another at the Massanutten northern tip to find an empty turnpike. Both commanders picked up the pursuit, Shields up the Luray Valley, Frémont on the western side of the hogback.

Frémont's cavalry brushed several times with the Confederate rear guard, but although Shields, across the ridge, could hear confused sounds of firing, he could not cross the Massanutten to hit Jackson in the flank, for his road ran east of the Shenandoah, and the New Market Gap bridges near Luray had been destroyed by Ashby's men. Torrential rains, swelling both branches of the Shenandoah River, hampered the movement of both sides, but by June 5, Jackson, still twenty-four hours ahead of his pursuers, had cleared the Massanutten and reached Harrisonburg.

Next day Ewell's division lay at Cross Keys, seven miles south of Harrisonburg, and Jackson, with his own troops and the wagon train, was at Port Republic, three miles beyond. Frémont's van, coming up on the western side of the Valley, had reached Harrisonburg. Shields' foremost elements were twelve miles away to the northeast at Conrad's Store, by Swift Run Gap; the rest of his force stretched back down the Luray road for twenty-five miles.

Jackson's entire command could now easily fade from the Valley. But Stonewall had different ideas. He wanted to defeat both his enemies. Ewell, at Cross Keys, would hold Frémont. The "Pathfinder" might immediately put twice the strength of Ewell's 6,500 into his attack, but Jackson well knew Frémont's vacillating nature in combat. Jackson would hurl his own force against the head of Shields' column before it could develop from the Luray defile, and smash it.

That is just what he did. Frémont moved on Ewell June 8, with greatly superior strength, but he thought he was opposed by Jackson's entire command and hesitated, uncertain of Shields' whereabouts. When, finally, he made his attack, Ewell repulsed it easily, his right flank chasing the Federals for more than a mile, taking all the fight out of Frémont. So ended the Battle of Cross Keys, as Ewell refused to let his eager brigadiers attack the new Union line.

Earlier that same day, Shields' cavalry came dashing into Port Republic and nearly captured the precious wagon train. Their rush almost swallowed Jackson himself, but Stonewall, putting himself at the head of an infantry regiment now coming up, sent the Federal troopers scattering by a bayonet charge, and the train was saved. Jackson then went over to observe the situation at Cross Keys. Completely satisfied with Ewell's handling of the battle, he ordered him to leave a covering force to observe Frémont, and with the remainder of his command to join the main army at Port Republic early next day. Shrewdly assessing the Federal general, Jackson was sure that Frémont would make no move after his repulse.

At dawn, June 9, Jackson attacked Shields. The Union troops resisted valiantly in a five-hour-long battle, which was not concluded until Ewell, who had burned the one bridge by which Frémont could advance through Cross Keys, came marching over to Port Republic. The combined force then pushed Shields' men back almost to Conrad's Store, where Federal reinforcements halted the pursuit.

By midnight Stonewall Jackson and his "foot cavalry" sat safely at Brown's Gap in the Blue Ridge, masters of the situation.

The wagon train and its booty were trundling down the road to Richmond. Frémont had retired to Harrisonburg, displaying all the martial ardor Jackson had expected, and McDowell would never join McClellan; urgent orders from Washington directed him to remain in the Valley, with Shields' division at Luray and the rest of his command at Front Royal. Jackson's mission had been magnificently accomplished and the Valley Campaign had passed into history.

With less than 18,000 men, Stonewall Jackson, between April 30 and June 9, had stymied 70,000 Union troops. He had marched his men some 400 miles, fought five battles on terms of his own choosing and defeated four different Union commanders. He had seized great quantities of stores urgently needed by the Confederacy. He had sent the Federal administration into consternation. He had changed the complexion of the entire Federal plan of campaign and had taught the military world a lesson in lightning war which would never be forgotten.

Meanwhile, McClellan was having troubles of his own.

# 10

# The Peninsula

y April 4, McClellan had
about 90,000 men at Fortress Monroe, with another 15,000 combat troops embarked and on their way from Alexandria. He started to advance north up the Peninsula, only to be confronted unexpectedly, that very afternoon, by a line of entrenchments extending southwestward across the Peninsula from Yorktown. He ordered a halt and went forward to inspect the hostile positions.

The grim ten-mile length of earthworks bristled with heavy gun-muzzles. From time to time, through gun-emplacements, there could be glimpsed the movements of many troops. Sporadic cannon fire opened on the leading Federal units and on reconnaissance parties, forbidding closer inspection. To McClellan all this added up one way: behind those ramparts lay an army awaiting attack and obviously ready to fight. How strong was it? McClellan's estimate was 50,000. His worst fears were realized; Pinkerton's reports justified. Defenses such as these could not be assaulted without heavy artillery, and the delay would, McClellan knew, permit Johnston to arrive from the Rappahannock. The Union commander appealed immediately to Washington for more troops and for siege artillery.

Lincoln, despite misgivings as to the Confederate strength— how could they have gotten there, and when?—ordered guns and reinforcements sent as McClellan had requested. But he also sent

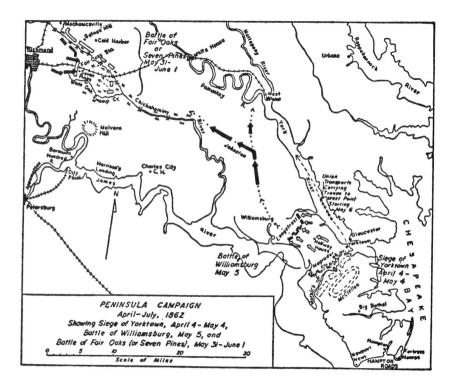

PENINSULA CAMPAIGN
April–July, 1862
Showing Siege of Yorktown, April 4– May 4,
Battle of Williamsburg, May 5, and
Battle of Fair Oaks (or Seven Pines), May 31–June 1

a crisp wire, on April 6: "I think you better break the enemy line from Yorktown to Warwick River at once."

McClellan paid no attention, continuing careful preparations for siege operations, to be followed by a great assault when artillery and reinforcements arrived.

Actually, McClellan was being bamboozled by an artist. Commanding the Yorktown defense was Confederate Brigadier

General John Bankhead Magruder—"Prince John" to his West Point classmates and the "old" Army. An avid devotée of amateur theatricals, Magruder was now staging his finest production. On April 4, he had approximately 15,000—not 50,000—men holding a line ten miles long. Most of those menacing cannon muzzles poking from Magruder's ramparts were "Quaker guns"; peeled logs of wood painted black. Intermingled among them were his few actual artillery pieces, engaged in the firing noticed by the Northerners. Practicing one of the oldest tricks of warfare, he had taken his few troops and marched them back and forth in areas which the Federals could observe, to be counted many times over.

Even the Federal observation balloon careening high as it tugged at the cable linking it to the Army of the Potomac could not detect Magruder's deceptions. Tethered as it had to be, well behind the Union lines to be out of range of the Confederate sharpshooters who invariably opened fire on it, the observers in this new development in war were completely fooled.

After energetic General Fitz-John Porter, commanding the Union V Corps, was carried away when the balloon he was in snapped its cable in a wind-gust, McClellan prohibited aerial reconnaissance by general officers. Porter on April 11 had gone on a wild ride over the Confederate positions, his runaway gasbag the target for trigger-happy Southerners, until the wind shifted and brought him back safely into the Union lines.

Commented McClellan to his wife: "You may be assurd of one thing; you won't catch me in the confounded balloon, nor will I allow any other generals to go up in it."

Magruder well knew, of course, that he could not hope to stop a determined thrust against any point in his long line. But under these conditions he didn't even have to try. By April 11, his command had grown to 23,000, and a few days later Johnston arrived to take command, bringing the total defensive force to about 60,000 men.

This was enough to hold the lines—perhaps indefinitely

against McClellan. Johnston reported to Richmond, after arriving and finding how Magruder had deceived the Federal general: "Only McClellan would have hesitated to attack."

But the Yorktown defenses were vulnerable to being enfiladed or bypassed by the Federal Navy. At present the Northern seamen were still operating most cautiously because of the potential threat of the *Virginia*. But Johnston realized that the ironclad had been neutralized effectively by *Monitor*. As the Union seamen grew bolder, even McClellan, Johnston realized, would be likely to utilize Northern seapower to overthrow or turn the Yorktown position.

President Davis ordered Johnston to hold on to the Yorktown line for the present. But with the arrival of the Union siege artillery, as well as the increasing boldness of the Federal Navy, and the growing threat of McDowell's corps at Fredericksburg, Davis approved Johnston's request that he be permitted to withdraw to defenses near Richmond.

McClelland, happy as a boy with a new toy, had been emplacing his new siege artillery for its projected bombardment of the entrenchments, scheduled to take place on May 6. No coordinated attack had been planned. Gunfire alone was expected to be enough to make Johnston "surrender or abandon his works in less than 12 hours." But suddenly Johnston wasn't there! On the night of May 3–4 he had quietly started marching his army northwest toward Richmond.

He left behind him another "first" in war: booby-traps. Let McClelland tell it in his own words:

"The enemy had made a free distribution of torpedoes in the roads, within the works and in places where our men would be apt to go—for instance, near wells and springs, telegraph-offices and storehouses—so that some of our men were killed. . . . Barbarous in the extreme. . . . I at once ordered that [the booby-traps] should be discovered and removed by the Confederate prisoners."

These mines were the invention of Brigadier General Gabriel

J. Rains, a West Pointer, whose report on his success included, as it turned out, a prophesy for the future:

". . . No soldier will march over mined land, and a corps of sappers, each man having two ten-inch shells, two primers, and a mule to carry them, could stop any army."

Rains was later put in charge of all mining operations in the Confederacy. He supervised, in particular, the placing of underwater mine fields in Charleston harbor, and on the James River below Richmond.

The departure of the Southerners was learned early on May 4, and McClellan's reaction was commendable. He ordered immediate pursuit of the Southerners, with four divisions to go by boat, under the protection of the Navy, up the York River to the junction of the Pamunkey and Mattapony Rivers. But this latter movement could not get under way until May 6, and when Franklin's division disembarked opposite West Point on May 7, it found itself engaged by the division of Confederate General Gustavus W. Smith. Johnston's rear guard was able to pass by unmolested.

General James Longstreet, with his own division and that of D. H. Hill, had been stoutly holding back the energetic pursuit of McClellan's main army, just below Williamsburg, until the remainder of Johnston's troops and their trains could slowly work their way to safety over the muddy roads. This rear guard had had to fight vigorously on May 5, but it accomplished its task and slipped out that night.

This evidence of Southern determination re-awakened McClellan's caution, briefly forgotten in the elation of capturing the Yorktown defenses. Now he moved warily up the Peninsula from Williamsburg, and from a newly established base at West Point. Not until May 25 did his advanced guard approach the Richmond defenses—in sight of the city's steeples seven miles away—near Fair Oaks Station on the Richmond-West Point railroad line. McClellan established his headquarters at White House where the railroad crossed the Pamunkey River, and began building up a supply base there.

As we know, President Lincoln had promised that McDowell's corps at Fredericksburg, reinforced to 40,000 men, would join the Army of the Potomac at Richmond. So McClellan now took up positions from which he felt he could best cover McDowell's approach, and at the same time be in position to attack Johnston when the reinforcing corps arrived.

Three corps—Porter's V, Franklin's VI and Sumner's II—were deployed north of the Chickahominy River, generally from Mechanicsville to the railroad bridge over the river. By thus extending his right wing to the west, McClellan made sure that Johnston could not interpose any force between the Army of the Potomac and General McDowell without abandoning Richmond. And to keep the Confederates occupied in the fortifications east of their capital, as well as to provide a base for subsequent attack, McClellan had placed Keyes' IV Corps south of the Chickahominy in the vicinity of Seven Pines and Fair Oaks Station. Heintzelman's III Corps protected the left and rear of the army below the Chickahominy between Bottom's Bridge and White Oak Swamp.

McClellan did not like having his army split by an unfordable stream, particularly since the Chickahominy was in flood, and its banks marshy or under water. However, there were many bridges over the stream, and he had more built. He felt sure that he could send reinforcements easily across these if the Confederates should concentrate against one portion of his army.

As usual, McClellan was obsessed by the delusion of overwhelming Confederate strength. Pinkerton had reported 200,000 men in the Southern forces defending Richmond, and the Federal commander feared lest both parts of his army be attacked and defeated simultaneously. So repeated telegrams went to Stanton and Lincoln, pleading that McDowell be sent him before the Army of the Potomac met with disaster. Oddly enough, and indicative of the illogical and devious reasoning of this peculiar

man, McClellan promised at the same time that as soon as Mc-
Dowell arrived he would attack Richmond, even though this
would bring his strength up only to about 140,000.

Johnston actually had about 63,000 men at this time. He felt
that if McDowell arrived to reinforce McClellan he would have
to abandon Richmond. (The Confederate Government was packed
to move if necessary.) But noting the way in which McClellan's
army was split by the Chickahominy, Johnston felt that he had a
chance to defeat him before reinforcements could arrive. It was
a risky business, to attack an army almost twice as strong as
his own. But he considered the situation desperate, and thus
warranting such risk. (He did not yet know, of course, that at this
very time McDowell was being ordered to move to the Valley to
counter Jackson's supposed threat to Washington.)

Magruder, with his own division and that of A. P. Hill—
about 20,000 men—would demonstrate against McClellan's right
wing, making motions as if to assault across the Chickahominy.
Meanwhile Johnston with about 42,000 men would attack Keyes'
corps—17,000 strong. This would be a double envelopment, and
Johnston felt that he could overwhelm Keyes before the isolated
Federal corps could be reinforced either by Heintzelman, or from
across the Chickahominy.

It was a good plan, but unfortunately for the Southern cause,
staff officers and commanders lacked the experience, and the
troops the training, to assure necessary coordination. Magruder
did his part well, and kept about 40,000 Northerners tied down
on McClellan's right flank. But the main effort against Keyes got
off to a slow start on May 31, with separate, piecemeal attacks.
By the time G. W. Smith's division moved against the right flank
of the IV Corps, Sumner had been able to get some troops across
the Chickahominy, extending Keyes' right flank up the stream.
The attack against Keyes' left was even slower; the Northern
troops here fell back slowly, and were soon reinforced by Heintzelman. Thus instead of making a double envelopment with superior numbers, 42,000 Confederates found themselves engaged

frontally by a like number of Federals. Nor could Johnston, despite his efforts, succeed in getting his units all to attack together. Trying to rectify the situation personally late in the day, Johnston was seriously wounded, and General Smith temporarily took his place.

The struggle was renewed early on June 1, but by this time the Northerners were ready, and easily held their lines. The attacks were called off by Smith about noon, bringing the indecisive battle to an end. McClellan's troops had suffered about 5,000 casualties, while the Southerners had lost about 6,100. Because of this, and the fact that the Confederates had failed to achieve their objective, McClellan was right to hail Fair Oaks as a Union victory. Had he counterattacked or pursued, or in any way employed more than half of his army in this battle, he would really have had something to crow about. All of the credit for Union success must go to the three corps commanders and their men, who, despite inexperience, fought bravely and skillfully, without instructions from McClellan.

Dejected as the Confederates were with their failure at Seven Pines—as they called the battle—far more serious was the loss of General Johnston, who would be out of action for several months. His battle plans had gone awry, but through no fault of his. He had proven himself a courageous and resourceful leader. In this crisis, with an invading army at the gates of the capital, the best possible replacement had to be found at once.

President Davis turned to his own military adviser, General Robert E. Lee. The afternoon of June 1, as the battle was ending, Lee took over his new command. And as he did, he gave it a name that would go down in history. The Army of Northern Virginia had been born.

McClellan now received a telegram from President Lincoln, informing him that McDowell's corps could not be released due to Jackson's activities in the Valley. This was a terrible shock to the Union general, who protested bitterly in telegrams to Washington that it would not be his fault if his outnumbered army was now to be overwhelmed. He rearranged his corps, to eliminate the dangerous exposure of Keyes which had enticed Johnston's attack, moving Franklin and Sumner across the Chickahominy north of Fair Oaks Station, and bringing Heintzelman up to Seven Pines. Keyes now held the left flank, extending down to White Oak Swamp Creek. Hoping against hope that Lincoln would change his mind and still send McDowell down to join him, McClellan left Porter's corps, reinforced, north of the river. That gave him 30,000 men on the north bank of the Chickahominy, and about 60,000 below.

Now, to add to McClellan's worries, Lee sent cavalryman James Ewell Brown ("Jeb") Stuart on a combined raid and reconnaissance mission behind the Union army. Stuart swung to the north on June 12, then southeast along the Pamunkey River, destroying part of the railroad line, and large quantities of McClellan's stores near White House. Continuing to the southeast, the raiders crossed the Chickahominy, and having ridden completely around the Federal army, returned to Richmond on the 15th. Stuart's dazzling exploit aroused tremendous acclaim throughout the Southland and equal dismay up North. Aside from the psychological effect on the Army of the Potomac and its leader, Stuart also brought back with him invaluable information concerning the Union right flank, which Lee put to prompt use.

With McClellan still astride the Chickahominy, Lee decided to use the same concept that Johnston had employed at Seven Pines, but this time he would concentrate against those Federals north of the river: Porter's V Corps. And this time, too, he would try to bring to bear an even greater preponderance of force in his main effort. He sent a message to Jackson directing him to leave only a detachment in the Valley, and to come secretly and quickly by railroad to Ashland Station north of Richmond. With Jackson and other reinforcements, Lee would have approximately 90,000 men available for battle—almost exactly the combat strength of the Army of the Potomac at that time.

Once again Magruder would employ his theatrical talents to

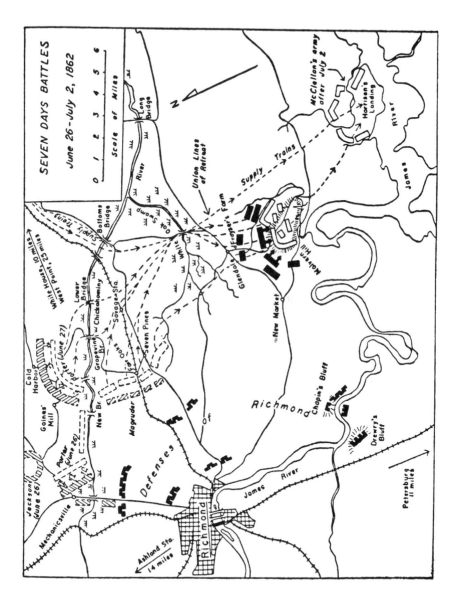

hold the interest of a large Federal audience, demonstrating with 25,000 men against the 60,000 Federals south of the Chickahominy. Lee with 47,000 men—A. P. Hill's, D. H. Hill's and Longstreet's divisions—would move north of the Chickahominy to engage Porter's right flank near Mechanicsville. Jackson, with 18,000, would move east, then south from Ashland Station to strike Porter from the rear. Jackson said he could be ready by June 26, so that was set as the date of the attack.

Like Johnston's a month before, this was an excellent plan; but as had happened at Fair Oaks, execution would be hampered by the inexperience of officers and men, and by the exhaustion still gripping Jackson and his men after their exertions in the Valley. A. P. Hill, who was to attack Porter's Mechanicsville position as soon as he heard Jackson's artillery, waited till late afternoon. Finally, at 3:00 P.M., despairing of Jackson's arrival, Lee ordered A. P. Hill to attack, and moved up D. H. Hill and Longstreet to follow his assault. But the well-entrenched Federals repulsed A. P. Hill's repeated attacks, and there wasn't time before dark to get D. H. Hill or Longstreet into the fight. Jackson didn't get on the field at all. About the time A. P. Hill was being repulsed, Jackson went into bivouac about two miles north of Porter's right flank.

That night Porter received word from Union cavalry of Jackson's position, and so withdrew about three miles to a new position near Gaines' Mill. The Confederates followed promptly in the morning, and Lee directed the same plan to continue. Again Jackson was late, and he failed to get behind Porter's right flank. But by afternoon Lee had about 65,000 men engaged north of the Chickahominy, and this was too much for Porter, with less than half that strength, to restrain. The Union line north of the Chickahominy began to crumble, and would probably have collapsed completely but for the timely arrival of units sent across the river by Franklin and Sumner. As it was, Porter was able to withdraw in good order and, on instructions from

McClellan, began crossing to the south side of the Chickahominy after dark.

Meanwhile, "Prince John" Magruder had been putting on a show worthy of comparison with his Yorktown production. The blowing of bugles, shouting of attack orders, columns of dust raised by troop movements, outpost skirmishes all along the line—all these kept the four Union corps south of the river on constant alert through June 26 and 27. McClellan was convinced that the main attack was coming here, rather than north of the river, and it was on their own initiative that Franklin and Sumner sent assistance to Porter on the twenty-seventh. They were not the only Union generals who began to see through Magruder's bluff by evening of the twenty-seventh.

Generals Phil Kearny and Joe Hooker of Heintzelman's corps reported that there was only a thin shell in front of them, and that they could march into Richmond almost without opposition. They were dumbfounded, therefore, when they received orders to prepare to withdraw, and learned that the Army of the Potomac was about to retreat. Both of them at once rode to tell McClellan of the situation as they saw it.

But McClellan, sitting gloomily in his tent when the two division commanders arrived, was unmoved by their efforts to have him change his mind. He had already sent word to Washington that he was attacked by superior numbers. The only way to save his army, he had reported, was to abandon his base at White House and move his entire army south to the James River, where a new base would have to be established with the help of the Navy. His telegram to Stanton had ended with these amazing words: "The government has not sustained this army. . . . If I save this army now, I tell you plainly that I owe no thanks to you or any other persons in Washington. You have done your best to sacrifice this army."

When McClellan refused to withdraw the retreat order, Kearny berated him with a violence that caused onlooking staff officers to expect McClellan to throw the division commander into arrest. McClellan took the abuse—but refused to change his orders. The die was cast. The army was retreating and changing its base.

The third day of the Seven Days' Battle, June 28, was the quietest. Porter's corps and the army's trains moved south over the bridges across White Oak Swamp while Keyes, slipping to his left, took up positions near Glendale, west of the swamp and northwest of Malvern Hill, covering the line of retreat. The other three corps readied themselves for departure that night, skirmishing with Magruder's men, and with Lee's troops, which had moved up to the Chickahominy in Porter's old positions.

Lee, who had not yet realized that the Union army was retreating, was trying to find out what McClellan was up to, and was preparing to attack across the Chickahominy in the morning, if McClellan didn't counterattack in the meanwhile. When, early on June 29, he discovered the withdrawal of the entire Union army, Lee guessed that McClellan was heading for the James, and gave immediate orders for pursuit.

Magruder was to press forward after the retreating Federals, while Jackson and D. H. Hill were to cross the Chickahominy over the Grapevine Bridge as rapidly as possible, striking the flank or rear of the receding Union columns. A. P. Hill and Longstreet were sent directly south over the New Bridge toward New Market, to try to intercept the retreating Northerners between White Oak Swamp and the James.

Magruder soon came on Sumner's corps, which, with part of Franklin's, was the Union rear guard. Sumner had taken up a defensive position near Savage's Station, and repulsed Magruder's repeated assaults. Magruder expected Jackson to come up on Sumner's right flank, but Stonewall had been delayed in rebuilding the bridges the Federals had destroyed, and didn't arrive till after dark. Meanwhile, Sumner, his mission accomplished, had withdrawn toward White Oak Swamp.

By morning of June 30, the entire Union army and its trains

had crossed White Oak Swamp. The bridges had been destroyed and the fording was covered by Franklin. Sumner, Heintzelman and Porter held a line from White Oak Swamp to the James, west of Malvern Hill, while Keyes was in reserve on Malvern Hill. The trains were continuing southward, behind this line, heading for Harrison's Landing and the protection of the Union Navy.

All day and into the night, Longstreet and A. P. Hill, following their orders from Lee, attempted vainly to break through the Federal line near Frayser's Farm and Glendale. Jackson, meanwhile, who had reached the northern side of White Oak Swamp with D. H. Hill, contented himself with exchanging artillery fire with Franklin, south of the swamp. During the night most of the Union army fell back to positions McClellan had selected on Malvern Hill, while Keyes' corps, covering the rear of the trains, moved down toward Harrison's Landing.

Next day, July 1, Lee pushed forward to find the Union army ready and waiting in strong positions on Malvern Hill, its artillery posted to sweep the cleared fields around its gentle slopes. Events of the past six days had given Lee considerable respect for the fighting ability of the Union soldiers, no matter what he may have thought of their commander. Before attacking, therefore, he wanted to be certain that his own guns were emplaced to cover his assaulting troops, and to neutralize the Federal batteries. He now discovered, however, that his gunners lacked the efficiency and the power of the Union artillery. By mid-afternoon many of his guns were still not emplaced, and those that were, were unable to fire very effectively. Though his infantry divisions were assembled, he was about to call off the attack for the day, when he noticed some movements in the Federal lines indicating to him another Union retreat.

Lee thereupon ordered immediate attack. But by now it was 4:00 P.M., and there was insufficient time to get orders to the various units for proper coordination of their moves. Huger and D. H. Hill, in the center, attacked vigorously, and as soon as Jackson realized what was going on, he sent reinforcements to

Hill. But the assaults were beaten back with heavy losses, and darkness fell before Longstreet or A. P. Hill, in reserve, could even start for the front. In a little over two hours Lee lost more than 5,000 men, while Union casualties were less than half that number.

The capable defense of Malvern Hill had been conducted by Fitz-John Porter, V Corps commander. McClellan had been absent, spending most of the day on a Federal gunboat in the James, inspecting his new base. The Battle of Malvern Hill was a clear-cut Union success, and would have been hailed as a great victory, save for one thing: McClellan ordered his victorious army to retreat to Harrison's Landing, leaving the field to the astonished Confederates.

So the Seven Days' Battle ended as it had begun: the Union troops repulsed the attacking Confederates, but the Union commander was determined that he would be defeated, and so he was.

The casualty figures for the battle are revealing. McClellan had 1,734 men killed, 8,062 wounded, and 6,053 missing (practically all prisoners), for total losses of 15,849. Lee lost 3,478 killed, 16,261 wounded, 875 missing, for a total of 20,614. These casualty figures, plus the fact that all Confederate attacks (except at Gaines' Mill) were repulsed, might have been depressing to the South. Yet when the battle was over the invading Union army had been driven from the outskirts of Richmond, and was huddling, twenty miles away, in a small encampment on the banks of the James River, under the protection of Federal gunboats. Regardless of casualty figures, this was victory, clear-cut and undeniable. It was celebrated as such throughout the Confederacy and the North was correspondingly despondent. Lee and the Army of Northern Virginia had established reputations whose luster would never be dimmed.

There was one other important result of the battle so far as the South was concerned. The still-inexperienced troops that had opened the battle at Mechanicsville on June 26, were relatively seasoned veterans by the time they occupied the abandoned Union positions on Malvern Hill on July 2. Lee had learned much about capabilities and peculiarities of his own principal generals. And these, every last man, had learned that their new commander was a wise, courageous, forceful and inspiring leader. This was a fighting team; they were winners, and they knew it!

Up in Washington, President Lincoln now took up a job of military fence-mending.

# 11

# Second Bull Run

The complete failure of the efforts of McDowell, Banks and Frémont to catch and defeat Jackson in the Valley had been in part due to the ineptness or caution of these Union commanders—particularly Banks and Frémont. In at least equal measure the failure had resulted from inadequate coordination and control of the independent efforts of these generals. The responsibility for this, of course, lay with two amateur strategists—Lincoln and Stanton—who had assumed direct control over Federal military operations.

Lincoln learned his lesson. Although he had not yet found a military man who had the wisdom and breadth of vision necessary for coordinating operations of armies spread across half a continent, some professional would have to be found who at least could translate the President's ideas into military plans, with due consideration for basic military requirements.

The first step in getting the chaotic command situation under control was to have one competent man to direct the three small forces that had failed against Jackson. So, on June 26, 1862, General John Pope, hero of Island No. 10, was assigned as commander of the newly created Army of Virginia, consolidating the commands of McDowell, Frémont and Banks. (Frémont soon after this was relieved and General Franz Sigel took his place.) The mission of this army, 47,000 strong, would be to cover Washington, to hold the northern portion of the Shenandoah Valley, and to threaten Richmond from the north so as to divert forces from Lee's army facing McClellan at Richmond. Lincoln didn't realize, as he signed that order, that the situation near Richmond was beginning to change dramatically, as Lee began the Seven Days' Battle that very day.

Though the President was distressed over the results of that battle, it merely served to confirm his thoughts on the need of a military professional to take the reins of command and supervision in Washington. Lincoln now turned to Halleck as the most obvious man for the job.

Lincoln was soon disappointed by Halleck's caution and indecisiveness. But he was pleased by the energetic way in which the new General-in-Chief tackled the confused administrative situation that prevailed in the War Department. He discovered that Halleck's keen mind, combined with his military training and experience, made the general a valuable adviser, and an almost indispensable chief of staff. Since Lincoln had no hesitation in making decisions, he accepted Halleck's shortcomings, and this relationship was to continue for almost two years.

Meanwhile John Pope had taken command of his new army, and had almost immediately alienated most of its members. On July 14, he made a bombastic address in which he implied that the troops in the East were not as good fighters as those he had commanded in the West, intimating that he would make real soldiers out of them regardless of their deficiencies. His own men naturally took this as an insult. So did McClellan, and all of the officers and men of the Army of the Potomac at Harrison's Landing.

But Pope was both energetic and able, as he had proven in his operations against Island No. 10. He also prided himself as a man of decision—a quality assessed by some others as stubbornness. Despite the early, unfortunate, impression he made on his men, he soon stamped his will on his new army, as he reorganized it in the region west of Fredericksburg and north of the Rappahannock.

McClellan, meanwhile, had urged that he be given reinforcements in order to continue his operations against Richmond. He also suggested that he be authorized to take his army across the James River in the general vicinity of Petersburg, to cut Richmond off from the rest of the South. He said that he could take Richmond if only he were given 30,000 more men. Halleck, who visited the Army of the Potomac at Harrison's Landing, agreed to let him have 20,000. A few days later McClellan reported that Lee had 200,000 men in Richmond, and so the Army of the Potomac, only 90,000 strong, could not advance without 40,000 reinforcements. This was too much for Lincoln; he had heard this same illogical story from McClellan before. On August 3, he ordered that the Army of the Potomac be withdrawn from the James River and brought by ship back to Washington, to be used for an overland advance against Richmond from the north. Nothing was said about the future relationship of McClellan, or his army, to Pope. It was assumed by many, including the bitter McClellan, that his army would be absorbed by Pope's.

At the same time, Lee was greatly concerned by Pope's activity in central Virginia. He had about 70,000 men near Richmond, and the combined armies of McClellan and Pope would amount to nearly 150,000. Lee apparently was not too concerned about McClellan, so long as that general was not reinforced or supported. He was less sure if his army had to face the combined forces of Pope and McClellan. Lee sent Jackson, with 12,000 men, to the vicinity of Gordonsville to observe Pope, and to try to ascertain his intentions. Jackson soon reported that Pope was very active, and that his army appeared to be getting ready for an advance. One of Pope's orders, signed from his "headquarters in the saddle," was captured and delivered to Lee. It is reported that Lee dryly remarked that Pope's headquarters were where his hindquarters ought to be, but he took the Union general's activity seriously enough to send reinforcements to Jackson. Stonewall now had three divisions, 24,000 men in all.

August 7, Jackson received word from spies that Pope was advancing across the Rappahannock with a view to concentrating his army at Culpeper. Jackson decided at once to try to defeat the leading portion of Pope's army before the rest could get across the river. But there was confusion in the orders, due partly to Jackson's usual refusal to tell his plans to his subordinates, and partly to poor staff work in planning the march. So instead of arriving at Culpeper early on the ninth, as he had planned, the head of his column was then just moving across the Rapidan west of Rapidan Station.

About noon, just west of Cedar Mountain, Jackson's advance guard ran into Federal cavalry outposts. A skirmish began, that quickly developed into a battle. Pope had received word of Jackson's advance and ordered Banks, his leading corps commander, to delay Jackson while the Union army concentrated. Banks, possibly hoping to gain revenge for the humiliation Jackson had handed him in the Valley—or more likely unaware of Confederate strength—attacked vigorously, almost recklessly, with less than 10,000 men. The Union troops smashed Jackson's left flank, even sending part of his own Stonewall Brigade into flight. For a few minutes the Confederate army was close to defeat. After personally rallying some of the fugitives, Jackson sent his reserve division—A. P. Hill's—into the battle, and by nightfall had driven Banks off the field and back toward Culpeper. Though Jackson won the battle, Banks had delayed his advance, and greatly increased his own prestige—probably more than he deserved—by the vigor of his activity.

Pope now began to push against Jackson with his concentrated army. Stonewall, realizing that he had lost his opportunity to defeat the Army of Virginia in detail, withdrew across the Rapidan on the eleventh.

It was now obvious to Lee that Pope's army was a considerably greater danger than McClellan's. It was also apparent that McClellan's army was about to be withdrawn from Harrison's Landing to join Pope. Lee was determined to prevent this at all costs. Leaving only 20,000 men near Richmond to observe McClellan, Lee moved with most of his army to join Jackson, arriving at Gordonsville on August 15. He had 55,000 men, which he divided into two wings, or corps. He placed James ("Old Pete") Longstreet in command of his right wing, or I Corps; Jackson commanded the left wing, or II Corps.

Pope—who also had 55,000 men—had concentrated his army along the railroad between Rapidan Station and Culpeper. But, with the arrival of Lee, Pope realized that a Confederate crossing of the Rapidan to his east could cut his line of communications, so he withdrew across the Rappahannock on the nineteenth.

Lee had, in fact, been contemplating just such a move as Pope had feared. But after the efficient Union withdrawal he had to devise a new plan. As he pushed after Pope to the line of the Rappahannock, Lee received information on August 24, which made him realize that prompt action was imperative.

Two corps of McClellan's army had reached northern Virginia on the twenty-second—Porter's at Acquia Landing, just twenty-five miles east of Pope's army, and Heintzelman's at Alexandria. More Union troops were on transports and could be expected to arrive within a few days. If Lee could not defeat Pope in the next few days, it would be too late. In this desperate situation he could see no possibility of success against an undefeated Union army of 150,000 men.

Lee produced a plan worthy of the situation. While Longstreet kept Pope's army occupied along the Rappahannock line, Jackson was to march north, then east, to cut the railroad line behind Pope. Giving Jackson only a one-day start, Lee and Long-

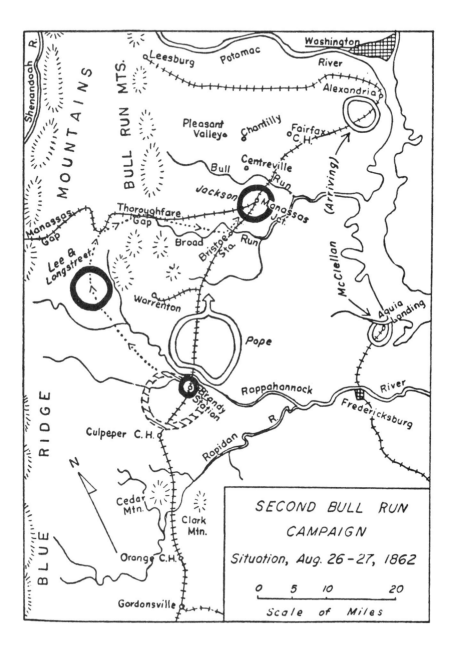

Shenandoah R.

Leesburg

Potomac

Washington

River

Alexandria

BULL RUN MTS.

MOUNTAINS

Pleasant Valley•

Chantilly

Fairfax C.H.

Centreville

Bull Run

Jackson

Manassas Jct.

Thoroughfare Gap

(Arriving)

Manassas Gap

Broad

Bristoe Sta.

Run

McClellan

Lee & Longstreet

Warrenton

Aquia Landing

BLUE    RIDGE

Pope

Rappahannock

River

Fredericksburg

Brandy Station

Culpeper C.H.

Rapidan

R.

N

Cedar Mtn.

Clark Mtn.

Orange C.H.

SECOND BULL RUN
CAMPAIGN

Situation, Aug. 26–27, 1862

0      5     10              20

Scale   of   Miles

Gordonsville

street would follow, to concentrate the army somewhere near Manassas, where Pope had established a great supply depot. Lee expected that Pope would rush northward when informed of the threat to his line of communications and his supplies. By rapidly concentrating his army near Manassas, therefore, Lee hoped that he would be able to crush the unsuspecting Pope before many additional reinforcements reached him.

The greatest danger, Lee realized, would be while Jackson was on the march, and Longstreet's single corps was opposite Pope's concentrated army along the Rappahannock. Therefore both Jackson and Longstreet would have to move fast. The time and place of the battle he could not forecast. He would have to rely on Jackson to select a good defensive position which he could hold until Longstreet arrived.

This was a bold plan, that able military theorists have criticized as "rash" and "perilous." But Lee felt, as he wrote at the time, that "the disparity of force between the contending forces rendered the risk unavoidable." These authors agree with Lee, and with the assessment of Lee's great biographer, Douglas S. Freeman, who wrote: "In detaching Jackson for the march against Pope's communications . . . examination of the circumstances will show that daring was prudence." At least it was for a general who had both a Jackson and a Longstreet to put his plans into execution.

Jackson's corps started at dawn of the twenty-fifth. The men carried three days' rations, there was a wagon train carrying artillery and small-arms ammunition, there were ambulances—and there was a herd of beef-cattle bringing up the rear. They marched northwest, to reach Salem on the Manassas Gap Railroad that night. Early next day they moved boldly eastward through Thoroughfare Gap. By evening Bristoe Station had been occupied, the railroad bridge over Broad Run destroyed, and after dark a strong force had seized part of the Union supply depot at Manassas. In two days the corps had covered fifty-four miles, and some units had traveled even further. That night the stern general went to sleep with the realization that his command had just completed one of the phenomenal marches of military history.

Next day the great store of Federal supplies—loaded on railroad cars on the sidings at Manassas—was looted by Jackson's corps. This pleasant task was interrupted briefly to crush a rash Federal brigade that advanced into Manassas from Centreville. Jackson ordered all liquor stores destroyed but otherwise gave his men a free hand to gather clothes, food delicacies, or whatever caught their fancy. Finally, as Pope's army began to press against his covering force at Bristoe Station, Jackson ordered all remaining Union equipment to be burned, and prepared to withdraw from Manassas.

Pope reacted just as Lee had hoped. Receiving word late on the twenty-sixth that a Confederate force had cut the railroad, he ordered a concentration of his army to smash the audacious raider. He did not realize that Lee and Longstreet had already left their positions on the Rappahannock, leaving only Anderson's division to try to simulate the activity of an army. All that was now on Pope's mind was to seize the opportunity he thought had been presented to him. Jackson's isolated corps, he fondly expected, would soon be destroyed or in flight.

But when Union troops marched into the debris of the wrecked supply depot at Manassas Junction, early on the twenty-eighth, Jackson had disappeared. All day Federal divisions marched across the countryside, searching for the elusive Confederate. Pope was certain he had not gone far, but grew increasingly annoyed as the day passed without any information.

Then, just before dark, Pope received some news. One of McDowell's divisions had been attacked at Groveton, just west of the old Bull Run battlefield. Jackson, Pope now learned, had hidden all day along a wooded ridge just north of the Warrenton Turnpike, southwest of Bull Run. Here an unfinished railroad cut and embankment provided the basis for a strong defensive position.

It is not clear whether Jackson attacked the Union division

as it marched down the road in front of him because he could not resist a splendid opportunity, or whether it was his intention to distract attention from Longstreet's advance through Thoroughfare Gap. In any event, it had this latter effect, so far as Pope was concerned.

Pope ordered all units of his army to concentrate to attack the Confederate position early on the twenty-ninth. He was elated;

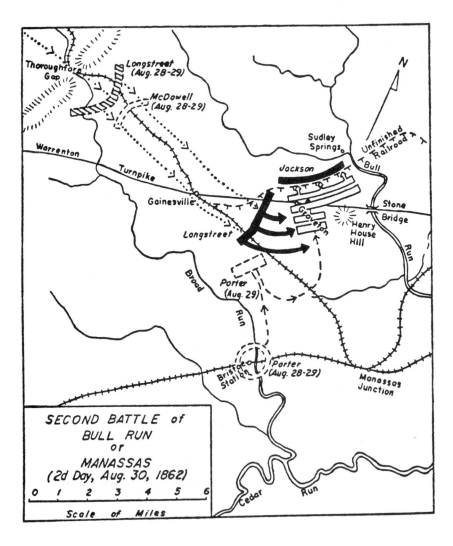

his enemy's rashness had given him the great opportunity of the war. Jackson would pay dearly for the stores he had captured and destroyed!

Pope apparently did have some concern that Longstreet's corps might be marching to join Jackson. Late that day he had received word that Buford's cavalry and another of McDowell's divisions had encountered some Confederates in Thoroughfare Gap, apparently part of Longstreet's command. But Pope was led to believe that this enemy force had been driven west of the pass. He assumed, apparently, that the cavalry screen would be able to hold the pass for as long as would be necessary to dispose of Jackson.

But Longstreet had not been driven west of Thoroughfare Gap. Early next morning, McDowell, who had lost contact with his division skirmishing to the west, was coming up from Manassas with the remainder of his corps to join the attack on Jackson's right flank when he got word that Longstreet's men were pouring through the Gap in great force.

Just west of McDowell, near Gainesville, was Porter's corps—the first of the Army of the Potomac elements to join Pope—also advancing to attack Jackson in compliance with Pope's orders. He had halted it now, to investigate great clouds of dust rising west of Gainesville—actually raised by the feet of Longstreet's men. McDowell and Porter discussed the situation, and they agreed that Porter would take up a position southeast of Gainesville, protecting the left flank of the Union army. McDowell would have one division (Reynolds') south of Groveton, while continuing northward with two others to join the attack against Jackson. Pope was informed of the situation on the left flank.

Meanwhile, Lee, gravely concerned about the Union attacks now raging against Jackson's lines, had urged Longstreet to move forward as rapidly as possible to attack the Union left flank. But now Longstreet's scouts discovered the positions taken up by Porter and Reynolds. Longstreet, properly, advanced with great caution, since he feared that otherwise Porter might turn his own right flank. Skirmishing with Porter's and Reynolds' outposts, the Confederates advanced very slowly, and Longstreet was not able to take up a position in extension of Jackson's line till dark.

Meanwhile Jackson had been receiving severe punishment from the rest of Pope's army. All day long the Northerners had pounded at the Confederate position, and had succeeded in pushing back A. P. Hill's division, holding Jackson's left, for a short distance. But Jackson's men held grimly to their railroad cut, encouraged by their dauntless commander, and by the sight of Longstreet's corps, which they could see advancing from the right.

That night Pope learned that Porter's corps and part of McDowell's had not obeyed his orders to join the attack against Jackson. Pope was certainly now aware that Lee and Longstreet were approaching from the west, but he apparently did not believe that they were close, or that Porter or Reynolds had in any way delayed their arrival. He was firmly convinced that if Porter and Reynolds' troops had taken part in the attack, Jackson would have been defeated before Lee and the rest of the Southern army could have arrived. Even that night, with Longstreet's men actually deployed in a battle line overlapping his left flank, Pope apparently did not believe it, despite the messages he had received from Porter and McDowell.

It is likely that Pope thought that Longstreet had moved into the same position that Jackson held. In describing his attacks of August 29, in a report to General Halleck written early on the thirtieth, he wrote of fighting ''the combined forces of the enemy.'' He also wrote that ''the enemy was driven from the field, which we now occupy.'' This would have surprised Jackson's men who, with the exception of the extreme left flank, held the same positions they had occupied forty-eight hours earlier. They also would have wondered how Pope could write, at dawn of August 30, that ''the enemy is retreating toward the mountains.''

Whatever the reason, Pope was convinced that there was, and had been, no danger to his left flank. Porter had received two orders to attack Jackson's right, and so far as Pope could see, had ignored them. What followed next is best described in Pope's own words:

"General Porter, with whose non-action of the day before I was naturally dissatisfied, had been peremptorily ordered that night to report to me in person with his corps, and arrived on the field early in the morning."

Porter, who knew that he had been skirmishing with Longstreet most of August 29, and that the Union left flank was seriously threatened by the Confederate dispositions, had apparently made no further effort to give his commander a complete picture of the situation. Porter heartily disliked Pope, and like all members of the Army of the Potomac, resented the slurring remarks Pope had made a few weeks earlier. Realizing that he was doing a good job protecting the Union left, he had become extremely annoyed when Pope sent repeated orders to "push forward into action at once" on Jackson's flank and rear. Now, having received Pope's "peremptory" order, Porter simply obeyed, again making no effort—or so it was later alleged—to clarify the confused picture which obviously existed in his commander's mind.

Pope was aware of Porter's animosity, which he heartily reciprocated. He strongly mistrusted his new subordinate, who had been, he knew, a favorite of McClellan's. Pope had reason to believe that Porter was slandering him in letters to McClellan and other Union generals. He also believed that McClellan, now back in Alexandria, was doing his best to discredit him and his Army of Virginia. These well founded suspicions, combined with his impetuous, stubborn, combative nature, caused him to believe that Porter was deliberately trying to make him fail as a commander, and to doubt Porter's messages about a threat to the left flank. Thus it was, that the weaknesses of two hard-fighting Union generals, each doing his best for Federal victory, conspired to set the stage for disaster.

During the morning Pope also pulled Reynolds out of his

position on the Federal left, to join the attack, which started about noon. He seemed to believe that a small force of cavalry could adequately screen the Union left.

At the same time, Lee's combined forces were reorganizing their positions, their battle front becoming a wide V, opening toward Pope's army. Jackson, on the north side, was still securely anchored along the railroad cut and fill. Longstreet, ready to attack, extended south from the cut, reaching well across the other side of the Warrenton Pike. Longstreet's reconnaissances during the night had found Porter's men in position and ready to fight. The Confederates were unaware of the pre-dawn withdrawal of Porter's corps from Longstreet's front, so Lee bided his time, waiting for Pope further to commit himself.

Shortly after noon, the Union onslaught came, again directed against Jackson's position. Porter's corps on the left, making the main effort, thus advanced under the very eyes of Longstreet's men. For the first time the Southerners realized that the Union left flank was now wide open; tailor-made for a crushing counter-attack.

Lee, who had at first ordered Longstreet to send reinforcements to help Jackson's II Corps repel the violent Northern assault, now directed the I Corps to attack directly to its front. As a matter of fact Longstreet's men were actually advancing when Lee's order reached him; "Old Pete" was too good a general not to realize for himself what a wonderful opportunity had been presented to him. Following a devastating concentration of artillery fire enfilading the entire Union line, the Confederate I Corps swept forward against the exposed Union flank. Porter's corps, caught as it was driving against stubborn Jackson, was rolled back and to the east.

Porter, of course, had suspected that something like this might happen. Though his corps took the brunt of Longstreet's attack, at least one of his divisions was quickly shifted to the left, slowing down the Southern advance. This was Sykes' division of Regulars; by coincidence, Sykes had been the man who, with a battalion of Regulars, had covered the Union retirement from First Bull Run.

But there was no holding the irresistible advance of the Confederates. Jackson's men now joined the attack, though their efforts were understandably weak. By dusk Pope's army was bent back in a horseshoe around Sykes' stubborn resistance on Henry House Hill.

It was now obvious to all of the Northerners, including Pope, that the battle had been irretrievably lost. But these men had become veterans, like the grim Southerners pressing them back across Henry House Hill to Bull Run. There was confusion, there was a feeling of despair shared by officers and men, but there was no widespread panic. As Sykes' troops fell back, the last Union division to cross the stream, they could be proud of a job well done. And the sullen, gloomy, beaten army that was marching northeast on the roads toward Washington was in good order, bearing little resemblance to the confused mob that had fled along these same roads thirteen months before.

Lee was naturally elated at his splendid victory, but hoped to be able to cause even more damage. On August 31, he sent Jackson north, then east, intending to strike the flank of the retreating Northern army. Longstreet would follow early next day, as Jackson turned southeast at Pleasant Valley, heading for Chantilly and Fairfax Courthouse.

That afternoon, just south of Chantilly, Jackson ran into Reno's IX Corps, and Phil Kearny's division of Heintzelman's corps, just arrived from the Peninsula. Jackson tried to drive through, in a blinding rainstorm, but the Federals were too strong for him. In the stubborn fighting brave Phil Kearny was killed in hand-to-hand action. The Battle of Chantilly ended at dark, with neither side able to gain any real advantage.

With it, the Second Bull Run Campaign came to a close, because Lee now realized that with practically all of McClellan's army now arrived, it would become extremely risky to press any closer to Washington. He had also received reinforcements, but these were barely sufficient to make up for the 9,197 casualties he had suffered at Bull Run and Chantilly. Though he had inflicted losses of more than 16,000 on the Northerners, and had crushed their morale, he could not hope to fight successfully against more than 100,000 Federals, supported by the fortifications of Washington. For the moment he was satisfied with the fact that in the three months since he took command, the Army of Northern Virginia had advanced from defeat outside of Richmond to victory at the outskirts of the Federal capital.

Dismay in Washington caused an immediate reshuffling of command. The Army of Virginia was dissolved; Pope was sent to a command in the West chasing Indians, and the troops reverted to the Army of the Potomac, with McClellan once again in the limelight. But in the face of popular clamor, a scapegoat had to be found for the Second Bull Run defeat. Pope pointed the finger at Fitz-John Porter. A few weeks later, shortly after the Battle of Antietam, Porter was relieved of command, tried by court-martial and hastily convicted of failure to obey orders. Dismissed from the service, Porter would not be cleared of this unjust charge until 1879, by a court of inquiry. In 1886 he was reinstated to his permanent rank of Colonel in the Regular Army. Porter had paid a heavy penalty for allowing his personal feelings to influence his actions and attitude in a battle he helped save from complete disaster.

# 12

# On a Bright September Morn

Invasion of the North began September 4, 1862. Four days after Second Bull Run, the Army of Northern Virginia crossed the Potomac near Leesburg, and by the seventh was concentrating at Frederick, Maryland. The move had been deftly screened from Union observation by Stuart's cavalry, extending all the way from Alexandria to Hyattsville, eleven miles southeast of Frederick.

Lee's army now consisted of nine divisions organized in two army corps: Longstreet's and Jackson's. Including the cavalry, it numbered 50,000 men and 230 guns. It was poorly clothed, badly equipped and short of transportation. It would have to subsist mainly on its own resources, at the end of an ever-lengthening line of communications reaching back to Richmond.

By contrast, the Army of the Potomac was shaking itself smartly together under McClellan's efficient administration. It consisted of six army corps and a cavalry division; in all, 97,000 men and 330 guns. The Union troops were well clothed, their ranks had been refilled, they were close to their base of supply and their confidence had rocketed now that their old commander was back.

Why, then, under such circumstances, had Lee—with Jefferson Davis' approval—chosen to invade the North?

The answer lies in two impalpable factors—morale and leadership. Lee's army was a "hot" team, flushed by recent victory. Its leader was taking a calculated risk. Lee had to strike somewhere, to keep the Federal forces off balance. Otherwise, it was only a question of time before another invasion of the Southland would have to be combatted. He was moving from the already strained resources of the Confederacy into a rich agricultural region where, he also hoped, the presence of a Confederate army would not only spur many sympathetic inhabitants to join the Southern cause, but also dampen Northern enthusiasm for the war. There also was an international political angle, as apparent to Lee as it was to Davis. Success of Southern arms on Northern terrain might well bring about the active intervention of Europe for which the Confederacy so devoutly hoped.

Lee was playing for high stakes against a dilatory opponent. If his invasion were successful, he would cut first the Baltimore & Ohio R.R. and then the Pennsylvania R.R. above it, thus breaking all communications between Union east and west except by the long, roundabout Great Lakes route. Philadelphia, Baltimore and Washington would lie at his mercy. At worst, Lee believed, immediate Federal retort to his audacious move would be to rally all available forces to defend Washington, and thus relieve much of the Union pressure on the Confederacy.

In short, Lee's decision was right in line with Dennis Hart Mahan's West Point theory: "Carrying the war into the heart of the assailant's country . . . is the surest plan of making him share its burdens and foiling his plans."

For two days Lee rested his men at Frederick, while he planned for the future. A cool reception was given both his troops and his proclamation urging the people of Maryland to rise against

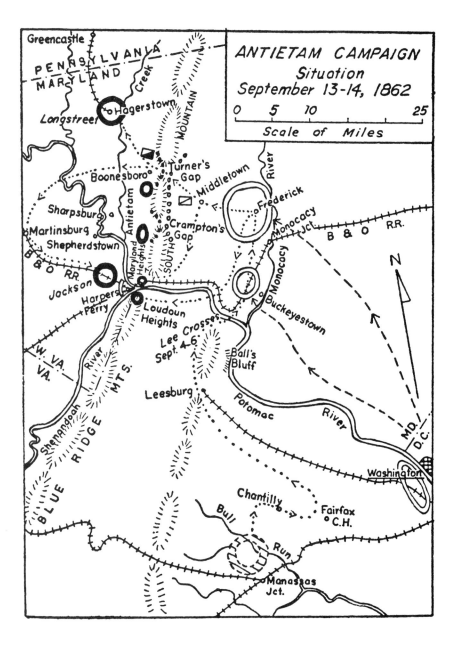

ANTIETAM CAMPAIGN
Situation
September 13-14, 1862

0    5    10                          25
Scale  of  Miles

the Union. Determined to push on to Harrisburg, he also felt that for safety's sake he needed to change his line of communications westward to the Shenandoah Valley.

So Lee, with an enemy nearly twice his strength assembled not more than forty miles away, decided to scatter his army wide in several small packets, to surround and capture Harpers Ferry, and destroy Washington's rail and canal communications with the west, while his advance guard began the invasion of Pennsylvania. This was indeed dicing with Fate. But, as Lee told one of his subordinates, McClellan's army "will not be prepared for offensive operations—*or he will not think it so* [italics supplied]—for three or four weeks. Before that time I hope to be on the Susquehanna."

Special Orders No. 191, Headquarters Army of Northern Virginia, directing the movement, was issued the night of September 9. Jackson was to take his corps back over the Potomac in a wide westerly arc, ripping up the B. & O. rail line on the way, drive the Federal garrison out of Martinsburg and then strike Harpers Ferry. Major General Lafayette McLaws, with two divisions of Longstreet's corps, would move to Maryland Heights on the north bank of the Potomac, overlooking Harpers Ferry. Brigadier General John G. Walker's division—also of Longstreet's corps—marching south to where the Monocacy meets the Potomac, would destroy the Chesapeake & Ohio canal aqueduct over the Monocacy, re-cross the Potomac into Virginia, and occupy the Loudoun Heights, which frown over Harpers Ferry from the south, just below the Shenandoah River mouth. The remainder of Longstreet's corps—two divisions—with the army's supply trains, would proceed northwest on the Hagerstown road; the first step on the ninety-mile proposed invasion path through the Cumberland Valley to Harrisburg. Major General Daniel Harvey (D. H.) Hill's division of Jackson's corps would follow Longstreet, as rear guard, with Stuart's cavalry still further behind to screen the movement. Lee himself would accompany Longstreet. Once Harpers Ferry was captured, Jackson, McLaws and Walker would rejoin the main command at Boonesboro, Maryland. All movements were to begin the morning of September 10.

The order was clear and unmistakable; a detailed program of the whereabouts of the entire Army of Northern Virginia for the next week or more. Its distribution was limited to the corps commanders and to those division commanders directly involved. But D. H. Hill received two copies; one through Jackson, his corps commander, and one direct. Hill kept Jackson's copy, but, in the shuffle and hustle departure someone in his headquarters— to this day nobody knows who—found no better use for the latter than to wrap up three cigars. And then he dropped the packet.

Forty-eight hours later the Army of the Potomac began to arrive in the Frederick area—McClellan, pressed by Lincoln, had been much quicker to pick up the pursuit than Lee believed possible. Two soldiers of Company E, 27th Indiana Infantry, lounging in their bivouac, saw and picked up a weatherstained packet on the ground. In idle curiosity they examined the wraper as they prepared to smoke the cigars, and had sense enough to realize they had stumbled on something for higher authority to scan. From company to regiment, and from brigade headquarters to division and beyond, the paper traveled in successive bounds. George B. McClellan had it—and with it the Army of Northern Virginia—in his hands on the morning of September 13.

Lee's army was split; more than half of it back across the Potomac in Virginia, the remainder spread over a twenty-five-mile-long area only fifteen miles away from him. Between McClellan and his prey lay South Mountain—the northern continuation of the Blue Ridge—cut by two main passes. Through Turner's Gap, the northernmost of these, ran the main highway from Frederick through Hagerstown. Eight miles south of it was Crampton's Gap, the direct road from Frederick to Sharpsburg. The Federal cavalry, in contact with Southern horsemen, was already at the entrances to both passes. The weather was good, the roads hard, there would be a moon that night. An immediate advance in force through the passes would place the Army of the

Potomac in the midst of these widely-scattered elements, which could then be gobbled up successively.

McClellan sensed the possibilities. His order that day spelled them out: "My general idea is to cut the enemy in two and beat him in detail."

His right wing and center column, bivouacked in the Frederick area, would strike at Lee and Longstreet up in Boonesboro, only a fifteen-mile march through Turner's Gap. His left wing, lying a bit to the south, between Buckeyestown and the Potomac, would push through Crampton's Gap, twenty miles away, to cut off the Confederate forces on Maryland Heights, relieve Harpers Ferry and be prepared to block Lee's retreat.

But . . . the movement was not to start until "daybreak in the morning"; thus wasting the remaining daylight hours of September 13, and its moonlit night.

In consequence, when the heads of the two Union columns probed the Gaps, about mid-day of the fourteenth, they were met by bitter resistance. Lee had, of course, discovered McClellan's unexpected arrival. D. H. Hill's division had turned back to Turner's Gap, with Longstreet hastening down from Hagerstown in support. McLaws, while preparing to bombard Harpers Ferry from the Maryland Heights, had detached part of his force to defend Crampton's Gap.

The battle of South Mountain was on; in two separate engagements. Up at Turner's Gap two Union army corps, under Major General Ambrose E. Burnside, struggled manfully to storm the heights, but not until 10:00 P.M. was the craggy defile flanked. By midnight, Hill withdrew his defenders toward Sharpsburg to escape annihilation. Down at Crampton's Gap the 18,000 Union troops under Major General William B. Franklin forced an opening, and by nightfall were established on the west side of South Mountain. McLaws, however, set up a delaying position north of Maryland Heights and the Federal commander, for some reason believing himself to be out numbered "two to one" by a force actually one-third his strength, advanced no further.

It had been an anxious day for General Lee, who as yet had heard nothing from Jackson at Harpers Ferry, and now knew McClellan had forced the South Mountain passes. He decided to withdraw across the Potomac at Shepherdstown and sent word to McLaws to abandon Maryland Heights and return to Virginia. But by noon on the fifteenth, as Lee stood with his rear guard near Sharpsburg, overseeing the withdrawal, a galloper brought stirring news. Jackson had captured Harpers Ferry and was already on the way to Sharpsburg!

Jackson had reached Bolivar Heights, dominating Harpers Ferry from the west, on the thirteenth. Next day, while he pushed in the Federal defenses, McLaws' artillery from Maryland Heights, and Walker's from Loudoun Heights, opened fire on the town below them; all this happening while the South Mountain battle was raging. Early on the fifteenth, as Jackson prepared to assault, the Harpers Ferry garrison had surrendered unconditionally.

From the Union point of view, there had been but one bright footnote to this operation. The Harpers Ferry garrison included the 8th New York Cavalry, some 1,300 sabers, commanded by Colonel Benjamin Franklin Davis. West Pointer Davis had no illusions as to Harpers Ferry's defensive capabilities. The night of the fourteenth, when its fall next day was practically certain, he—like Forrest at Fort Donelson—got permission from the garrison commander to get his horsemen away.

Crossing the pontoon bridge to the Maryland side, Davis led his command along the river road right under the noses of the Confederates on Maryland Heights above, galloped through a picket, thundered through Sharpsburg and up the Hagerstown road. Then a wagon train loomed in the moonlight, moving south. Davis, born in Mississippi, had no difficulty in posing as a Confederate officer. As a result Longstreet's reserve ammunition train of some forty wagons and a 200-man escort was bagged. It ended up with Davis' command, at Greencastle, Pennsylvania, next morning.

By that time Harpers Ferry had surrendered and Jackson had garnered 11,000 prisoners, 13,000 stands of arms and 73 guns. Joined now by McLaws from Maryland Heights, and Walker from Loudoun Heights, he was marching on Sharpsburg.

To General Lee at Sharpsburg, the situation at mid-day had now radically changed. McClellan's masses were moving through the South Mountain gaps at a snail's pace. He had Longstreet's corps in hand, and Jackson would be with him by the sixteenth. There would be no more retreat; the Army of Northern Virginia would stand at Sharpsburg.

It was, perhaps, the most daring of Lee's many audacious decisions. To the west and close behind his position the Potomac ran in a long, winding arc. Lee had deliberately placed himself in a *cul-de-sac*, with the unbridged river on his right, left and rear. At the moment he had less than 20,000 men; McClellan had double that number already west of South Mountain, and the rest of his army was coming through the passes. An energetic Union advance would have crushed Lee.

But that was not McClellan's way. Establishing his head-quarters not far from Antietam Creek, on the Boonesboro road, the Union commander carefully plotted his proposed offensive, taking time out to send self-laudatory messages and promises of great victory back to Washington. Unfortunately for him McClellan was between the devil of Halleck and the deep blue sea of Lincoln. The President, hoping against hope for victory, had wired him to "destroy the rebel army, if possible," while timorous Halleck, the newly-appointed General-in-Chief, flashed over the same wire: "Scouts report a large force still on the Virginia side of the Potomac. If so, I fear you are exposing your left and rear."

In fact, McClellan still believed that Lee had more than 100,000 men to oppose him. So while he planned to strike Lee's left with his own right wing, he was keeping Franklin back at Maryland Heights—like a hopeful cat watching an empty rat-hole—to prevent long-since-departed McLaws from pouncing on his own left. So all through September 16 the Army of the Potomac slowly built up, with its main concentration on its right.

Antietam Creek flowed from north to south between the opposing armies, emptying into the Potomac below Sharpsburg. In the battle area it was crossed by three bridges and several known fords (actually the Creek was fordable at almost any point; a fact unknown to McClellan, who had made no reconnaissance). Beginning at the north, the Upper Bridge spanned it opposite the extreme left of the Confederate position. The Middle Bridge carried the Boonesboro-Sharpsburg road. Just south of Sharpsburg a stone bridge—which would go down on history's rolls thereafter as the Burnside Bridge—led into the right of Lee's position.

Between the west bank of the Creek and the Hagerstown Pike, which ran north and south through Sharpsburg, lay farm land; mostly fields of corn now standing head-high and more, with several patches of woods north of the town.

McClellan's plan was to strike a hammer-blow southward down the Hagerstown Pike on September 17, with three army corps—Hooker's, Mansfield's and Sumner's—rolling up Lee's left. At the same time Burnside's corps would attack the Stone Bridge to pin down the Confederate right. "With whatever reserve I might then have in hand," as McClellan put it, he would then attack the Confederate center. (Reserves he would have in plenty; Pleasanton's cavalry and Porter's corps on the field when the battle started, and Franklin's corps belatedly moved up from Maryland Heights during the day.)

Meanwhile, behind Antietam Creek, Lee was taking advantage of this blessed gift of time. Jackson—after an all-night march—arrived early on the sixteenth with McLaws and Walker twelve hours behind him. By dawn the next day the only absentee was A. P. Hill, left with his division to complete the Harpers Ferry surrender, to parole prisoners, and to start the captured matériel back into Virginia.

The Army of Northern Virginia took position facing east,

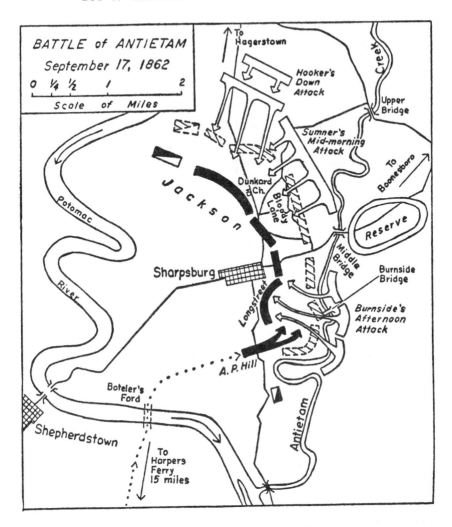

BATTLE of ANTIETAM
September 17, 1862

generally along the Hagerstown Pike. Jackson was on the left, his northern flank cemented to the Potomac by Stuart's cavalry. Longstreet, on the right, included Sharpsburg itself in his position, which stretched down to the Stone Bridge. A small cavalry brigade covered the remaining one-mile gap between Longstreet's right and the Potomac at the Antietam Creek mouth.

Lee suspected his opponent's intention, for late in the afternoon of the sixteenth both Hooker and Mansfield crossed the Creek by the Upper Bridge and fords, skirmished with the Confederates in the immediate area and bivouacked about one mile north of the Southern position.

At dawn of the seventeenth the Union assault began, covered by heavy fire from its artillery, well-placed on high ground just west of the Creek. But the proposed great main effort broke down into three separate and disjointed attacks. Hooker fought his way into Jackson's position only to be repelled by reinforcements from Jackson's and Longstreet's reserves. Mansfield, following, didn't do much better. The Federal tide at first breached Jackson's defenses and reached the Dunkard Church on the Pike, a scant mile north of Sharpsburg. But, with more men sent him by the idle Longstreet, Jackson was able to re-establish his line.

Sumner, using the Middle Bridge, didn't get across the Creek until after 8:00 A.M. By this time Hooker and Mansfield had shot their bolts and were reorganizing. Sumner's attack broke in two parts—his right assisting the other two corps, his left entangled with a Confederate division holding a sunken road between cornfields. It was here the most sanguinary struggle of the day took place. When the Confederates finally were enfiladed and driven out the "Bloody Lane," as it is called to this day, was heaped high with corpses. By noon, with the left wing of the Southern line bent back across the Pike, all Lee's reserves expended and Longstreet's corps depleted, the Federal assault was checked. The battered Union troops fell back east of the turnpike and halted. There would be no further fighting north of Sharpsburg that day.

But on Lee's right, now held by only one division, action tardily flamed. Burnside's so-called "diversion" in that sector had been amazingly late in starting—and this delay enabled Lee to send reinforcements to Jackson from his right flank. Burnside's literal-minded compliance with his orders to "carry" the bridge made matters worse. Three times the Union troops charged the causeway now bearing his name, though the Creek could have been forded anywhere. Not until 1:00 P.M., and after heavy losses, was he successful. Once across, it took him two hours to reorganize his troops before pushing on to high ground beyond at Sharpsburg's southern edge, where a mere 2,000 Confederates were clinging.

All the while, it must be remembered, McClellan had held Porter's V Corps close to the Creek but entirely out of the battle. By this time, too, Franklin's corps was slowly moving to assembly points behind the right of the Union line. More than 20,000 fresh Union troops were thus left unemployed while the battle reached its climax.

Yet despite this appalling waste of men, it did not seem that the Southerners could stop Burnside's final assault, as the Union left wing reached the brow of the hill and lapped at the very edge of the village.

But out of the cornfields on Burnside's left burst a close-knit line of infantry, firing as they came. They wore blue coats, but they gave the Rebel yell, and they meant business. A. P. Hill's division, its Harpers Ferry chore accomplished, its rags discarded for captured Federal uniforms, had completed an amazing seventeen-mile march. Rushing up from Boteler's Ford across the Potomac to the sound of the guns, Hill saved the day for Lee. Burnside's flank was thrown into confusion. It recoiled. Falling back from the heights, in the gathering darkness, the corps regrouped down by the Creek as the firing died away. The battle of Antietam Creek was ended.

Lee, with less than 40,000 effectives, had stopped McClellan's 90,000—though only 66,000 of these actually took part in the battle. Some 12,400 Federals and 13,700 Confederate soldiers lay dead or wounded when the sun went down on the field of the bloodiest one-day battle of the entire war.

All that night and all the next day the opponents faced one another warily; Lee with all his resources expended, McClellan with 23,000 fresh troops in hand. On the night of September 18,

Lee, unmolested, withdrew unhurriedly across the Potomac, his Army of Northern Virginia still a fighting force.

Who won at Antietam?

Tactically, Lee did. McClellan, repulsed in his assault, had dared make no further attack, as the Southerners contemptuously held their positions on September 18. Strategically, since Lee's invasion of the North had been ended, and the Army of Northern Virginia then retired from the field, it was a Union victory, with far-reaching effects. President Lincoln used it as springboard for his preliminary Emancipation Proclamation, long-delayed for just such an opportunity. England, faced now by the fact that any official pro-Southern move would *ipso facto* infer a pro-slavery bias, would decline Napoleon III's later suggestion that Europe force an armistice between North and South. The war became America's business only, and Confederate hopes for European intervention went by the board.

And what shall we say of McClellan, the general with all the trumps of the deck in his hand, who could have ended the Civil War on the banks of a Maryland creek in 1862?

It is perhaps better to say nothing. Antietam speaks for itself.

# Some Generals Shrink from Combat

Having observed the fortunes of Jackson, McClellan, Lee and Pope in the East, it is time we take note of the activities of their counterparts in the West.

## HALLECK: CRAWL TO CORINTH— AND WASHINGTON

Enraged that a great battle should have been fought without his presence, General Halleck came charging down from St. Louis on April 11, 1862, four days after Shiloh, to take personal command of both the Armies of the Tennessee and of the Ohio. Peevishly he eased Grant out of any further active role by appointing him second in command, and then giving him nothing to do.

Careful preparations were at once begun to advance against

Corinth, which Halleck, like Grant, considered to be a railroad junction vital to the Confederates. By the end of April, 100,000 men had been assembled in the Shiloh battlefield area and Halleck felt himself strong enough to tackle Beauregard, who now stood twenty-one miles away at Corinth, with perhaps 35,000 men.

But Halleck's pace was a crawl. In consequence, Beauregard, who would have been overwhelmed by a swift Federal advance, was able to move away everything of vital military importance in Corinth and to prepare a new defensive line further south. On May 30, he coolly evacuated the city. Next day the Northern troops, somewhat redfaced, marched in, unopposed.

Halleck still had it in his power to win the war. With New Orleans and Memphis in Federal hands, the economic squeeze on the Confederacy—envisaged a year earlier by General Scott—was beginning to tighten. The sole obstacle to complete Northern possession of the Mississippi was Vicksburg, before which Farragut, because of Halleck's failure to cooperate with land forces, had twice been frustrated.

Opportunity still existed at the beginning of June. A Federal army of 100,000 men advancing from Corinth to Vicksburg could have been stopped only by a drastic depletion of Lee's army in Virginia. Certainly Beauregard, unless so reinforced, could not have stopped it.

An alternative move of almost equal importance could have been made against Chattanooga, which should have been seized two months earlier. Even as late as mid-June a prompt, energetic, full-scale advance against it promised its capture.

But Halleck, irresolute, seeing too many things at once, met the situation with half-measures only. Splitting his forces, he sent General Buell and the Army of the Ohio to seize Chattanooga; he retained the Army of the Tennessee in the Corinth-Memphis area and along the line of communications all the way back to Cairo.

# BUELL AND BRAGG—MINUET IN TENNESSEE AND KENTUCKY

On June 10, Buell started east along the Memphis & Charleston R.R. toward Chattanooga, some 200 miles east of Corinth. Thanks to the energy and foresight of one of his subordinates, most of the route was already in Northern hands and no Confederate force of any size existed to dispute possession of the city with Buell's 50,000 men.

The western approaches to Chattanooga had been seized by Brigadier General Ormsby McK. Mitchel early in April. When Buell had left Nashville to join Grant at Pittsburg Landing, he had left Mitchel with 9,000 men in the Nashville-Murfreesboro area of central Tennessee. Realizing that Chattanooga was only lightly held by the Confederates, Mitchel and a Northern spy named James J. Andrews prepared a bold and imaginative scheme for capturing the city.

Mitchel with his division would march rapidly southward approximately 100 miles from Murfreesboro, Tennessee, to Decatur and Huntsville, Alabama, seizing the westward approaches to Chattanooga via the Memphis & Charleston R.R. Andrews' espionage activities had given him an intimate knowledge of train schedules, troop concentrations, and the region in general. While Mitchel was on the march, Andrews with a party of twenty bold soldier volunteers would burn bridges and tear up track along the railroad leading to Chattanooga from the southeast, through Atlanta and Marietta, Georgia. With Confederate reinforcement thus blocked, Mitchel would then be able to capture the city without opposition. He expected that additional troops would be rushed to him promptly, and in fact there were more Union troops available in Tennessee than could be matched by the Confederates in the surrounding region.

The scheme came very close to success. Andrews made an unfortunate last-minute change in the schedule which was to throw his plans out of kilter. On April 12 (instead of the eleventh as planned), he and his men stole a train near Marietta, but he was delayed by an unexpected Confederate troop train movement. Thanks to this delay, and the availability of additional Confederate troops, brave and resourceful Southern train crews and soldiers promptly pursued the stolen train. The Northern dare-devils had time neither to burn bridges nor to tear up track as their locomotive raced northward towards Chattanooga, though they were able to cut the telegraph lines in several places. This pursuit has come to be known as the Great Locomotive Chase—one of the most dramatic tales of the Civil War. Andrews and his men were captured, and most of them were executed as spies.

Meanwhile Mitchel's plans had gone according to schedule. On the eleventh he had seized Huntsville, after a swift march from Murfreesboro. He then rapidly pushed his forces eastward and westward along the railroad to capture Decatur and Stevenson. Though Andrews' failure had prevented the capture of Chattanooga, Mitchel was able to maintain a precarious hold on the railroad in northern Alabama for the next two months. Thus when Buell started for Chattanooga from Corinth on June 10, almost half of his route was already in Federal hands.

A little more than two weeks later, Buell's main army had made contact with Mitchel's exposed division in the vicinity of Decatur and Athens. Now, despite the relatively easy prospect of movement over Mitchel's railroad to the vicinity of Chattanooga, Buell became unduly worried about his supply situation. He was naturally concerned about the activities of Confederate cavalry Colonel John H. Morgan, who during most of July was raiding Federal communications in Tennessee and Kentucky. But Buell's situation was not directly affected. Nevertheless, for two weeks the Union army marked time in the Decatur-Huntsville area.

During this period over-all command in the West on both

sides shifted. Halleck, on July 11, was ordered to Washington to assume the post of General-in-Chief. He turned command of the Army of the Tennessee back to Grant. The brief unity of command in the Western field was ended; Grant and Buell becoming independent commanders responsible to Washington.

On the Confederate side, the illness of General Beauregard resulted in command of Southern forces south of Corinth falling to Major General Braxton Bragg, one of the enigmatic figures of the war. A West Pointer, Bragg's close combat affiliation with President Davis in the Mexican War, where both had played heroic roles, forged a personal loyalty between the two men which would directly affect the fortunes of the Confederacy. Bragg, a stern, grim disciplinarian, was known as a "dyspeptic martinet" to many of his subordinates.

Finding himself undisturbed in his present position by the Union armies, Bragg began an eastward movement about July 8, obviously in response to Buell's threat to Chattanooga. But since Bragg and his men had well over 200 miles to go by road and railroad, and since the advance guard of Buell's army held the railroad lines within twenty miles of the city, there seemed little chance that the Confederates could forestall Buell. Not even the annoying activities of the Confederate cavalry General Nathan Bedford Forrest, who raided Buell's communications at Murfreesboro on July 13, should have had any effect. There were plenty of troops to hold the line of communications, and to drive the raiders away, which they did.

But, incredible though it may seem, on July 29 Bragg arrived at Chattanooga, while Buell was still fussing about railroads and supplies west of the city. Having saved the key to the Confederacy's heartland, Bragg now decided to take advantage of Buell's dilatoriness by an offensive of his own. Including the command of General Edmund Kirby Smith, based at Knoxville, Bragg had a total of about 50,000 men available for operations in southern and eastern Tennessee, and had been promised reinforcements. He decided to strike north, expecting to gain numbers of recruits for his army in Tennessee and Kentucky, and perhaps wrest these two states completely from Federal control.

The first indication which the Federals had of Bragg's intention was on August 9, when Morgan's cavalry again swept into central Tennessee from the eastern mountains. On the twelfth he captured the town of Gallatin, with its small Federal garrison, northeast of Nashville, then turned north towards Kentucky. Kirby Smith left Knoxville on the fifteenth, heading for Cumberland Gap, with a force of close to 15,000 men. Next day Bragg, with about 35,000, started north from Chattanooga.

Buell had approximately 45,000 men available northwest of Chattanooga. General George Thomas, whose division had been transferred to Buell from Grant's army, urged an immediate concentration to head off Bragg, and to force him to battle in southeastern Tennessee. But while Buell hesitated, Bragg slipped north between the Federal army and the mountains. Fearing for his communications, Buell now hurried northwest toward Nashville on a road paralleling Bragg's. This was the fastest movement his army had made all year, and he reached the Tennessee capital at the beginning of September.

Kirby Smith, meanwhile, marched north, moving directly into the heart of the Blue Grass state. On August 30, he overwhelmed a smaller Federal force under Major General William Nelson at Richmond, Kentucky, capturing 4,300 prisoners. Only about 1,100 Federals escaped. Continuing northward, Kirby Smith captured Lexington on September 2.

The steady advance of Bragg and Kirby Smith and the sweeps of their cavalrymen across Tennessee and Kentucky had caused great alarm in the West, as well as in Washington—already sufficiently alarmed by Lee's successful offensive against Pope in the second Bull Run campaign. All available troops west of the Appalachians were rushed to the important Ohio River cities of Louisville and Cincinnati. The governors of Ohio, Illinois and Indiana called out numbers of militiamen to meet the threat. Grant, who had already given Thomas' division to Buell, sent two more on August 16, and a fourth on September 2, placing his own exposed position in serious jeopardy.

But Buell, with the only major Union force in the area of operations, for some unaccountable reason stayed in Nashville for over a week, while Bragg and Kirby Smith were left free to operate to the east and north. Bragg captured Munfordville on the sixteenth, after a gallant defense by an outnumbered Federal garrison. Buell, with about 40,000 men, had moved to Cave City, less than fifteen miles away. For four days Bragg and his 30,000 men lingered at Munfordville, seemingly daring Buell to fight. When the challenge was unanswered, Bragg again moved northeast on the twenty-first towards Frankfort.

Buell, it seemed, had merely been waiting for Bragg to get out of the way. He immediately marched through Munfordville, but rather than making any effort to seek out his enemy for a battle, headed for the security of heavily-garrisoned Louisville.

Thoroughly disgusted, the Washington government ordered Buell on the twenty-fourth to turn over his command to General Thomas. On the twenty-ninth, however, Thomas declined the responsibility, and since there was no other senior, experienced general in the region, Buell got a reprieve. For a while it appeared he had learned his lesson. A quick reorganization of his army was followed by an advance south from Louisville on October 3. By the seventh the advance elements of his 60,000 men were now approaching Perryville and Harrodsburg.

Bragg, by this time, had been reinforced to some 60,000 men also, but his units, trying to round up recruits and also to live off the impoverished countryside, were widely scattered. Believing that Buell was heading towards Frankfort, Bragg began concentrating south of that city.

Near Perryville itself remained only 16,000 Confederates; Hardee's corps, part of Polk's, and some cavalry. The weather was dry, water scarce, and Perryville was a valuable watering point. Savagely the Southern troops present contested for it with the Federals. Fighting broke out early on October 8; soon two-thirds of Buell's army—about 37,000 men—was hotly engaged with Polk and Hardee.

Early in the battle the Confederate veterans came close to driving the much more numerous, but less seasoned Union troops off the field. As Northern reinforcements moved to the sound of the guns, the Confederate onslaught was brought to a halt. But Buell did nothing to coordinate the activities of his now over-whelmingly superior force. His right flank division, almost 20,000 strong under General Crittenden, was held immobilized for several hours by the brilliant diversionary tactics of some 1,200 cavalry under young Brigadier General Joseph Wheeler, while Polk and Hardee repulsed counterattacks by the Federal left wing.

Perryville was a drawn battle, with most of the honors going to the Confederates, who held off a force more than double their size. Casualties were heavy on both sides, the Federals losing 4,211 killed and wounded, while Southern losses were 3,396.

Bragg by this time realized where Buell's army was, and ordered the withdrawal of Polk's and Hardee's brave divisions from Perryville to Harrodsburg, where he collected his army on October 9 and 10. Buell was satisfied with moving into Perryville on the ninth, making no effort to strike Bragg's still-incomplete army, gathering less than ten miles away.

On the tenth, however, the shoe was on the other foot. The two armies were now concentrated, and each had close to 60,000 men. But Bragg's was composed mostly of veterans, now some-what rested from their arduous marches, and with the confidence born of a successful invasion. The preponderance of combat power, therefore, was probably with the Confederates. It was to the consternation of his hard-fighting subordinates, therefore, that Bragg on the eleventh suddenly and inexplicably turned southeast to march back through the Cumberland Gap into Tennessee. There is no reasonable explanation of Bragg's loss of nerve, other than that the strain of the campaign had suddenly become too much for him.

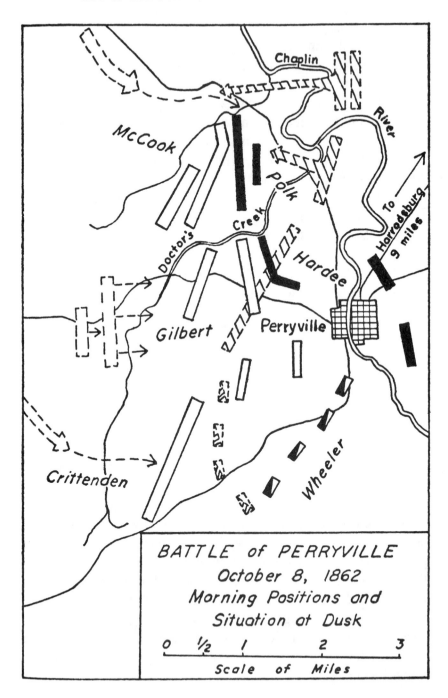

BATTLE of PERRYVILLE
October 8, 1862
Morning Positions and
Situation at Dusk

0   ½   1           2           3

Scale   of   Miles

Buell made no real effort to pursue, and his perfunctory moves to follow Bragg were hampered by another of Morgan's raids. The Confederate cavalryman, completely circling the Union army, captured Lexington on October 19. As Buell dawdled, the government in Washington decided he had forfeited his reprieve. Peremptorily he was relieved on October 23, by Major General William S. Rosecrans, who, as we shall see later, had gained combat reputation as a division commander under Grant. By November 6, Rosecrans was marching into Nashville.

# GRANT—A SOLDIER DOES THE BEST HE CAN WITH WHAT HE HAS

As we have seen, when Halleck went to Washington, Grant again assumed command of the Army of the Tennessee. He had to stay in the general vicinity of Corinth and Memphis, since he didn't have enough men to do more than to hold these key cities and his line of communications north to Cairo. Furthermore, he was soon required to give up four divisions to help Buell meet Bragg's threat in Kentucky and Tennessee.

So, with about 45,000 men, Grant organized himself as best he could to hold Corinth, Memphis, and the long river and rail lines through hostile country back to the Ohio River at Cairo, Illinois. Fortunately for him the Confederates initially had little strength with which to threaten his exposed position, aside from frequent, annoying cavalry raids. But as Grant's strength dwindled, that of the Southerners in his area began to increase. Earl Van Dorn and Sterling Price, two experienced and capable Confederate generals, were now in the field in this area. Van Dorn had a force of about 15,000 men, while Price had brought some 17,000 from Missouri and Arkansas.

Grant, at Corinth, had no intention of permitting them to unite and become a serious threat. When Price moved into Iuka on September 17 (Grant had evacuated the town as being an unwise overextension of his depleted command), Grant at once moved to attack him. Rosecrans, with 7,000 men, was to strike Iuka from the south, using the two available roads; Ord's division, 6,000 strong, would attack simultaneously from the north. Between them, Grant hoped, they would drive Price back against the Tennessee River.

The plan miscarried. Rosecrans, approaching by one road only, attacked on the nineteenth, without Ord, and was repulsed after hard fighting. Both Federal commanders attacked in unison next day, but to Grant's disappointment Price, instead of being rocked back to the river and destroyed, nimbly withdrew southward over the road that Rosecrans had originally overlooked.

Unable now to prevent a junction of his two opponents, Grant redistributed his available maneuvering forces, to take care of all eventualities. Rosecrans held Corinth with 23,000 men. Ord was pulled back north and west to the vicinity of Bolivar and Jackson. Grant established his own headquarters at the latter town, to be centrally located.

Price and Van Dorn united west of Corinth October 1, Van Dorn taking command, as the senior. Two days later he swept in against Corinth from the northwest, driving Rosecrans' men from their initial positions, but he failed to break through into the town.

Grant, at the first news of the attack, hurried 5,000 men from Bolivar to concentrate on the Confederate rear. Once again he was trying for a double envelopment and the destruction of the enemy, and again he was disappointed. Van Dorn, after one more unsuccessful assault next day, gave up the attempt and, because Rosecrans failed to obey Grant's order for close pursuit, slipped from the pincers. In those three days of bitter fighting the Confederate losses were 4,233 in killed, wounded and prisoners, while Union casualties were 2,520.

Despite Grant's chagrin that neither Iuka nor Corinth had resulted in total destruction of his enemies, the fact was that firm

Federal retention of the strategic outposts of Memphis and Corinth was now assured. And it had been demonstrated once again to Washington that here was one Federal general who was willing to fight the Confederates under any and all conditions, without boast, complaint or recrimination.

# 14

# Valley of Death
# in the East

**F**or more than a month after the
Battle of Antietam, McClellan remained north of the Potomac,
content to rest on his meager laurels. Lee, the Federal commander
held, had been "greatly superior in numbers," and he—McClellan—had driven him out. A half-hearted Union attempt to pursue
Lee, two days after the battle, had been sharply repulsed. A
flamboyant raid by Stuart's Confederate cavalry in early October,
across the Potomac, up into Pennsylvania and completely around
the Army of the Potomac, added to McClellan's anxieties.

Meanwhile, in the vicinity of Winchester, the Army of
Northern Virginia was recuperating in marvelous fashion. Stragglers from the invasion march had returned by thousands, and
replacements had also come in. Doubtless, the passage of a second Conscription Act by the Confederate Congress, September
27, raising the draft age limit to 45, and eliminating loopholes in
the original draft act, had something to do with this resurgence
of manpower. In any event, the ranks were filling, and supplies

came in. Lee had "present for duty" nearly 80,000 men of his total 90,000 strength, and some 300 guns. He lost no time in reorganization. Jackson and Longstreet were now both lieutenant generals, and "Beauty" Stuart, earlier promoted to major general, counted nearly 8,000 sabers in his three hard-riding brigades of cavalry. The Confederate Army's morale was high—hadn't it twice stopped McClellan in his tracks?—and it was ready to go again.

Not until October 26, did McClellan re-enter Virginia, spurred at last by President Lincoln's vexed and urgent order of October 6 to "cross the Potomac and give battle to the enemy or drive him out . . . now, while the roads are good." He moved via Harpers Ferry, leaving behind him one army corps to guard against another Confederate invasion.

Lee's reaction was prompt. He sent Longstreet's corps down to the Culpeper Courthouse area, south of the Rappahannock. He left Jackson in the Valley, while Stuart's cavalry fringed the Blue Ridge passes, watching to see which way the Union cat jumped.

Once again then, Lee was dividing his forces in the face of an enemy grossly superior in strength; his future dispositions dependent upon his opponent's moves. If McClellan tried an overland drive on Richmond, Longstreet's corps would check him by a holding operation while Jackson popped through the Blue Ridge to strike his line of communications with Washington. If the Federal advance came up the Shenandoah Valley, Jackson's corps was ready to snub it, while Longstreet threatened either Washington or the Union line of communications. If McClellan tried to repeat his water-borne Peninsula invasion, there would be time to shift and concentrate the entire army against him.

There was, however, one very real danger inherent in Lee's dispositions. If McClellan simply planted his army between the divided Confederate forces, and upon their direct communicating road, Lee would be unable to concentrate; furthermore, in theory, McClellan would then be in position to attack and defeat the Southern army in detail.

That was exactly what McClellan seemed to have in mind. Coming south through the corridor between the Blue Ridge and the Bull Run mountains, the Army of the Potomac turned east through Thoroughfare Gap and by November 2, began concentrating on the general area of Warrenton; astride the shortest and most direct route between Jackson and Longstreet, who were some forty-odd miles apart in air line. There the Union army sat.

Lee, counting on his knowledge of McClellan's military characteristics, waited for further developments. He didn't have to wait long; the sands were running out for McClellan. On November 7, he was summarily relieved of command and General Burnside was appointed in his place. The Administration was fed up with McClellan. Militarily, he had proven himself to be overcautious and inept in combat; politically, he had become a problem. Possessed of a definite ambition for the Presidency, he had committed himself to become the standard bearer of the anti-war Democratic Party. Thus he was not only out of sympathy with the Republican Administration, he was also in effect a potential rival of President Lincoln. His political enemies—and they were many—were accusing him now of prolonging the war to satisfy his own and his Party's interests. So his official head rolled.

His successor, Burnside, was an amiable man of great integrity, whose modesty and patriotism had made an impression on President Lincoln. A West Pointer graduated too late to participate in the Mexican War, Burnside had resigned from the army in 1853, taken up arms manufacturing in Rhode Island (without too much success), and later shifted to railroading with the Illinois Central. When war broke out Burnside had come back to Rhode Island, organized a militia regiment—which automatically procured him its colonelcy—and then later participated at First Bull Run as a brigade commander. His command of the ground forces in the successful Roanoke Island joint expedition in February, 1862, earned him a major generalcy. He had not distinguished himself at Antietam, as we have seen, but he would be malleable and so Halleck preferred him to cantankerous Hooker, elderly

Sumner, or to Franklin, a capable soldier whose only fault was that he was a very close friend of McClellan.

Burnside had not sought his new command; in fact he doubted his own ability—an opinion shared by most of his subordinate commanders. He was embarrassed, too, that he should supersede McClellan, whom he liked. But orders were orders. He knew that he now had to do something, and do it quick; the entire North was clamoring for action. A witch hunt was on in Washington; McClellan in disgrace, his most brilliant corps commander, Fitz-John Porter, facing trial by court martial for alleged cowardice and disobedience at Second Bull Run. Where the official ax would next fall and upon whose neck, no man could predict.

Burnside, combining industriousness and stupidity—dangerous characteristics in an army officer—failed to realize that the Army of the Potomac was now most strategically placed for offensive action; between the two halves of the Army of Northern Virginia. He decided instead to strike at Richmond. It was the old story over again; the selection of a geographical goal, rather than the destruction of the enemy's force in the field.

His plan was to cross the Rappahannock at Fredericksburg, and follow the railroad line to the Confederate capital. To preserve his line of communications, his base would be situated at Aquia Creek, linked to Washington by water. Since the Rappahannock bridge at Fredericksburg had been destroyed, he would move pontoon bridging matériel down from Harpers Ferry, where it was spanning the Potomac.

With some reluctance, President Lincoln approved the plan, and the Army of the Potomac began its eastward movement. Burnside had reorganized it into three so-called grand divisions— each comprised of two army corps—as well as a reserve corps which was scattered from Harpers Ferry to Washington and took no part in the operation. In hand, Burnside now had some 120,000 men and 374 guns. Sumner's grand division reached the area opposte Fredericksburg November 17, and could have crossed—

the river was still fordable in a few places—and driven off the small Confederate cavalry detachment then guarding the heights on the far bank. But Burnside would have none of it. He feared a rise in the river would leave him with his army split.

So the Union army gathered near Falmouth, across the river from Fredericksburg, to await the arrival of the pontoon bridges. Franklin's grand division arrived November 19, Hooker's next day. Lee, while sending Longstreet's corps down to occupy the high ground west of Fredericksburg, still couldn't believe that Burnside would risk a river-crossing at that point. He merely alerted Jackson, up in the Valley. Stonewall could decide if and when to move to the Culpeper area to replace Longstreet.

Longstreet reached Fredericksburg November 20, and at once established himself along the heights overlooking it. And still the Union pontoons hadn't arrived. But cold weather had, bringing rain and snow with it, and the Rappahannock rose while Burnside waited and Lee watched.

On the twenty-fifth the long-awaited bridging equipment finally reached Aquia Creek and began inch-worm movement over the muddy roads to Burnside's bivouacs fifteen miles away. Jackson, meanwhile, had crossed the mountains and halted at Orange Court House. Lee, at last convinced that Burnside really intended coming across, ordered Jackson down to Fredericksburg. Arriving November 30, ahead of his corps, Stonewall was told to go into position on Longstreet's right. The stage was being set for the most atrocious blunder of the entire Civil War.

Breaking out of a chain of hills just above Fredericksburg, the Rappahannock, here some 150 yards wide, bends sharply from easterly to southeasterly flow, through a natural amphitheater. It brushes close under Stafford Heights along its left bank, on which the Army of the Potomac was then concentrated. But on the right shore, where Fredericksburg sits in fertile bottom land, the flat ground extends back from the river for a distance varying from one to two miles before the westerly ridge hugs it in an irregular arc. Upon these heights lay the Army of Northern

Virginia. Union artillery emplaced on Stafford Heights commanded Fredericksburg and could reach part way across the flats, but the westerly hills were beyond its range. On the other hand, Confederate guns on the western heights, while they could not reach across the water, commanded the flatland area and the town itself.

What Burnside proposed was to make a river crossing in the face of an enemy already established on the far side, then assault that enemy in his positions along the ridge beyond. His plan was to throw two sets of pontoon bridges across the river; three bridges opposite Fredericksburg itself, and two others some two miles downstream. Sumner's grand division was to make the crossing on the right; Franklin's on the left. Hooker's, in the center, would provide general support as needed. A 150-gun concentration of Union artillery on Stafford Heights would cover the troops crossing the river. But in the ensuing assault on the western ridge, artillery support could be furnished only by whatever guns could be transported with the troops making the crossings.

To further handicap the Army of the Potomac, on reaching the plain Burnside's two assault forces would be fighting independent and divergent actions, separated from one another by Deep Run; a rugged, almost impassable east-west gash splitting the area between the proposed crossing points.

These terrain features and the almost insuperable problem they presented should have been apparent to Burnside. They were plain to any observer on Stafford Heights, which overlooked all the proposed battle area. They were known to Burnside's subordinate commanders, who on the night of December 10, it seems, voiced their general apprehensions to him. They had been apparent from the start, of course, to Lee who, with good reason, had for a long time doubted Burnside's suicidal intentions.

On the Confederate left, Longstreet's corps—holding from the river to Deep Run—was entrenched on the faces of three particularly formidable hills, known collectively as Marye's Heights. Taylor's Hill on the left was unassailable, and on the right of the sector was extremely rugged Telegraph Hill—which would become known in the future as Lee's Hill, for from it he directed the battle. Marye's Hill, in the center of Longstreet's sector, directly opposite Fredericksburg, jutted more gently out into the plain and across its lower portion was belted by the Telegraph Road, a sunken highway faced by a stone wall shoulder-high—a magnificent ready-made emplacement. In front of this again, and just at the western edge of Fredericksburg, ran a wide drainage ditch, practically impassable except at the street bridges, which the Confederates had partially destroyed. In Fredericksburg itself—which had been evacuated of its residents—Longstreet had placed a brigade of Mississippi sharpshooters, who manned the waterfront houses. Longstreet's guns, on the Heights, had been cunningly sited so as to put criss-cross fire on the plain below. "When they opened up," as his chief of artillery said, "a chicken could not live there."

Jackson's corps continued the Confederate line from Deep Run southward along the ridge to the Massaponax. In the plain below, on the extreme right, Stuart's cavalry and horse artillery, facing generally north, blocked the flatland from the ridge to the river.

In front of Jackson's position on the Confederate right— Franklin's objective—no terrain obstacles existed. But the wooded ridge afforded splendid cover for his riflemen, and his guns, too, covered the plain over which the Union troops must advance. In all, including Stuart's artillery on the far right, 306 Confederate guns were ready to play upon the attackers.

Burnside's plan went into operation on December 11, when the pontoon bridging began. Franklin on the Union left had but little opposition; the bridges were completed by noon, a brigade of infantry was across by nightfall, and during the next day both of his army corps—some 60,000 men and 100 guns—were concentrated on the flats below Jackson's position.

But on the Union right, in Longstreet's sector, the Confederate sharpshooters in Fredericksburg at once began mowing down the engineers and line troops trying to erect the bridges. The huge Union gun battery on Stafford Heights was turned on the town, but although it blasted the place to ruins, the Mississippians, in the rubble, continued their devastating musketry. Finally four Union infantry regiments, who volunteered for the task, rowed across in pontoon boats and drove the sharpshooters out. Then the bridges went across. By nightfall, one Federal division had a toehold in town, and during the next day Sumner's entire grand division, together with 104 guns, was tight-packed into the ruined town, concealed from Confederate view by the rubble.

On the thirteenth, with the valley shrouded in heavy fog, Burnside's assault commenced. It was doomed from the start. The Union leader's attack orders, both dilatory and ambiguous, did not reach Franklin on the Union left until 7:30 A.M., although he had expected to attack at daylight. His assault elements, three divisions in brigade column, groped in the fog across the road and railroad tracks paralleling the river. Then the fog lifted and Stuart's artillery poured heavy fire into the Union left flank, necessitating a readjustment. While one division faced south against the unexpected challenge, the main attack proceeded, only to come now under the fire of Jackson's guns planted on the crest at their front. But the Union batteries accompanying the attack came into action, and momentarily silenced the Confederate fire. By this time Franklin's entire grand division had come into line and two additional divisions of Hooker's command were coming across the river in support. Under cover of their own guns Franklin's array heaved forward into the woods fringing their front, only to meet deadly short-range small-arms fire from Southern infantry deep-lined in the thickets.

One Federal division (Meade's) gained the woods at last, only to be thrown out by a counter-attack, which drove the Union force back onto the plain. All afternoon the fighting raged back and forth, ending with the Confederate positions still intact, and Franklin's troops holding fast to the railroad line and the plain, near the river.

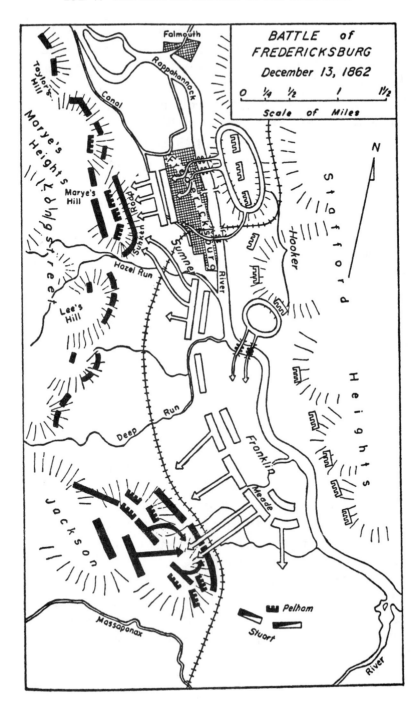

BATTLE of
FREDERICKSBURG
December 13, 1862

Scale of Miles

On the Union right, meanwhile, Burnside's vacillation had held up Sumner until 11:00 A.M., when the fog lifted and disclosed Fredericksburg crawling with Union troops. Confederate guns from Marye's Heights immediately opened fire. Through this fire Sumner's advance elements, two divisions in column, debouched from the ruins and began to cross the wide drainage ditch. Despite the fire, the Federal forces deployed into lines of brigades in column and moved towards Marye's Hill. At 200 yards range the Confederate infantry fire opened from the sunken road and stone wall, and three Federal brigades in succession melted away.

The next division, in the same formation, charged through their remnants to meet the same fate under the hail of musketry fire, delivered by Longstreet's men ranged four deep behind the stone wall. The Federal tide, torn by both small arms and cross-ranging artillery fire, ebbed to the ditch and hung on. Federal batteries, attempting to come into action, were shot to pieces. Only seven out of nineteen that had crossed ever got into action.

Burnside now ordered Hooker, commanding the reverse grand division, and who still had in hand three of his divisions, to take up the assault. The task, Hooker felt, was impossible, but Burnside was adamant.

"That height," he ordered, "must be carried this evening!"

It was 4:00 P.M. when Hooker signaled his assault. By that time Longstreet had shifted one of his divisions from Telegraph Hill to Marye's Hill, and the Confederate firing line in the sunken road below was now six files deep. Against the storm, brigade after brigade of Federal troops were tossed, in vain. No less than fourteen successive and separate charges were made that day by the seven Federal divisions engaged on the right. At twilight Hooker ordered his troops back, and the cannonading died away.

"Finding that I had lost as many men as my orders required me to lose," was his bitter comment, "I suspended the attack."

The Battle of Fredericksburg was over. Lee's army held the impregnable heights; Burnside's forces below were clinging to the ruins of Fredericksburg and to the railway line near the water paralleling the Valley of Death. Between the hostile lines more than 12,500 fallen Union soldiers lay dead and wounded, in a succession of ghastly windrows; of these some 6,000 were heaped in front of Marye's Hill. Lee's losses were about 5,300 men in all.

Burnside, unsatisfied, wanted to renew the attack; even proposing that night to his shocked and almost mutinous corps commanders, that he lead his old corps, the IX, in column of regiments next day to storm Marye's Heights. Finally dissuaded, he withdrew all his troops across the Rappahannock on the night of December 15. There was no Confederate counterattack. Even Jackson, who at first desired it, realized that to assault the Union troops in the plain, protected as they were by the Stafford Heights batteries across the river, would be disastrous.

While the Army of the Potomac huddled in the muddy confines of its Aquia Creek cantonments, Burnside now decided on another forward movement. He was halted by President Lincoln's firm order to take no further step without informing him. A delegation of Burnside's generals—including Hooker—had protested to the President. Enraged, Burnside, despite the Presidential order, on January 20 attempted a movement to cross the Rappahannock fords above Fredericksburg. This abortive effort, remembered by the soldiers as "the Mud March," literally bogged down next day in a severe storm. Burnside then wrote out an order dismissing Hooker and three others of his generals from the service, and relieving several others from command.

This he presented to President Lincoln in Washington, for approval, together with the alternative that otherwise he himself be relieved from command. Kindhearted Lincoln accepted the alternative, but refused to permit despondent Burnside to resign. He was returned to the command of his own IX Corps and with it was sent to duty away from the Army of the Potomac.

Once more President Lincoln had to dip his hand into the

grab bag in search for a general. On January 25, 1863, Major General Joseph Hooker, Burnside's most vocal critic, was appointed to command of the Army of the Potomac.

Before we take up the story of "Fighting Joe" Hooker, we must turn again to the West.

# Balance Sheet in the West

**T**wo prominent politicians were at this time clamoring for more important roles in the war in the West: Nathaniel P. Banks, Republican from Massachusetts, and John A. McClernand, Democrat from Illinois. Both were major generals. Banks, thanks to the Northern topsy-turvy promotion racket, was senior to Grant; McClernand, Grant's subordinate at Donelson and Shiloh, had just attained his second star.

Lincoln, remembering Scott's Anaconda Plan, and thus thinking in terms of concentrated drives from New Orleans and Memphis to open the Mississippi and increase the squeeze on the Confederacy, found himself caught between these political generals' importunities. Caught, too, was Halleck, who now that he was secure in the top military position, apparently forgot his previous jealousy of Grant, and could appreciate his virtues.

As for Banks, Lincoln made a Hobson's choice. Ben Butler, then in New Orleans, commanding the Department of the Gulf, was definitely not the man to lead a major expedition up the Mississippi, yet he was a prominent Massachusetts politician and that important state had to be kept in line politically. So Butler was relieved and Banks replaced him. He received orders on November 9, 1862. He was authorized, as ranking general officer in the Southwest, to assume command of any military force coming from the north; the "line of division between your department and that of Major General Grant is therefore left undecided for the present. . . ." This might have been a shunting aside of Grant, for political reasons, or it might be that he was being held to pull military chestnuts out of the fire later, if necessary.

Boastful and ambitious McClernand, coming to Washington on leave of absence, suggested to the President and to War Secretary Stanton that were he promised command of an expedition to capture Vicksburg from the north, he could raise the necessary forces from among his political followers in the West. Lincoln accepted the idea and Stanton secretly issued the necessary orders on October 21, 1862. Whether Lincoln and Stanton took Halleck into their confidence at this time is not clear. In any event, while they had accepted McClernand's offer and promised him command, the orders he later received from Halleck were subject to varying interpretations.

As the troops recruited by McClernand began to arrive in Memphis, Grant queried Halleck as to the status of these units, and of any expedition to be undertaken in his Department. On November 11, Halleck replied:"You have command of all troops sent to your Department, and have permission to fight the enemy where you please." Grant was satisfied.

Meanwhile the Army of the Tennessee had received enough reinforcements to permit Grant to advance south of Corinth. With the assurance he had received from Halleck, Grant pushed along the railroad towards Holly Springs and Granada, Mississippi. Steadily he forced back the Confederates, now commanded by Lieutenant General John C. Pemberton, West Pointer from Pennsylvania, married to a Southern woman, who had resigned from the U.S. Army to accept a Confederate commission. He now commanded all Southern troops in Mississippi.

As winter weather began to affect the roads, Grant thought of that broad highway—the Mississippi River. On December 5, he requested Halleck's permission to send General Sherman down the river to seize Vicksburg, while he continued to press ahead by land. Sherman's force, of course, would include the new units which had been streaming into Memphis as the result of McClernand's recruiting. On December 8, Halleck assented, and Grant immediately issued the necessary orders to Sherman, who began making his plans in cooperation with Rear Admiral David D. Porter, now in command of naval units in the Memphis area. Sherman was expected to depart for Vicksburg "as soon as possible," about December 20.

Word of Sherman's plans reached McClernand, still in Illinois, in mid-December. He sent a frantic telegram to Stanton saying he was being "superseded." Apparently there was a hasty and serious consultation between Stanton and Halleck—and probably the President was brought in. An important political commitment had been made to McClernand, but a military commitment had also been made to Grant, the proven, competent general who was in command. The solution was to direct Grant on December 18, to organize his expanding army into four corps, one of which was to be commanded by McClernand, adding that it was "the wish of the President that General McClernand's corps shall constitute a part of the river expedition and that he shall have the immediate command under your [Grant's] direction."

While Grant would much rather have had the expedition commanded by his trusted Sherman, he was satisfied with this order which assured his overall control of the operation. He immediately sent word to Sherman that McClernand was to take command, and sent a message to McClernand that he should report to Memphis without delay. McClernand, exasperated by what he considered to be a double shuffle by Stanton, Halleck, and Grant, was to find himself still further frustrated by the actions of a Confederate cavalryman: Nathan Bedford Forrest.

Forrest had crossed the Tennessee River to harass Grant's line of communications. On the night of December 18, one of his regiments destroyed a section of the railroad and telegraph north of Jackson, cutting off all communications between Corinth and Memphis. Grant's message to Sherman was therefore held up for two days and Sherman, unaware of the change in command, left Memphis with his troops on the twentieth. Fuming McClernand arrived there only on the twenty-eighth, to find his expedition had gone on without him.

Grant, meanwhle, was being occupied with more amazing Confederate activities on his long line of communications from Cairo. While Forrest was raiding in northwestern Tennessee, Van Dorn slipped behind Grant's lines in northern Mississippi. On the twentieth he surprised the Federal garrison at Grant's major supply depot at Holly Springs, captured the place, and destroyed warehouses and stores estimated to be worth upwards of $1,000,000. Prompt action by Grant resulted in forcing the two bold Confederates from his line of communications, but they had caused him great damage, had stopped his advance into Mississippi, had put his army on half-rations, and had given Southern morale a needed boost.

Grant, realizing now that a continuation of the land advance to Vicksburg would require too large a diversion of troops to guard his line of communications, decided to take personal command of the river expedition, if Sherman were delayed in his efforts to capture Vicksburg.

Porter and Sherman, meanwhile, had steamed rapidly down the Mississippi with more than fifty transports and accompanying gunboats. The expedition was at the mouth of the Yazoo River, just above Vicksburg, on Christmas Day. Next day the force ascended the Yazoo, Sherman planning to seize the high ground along the left bank of that river, and then to press ahead to cut off and capture Vicksburg.

The possibility of such an approach to the key river fortress had, however, been considered by Pemberton. By the time Sherman reached a position from which to attack, the strong defenses of Chickasaw Bluffs were manned by 14,000 ready Southern veterans of the Iuka-Corinth campaign. For three days Sherman probed in vain for an accessible approach to Vicksburg up the steep bluffs, and past the grim defenders. Finally, after his assaults were repulsed on December 29, he admitted defeat. He had had 1,776 casualties, while the well-protected defenders had lost only 207. Returning to the mouth of the Yazoo, he was met by McClernand, who assumed command.

We leave Vicksburg now for the moment, to observe the situation at the mouth of the Mississippi. General Banks had arrived in New Orleans on December 14, with a large body of troops, and had taken over the command from Butler. He immediately pushed up the river, with commendable energy, and on December 17 captured Baton Rouge. He now learned of the recent construction by the Southerners of a powerful fortress at Port Hudson, Mississippi, overlooking the point where the Red River flows into the Mississippi. Rumor had it that this place was as strong or stronger than Vicksburg, and so Banks had to pause to reconsider his plans. Meanwhile he had sent a regiment to occupy Galveston, which the Navy had seized early in October. The Federal troops arrived at the Texas seaport on December 25, just in time to fight off a Southern attempt to recapture the town. In a fiasco for which an incompetent naval officer was primarily responsible, the Confederates, at first beaten off, made another attack, capturing the town with its newly-arrived Federal garrison. Here was news to match that from Vicksburg, and to the South it was an omen of the prospects of all the efforts of General N. P. Banks.

To the Southern populace and officialdom the year 1862 thus ended with a favorable balance sheet along the Mississippi River and the Gulf Coast. On December 7, Confederate Maj. Gen. T. C. Hindman, with about 10,000 men had been checked by an equal number of Federals under Brig. Gens. James G. Blunt and Francis J. Herron at the battle of Prairie Grove, Arkansas. Hindman had been forced to withdraw, leaving northwest Arkansas in Federal hands. And then there had been the unexpected loss of Baton Rouge. But by New Year's Day these two reverses were more than offset by the victories at Chickasaw Bluffs and Galveston. Added to Fredericksburg, they greatly brightened hopes of Southern independence. Vicksburg, too, was securely in the hands of the jubilant Confederates. Grant's overland operations had been halted, and they had thrown back Sherman's river expedition with even more dramatic finality. They now had increasing confidence that they could retain their grip on the Mississippi at Vicksburg, despite the strongest efforts which the North could exert.

But Confederate eyes—and those of the Union too—were also pinned on the outcome of the great battle in central Tennessee, where the armies of Generals Bragg and Rosecrans were locked in desperate conflict.

We left Rosecrans and his Army of the Ohio at Nashville on November 6, the day after a daring double raid against the outskirts of the Tennessee capital by Confederate cavalrymen Forrest and Morgan. Bragg, after withdrawing to Knoxville and Chattanooga, had again moved north, to Murfreesboro. As the two armies remained thus, some thirty-five miles apart, week after week, official Washington became impatient. On November 27, and again more firmly on December 4, Halleck warned Rosecrans that if he did not soon take the offensive against Bragg, President Lincoln would have him replaced by a more energetic general.

Rosecrans' slightly haughty, but soldierly, reply ended with the terse statement: "If my superiors have lost confidence in me they had better at once put someone else in my place. . . ." Rosecrans hastened his preparations, but he did not move within a week, and he was not relieved from command.

Rosecrans, who had no cavalry leaders or units of comparable ability, was greatly hindered by the activities of Forrest and

Morgan. On December 7, Morgan surprised, defeated and captured the Union brigade garrisoning Hartsville, east of Nashville, and returned to Murfreesboro with 1,800 prisoners. For this exploit he was promoted to Brigadier General. At the same time Forrest was reported moving west through Columbia, Tennessee. A week later Rosecrans learned that the wily cavalryman was crossing the Tennessee River northeast of Jackson, and now Grant would have to worry about him. As we know, Forrest's raid, combined with Van Dorn's, created turmoil on Grant's line of communications.

But on December 22, Morgan was again striking along Rosecrans' line of communications. Frustrated, Rosecrans could only alert the garrisons to his north, as the raider struck deep into Kentucky. But Bragg had made a mistake this time, in unleashing Morgan while Forrest was still away. In a few days he would sorely miss these two brilliant cavalrymen, because, on December 26, Rosecrans moved his army southward from Nashville, determined to seek, and win, a battle. He had collected ample supplies in Nashville, and felt that he could ignore Morgan, who was now the concern of General Wright in Kentucky. His army was organized into three wings—or corps—under the command of Thomas, Alexander D. McCook, and Crittenden. With about half of its total strength guarding key cities on the line of communications, the army totalled about 44,000 effective troops.

Bragg, for his part, had been subjected to increasing criticism in the South for lack of aggressiveness. Ever since his withdrawal from Kentucky, his old friend, President Davis, had been under increasing pressure to relieve him from command. In partial response to this pressure, Davis had, on November 24, placed General Joseph E. Johnston in command in the West, over both Bragg and Pemberton. And at one time Davis had evidently been close to ordering Johnston to take personal command of Bragg's army. So there was considerable tenseness in each of the rival headquarters as the Union army moved south from Nashville; both generals knew they had to fight if they wished to retain their commands.

Bragg, however, seemed to have recovered much of the confidence he had lost after Perryville. He had about 38,000 troops—mostly veterans—in the vicinity of Murfreesboro. His outposts engaged the cautiously advancing Federals a few miles north of that town on the twenty-ninth, and skirmishing was brisk throughout most of the thirtieth. That day, too, the Federals learned that the absence of Forrest and Morgan had not left Bragg without capable cavalrymen. Brigadier General Joe Wheeler, hero of Perryville, made a circuit behind Rosecrans' army, creating havoc in the Northern supply trains.

Thanks to the superiority of his cavalry, Bragg now had a better picture of the Federal dispositions than Rosecrans had of his. That night the Confederate leader made his plans and issued his orders. His army was athwart the road and railroad from Nashville, just northwest of Murfreesboro. These routes crossed the West Fork of Stones River about half a mile above the town. To secure these crossings, as well as the northern approaches to Murfreesboro, Bragg had placed his army astride the river. Apparently he had weighed the obvious disadvantages of such a position, and had decided that there were enough fords and bridges to make the risk acceptable. Particularly since he hoped to be able to seize the initiative, envelop Rosecrans' right flank and crush the Union army against the river.

Hardee's corps, some 12,000 strong, west of the river, would strike the hammer blow at dawn, December 31. Polk, also across the river and covering the bridges, would contain the Federal center. On the east bank was Breckenridge's division (detached from Hardee's corps), destined to hold the high ground and protect the Confederate northern flank against the Union troops seen massing at the fords. When Hardee had hit Rosecrans' right flank, Polk would press forward.

By coincidence, Rosecrans' battle plan also envisaged an

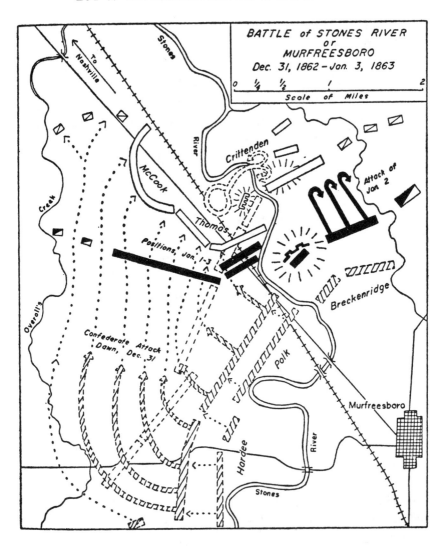

**BATTLE of STONES RIVER**
**or**
**MURFREESBORO**
**Dec. 31, 1862 – Jan. 3, 1863**

Scale of Miles

envelopment of his enemy's right flank. His left flank, part of Crittenden's corps, was to cross the river early in the morning, to envelop the Confederate right. The remainder of Crittenden's corps, with one division of Thomas', was to hold the center, along the road and railroad. McCook's corps was extended to the right, to occupy the attention of Bragg's left.

Rosecrans' plan was a poor one. The force which was to make his main effort was far too small for its mission, and furthermore it could get into position for attack only by a slow, daylight river crossing in sight of an alert enemy. Bragg's dispositions were much more sound, particularly in the light of his correct assessment of Rosecrans' intentions, and the simple, reasonable plan he had conceived.

Hardly had Crittenden's divisions begun fording the river, shortly after dawn on December 31, when they received sudden orders to return. Hardee's attack had struck like a thunderbolt, and the entire Union right wing was falling back in confusion. Fortunately for Rosecrans, the necessity for abandoning his plan almost before it had gotten started, by accident turned out to be a major contribution to the salvation of his army. Breckenridge had reported the Federal crossing of the river to Bragg, but owing to the wooded terrain, and the general confusion of the battle as its tempo increased, the Confederates did not realize that the Northerners had soon withdrawn to the west bank. And so Breckenridge's men were kept ready in their defensive positions east of the river, waiting for an attack that never came. By mistake, Rosecrans had created a diversion which kept one-fifth of the Confederate Army out of the battle most of the day. Had Breckenridge been available to Hardee on the Confederate left early in the afternoon, it is difficult to see how the Union Army could have escaped the greatest disaster of the war.

As it was, Hardee threw McCook back five miles before he was finally brought to a halt about 2:00 P.M. by the concentration of additional Federal forces in front of him, and by the exhaustion of his own men. The Federal line had been bent back at right angles. Rosecrans' back was now against the river, and his troops were just barely holding on to the vital Nashville turnpike, his only route for supplies and reinforcements.

The Federal center had also been pushed back by Polk's corps, its defense hindered by the fact that the aggressive Confederate cavalry was still playing in the Union backfield, and had dispersed several ammunition trains. By 4:00 P.M., however, thanks to fine troop leading by division and brigade commanders, the Army of the Ohio had caught its second wind. Ammunition was now reaching the troops, and the Confederates just didn't have enough reserve strength to exploit their initial and startling success.

Bragg now did make use of Breckenridge, throwing him in just west of the river to bolster Polk, and to try to dislodge the Union left. But it was too late, and this was the wrong place. The Confederate assaults were repulsed, and the first day of the battle of Stones River came to an end, with Rosecrans' army still intact, though badly shaken by the fury of the Confederate onslaught. Bragg's army was in only slightly better shape. Losses had been heavy, troops were tired, and the edge had been taken off the initial success by the valiant stand of the Northerners late in the day.

Aside from some outpost skirmishing and reorganization of positions, there was relatively little activity on January 1, 1863, as the two armies licked their wounds and glared at each other. Rosecrans' army, bent back against the river, was in jeopardy. But he determinedly held his position, although he sent a division across the river to secure a possible line of retreat. Bragg did not feel that he had the strength to resume the attack without resting his men.

Early on January 2, Rosecrans sent more troops east of the river. It became obvious to Bragg that this concentration might permit his own positions on the west bank of the river to be taken under enfilade fire by the Northerners. He ordered Breckenridge to recross the river to his old positions, and to drive the Northerners back. The attack, launched late in the afternoon, was initially successful, driving several Federal units into the river. But Breckenridge's left flank now came under heavy enfilading fire from Union artillery massed on high ground on the far (the west) side of the river. More than fifty guns poured shot and shell into the advancing Confederates, causing horrible losses. It was more than they could stand, and as the day ended Breckenridge fell back to his starting line, with more Union infantry pouring across the river to secure the Federal left flank.

Early on January 3, more Northern reinforcements and a large supply train arrived from Nashville. Rosecrans, however, felt that he needed additional ammunition before he could advance, while Bragg, depressed by repulse, stayed relatively inactive. There was some skirmishing, and Wheeler's cavalry again created trouble in the Federal rear. However, that night Bragg retired from Murfreesboro, and the great battle was at an end.

Almost sixteen years earlier Bragg had commanded one of two lone artillery batteries that faced without flinching the terrifying advance of the entire Mexican Army on the rocky plateau at Buena Vista. His professional skill and cool determination had helped to save that day, in response to iron-nerved Zachary Taylor's famous exhortation: ''A little more grape, Captain Bragg.'' But responsibilities of army command require more of a soldier than the simple, necessary, ability to carry out orders no matter what the odds or risks.

Tactically, Stones River had been a draw, but Bragg's withdrawal turned it into a strategic success for the more determined Rosecrans. Bragg, a competent soldier, had twice come close to glory; had twice faced the supreme test of top command; and twice his nerve had failed when determination and perseverance would almost assuredly have won him a big victory.

Casualties were heavy on both sides; Federal losses had been 1,677 killed, 7,543 wounded, and 3,686 missing, a total of 12,906. The Confederates had 1,294 killed, 7,945 wounded, and about 2,500 missing, for a total of approximately 11,740.

While it had lacked the decisiveness and brilliance of Lee's recent victory over Burnside, Stones River was a Union victory nonetheless, and to a desperate Northern government, and a despondent Northern people, this was enough. It redressed the balance of Fredericksburg.

# 16

# The Perfect Battle

**M**y plans are perfect. May God have mercy on General Lee, for I will have none."

Thus spoke "Fighting Joe" Hooker, President Lincoln's New Year's gift to the Army of the Potomac, shortly after his appointment in January, 1863.

Hooker—a West Pointer—was both a fighter and a vainglorious opportunist. He had won three brevets for gallantry in action in the Mexican War. Later entering civil life, he returned to the colors in early 1861, as a brigadier general of Volunteers. His nickname was coined by his own division during the Peninsula Campaign. He had openly raged against McClellan's diffidence in the Seven Days; he had blasted Burnside's inefficiency at Fredericksburg. Now he was in Burnside's shoes. President Lincoln's letter to him on January 26 is self-explanatory:

> I have placed you at the head of the Army of the Potomac.
> Of course I have done this upon what appears to me to be

sufficient reasons, and yet I think it best for you to know that there are some things in regard to which I am not satisfied with you. I believe you to be a brave and skillful soldier, which, of course, I like. I also believe you do not mix politics with your profession, in which you are right. You have confidence in yourself, which is a valuable, if not an indispensable, quality. You are ambitious, which, within reasonable bounds, does good rather than harm; but I think that during General Burnside's command of the army you have taken counsel of your ambition, and thwarted him as much as you could, in which you did a great wrong to the country and to a most meritorious and honorable brother officer. I have heard, in such a way as to believe it, of your recently saying that both the Army and the Government needed a dictator. Of course, it was not for this, but in spite of it, that I have given you the command. Only those generals who gain successes can set up dictators. What I now ask of you is military success, and I will risk the dictatorship. The government will support you to the utmost of its ability, which is neither more nor less than it has done or will do for all commanders. I much fear that the spirit that you have aided to infuse into the army, of criticising their commander and withholding confidence from him, will now turn upon you. I shall assist you as far as I can to put it down. Neither you nor Napoleon, if he were alive again, could get any good out of an army while such a spirit prevails in it. And now beware of rashness. Beware of rashness, but with energy and sleepless vigilance go forward and give us victories. Yours, very truly, A. Lincoln.

An extraordinary document, this; a measure both of the patient man who wrote it—the man who sought generals who would fight—and an appreciation of the man to whom it was sent.

Hooker tore into the sorely abused Army of the Potomac like a whirlwind, restoring its morale, forcing it to pull itself by its collective bootstraps out of the mud and mess of the Aquia Creek cantonments, and Burnside's clumsy organization. By April's end Hooker had the largest, best organized and best equipped army yet to be assembled on this continent—seven corps of infantry and one of cavalry. Its strength was 122,000 foot and 12,000 horse, organized into 57 brigades of infantry and 7 of cavalry, together with 400 guns. For the first time in this war the Union cavalry had been assembled for coherent tactical operation.

Meanwhile Lee, across the Rappahannock, had confined operations during the winter to cavalry raids. Stuart's horsemen had been continuously harassing the Northern line of communications from Falmouth to Washington, and had ranged westward as far as the line of the Orange & Alexandria R.R.

There was reason for Lee's inactivity. The Army of Northern Virginia was short on equipment, rations and clothing. Longstreet, with two divisions, had been sent down into the lower James River area to gather provisions. Lee retained some 60,000 men—of whom 6,500 were cavalry—and 228 guns, organized in six infantry divisions (twenty-eight brigades), and two brigades of horse. Morale in the army was, of course, topnotch; Lee's invincibility had become legend; his men—with good reason—considered themselves to be unbeatable.

Hooker had prepared a plan, which, he felt, would destroy his enemy. It would be a nutcracker operation. Two of his army corps, some 40,000 men under Major General John Sedgwick, would force a crossing of the Rappahannock just below Fredericksburg, to distract Lee's attention. At the same time Hooker himself would lead his main effort across the river, well above the town, into the Wilderness, circling Lee's left. He would then throw this overwhelming force of five army corps—some 73,000 men in all—straight at the rear of the Southern Army. Preliminary to the operation, the Federal cavalry corps under Major General George Stoneman—less one small brigade—would sweep far to the west, ride around Lee's left flank, and cut his communications with Richmond. Against such strategical combination Lee, in theory, would have to retire at once or face annihilation.

The Union offensive was delayed for two weeks by storms and high water. Not until April 27, did Stoneman's cavalry stream away on its long end run, not to return until the campaign was over. (Actually this cavalry raid accomplished nothing.) Next day the troops of the main effort started their long march northwest to the river fords. On the twenty-ninth, Sedgwick, commanding the holding attack, began throwing two pontoon bridges across the Rappahannock and established a bridgehead on the west side—in the same general area as that of Franklin's previous attack—just south of Fredericksburg. At the same time, Hooker's main body began its crossings of the Rappahannock and Rapidan, northwest of Fredericksburg, into the Wilderness, to get in the left rear of Lee's army.

Hooker had hoped that the cavalry raid and Sedgwick's demonstration would distract attention from his turning movement. But Stuart was doing a magnificent job of screening Lee's left along the Rappahannock. (Lee had prohibited his cavalry commander from engaging the Federal cavalry corps; only two Southern regiments had been detached to observe its movements.) As a result, Lee possessed full details of the strength and direction of the Union movement across the river and into the Wilderness.

Thus oriented, Lee, daring as usual, decided to hit the main Union attack head-on, despite the disparity in numbers. Anderson's division was sent post-haste towards the focal point of the meager road net leading out of the Wilderness, a one-house road junction named Chancellorsville, nine miles west of Fredericksburg on the Orange Courthouse Turnpike. Anderson's orders were to make contact and dig in (this, incidentally, was the first planned use of extemporized field fortifications in mobile action in the war.) About this position, Lee would then build up his strength to contest Hooker's advance.

On the morning of the thirtieth Anderson made contact with Union troops advancing just south of Chancellorsville. He fell

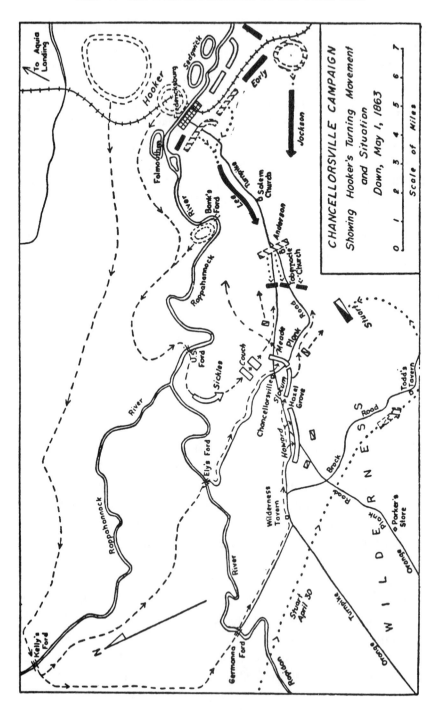

CHANCELLORSVILLE CAMPAIGN

Showing Hooker's Turning Movement
and Situation
Down, May 1, 1863

Scale of Miles

0   1   2   3   4   5   6   7

back three miles and threw up entrenchments near Tabernacle Church. Lee now ordered the rest of his army westward, except for General Early who was left with 10,000 men on Marye's Heights to contain Sedgwick's demonstration. McLaw's division arrived that night and took up position on Anderson's left, while Jackson with three more divisions was marching up from Fredericksburg. Meanwhile more than two divisions of Sedgwick's Federal troops had already crossed the river there, and were concentrating on the flats in front of Early's position.

The importance of the Chancellorsville road junction had not been lost on the Union commander. By nightfall of the thirtieth, three of Hooker's army corps had converged in that vicinity, with Sykes' division of Regulars out front, pressing Anderson. Union hopes were high; thus far everything had gone on schedule.

With the morning, Hooker's great push was launched. Federal columns moved eastward out of the tangled scrub of the Wilderness on the three roads leading toward Fredericksburg and—so Hooker dreamed—the rear of Lee's army. Meade's V Corps was on the river road fringing the Rappahannock, Couch's II Corps was on the Turnpike, and Slocum's XII Corps paralleled it on the Orange Plank Road. Behind them again came two more corps; Howard's XI, and Sickles' III. There was just one thing wrong with the Federal picture; only one small brigade of cavalry was present; totally inadequate for reconnaissance across that wide front. Hooker, when he sent his cavalry corps away, had in effect blinded himself.

The fog hung low that morning of May 1, over the thickets and fields. Sykes' division, spearheading Couch's movement down the Turnpike, flushed a line of Confederate skirmishers, and deployed astride the road, three miles east of Chancellorsville. At the same time, less than a mile to the south, Slocum's advanced elements also met resistance on the Plank Road. They, too, deployed, preparatory to attacking.

The Union advance was in fact now opposed by five Confederate divisions (Jackson had arrived) lined across the two roads, which joined just east of Tabernacle Church. Hooker, at the first sound of firing, ordered an attack. A sharp fire fight built up as the overwhelming strength of the two Union army corps massed for action. Meanwhile, to the north, and less than two miles away, the Union V Corps was proceeding, unopposed, on the river road towards Fredericksburg. The Union positions were good, the ground favorable. A determined advance would have sealed Lee's fate. Couch and Slocum pressed on.

To their horrified shock, at 1:30 P.M., came a peremptory order from Hooker, back at Chancellorsville: Withdraw at once! A similar message also brought Meade up short on the river road. Immediate appeal and expostulations by all the corps commanders were of no avail. The Army of the Potomac would fall back, Hooker told them, and dig in for a defensive action around Chancellorsville.

For the first time in his life "Fighting Joe" Hooker was dodging a fight. There is no logical explanation for this pitiable exhibition of a superb army, launched in a great offensive, being commanded to fall back at the first show of opposition and go on the defensive.

Granted that, through his own fault, Hooker had deprived himself of his eyes—his cavalry—and had no knowledge of the strength and dispositions of the enemy on his immediate front that morning, he still knew he must outnumber his opponent by two to one. The fact was that night he wired Sedgwick at Fredericksburg to send Reynolds' I Corp, 17,000 strong, to reinforce him, gives some indication of the confusion existing in the man's mind; he already had 73,000 men on the field.

So it was that by nightfall the Union Army, which that morning had advanced so jauntily to attack, was back in the fringes of the Wilderness, disgruntled and disappointed, throwing up entrenchments for a defensive action.

The new disposition was along a five-mile arc, with the left resting on the Rappahannock at Scott's Dam. From the river to Chancellorsville, Meade's corps held the line, facing southeast.

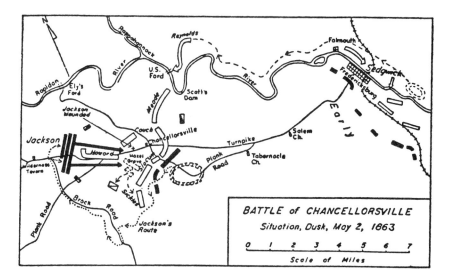

BATTLE of CHANCELLORSVILLE
Situation, Dusk, May 2, 1863

Scale of Miles

Around Chancellorsville itself, the Union position formed a horseshoe bulge: Couch faced east and Slocum continued the bulge, facing south and west. Behind the bulge stood Sickles, in reserve. West of Slocum, the pike was open for a half mile, then Howard's corps extended along it for another mile, facing generally south and holding the right of the line.

Lee built up his strength in front of the center of the Federal position along a two-and-a-half mile line. His skirmishers felt out the Union dispositions, while his cavalry ranged both flanks, probing, in particular, the Union right. That night, in the woods, Lee and Jackson conferred. The Union strength, it appeared, was too great for a successful frontal attack by the 43,000 Confederate troops. Its left flank, anchored on the river, would be unassailable. But the right flank was up in the air. So, as Jackson gravely scratched diagrams on the ground by a campfire's flickering light, a breath-taking plan grew.

While Lee, with two divisions—17,000 men—held the front

against an enemy three times his strength, Jackson with 26,000 would turn the Union right flank. As historian Freeman puts it, "The boldness of the proposal stirred Lee's fighting blood."

With the dawn, May 2, Jackson's "foot cavalry" disappeared southwest in the woods, through a mine trail to the Brock Road, thence northward to Wilderness Tavern; a ten-mile march, skirting the entire right of the Union front. From Federal patrols out on that right, came word of some sort of troop movement behind the Confederate lines, and the three observation balloons bobbing high over Falmouth Heights reported dust clouds sifting above the trees. The clicking field telegraph brought this corroborating word to United States Ford on the Rappahannock, the Union message center, whence it traveled by courier to Hooker at Chancellorsville. Jumping to conclusions, the Federal commander decided that Lee was retreating. He ordered Sickles' corps out in pursuit and at the same time sent word to Sedgwick, back at Falmouth, to attack the Fredericksburg Heights at once.

Sickles' advance momentarily endangered Jackson's wagon train, in the rear of his column. But Stonewall simply sloughed off two small brigades to protect his train and hurried on with his main body. Sickles managed to capture one of these rearguard regiments but was, in turn, so vigorously assailed by Anderson's division on the left of Lee's attenuated holding force that the Federal movement halted. Pleasanton's cavalry came forward to reinforce Sickles.

While these things were going on in the Chancellorsville area, there was great activity in Fredericksburg. Early, through a misunderstanding of orders, withdrew his entire force on the heights and started marching to join Lee. Fortunately for the Confederates, the mistake was discovered in time and Early was turned back. He reoccupied his trenches just as Sedgwick, having started Reynolds' corps north to join Hooker, prepared the remaining half of his force for the assault directed by Hooker's later orders.

Meanwhile, Jackson, arriving ahead of his troops well to the westward of the extreme right end of Howard's corps, discovered that he was looking right down the Union line of entrenchments, stretching eastward before him. Its occupants, their arms stacked, were completely unaware of any danger. It was then two o'clock in the afternoon. By six o'clock, his preparations made, Jackson launched his thunderbolt—his three divisions in as many lines—perpendicular to the Union positions.

Heralded only by a sudden rush of wildlife—deer, rabbits and turkeys—feeling before their advance, Rodes' division of Jackson's corps burst out of the woods upon the unsuspecting Union troops. Two of Howard's divisions, thus caught in flank, fled east through Chancellorsville and passed Hooker's headquarters, in panic. The third managed to face to its right, and for a short time checked the Confederate advance. Then Colson's division—Jackson's second line—reinforced Rodes', and the Confederate assault rushed down the turnpike on to the rear of Sickles' corps, almost cutting it away from the rest of Hooker's command.

By this time darkness had set in. The 8th Pennsylvania Cavalry Regiment, far out on Sickles' right flank, turned back and charged into the attacking units which, intermingled and exhausted, were losing their impetus. At the same time, some thirty-four Federal guns, on a knoll called Hazel Grove, swung about and opened fire, and Sickles, reinforced by a brigade from Couch's corps on the other side of the horseshoe bulge, rallied his command.

All during this period Lee's troops on the face of the Union position had been doing their best to keep the remainder of Hooker's command occupied. By 10:00 P.M. the horseshoe bulge had thus become a box, its open side to the river. Sickles was holding off Jackson on the west; Slocum, facing south, and Couch, facing east, confronted Lee's two aggressive divisions.

But Jackson had no intention of letting his momentum die. He hoped to cut Hooker off entirely from his communications with United States Ford on the Rappahannock. A. P. Hill, commanding the third division in column, took over the attack, Jackson himself riding ahead in the night to reconnoiter. A North Carolina regiment, mistaking the party for a Federal cavalry detachment, opened fire and Jackson fell, mortally wounded, at the instant of his greatest glory.

Little more happened that night. Movement was virtually impossible in the woods. A. P. Hill, who took command when Jackson was hit, was himself later wounded and J. E. B. Stuart assumed control of Jackson's old command. On the Union side, Hooker, who was trying to regain control of his shattered strength, ordered Sickles to counterattack the Confederate flank near Hazel Grove, but in the darkness that episode ended in another case of mistaken identity; two Federal forces firing on one another for more than an hour, without much damage being done. During the fight, Reynolds' corps had arrived in Hooker's lines. It was sent to the Union right flank, together with Meade's corps, shifted from the far left. Howard's corps, rallied after its ignominious rout, replaced Meade on the Union left.

Dawn of May 3, ushered in a renewal of the Confederate attack. The Army of the Potomac now lay in a sort of arrowhead formation, its base on the river, its apex pointing south. Stuart on the west and Lee on the east were pounding on that apex. But Hooker, had he been able to resist the counsel of his fears, still had victory dangling before his grasp as the morning wore on. His two right flank corps—Reynolds' and Meade's—some 30,000 strong, who had not been engaged at all the previous day, could easily have encircled Stuart's left and rolled his entire corps back. Down at Fredericksburg, Sedgwick was driving Early's slender force from Marye's Heights, after a stout defense.

But Hooker had no fight left in him. Dazed by a Confederate shell striking a porch pillar against which he was leaning at his headquarters, he now turned over his command to Couch, with peremptory orders to retire to a position in rear of Chancellorsville, a plan which he had determined on during the night. So, behind the fresh troops of Reynolds and Meade, the remainder of the Army of the Potomac sullenly fell back. It was withdrawing at the very moment that Lee, learning that Early had been driven from the Fredericksburg lines, was hurriedly sending back one of his own divisions to check Sedgwick's advance against what was now his rear.

The rest was anticlimax. While Stuart, with what was left of Jackson's old II Corps, some 25,000 in all, was harrying Hooker's 70,000-odd men pressed back on the Rappahannock, Lee and Early with 21,000 men pushed Sedgwick's 19,000 also back to the Rappahannock west of Fredericksburg and six miles away from Hooker.

This phase of the battle lasted through May 4. Sedgwick succeeded in escaping across the river that night. Lee, the next day, shifted the bulk of his troops once again to Hooker's front, prepared to assault at daybreak, May 6. But when his skirmishers pressed toward the river they found the bird had flown. The Army of the Potomac, under cover of a driving rainstorm, was back north of the Rappahannock, leaving behind "its killed, its

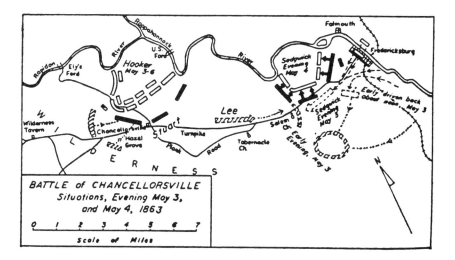

BATTLE of CHANCELLORSVILLE
Situations, Evening May 3,
and May 4, 1863

Scale of Miles

wounded, fourteen pieces of artillery and 20,000 stand of arms.'' Union losses in the battle of Chancellorsville were 16,792 killed, wounded and captured. The Confederates lost 12,754.

Thanks to his own generalship and the spectacular genius of Stonewall Jackson, Robert E. Lee had won the perfect battle. But in the doing he had lost the one man he could not spare. Jackson died four days later.

# 17

# Gettysburg

**B**y late May, 1863, Confederate President Jefferson Davis and his cabinet were on the horns of a dilemma. Should Southern strength be massed now in the East or in the West?

Despite the ascendancy which Lee had gained in Virginia, the Southern military picture was gloomy elsewhere. Vicksburg, the last important Southern foothold on the Mississippi, and vital link to the western states of the Confederacy, was now seriously threatened by Grant. At the same time, there was considerable doubt if Bragg at Tullahoma could keep Rosecrans from capturing Chattanooga, gateway to Georgia and Alabama, and in Kentucky a small army under Burnside was threatening Confederate Buckner at Knoxville.

Around the periphery of the Southern coastline the Union naval blockade was binding ever more tightly. Only two ports east of the Mississippi still remained in Southern hands: Mobile and Charleston, their approaches closed by Union men-of-war.

Northern invasion of the coastal regions was threatened in a dozen places, necessitating local concentrations of Confederate troops which could otherwise reinforce the armies in the field.

President Davis and his Cabinet asked Lee's advice. Lee, despite his deference to civilian authority, had no choice but to go to Richmond to present his own strategic opinions.

He felt it essential that he should seize the initiative. The morale of his army was soaring as a result of his unbroken string of victories. Yet it was short of rations and supply, and could not readily subsist itself in the denuded area along the southern bank of the Rappahannock. This magnificent fighting machine should not be left on the defensive where its spirit and energy would slowly dwindle. But a direct attack on Hooker's more numerous, well-supplied army, entrenched on Stafford Heights opposite Fredericksburg, was unthinkable.

But if the Army of Northern Virginia should cross the Potomac River and invade the North, Hooker would be forced to follow, and could then be maneuvered into battle in the open. There was no doubt in the mind of President Davis or his advisers as to the outcome of such a conflict. Whether or not Hooker accepted battle, the war would be ravaging Union territory, rather than Virginia; Lee's army would be living off a rich countryside. Meanwhile the Shenandoah Valley, freed of invaders, could produce plentiful harvests to tide the army, if necessary, through the winter and future campaigns. The threat such an invasion would pose to Northern cities would be likely to force the Federal Administration to rush reinforcements from the Western theater, thus immobilizing Grant and Rosecrans, and possibly permitting Johnston, Pemberton and Bragg to resume the offensive in Tennessee and Kentucky. At the very least, the entire Northern plan of campaign for 1863 would be disrupted.

A successful invasion of the North, furthermore, would revive lagging foreign interest. The South's financial credit abroad would be strengthened. There was also hope of foreign recognition, and possibly assistance from the sympathetic governments of France and England. Up North, too, they knew, the war spirit was lagging, so much so that the Union had had to come to conscription, by the unpopular Act of March 3, 1863. If an invading army were to threaten the great centers of population in the North, terrorizing the war-weary populace, clamor against the war might force Lincoln's administration to a negotiated peace, or even result in its overthrow.

Summing up, Lee warned the Cabinet that while the proposed invasion was risky, a war against an enemy possessing superior resources could be won only by taking some risks. His concept did not meet unanimous approval in the Southern high command. Longstreet, in particular, was vehement in objecting to a hazardous invasion with possibility of enormous Confederate casualties. He proposed, instead, that Hooker be contained on the Rappahannock while Lee, taking one corps from the Army of Northern Virginia, join Bragg and Johnston in the West and crush Rosecrans. This, he argued, would cause the abandonment of Grant's Vicksburg campaign and probably both Tennessee and Kentucky would fall to the South. Longstreet's ''great strategic plan,'' as Steele terms it, utilizing the railroads for operations on interior lines, could well have held better chances of success than Lee's proposed invasion.

But Longstreet was overruled and Lee's plan officially approved in Richmond on June 16. As a sop to ''Old Pete,'' Lee personally assured him that by superior speed and leadership the Army of the Potomac would be so outmaneuvered that Hooker would have to attack and take the losses Longstreet feared.

In anticipation, Lee had already begun to shift his army northward; now the tempo quickened, still under conditions of the utmost secrecy. The Army of Northern Virginia now had a strength of 76,224 men and 272 guns, and was reorganized into three infantry corps of three divisions each, plus a cavalry division of seven brigades. Longstreet continued to command the I Corps, which had returned from North Carolina; Ewell, now a lieutenant general, had Jackson's old II Corps, and A. P. Hill, also promoted to lieutenant general, had the newly created III Corps. Stuart retained command of the cavalry, some 12,000 strong.

Lee marched northwest toward the Valley, with Longstreet and Ewell; the movement screened by Stuart's cavalry, holding the line of the Rappahannock River. Hill would follow later; meanwhile he was to keep up a semblance of army activity at Fredericksburg and to prevent Hooker from interfering with the movement of the main body.

North of the Rappahannock there were many rumors of Confederate plans. Early in June, Hooker thought he detected fewer troops holding the Fredericksburg lines. But when Sedgwick was sent to carry out a reconnaissance in force on June 6, Hill responded so vigorously that the Northerners were convinced Lee's entire army was still in their front. Not till the tenth did Hooker finally obtain information revealing that a major Confederate troop movement was under way.

Since Chancellorsville, the Union and Confederate cavalry had been skirmishing along the upper Rappahannock, in westward extension of the main armies, but no large-scale actions had been undertaken either by Stuart or by Major General Alfred Pleasanton, who now commanded the Union cavalry corps. Early on June 9, Pleasanton crossed the river with about 12,000 men. Stuart and his command were completely surprised. But "Jeb," rallying his men, was able to fight the attackers to a standstill in the largest purely cavalry battle of the war. After a very confused action that ranged all around Stuart's headquarters near Brandy Station, Pleasanton, by dark, had returned to the north bank of the Rappahannock.

This drawn battle had far-reaching results. Heretofore both armies had accepted without question the superiority of Southern cavalry over that of the North. But Brandy Station had been fought with almost equal numbers and with almost equal casualties. Worse, from Stuart's point of view, was public criticism for having allowed himself to be surprised. Most important, however, was that during the battle the Northerners captured some documents from Stuart's headquarters, indicating that a major movement of the Army of Northern Virginia was afoot, and that at least part of it was headed for Northern soil.

Hooker immediately shifted some troops to his right, up the Rappahannock, and alerted the rest of his command for early movement. He sent a message to Washington suggesting that he now march with his army to Richmond to seize the Confederate capital. Lincoln rejected this in terms which show how much the President had learned in two years of war: "I think Lee's army, and not Richmond, is your sure objective point. . . . If you had Richmond invested today, you would not be able to take it in twenty days; meanwhile your communications, and with them your army, would be ruined." Halleck sent instructions to the effect that Hooker was to keep his army between the Confederates and Washington. Neither he nor the President had any confidence that Hooker would now be able to carry out an offensive action any better than he had in May.

Late on the thirteenth Hooker began to move northward. His effective combat strength was not much more than 90,000, divided among seven infantry corps, and one of cavalry, each averaging about 12,000 men. Pleasanton commanded the cavalry; the infantry corps commanders were: Reynolds, I Corps; Hancock, II Corps; Sickles, III Corps; Meade, V Corps; Sedgwick, VI Corps; Howard, XI Corps; and Slocum, XII Corps.

That same evening, Ewell, whose corps led the Confederate army, approached Winchester, held by General Milroy and 9,000 men. After a short engagement on the fourteenth Milroy was driven back towards Harpers Ferry, hotly pursued by Ewell. In a running fight, which continued on into the fifteenth, Milroy's command was completely smashed, almost half being captured.

The same day Ewell's leading elements crossed the Potomac at Shepardstown, while Jenkins' cavalry brigade dashed ahead, reaching Chambersburg in the evening. Though Lee's army was now as stretched out as it had been in the Antietam campaign, his movements had been made more cautiously; this time he had gotten the jump on his enemy. As Ewell marched northward through Maryland into Pennsylvania, and Hill hastened directly to the Valley from Fredericksburg, Longstreet left Culpeper on June fifteenth, keeping east of the Blue Ridge to protect the passes. Further east, Stuart held the line of the Bull Run Mountains.

From the seventeenth to the twentieth Pleasanton probed against Stuart, having somewhat the best of a number of small cavalry encounters, but without penetrating the skillfully maintained screen. After Longstreet turned westward into the Valley, Stuart withdrew to the line of the Blue Ridge, closely followed by Pleasanton. The Southern cavalryman now held the passes while Hill crossed the Potomac on the twenty-third at Shepherdstown, Longstreet crossing on the twenty-fourth at Williamsport.

Hooker, meanwhile, was carrying out his instructions to keep between Lee and Washington. In the capital itself there was considerable alarm. Lincoln called on the states to furnish 100,000 militiamen for six months or less, at the same time that Halleck was alerting Major General Darius N. Couch, commanding the newly-established Department of the Susquehanna. Meanwhile Major General John A. Dix, commanding Union troops at Fort Monroe, was ordered to make a demonstration up the Peninsula against Richmond. It was hoped that this might result in some of Lee's army being ordered back to protect the Confederate capital.

The Confederate government was not seriously alarmed by this threat, but it did cause President Davis to decide against a recommendation by Lee that troops be taken from the Richmond garrison and from the North Carolina coast to create a small new army at Culpeper. Lee believed—with good reason—that the establishment of such a command, "even in effigy," would cause the Federal government to order Hooker to leave troops in Northern Virginia to protect Washington.

Had it not been for Dix's demonstration, therefore, Hooker

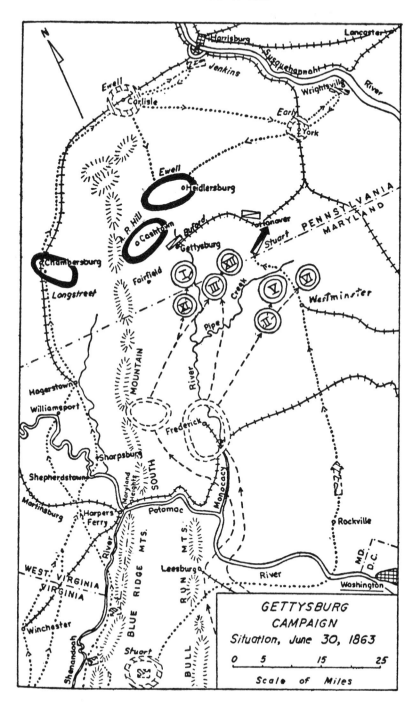

GETTYSBURG
CAMPAIGN
Situation, June 30, 1863

0    5         15        25

Scale  of  Miles

would probably have moved into Maryland with considerably less than the 90,000 men who started across the Potomac on June 25. He was displaying again some of the jitteriness that had wrecked his well-laid plans for the Battle of Chancellorsville. Like McClellan, he began to believe that he was not receiving the whole-hearted support of the War Department in Washington.

A showdown came on the twenty-seventh. Hooker, now at Frederick, had been told that the 10,000 men of the garrison of Harpers Ferry were under his command. The town had been evacuated, but the strong fortifications on Maryland Heights, overlooking the town from the north bank of the Potomac, had been held. Thus use of Harpers Ferry was effectively denied the Confederates, and the valuable railroad bridge, only recently rebuilt, was protected from possible destruction by Lee's men. Hooker wanted to evacuate Maryland Heights. He proposed that the garrison be combined with a force of three corps under Reynolds, which would operate against Lee's rear and communications, while Hooker and the remaining four corps advanced northward from Frederick.

Halleck, overruling Hooker, insisted that a sufficient force be left at Maryland Heights to deny Harpers Ferry to the Confederates. Nor would he permit Hooker to divide his army in the face of Lee.

Hooker—who claimed that Lee's army was larger than his own—now submitted his resignation. Possibly this was a bluff, on the assumption that there was no one suitable to replace him. He did not have to wait long for a reaction. Before dawn on June 28, he was visited by a special courier from Washington, carrying orders that he turn control of the army over to Major General George Gordon Meade. The Army of the Potomac had gained its fifth commander in ten months.

Meade's specific mission was to find and fight Lee, but at the same time to cover Washington and Baltimore from possible Confederate attack. Few generals have assumed command under more difficult circumstances.

The job was made no easier when, a few hours later, Meade received some startling news, which at first he could hardly believe. Stuart's cavalry was raiding at the outskirts of Washington. He had captured a supply train of more than 125 wagons, destined for the Army of the Potomac, at Rockville, less than ten miles from the District line.

"Jeb" Stuart was indeed between the Union army and the capital it was supposed to be protecting. But he had only three brigades, not enough for him to think even of a demonstration against the fortifications around Washington. His less ambitious—but nonetheless spectacular—intention was to ride completely around the Union army, and join Ewell somewhere in Pennsylvania. *Why* he was where he was, with the objective he had in mind, has become a matter of controversy never satisfactorily settled.

Lee had much on his mind in those late June days, as he supervised the cautiously bold movement of his army into Federal territory. As a consequence, a serious weakness in his command organization began to make itself felt. His staff consisted essentially of a few junior officers of the Adjutant General's Department, and the general's personal aides. These men, though mostly able and energetic, were hardly more than clerks and messengers. Above all, there was no chief of staff, no experienced officer to whom the general could delegate authority to make routine decisions, and who would make sure that *all* orders to *all* commands were consistent with each other, and with the objective of the commander.

Lee realized that his right flank would be most vulnerable to possible Federal reaction. The leading corps—Ewell's—would, in particular, need cavalry to cover the right as well as in front. Stuart, as soon as he had finished his mission of screening the crossing of the Potomac, was expected to hasten North to join Ewell. There he could best perform his accustomed reconnaissance role as eyes and ears of the army, at the same time providing a screen to deny information to the enemy. The orders issued to

Stuart, however, were fragmentary and poorly written. One read in part as follows: "You will, however, be able to judge whether you can pass around their army without hindrance, doing them all the damage you can, and cross the river east of the mountains. In either case, after crossing the river you must move on and feel the right of Ewell's troops, collecting information, provisions, etc."

The army's cavalry commander, after two years of war, should not have required specific directions to keep the commanding general constantly informed of his own whereabouts, as well as of the location and movements of the enemy. Nor should there have been any need to remind him that his mission to "move on and feel the right of Ewell's troops" was overriding; its earliest accomplishment vital not only to the success of the invasion, but also for the very safety of the entire army. A good chief of staff, as aware of the shortcomings as of the capabilities of "Jeb," would have made sure that orders were complete and specific, and that the limits on his discretionary instructions were clearly defined. As he interpreted them, these instructions gave Stuart the opportunity he had been seeking: he would ride completely around the Union army, and in this glorious exploit wipe out the memory of the setbacks at Brandy Station and in the Bull Run Mountains. Leaving two brigades still in the Blue Ridge passes, Stuart crossed the Potomac a few miles above Washington early on June 28, with his three remaining brigades.

That morning, as we know, Stuart captured the supply train at Rockville. He decided that he would take with him these brand new wagons, with their valuable contents, and their plump mules. His union with Ewell, somewhere in southern Pennsylvania, would be a triumphant one. For the next four days Stuart worked his way north, constantly skirmishing with Federal cavalry, almost getting captured twice, but never relinquishing his hold of the captured wagon train.

It was on the twenty-eighth, also, that General Lee, late in the evening, received his first word of the passage of Hooker's army over the Potomac—and learned also that it was now Meade's army rather than Hooker's. The Federal army was reported to be in the vicinity of Frederick, but the information was vague. Lee, in frustration, is reported to have said: "I do not know what to do, I cannot hear from General Stuart, the eye of the army." It has never been satisfactorily explained why the two brigades left in the Blue Ridge, or another brigade of cavalry, then raiding westward against the Chesapeake & Ohio Canal, did not join Lee before the end of June. Jenkins' brigade, along the Susquehanna River with Ewell, was all the cavalry Lee had with him.

The Confederate army at the time was spread in a wide arc between Chambersburg and the Susquehanna. Jenkins was skirmishing with Union militia along the banks of the river, just opposite Harrisburg. Ewell with two divisions was in Carlisle, while Early's division, in York, had a brigade thrown out to the Susquehanna River at Wrightsville. Longstreet was at Chambersburg, while A. P. Hill's corps was between Chambersburg and Cashtown.

Lee, with incomplete information about the Union Army's dispositions and movements, concerned about a possible threat to his communications, and fearful of being surprised while his army was scattered and without its cavalry "eyes," determined to concentrate at once in the Cashtown-Gettysburg area. From here he could move against Meade's flank if the Union general threatened the Confederate line of communications. Or, if Meade moved directly northward, Lee was prepared to fight an offensive battle on carefully selected ground. The orders for the concentration went out late that night.

Meade was much better informed of the dispositions of his enemy. Prompt and accurate reports were being received from loyal Pennsylvanians, and from the militia units along the Susquehanna between Harrisburg and Lancaster. With Pleasanton's cavalry screening the advance, he moved towards Hanover, keeping himself between the Confederates and the Baltimore-Washington area. On the 29th he got word of the southwesterly movement of Ewell's corps, and properly interpreted this as a concentration of Lee's army. As he probed cautiously north—his cavalry playing hide-and-go-seek with Stuart near Hanover—Meade selected a strong defensive position along Pipe Creek, midway between Westminster and Hanover.

This was the situation on June 30: two great armies, each commander on the defensive, cautiously probing for the other, expecting—almost inviting—attack. That afternoon Confederate Brigadier General Johnston J. Pettigrew, of Hill's corps, received orders from his division commander, Henry Heth, to march from Cashtown to nearby Gettysburg to seize a large supply of Union shoes reportedly stored there. But as his column came swinging down the Chambersburg Pike about two miles northwest of Gettysburg, it was brought to a sudden halt by fire from Federal outposts.

Buford's cavalry brigade, covering the left front of the Union army, had ridden into Gettysburg a few hours before. Buford, recognizing the strategic importance of the town, had put out his screen to the northwest shortly before Pettigrew's men appeared.

Pettigrew returned to Cashtown and reported the presence of Union cavalry at Gettysburg. Heth, with the permission of A. P. Hill, determined to leave next day at dawn to flush the cavalry out of Gettysburg. This would provide more information about the Union army, whose location was only vaguely known— and would also get those badly needed shoes for the division.

Between 9:00 and 10:00 A.M. on July 1, Heth's advance guard met vigorous resistance just west of Willoughby Run. The Battle of Gettysburg had begun.

The principal strategic importance of Gettysburg is the confluence there of a number of major roads, radiating north, south, east and west. The sleepy college town lies in a depression amid rolling hills. To the westward, between Willoughby Run and the town, lies long, low Seminary Ridge, running almost due north and south for several miles. Directly south of Gettysburg, high

Cemetery Hill rises abruptly, to dominate the town. Further east, rugged Culp's Hill juts up between Cemetery Hill and Rock Creek. The Baltimore Pike passes between these steep heights as it turns north into Gettysburg. From Cemetery Hill, broad Cemetery Ridge slopes gently southward, to terminate in the prominent knobs of Round Top and Little Round Top—really small mountains—rising high above the rolling hills and valleys. Cemetery Ridge runs parallel to Seminary Ridge, less than a mile to the west. In the shallow valley between these two elevations the Emmitsburg road runs southwestward, to pass over the southern extension of Seminary Ridge just west of the Round Tops.

On that hot, sunny first day of July, 1863, the main concentration of the Confederate army lay to the west of Gettysburg, along the Chambersburg Pike. But two of Ewell's divisions were also converging on Gettysburg from the north, along the York and Harrisburg roads. Union cavalryman Buford, under increasing pressure from Heth, sent back an urgent message to Reynolds, whose I Corps was only five miles south of the town. In addition to his own corps Reynolds also commanded the Union left wing, comprised of the I, III, and XI Corps. Upon receiving Buford's message, he immediately marched for Gettysburg and ordered the other two corps to join him there. Meade was informed of the situation.

On the Confederate side Lee ordered Hill to move from Cashtown to support Heth, and Ewell was also informed about the meeting engagement. Longstreet, still near Chambersburg, was given orders to march eastward at once. The Confederate commander then rode from Cashtown down the Chambersburg Pike, arriving on the high ground west of Willoughby Run about 2:00 P.M.

By that time a violent battle was raging north and northwest of Gettysburg. The van of Reynolds' I Corps arrived just in time to prevent Heth from driving Buford off Seminary Ridge. Both sides quickly built up their lines; Hill's troops pouring east down the Chambersburg Pike, Reynolds' northward up the Emmitsburg

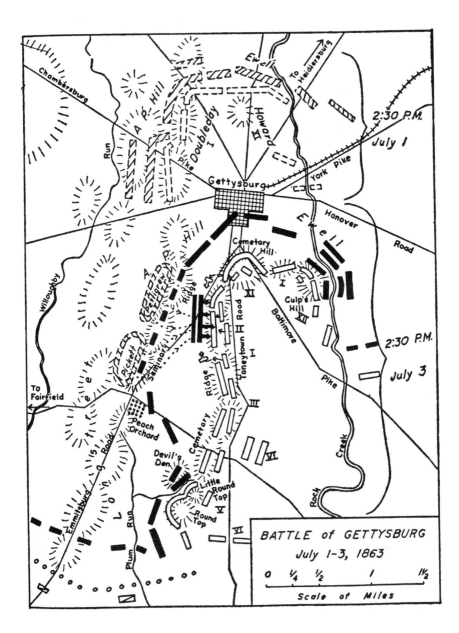

BATTLE of GETTYSBURG
July 1-3, 1863

Road. Early in the fight Reynolds was killed by a Southern sharp-shooter; Abner Doubleday assumed command of the I Corps.

About noon, Ewell, coming down from Heidlersburg, had driven back the right flank of the I Corps, but at this critical time Howard's XI Corps had arrived to extend the Union line north of Gettysburg. The Confederates, however, were concentrating more rapidly than the Northerners, and, by the time Lee arrived, Hill and Ewell each had two divisions on the field, giving them a three to two numerical advantage. Attacking aggressively, Ewell enveloped the right flank of the Union XI Corps, driving it back through Gettysburg. This exposed the right flank of the I Corps, which was also forced back.

Losses were heavy in both Union corps, and it is doubtful if they would have been able to contain the increasing Southern pressure if Howard had not had the foresight to place his reserve division on Cemetery Hill. The retreating Northerners rallied on the high ground south of the town, the XI Corps holding Cemetery Hill, one division of the I Corps on Culp's Hill to the right, the remainder of the I Corps organizing and digging in on the left along Cemetery Ridge.

It has generally been considered that Ewell could have seized the heights south of Gettysburg in mid-afternoon had he pressed promptly after the defeated Northerners. But the fragmentary orders he had received from Lee were ambiguous, the net impression of these being that he was to seize Cemetery Hill "if possible," but to avoid precipitating "a general engagement" until more troops arrived. Had there been a well-organized Confederate staff preparing the orders, Lee's intentions would have been made known to Ewell; the relative importance of capturing the hill, and of avoiding a general engagement, would have been clarified, as would the significance of the enigmatic, and discretionary words, "if possible."

It is questionable, however, whether Ewell would have been able to capture the hill from the waiting Northerners before his third division arrived, about 5:30 P.M. By this time the Union XII

Corps was arriving on the field, one division east of Rock Creek, in extension of the Culp's Hill line, another establishing positions left of the I Corps along Cemetery Ridge. Shortly after this the leading division of the III Corps was also going into bivouac along Cemetery Ridge. Even had Ewell been able to drive the tired defenders from Cemetery and Culp's Hills that afternoon, his equally exhausted troops would by dark have been hard pressed to keep the heights.

As it was, when darkness fell over the first day's battlefield, all of Hill's corps was assembled west of Gettysburg, while Ewell held the town, with his fresh division northeast of Culp's Hill on the far side of Rock Creek. Longstreet's corps was still far to the west—Pickett's division back in Chambersburg guarding the army's trains—but ''Old Pete'' himself joined Lee on Seminary Ridge by 5:00 P.M. Lee and his senior corps commander were soon engaged in animated discussion of the situation, and of the actions to be taken on the morrow.

Lee believed the battle could be won early on the 2nd by enveloping the Union left on Cemetery Ridge. Longstreet would make the main attack against this flank, while Ewell enveloped the Federal right at Culp's Hill. Hill would keep the Union center engaged by a secondary attack. Lee realized that this involved a considerable extension of his line, but Ewell had expressed complete confidence in being able to take Culp's Hill. (This confidence, evidently, was due to a report of a subordinate whose reconnaissance had been inadequate.)

Longstreet was strongly opposed to attacks against troops entrenched on high, easily defensible ground. And since the Union army was probably concentrating rapidly, the proposed envelopment might fail. Instead, he urged a turning movement around Meade's left flank. Such a maneuver would directly threaten the Federal line of communications with Washington, without exposing the Confederate communications. The Union army would then be the one which would have to attack, and take attacker's losses. Lee, however, was apparently doubtful of the wisdom of making such a movement without cavalry to reconnoiter ahead, and to screen the movement. He was certain that the Union left flank was in the air, and he made clear to Longstreet his determination to envelop that flank. Shortly after dusk, and just as he was about to go to the town of Gettysburg to talk to Ewell, he said to Longstreet and Hill: "Gentlemen, we will attack the enemy in the morning as early as practicable."

This statement of Lee's has been interpreted by many as indicative that he had given orders to Longstreet to attack at dawn, or as soon as possible thereafter. The evidence is clear that this was not the case. Ewell was instructed to attack when he heard Longstreet's guns; no hour was set, though Lee hoped the attack would be early. Furthermore, Lee gave no specific orders to Longstreet until the army's engineers made an early morning reconnaissance of the Union left flank.

Meanwhile Hood's and McLaw's divisions of Longstreet's corps had marched down the Chambersburg Pike until midnight, the head of the column going into bivouac a little more than four miles from Gettysburg. But they were on the road shortly after dawn, and were waiting for orders, near the Pike, by the time Lee was ready to give his instructions to Longstreet.

It was probably around 10:00 A.M.—Longstreet says 11:00 A.M.—when Lee finally issued the order. The engineers had been up on Little Round Top—which they found unoccupied save for a small group of Union signalmen—and discovered that the Union left flank, spread out before them to the north, was completely in the air; not even protected by cavalry! (Buford's brigade had been along the Emmitsburg Road, south of Seminary Ridge, the night before, but through a misunderstanding had been withdrawn by Pleasanton shortly after dawn.)

Earlier in the morning Lee and Longstreet had again debated the relative merits of a flank attack and a turning movement. But the reconnaissance report confirmed Lee's previous estimate. Longstreet was directed to take his corps south, behind Seminary Ridge, to a position from which he could strike northeastward, up the Emmitsburg Road and along Cemetery Ridge, directly toward Cemetery Hill. The instructions were quite specific— details of course being left to the corps commander. Longstreet, ever the good soldier, realized that he had been overruled, and that he must obey orders. Though he has been criticized for ''sulking,'' for procrastinating, and for failing to act promptly and energetically, there appears to be no factual evidence to support such accusations. There were delays, there were misunderstandings, and the attack didn't get started as promptly as Lee had hoped. Such, however, is the normal course of combat operations; rarely does everything go perfectly.

A march of four or five miles to the southward was necessary, in order to get the troops to their starting position. The route of march was chosen to avoid observation, if possible, from the Union signaling station on Little Round Top. There were further delays and some countermarching as a result of the efforts to avoid being seen. Finally, Longstreet, realizing that the movement must have been observed, ordered Hood to march promptly to the designated assembly area. Some time after 2:00 P.M. the divisions were forming for the attack, and had sent scouts forward. Longstreet ordered Hood, on the right, to start the attack up the Emmitsburg road; McLaw's would follow in echelon to the left rear. Once these two divisions were engaged Anderson's division of Hill's corps would in turn come up on McLaw's left rear. The Confederates frequently used this echelon type of attack. The advance by echelon sacrificed the shock effect of a concerted attack, but it was simple, relatively foolproof, and it frequently had a kind of cumulative, swinging-door effect, best exemplified by the successful Confederate attacks at Second Bull Run and Murfreesboro.

Now there was another delay, as Longstreet's and Lee's impatience mounted. Hood's artillery had begun firing southwest of Cemetery Ridge, but now he requested permission to move further east, to swing further behind the Union right flank. He had discovered that the Union forces west of the ridge were much stronger than expected. Longstreet impatiently replied that Hood was to attack as ordered.

But Hood realized that the situation was quite different from that visualized by either of his superiors. Twice more he requested permission to move east, *around* the Union left, instead of striking directly at the very large forces stretching in the peach orchard and wheat field between the Emmitsburg Road and Cemetery Ridge. Finally Longstreet rode up personally, and after hearing Hood's reasons for wishing to go around the southern slope of Round Top, replied simply but peremptorily: ''We must obey the orders of General Lee.''

The attack started. But it was nearly 4:00 P.M. The Union situation was now far different than that envisaged by General Lee early in the morning.

It is doubtful, in fact, if that situation was ever quite as Lee thought it was. Save for the lack of cavalry to cover the flank— a bonus Lee had no right to expect—the strength of the Union left flank had been considerably greater than the Southern leader realized.

Meade had not expected to fight a battle as far north as Gettysburg, and when he arrived on the field shortly after midnight, July 1, was still contemplating a withdrawal to the Pipe Creek line. He was still hesitant even when he saw the natural strength of the ''fishhook'' position his corps commanders had established. However, while trying to make up his mind, and as more of his divisions marched up from the southeast, he devoted himself to reorganizing and strengthening the defensive line.

Just after dawn a division of the Union XII Corps had been ordered from its position on Little Round Top to join the remainder of the corps southeast of Culp's Hill, on the right of the Union line. (It had evidently been just after the departure of this division that Lee's reconnaissance officer had found Little Round Top unoccupied.) This left Sickles' III Corps, backed up by Sykes' V, holding the Union left. Meade's staff apparently assumed that Sickles would occupy Little Round Top after the departure of XII

Corps troops. Sickles, however, had other things in mind. He noticed the high ground several hundred yards to his front, where the Emmitsburg and Fairfield Roads intersected near the peach orchard on the east slope of Seminary Ridge. This ground was higher than the southern end of Cemetery Ridge, so, without permission from Meade, Sickles unwisely advanced about half a mile. He placed one division along the Emmitsburg Road, the other was faced to his left in the wheatfields south of the Fairfield Road. The apex of this resultant salient angle was the peach orchard. Sickles' left flank was on the Devil's Den, a rugged, rocky hill just west of Little Round Top, and slightly lower.

The Southern assault precipitated a furious battle along the entire length of Sickles' salient, Hood's division soon being joined by McLaw's, and then by Anderson's. The fighting in the peach orchard and in the wheatfields was as bitterly contested as any of the war. The V and II Union corps were soon caught in the fight, as they came to the assistance of the exposed III Corps. But the energy of the Southern assault could not be withstood. Slowly Longstreet's men pushed their way through the orchard, and across the Emmitsburg and Fairfield Roads. Hood's right flank units, overlapping the Devil's Den, and seeking for a vantage point to drive the stubborn Federals from the rocky crags, swung across the narrow ravine between the Devil's Den and Little Round Top, just five hundred yards away. From the crest of Little Round Top they would not only have overlooked the Devil's Den, but would have dominated the entire Union line on Cemetery Ridge—within easy artillery range. Then suddenly, as they were toiling to the summit of the knob, the Southerners were met by a hail of small arms and artillery fire.

Just a few minutes earlier Brigadier General Gouverneur K. Warren, Engineer Officer of the Army of the Potomac, had climbed to the crest of Little Round Top. He was carrying out a mission from General Meade "to examine the condition of affairs" on the threatened and embattled left flank. He arrived at the summit to find only the small signal party. Spread out below him was the battlefield. He saw not only the fierce fighting at the peach orchard, but—as he later described it—also "the glistening of gun barrels and bayonets of the enemy's line of battle . . . far outflanking the position of any of our troops; so that the line of his advance from his right to Little Round Top was unopposed."

Warren sent an urgent dispatch to Meade for reinforcements, then, dashing down the hill, he came upon a brigade of infantry and battery of artillery of the V Corps. In the name of General Meade, he ordered both of these to hasten back to the crest, which they reached only moments before the Confederate skirmish line would have arrived. Now began one of the most violent struggles in American military annals. Neither side would be denied, and prodigies of valor were performed by men in blue and in gray. On the Union side the 20th Maine Volunteers particularly distinguished themselves, their commander finally ordering a desperate counterattack with fixed bayonets, after all their ammunition had been exhausted. But even this could not have stopped the Southerners if Federal reinforcements had not arrived. Meade had acted promptly; Little Round Top was secure.

Meanwhile Hood, McLaw and Anderson had by 7:00 P.M. been able to press their way from the peach orchard all the way to the base of Cemetery Ridge, and had seized several positions on the slopes. But now that Little Round Top was firmly in Union hands, with the V and II Corps bolstering the decimated III Corps, further Southern assaults proved unavailing. Lee's great attack on the Union left had been partially successful; the Federals had been driven back three-quarters of a mile, and had suffered fearful casualties. But Longstreet's losses had been even greater.

The situation on the Confederate left was slightly better. Ewell, unaccountably, waited for two hours after Longstreet's attack before he started his own. A typically vigorous charge by Early's division briefly seized the crest of Cemetery Hill, but Ewell failed to coordinate the attacks of his divisions. Union reinforcements drove Early off the crest before dark, just as Rodes' division, belatedly ordered to join the battle, was advancing from the town of Gettysburg. Ewell decided to call off the attack for the evening. Meanwhile Johnston's division had penetrated the defenses of Culp's Hill—weakened by Meade to reinforce his left—but the attack came to a halt at dark, with the Confederates holding only a portion of the Union trenches. From these captured positions, however, they could threaten the rear of the entire Union line, as well as the Baltimore Pike—the Union supply route.

As to the Confederate III Corps, Longstreet later bitterly wrote: "Hill made no move whatever, save of the brigades of his right division that were covering our left." This is an overstatement, and fails to credit Anderson's division for its fierce struggle on the slopes of Cemetery Ridge. But certainly Hill's other two divisions saw little action on that bloody day. Beyond question, the unaccustomed lack of energy displayed by Ewell and Hill on July 2, combined with the lack of coordination between corps, and within the divisions of the corps, permitted Meade to shift forces from his right and center, thus assuring the failure of Longstreet's attack on the Union left.

Lee, surprisingly, overrated the partial successes achieved by Longstreet and Ewell. He felt that a complete victory could be gained on the next day, if only the actions of his units were better coordinated. Pickett's division of Longstreet's corps would arrive from Chambersburg by morning; two of Hill's divisions and one of Ewell's had hardly been engaged on the 2nd. With fresh troops he planned to continue the assaults against both of the Union flanks.

But Meade realized that Johnston's position on Culp's Hill threatened his entire position. Before dawn the Union commander shifted the remainder of the XII Corps back to the right flank again. The corps attacked at dawn. After a fierce struggle of several hours, Johnston's division was driven from the captured trenches, then forced back to Rock Creek. Ewell's other two divisions did little to help. Apparently he did not wish to make another costly assault against Cemetery Hill, and he failed to make any other diversion to assist Johnston.

This change in situation on his left flank caused Lee to modify his plan. Instead of a double envelopment by his over-extended army, he would penetrate the Union line south of Cemetery Hill, where it appeared to be at its weakest, and where crossfire from Union guns would be least effective. He selected a point about three quarters of a mile south of the intersection of the Emmitsburg and Taneytown roads. A clump of trees on the ridge clearly marked the spot. Success here would break the Union army in two, and threaten it with destruction. Longstreet was to command the attack. In addition to Pickett's fresh troops, he would have Heth's division (commanded by Pettigrew, Heth having been wounded on the 1st), and brigades from Anderson's and Pender's divisions. The remainder of the army would keep the Union troops on their fronts engaged by aggressive demonstrations.

Longstreet was again bitterly opposed to the plan of his chief. But orders were orders, and so he made the necessary preparations for the great attack. In about two hours the 15,000 men of the attacking force were ranged in several long lines behind Seminary Ridge, while every available cannon was wheeled into position along the Ridge. Col. E. P. Alexander, artillery officer for the I Corps, was responsible for this massive concentration of firepower. Some 110 guns were in position to hammer the Union lines and to support the attack, while about 60 more, mostly in the III Corps sector, were to contribute to the planned bombardment.

At 1:07 P.M. a signal gun heralded the opening of the greatest artillery duel ever seen on the American continent. The Confederate cannon swept the far ridge, smashing guns and entrenchments near the crest, but doing even greater damage to the Federal reserve formations massed on the high, level ground behind. Then, slowly at first, the Union batteries began to reply, until more than eighty weapons on Cemetery Ridge—all that could be brought to bear on the Confederate gun positions—were adding to the satanic uproar started by Alexander's guns. After about half an hour of noise, smoke, and destruction beyond anything ever before seen by soldiers on either side, the Union fire began to dwindle.

Alexander now sent a message to Pickett: "If you are coming at all you must come at once, or I cannot give you proper support . . ." As Pickett was carrying this to show Longstreet, another message from Alexander arrived: "For God's sake, come quick . . . or my ammunition won't let me support you properly."

It was almost 2:00 P.M. when Pickett asked: "General, shall I advance?" Longstreet, struggling with his emotions as he thought of the slaughter to come, said nothing. Pickett repeated his question. Silently Longstreet, looking at the ground, nodded his head. Pickett saluted, saying, "Sir, I shall lead my division forward." Mounting his horse, he galloped off to his troops. The long lines began to move over the crest of Seminary Ridge.

Then followed a scene of grandeur never to be forgotten by the survivors among the thousands of awestruck men in blue and gray manning their battle positions on Cemetery and Seminary Ridges. Through their massed guns, and between the intervals in Anderson's lines, swept ten brigades of Confederate infantry, battle flags waving proudly. Northern soldiers felt their stomach muscles tighten as a mile-long hedge of menacing bayonets, twinkling in the hot July sun, advanced steadily across the open ground between the ridges. Behind them some of the Confederate guns had started to fire again, over the heads of the advancing infantry, while Alexander was limbering up other batteries to accompany the charge.

Now the Confederates learned that their artillery fire had not silenced the Northern guns. Brigadier General Henry J. Hunt, Artillery Officer of the Army of the Potomac, had realized the implications of the great Confederate bombardment, and had ordered the Union guns to cease fire until the infantry attack began.

Now the entire length of Cemetery Ridge was belching fire, and great gaps were being blown in the advancing lines. As the Confederates came on, apparently oblivious of the carnage strewed behind them, more and more Federal artillery pieces joined the fight, until more than two hundred were pouring destruction across the narrow stretch of open farm land.

Now the Southerners were within musket range, and Union infantrymen, who had been watching this scene with dreadful admiration, lost themselves in the familiar routine of battle. The leading Confederate line stopped, fired a volley, then rushed on towards the crest and the smoke-covered Union entrenchments. But now Howard, whose XI Corps held Cemetery Hill, saw that the left flank of the attackers—Pettigrew's brigades—was "in the air." He sent artillery and infantry units in front of his main line to open fire on this exposed flank. Combined with the terrible hail from their front, this was more than Pettigrew's men could take. His brigades broke, and began to fall back.

On the Confederate right, at the same time, Pickett's right flank was "drifting" to the left as a result of similar enfilade fire from units which had swung out in front of the Union I Corps' lines. But this was not yet enough to stop the indomitable Virginians. On they swept—the "Rebel Yell" now ringing defiantly in Northern ears—over a stone wall which had been held by the Union II Corps, and right up to the clump of trees that Lee had pointed out to Longstreet and Pickett.

They had broken through! Armistead, leading his brigade, hat on the tip of his sword, reached the leading Union guns behind the stone wall, had his hand on one of them, only to be shot down. The other two brigadiers of the division had already fallen, and there were all too few survivors in that gallant band of gray-clad soldiers who had fought their way to the crest of Cemetery Ridge. Now the waiting Union reserves advanced to the counter-attack. It was all over.

Back down the slope of Cemetery Ridge came the survivors, the long, orderly formations broken into confused clumps of men.

Some were running, but most were walking, sullenly, defiantly. On the far ridge Lee and Longstreet choked down their heart-numbing sorrow and despair as they readied their remaining troops for an expected counterattack. Then they rode forward to rally the broken units drifting back from the Confederacy's high tide.

Meade had fought a workmanlike, though completely passive, defensive battle, in which he had well utilized his advantages of numbers and positions. Logistically, from the beginning of the battle, he had been sitting pretty. Brigadier General Herman Haupt, director of transportation for the Union armies in the East, had performed a seeming miracle of supply and evacuation from an extemporized railhead at Westminster. Fifteen trains a day shuttled from Baltimore, carrying food and munitions to the front and wounded men to the rear.

But Meade lacked the self-confidence—and perhaps the ability—to seize one of the great opportunities of the war. The Confederate army could have been smashed by counterattack that afternoon of July 3. It could have been defeated on the fourth, as Lee sat there, awaiting an attack which never came, and preparing for the dreary retreat which he feared must culminate in disaster. Finally, it could have been crushed against the flood-swollen Potomac, after Lee had skillfully brought it back through the Pennsylvania mountains, to find his bridges destroyed and the river impassable. Meade, however, to the despair of President Lincoln, was content to harass the Southerners, and could never quite bring himself to the offensive measures necessary to reap the fruits of his great defensive victory, and possibly to win the war in 1863.

Who was responsible for the Confederate debacle at Gettysburg? Lee, as the commander, must of course bear ultimate responsibility, as he freely admitted at the time. But would the outcome have been different if, as many assert, his subordinates had not failed him in several crucial instances?

It is difficult to find fault with Lee's generalship before the battle. The strategic concept of the invasion was debatable, and the bold, extended advance itself has been criticized. But the fact is that Lee properly judged the reactions of the Washington administration—always over-timid of its own safety—and, when the armies met, his was the first concentrated, and he was able to seize and maintain the initiative. Even the absence of Stuart, which so hindered his pre-battle movements, did not prevent this.

This lack of cavalry was of course as chargeable to the discretionary orders Lee sent Stuart as to the foolish ardor which caused "Jeb" to grasp at an apparent opportunity for glory. What would have happened had Stuart remained in touch with Lee during those fateful last days of June will always be a subject for speculation. The exhausted horsemen did arrive on July 2, and fought an inconclusive engagement with Gregg's cavalry brigade east of Rock Creek on the third. It is doubtful if Stuart could have contributed much more to the battle, as staged, had he been present from the outset.

Hill and Ewell have been justly charged with lack of energy, for failing to coordinate their actions with Longstreet's two attacks, and for failing to coordinate the operations of the divisions within their corps. As a consequence both generals lost opportunities which should have been seized. Yet much of their apparent indecision and lack of aggressiveness was due to incomplete orders and inadequate supervision. This would not have occurred had Lee provided himself with a suitable staff.

Most Southern writers have considered Longstreet the prime villain of Gettysburg. But the authors of this book can find no evidence of dilatoriness on his part, either on July 2 or 3. He had disagreed with his commander—and he appears to have been right and Lee wrong—but when overruled he carried out his orders as well as he could and as promptly as the circumstances permitted. It is significant that Lee never hinted that Longstreet had failed him, and "Old Pete" continued to be his most trusted subordinate to the end of the war. Longstreet's greatest failure at Gettysburg—for which he perhaps has not been sufficiently criticized—was in the handling of his right flank divisions on July 3. Hood's and McLaw's divisions should have been more energetic in engaging the attention of the Union left wing at the time of Pickett's and Pettigrew's charge. As it was, the only important action by these units was in driving off a Union cavalry charge against the Confederate right flank late in the battle.

One thing frequently forgotten in the debates over Gettysburg is the fact that the favors of fortune were quite evenly divided between the two armies. There were comparable numbers of stupid mistakes and of opportunities lost by Union leaders. Under the circumstances, and without some stupendous Union blunder, it is doubtful if the Confederate army really had a chance of driving the numerically superior and equally battle-wise Northerners off the easily defended heights south of Gettysburg.

Lee's greatest mistake was his failure to realize that the Confederate attacks were almost certainly doomed to be repulsed. No blunders by his subordinates can excuse such a failure by a general of Lee's ability. He sadly acknowledged this to Longstreet and others on the evening of the third, adding: "I thought my men were invincible."

But Lee the man never more thoroughly demonstrated his nobility than he did in the minutes and hours after the ill-fated charge of July 3. When Wilcox came staggering back with the fragments of his brigade, Lee rode up to him, clasped his hand and said: "Never mind, General, all this has been *my* fault—it is I that have lost this fight, and you must help me out of it in the best way you can."

As though to make up for his failures on July 2 and 3, he gave a sparkling demonstration of leadership in his skillful, unhurried retreat through rain and mud in the mountain passes, and in his remarkable crossing of the swollen Potomac. And when the Army of Northern Virginia was again safe on Southern soil on July 14, he soon discovered that his country and his men still retained their confidence in his genius; a confidence amply justified in the two years of fighting that remained.

# 18

# Vicksburg

It will be recalled that at the end of 1862, Grant had come to the conclusion that the overland approach to Vicksburg would require too large a diversion of forces to protect his lengthening line of communications through hostile country. The approach to Vicksburg by the Mississippi River, however, held out much more promise. The Union Navy controlled the river north of Vicksburg. Effective interference with the line of communications would be impossible, and yet no large army forces would need to be deployed along this line south of the main base at Memphis.

Accordingly on January 10, 1863, Grant established his headquarters at Memphis, where he could supervise McClernand and be but two days' steamboat run from Vicksburg. He withdrew his units south of Holly Springs to the vicinity of Corinth; the extra forces made available by this contraction of his lines would permit a substantial reinforcement to the Vicksburg expedition.

The day after he arrived in Memphis, Grant got a report

from McClernand that he had taken his expedition up the Arkansas River to attack Fort Hindman at Arkansas Post, thirty miles or more west of the Mississippi. Grant immediately ordered a return to the vicinity of Vicksburg, the capture of which was the object of the expedition, telling McClernand to "abstain from all moves not connected with . . . the reduction of that place."

McClernand actually captured Arkansas Post—largely as the result of the capable efforts of acting Rear Admiral David Porter and his gunboats—the same day Grant sent his message. Smarting under the rebuke, McClernand replied in a belligerent, self-justifying letter. Without informing Grant, McClernand sent a copy of this reply to President Lincoln. He did, however, obey his orders, and returned to Milliken's Bend on the Mississippi, a few miles above Vicksburg on the Louisiana side of the river.

Grant, with the approval of Halleck, decided that he had better take personal command of the expedition. Hardly had he arrived at Milliken's Bend on January 30, than McClernand challenged his authority. Basing his case on his understanding with President Lincoln and Secretary Stanton, McClernand wrote Grant that he was in command of the expedition, and that "two generals cannot command this army." Grant, ignoring the insubordinate nature of the letter, replied by formally assuming command of the army; and issuing an order making it quite clear that McClernand was in command of the XIII Army Corps only. Still insubordinate in manner, McClernand acquiesced to Grant's orders, but again wrote directly to Lincoln asking for reaffirmation of his sole rights to command Union forces in the expedition against Vicksburg. Lincoln ignored the letter. Apparently he felt that Grant could handle his obstreperous subordinate.

Having established his authority without question, Grant looked over the situation.

The city of Vicksburg was perched on cliffs nearly three hundred feet over the swirling waters at a bend of the Mississippi. At this point the river, which had been sweeping in a great arc from southerly to northeasterly direction, encountered the line of high, forbidding bluffs, and made a dramatic 180-degree right turn to the southwest, before swinging south again to continue its route to New Orleans and the Gulf. These heights—the Chickasaw Bluffs, where Sherman had been repulsed one month earlier—stretched northward of Vicksburg, overlooking the swampy flatlands where the Yazoo River joined the Mississippi, about a dozen miles upstream from the city. They provided a ready-made rampart protecting Vicksburg from the north and northeast, reaching the Yazoo River at Hayne's Bluff. From here the heights extended generally northeastward, paralleling the slow-moving, navigable Yazoo. Inland from Vicksburg and adding to its natural strength, the ground was rough, cut by deep ravines and covered with heavy forest.

The natural defenses of the city had been augmented by earthworks, trenches and artillery batteries. The powerful guns dominated the river for five miles to the north, and almost ten to the south, commanding also the long finger of land projecting from the Louisiana side toward the city into the river's hairpin bend. Vicksburg was deemed impregnable by its defenders, and there was little to encourage Union soldiers to think otherwise.

About fifteen miles northwest of Vicksburg—about twenty-five by the winding river channel—was Milliken's Bend. Here, along the levees on the Louisiana side of the river, most of the Federal army was encamped, and a few miles further south, at Young's Point, Grant had his headquarters. His army was divided into three corps: McClernand's XIIIth, Sherman's XVth, and McPherson's XVIIth. His total strength on the last day of January was about 36,000.

It was evident to Grant that approach via the Chickasaw Bluffs from the north was not feasible, and a direct assault against the city from the river was out of the question. This left only an approach from the south. The problem was how to get there. The low country west of the river was almost completely under water, the Mississippi and its tributaries having overflowed their banks wherever unrestrained by levees. The guns of Vicksburg made it

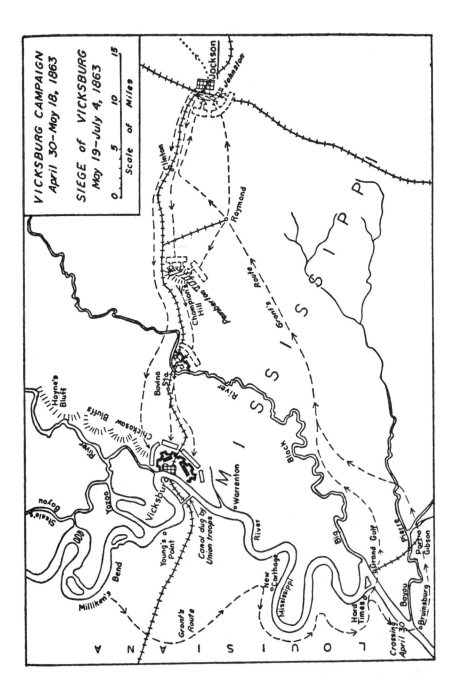

VICKSBURG CAMPAIGN
April 30–May 18, 1863

SIEGE of VICKSBURG
May 19–July 4, 1863

Scale of Miles

0    5    10    15

impossible to transport troops below the city by steamer; even the passage of the fort by ironclad gunboats was a hazardous undertaking rarely attempted by bold Admiral Porter and his stalwart sailors. Some way had to be found, it was obvious, to bypass the guns of Vicksburg and those on the bluffs both north and south of the city.

Grant apparently had determined upon his general concept for the offensive against Vicksburg from the south as early as February 2. But since effective movement of troops would be difficult until floodwaters had subsided, he realized that he would have to wait for at least two months. Meanwhile, it was necessary to keep the troops busy, for the sake of their health and their morale. Furthermore, Grant was never a man to close his mind, and he wished to explore all possibilities. So he pushed four major projects which would at least help to pass the time quickly, which would all directly or indirectly contribute towards the ultimate plan of campaign, and any one of which might provide an easier approach to the goal.

First of these was the great effort to build a canal bypassing the long loop of the Mississippi that ran under the Vicksburg heights. Started by Farragut seven months earlier, it was hoped that once the cut was made, the river current would dredge a deep channel. The scheme proved impractical, and Grant, while directing that work continue, in order to keep officers and men occupied, turned most of his attention in other directions.

The most promising alternative was through the Yazoo Pass, 150 miles north of Vicksburg—more than 200 miles by the river. Here, opposite Helena, Arkansas, a bayou, or backwater, of the Mississippi afforded an approach to the Cold Water River, a tributary of the Yazoo. Here the Mississippi levee was cut, and on the flood Federal gunboats rode through a network of streams and channels in the forests towards the Yazoo at Greenwood, 100 miles northeast of Vicksburg. If successful the formidable defenses of Hayne's Bluff and the Chickasaw Bluffs would be bypassed. But the vessels floundered in the flooded woodlands, where the Confederates barred progress by timber slashings and sniping. Finally a Southern earthwork on the Tallahatchie—Fort Pemberton—stopped further progress, and this project was abandoned on March 16.

A similar effort to bypass the Bluffs further south was tried; along Steele's Bayou, some twenty miles north of Vicksburg. Admiral Porter with several of his most powerful gunboats moved up the bayou in the latter part of March, followed by Sherman and part of the XV Corps. Again the Confederates made extraordinary efforts to halt movement, finally trapping Porter's gunboats front and rear, with felled trees and log rafts, protected by small arms fire. The water was now falling rapidly. But Sherman's troops, wading up in support, cleared away the barriers, permitting the Federal craft to escape.

A final project—considered but never seriously undertaken—was a bypass on the western side of the Mississippi, through Lake Providence, linking bayous and streams in a 200-mile detour ending more than 100 miles south of Vicksburg, opposite to and midway between Natchez and Port Hudson.

Newspaper reporters with the army wrote dismal stories about mud, discouragement, and failure of the efforts to find a bypass. The Northern people, and even the government in Washington, began to get a picture of a dull, unimaginative general, striving futilely to get himself out of a physical and psychological morass. Vicious, false rumors were printed asserting that Grant, facing failure, had become a sodden drunkard. Grant ignored the newspaper attacks, and the government was quickly reassured by the reports of trusted, competent observers.

But President Lincoln was under great pressure to remove the uncommunicative general. And though morale was high in his hard-working army, even some of Grant's most loyal subordinates were worried about the situation. Sherman urged him to give up the expedition and to return to the overland route from Memphis. Grant knew that the government desperately needed a victory, and that such a withdrawal would deal a deadly blow to Northern morale. Characteristically he pressed on with the activities he had undertaken, keeping his own counsel.

While this was going on, Porter attempted to break up Confederate river traffic below Vicksburg. During February, his fast ram *Queen of the West* and the ironclad *Indianola* braved the fortress guns and did much damage downstream. The *Queen* was finally ambushed by Southern troops on a Red River bend and captured, unharmed. Under Confederate command she now challenged the *Indianola*, just below Vicksburg, and assisted in her capture. But before the *Indianola* could be repaired Porter, in a clever ruse, let a dummy ironclad—actually a camouflaged coal barge—drift past Vicksburg, causing the *Indianola*'s captors to panic and hastily destroy their prize.

Then Farragut came up the river once again. On March 14, he tackled Port Hudson's powerful defenses. His flagship *Hartford* and one gunboat ran the hail of fire, but his other vessels were driven back with considerable damage. Bank's forces, who were to cooperate by attacking the land side of the Confederate defenses, did not materialize. However, Farragut's vessels, now both above and below Port Hudson, effectively closed the river to Southern traffic until the campaign was ended.

The efforts to find a bypass to avoid Vicksburg had failed— as Grant had really expected they would—but the troops, kept occupied, were in good health and spirits. And, with April, the weather improved, the high water was subsiding, and overland movements could be undertaken. On April 2 and 4 Grant informed Halleck he would move down the west side of the Mississippi— partly by marching, and partly by boats on the bayous—to Hard Times opposite the Confederate forts at Grand Gulf, forty miles south of Vicksburg. There the river could be crossed. This could be done only with help from the Navy.

Never has there been closer or more effective inter-service coordination than existed between Grant and his army on the one hand, and Admiral Porter and his naval squadron on the other.

During the hours of darkness on the seventeenth, Admiral

Porter began the hazardous southern movements of gunboats, and transports heavily laden with supplies, for the new base at Hard Times. Though frequently hit, the gunboats escaped serious damage, and gave as much as they received. The transports, however, despite protection from barges lashed alongside piled high with coal, grain bags, cotton bales, and various supplies, suffered heavily from the accurate Confederate fire. Some were sunk, some caught on fire, and all required major repairs. On this and subsequent nights, however, the brave crews—mainly volunteers from Grant's army—brought most of them through, and by the end of the month a number of boats were available to ferry the troops across the river.

While the defenders of Vicksburg were becoming alerted by this movement of boats down the river, they were thrown into a state of alarm by another kind of movement a few miles further east. On April 18, Colonel Benjamin H. Grierson, with three regiments of cavalry, left the town of LaGrange, Tennessee, to commence the most successful cavalry raid of the war. It had been Grant's idea that a raid through central Mississippi, coordinated with his own offensive against Vicksburg, would greatly confuse the Southerners. Grierson did not disappoint him. After a rapid, skillful and destructive ride through the entire length of the state of Mississippi, Grierson reached Baton Rouge, Louisiana, on May 3. While he tore up railroad tracks, cut telegraph wires, burned bridges and destroyed supplies, much larger numbers of Confederate troops marched and countermarched around the state in vain efforts to chase and intercept him. And while this turmoil was occupying not only General Pemberton's attention, but also distracting Bragg up in Tennessee and Johnston, the over-all Southern commander, Grant, on April 30, began to move his army across the Mississippi.

To still further mystify the Confederates, part of Sherman's corps was left north of Vicksburg to demonstrate in front of the same Chickasaw Bluffs where he had been repulsed exactly four months before. In cooperation with gunboats left north of Vicksburg for this purpose, Sherman on the twenty-ninth and thirtieth ostentatiously moved up the Yazoo and prepared for an assault. Pemberton rushed reinforcements to meet the expected attack. Sherman then quickly returned to the west bank of the Mississippi, and hurried south after McClernand's and McPherson's corps to Hard Times and the waiting ferries.

Meanwhile McClernand's and McPherson's corps were being ferried across the Mississippi, landing unopposed at Bruinsburg, ten miles south of Grand Gulf. The Confederate garrison there attempted to resist the Union advance at nearby Port Gibson, but was driven back across Bayou Pierre, and on the 3rd Grand Gulf itself was evacuated. This permitted Sherman's corps, just now arriving from its Yazoo River demonstration, to cross the Mississippi directly at Grand Gulf.

Pemberton was at Jackson, capital of Mississippi, when Grant began the crossing. He hastened to Vicksburg to take direct command against the Federal threat. Here he had about 35,000 men, out of a total of approximately 50,000 who were in the Jackson-Vicksburg-Grand Gulf area on April 30. (An additional 15,000 of his command, down in the Port Hudson area, were occupied by Banks' threatening advance toward that place.)

General Joseph E. Johnston, over-all Confederate commander in the West, was at Tullahoma, with Bragg's army. As soon as he was informed of Grant's crossing, Johnston ordered Pemberton to unite his scattered forces and attack Grant immediately, even if this meant the temporary abandonment of Vicksburg. On the ninth, in compliance with a directive from the Confederate Secretary of War, Johnston himself hastened toward the scene of action, ordering Bragg to send reinforcements to join him at Jackson.

Grant had by now learned that Banks, who had been expected to join him, would be unable to move past Port Hudson for several weeks at least. Grant had to recast his plans, therefore; the major factor in his decision would be the logistical situation of his army. By May 6, he had most of his troops across the river.

His advance divisions had pushed some twenty-five miles inland, had seized crossings over the Big Black River, and were pushing cavalry reconnaissance toward Warrenton and Vicksburg. But further advance seemed impossible until adequate supplies could be brought across the river to establish a base on the east bank, and until he was able to bring up additional troops to hold open the line of communications for an advance against Vicksburg. Despite an auspicious beginning, it seemed inevitable that the delay in waiting for supplies and reinforcements would give the Southerners an opportunity to concentrate against him, and to keep him bottled up along the river south of Vicksburg.

As Grant saw the situation, his immediate enemy, Pemberton, at Vicksburg, and the additional force now gathering at Jackson, forty-five miles to the east, should they unite, would outnumber his own 41,000 men. He decided, in Napoleonic fashion, to move his army in between them. Concentrating first against one, then against the other, he would defeat them in detail. Rations for three days were issued to the troops. For ammunition transport there was a wagon train of 120 captured vehicles—''a motley train,'' Grant described it—consisting of farm wagons, fine carriages, anything with wheels that could be found in the region.

What of other supplies? How would the men eat after their three days' rations were exhausted? Sherman remonstrated that there was only one road; the line of communications would become a shambles since it would be impossible to establish an efficient procedure to supply the three corps of the army over that road. Grant calmly replied that there would be no line of communications. The army would live off the country!

The move inland commenced on May 7, on a broad front, ready to concentrate against whichever enemy force first exposed itself to attack. Troops scoured the countryside for grain, cattle and chickens, which were in abundance. On the twelfth, Grant's right flank drove the Confederates out of Raymond after a short battle. Next day McPherson's corps, in the center, seized Clinton on the railroad between Vicksburg and Jackson, and turned towards the Mississippi capital. Sherman, now the right flank, approached the city from the southwest. McClernand was ordered to take up a position to the west, to prevent Pemberton from interfering.

That Confederate commander had failed to heed Johnston's sound advice to concentrate and to strike hard. Certain that Grant could not move far from his supposed base at Grand Gulf, he had distributed his force along the crossings of the Big Black River, and waited for Grant to attack. When, to his surprise, Grant moved northeastward towards Jackson, Pemberton believed he had a wonderful opportunity to strike the Federal line of communications. Again he had received orders from Johnston, now hurrying to Jackson, to concentrate against Grant's army. Instead, Pemberton poked south, expecting to capture unprotected wagon trains and to paralyze the Union army. All too late he discovered that there was no line of communications for him to attack!

Johnston, meanwhile, had arrived at Jackson on the thirteenth, to find that the Union Army was at the city gates, and securely in position on the railroad to Vicksburg. Reporting the situation to the Confederate Secretary of War, he added simply: "I am too late." But Joe Johnston was not a man to give up even when the situation seemed hopeless. He sent urgent orders to Pemberton: "If practicable, come up in [Grant's] rear at once . . . All the strength you can assemble should be brought. Time is all-important." But Pemberton, obsessed by Jefferson Davis' directive to hold Vicksburg, would not come. On the fourteenth McPherson's and Sherman's corps assaulted the entrenchments west and south of Jackson, forcing Johnston to abandon the city. Entering Jackson with the leading units, Grant left Sherman to destroy all Confederate supplies, the railroads, and manufacturing facilities. The rest of the Union army he hurried back westward to deal with Pemberton.

On the sixteenth McClernand's corps met Pemberton's troops holding a strong position on Champion's Hill, east of the

Big Black River, covering the roads and railroads leading towards Vicksburg. McClernand's right flank division became heavily engaged, and unaccountably he stopped the rest of his corps, allowing his exposed division to take a beating from Pemberton's 22,000 men. But McPherson moved forward promptly and saved the isolated division from defeat as it recoiled from the stout Confederate counterattack. Grant hurried forward, assumed personal command of the critical battle area on the right flank, and ordered McClernand to advance on the left with his three other divisions. In this way the Confederate line of retreat across the Big Black River would be cut.

McClernand, however, moved slowly and cautiously. When the right flank divisions under Grant's personal supervision drove the Confederates out of their positions in considerable confusion, they were able to slip back past McClernand. Closely pursued by Grant, the Southerners reached the protection of an entrenched bridgehead and crossed the Big Black River safely. While Grant brought up sufficient force to attack the entrenchments, Pemberton had a few brief hours' respite to reorganize his army and to decide what to do next.

Johnston had sent further messages, urging Pemberton to abandon the already-useless fortress of Vicksburg, to move north, and to join him for a combined attack against Grant. There is some question whether this would have been possible, because Grant had already ordered Sherman to leave Jackson and dash for the Big Black to the north of McPherson and McClernand. But Pemberton refused to comply with Johnston's instructions. Unlike Johnston, he failed to realize that the loss of the city was now inevitable, and that to stay there would merely mean the loss to the Confederacy of his remaining 30,000 men.

On the seventeenth McPherson's corps seized the Big Black River bridgehead by an impetuous attack, and Pemberton had to burn the bridges, abandoning some of his men on the east bank of the river. With Sherman now starting to cross further north, Pemberton withdrew to the city. Next day the leading elements of Grant's army were firing into the town, and on the nineteenth the siege began.

With the arrival of reinforcements in the final days of the operation, Grant's army had reached a strength of about 54,000 men. Keeping his army together he had, in nineteen days, marched about 200 miles, defeated detachments of a numerically superior enemy army in 5 battles and several skirmishes, meanwhile supplying himself from the countryside. He had inflicted losses of about 8,000 men and eighty-eight guns on the Southerners, at a loss to his army of less than 4,400 casualties, and had locked his principal opponent and some 30,000 men in a fortress. On May 26, President Lincoln, in a letter to a friend, wrote that whether or not Grant captured Vicksburg, his "campaign from the beginning of the month up to the twenty-second day of it, is one of the most brilliant in the world." A somewhat more authoritative student of military history, Grant's formerly jealous commander Halleck, later wrote: "In boldness of plan, rapidity of execution, and brilliancy of results, these operations will compare most favorably with those of Napoleon about Ulm."

Of course there is some doubt as to what cautious Halleck would have said earlier, had he known in advance that Grant planned to cut loose from his communications. But Grant, knowing Halleck, waited to inform him of this unprecedented decision until he knew that he would be out of touch by telegraph, and actually on his way to Vicksburg. In the opinion of these authors, this campaign was the most brilliant ever fought in the Western Hemisphere.

The campaign was over, but Vicksburg was not yet in Federal hands. On May 19, hoping the Southerners would be too disorganized to make effective use of the strong fortifications, Grant tried an assault. But Pemberton, now that he was penned in, had no intention of giving up easily, and the attackers were thrown back. On the twenty-second another assault was made but it, too, was soon halted by the resolute defenders. Then McClernand reported that he had seized important works, and in compliance with his urgent request, Grant ordered the other corps to renew their attacks to permit exploitation of this success. But Grant soon discovered that McClernand's report was false, and quickly ordered the attacks to stop. The defenders, some 22,000 combat soldiers, were too numerous and too well protected to permit success to 34,000 attackers.

The Union Army now buckled down to besiege Vicksburg. Grant established a base on the Yazoo River, and put Sherman in command of a mobile force between the Yazoo and the Big Black Rivers to block any attempt by Johnston to relieve the city. The Federal lines were pushed ever closer to the city, which was subjected to almost continual bombardment from Grant's siege guns, and from Admiral Porter's ironclads. Mines were dug and exploded deep under the Confederate earthworks. Makeshift trench mortars were manufactured from hardwood, reinforced with metal bands. Hand grenades were hurled between the opposing lines. Grimly, inexorably, the presure increased, the stranglehold tightened. The defenders and the city inhabitants, burrowed deep in caves, went on short rations, but continued to fight with a determination and gallantry that excited as much admiration in the North as in the South. Helplessly Johnston hovered to the east, lacking the strength necessary to attack Sherman's waiting force.

During the siege, McClernand, who had been a constant hindrance and irritation to Grant, once more became insubordinate. This time, despite earlier Presidential instructions that McClernand was to command an army corps, Grant summarily relieved him. The political general screamed for help from Lincoln. But the President, well-informed about the case, refused to intervene.

Federal reinforcements poured in, and by the end of June, Grant had more than 71,000 men. He now felt strong enough to try another assault, which was ordered for July 6. Arrangements were almost completed when, on July 3, Pemberton proposed an armistice to arrange the terms for a capitulation ''to save the further effusion of blood.''

Grant replied that ''the useless effusion of blood . . . can be ended at any time you may choose, by the unconditional surrender of the city and garrison. Men who have shown so much endurance and courage as those now in Vicksburg, will always challenge the respect of an adversary, and I can assure you will be treated with all the respect due to prisoners of war.'' Pemberton surrendered early on July 4.

As the Confederate units, 29,511 officers and men, marched out to lay down their arms between the opposing lines, Grant's troops, with one exception, maintained respectful silence. That exception was a Federal division which gave three cheers for ''the gallant defenders of Vicksburg.'' Immediately, as Grant describes it, ''the men of the two armies fraternized as if they had been fighting for the same cause.''

The repulse of a Confederate assault on Helena, Arkansas, later the same day, was an anticlimax. So too was the surrender of Port Hudson to Banks five days later. The Confederacy had been broken in two, and Grant's army had done it. The war was not ended, but the result was now inevitable if the Northern people would match the perseverance of the indomitable general and his close-knit army.

# 19

# Fatal Name—
# Fateful Gateway

**W**hile Grant's Vicksburg campaign was building to its climax, Rosecrans, with his Army of the Cumberland, sat like a bump on a log at Murfreesboro, Tennessee, for nearly six months following the battle of Stones River. Forty miles away, Confederate General Bragg and his Army of Tennessee remained unmolested at Tullahoma. Not until June 23, 1863—just eleven days before Vicksburg fell—did Rosecrans respond to the continued urgings of Halleck to move, or at least to demonstrate against Bragg, who had been depleting his army to reinforce Johnston's attempt to extricate Pemberton.

Then a nine-day march, well-conducted, through miserable, rainy weather, brought a bloodless victory to Rosecrans. Bragg, in no condition now to oppose the Federal move, abandoned Tullahoma and withdrew to Chattanooga, reaching it the day after Vicksburg surrendered. Rosecrans then sat on his hands in Tullahoma for eight more weeks.

Grant meanwhile had strongly urged that his Army of the

Tennessee advance immediately on Mobile, while Rosecrans continued to push on to Chattanooga, in pursuit of Bragg's weakened army. But, as had happened after Shiloh and after the capture of Corinth, the reeling Southerners were given another chance. Halleck disapproved the proposal, and to Grant's dismay ordered him to send troops to assist Banks in southern and western Louisiana, and to send more to Missouri and to Arkansas, and back along the lines of communications which Forrest and Morgan were raiding spectacularly.

Forrest's activities, of course, could not be ignored, and were gaining Grant's reluctant admiration for a "brave and intrepid cavalry general." But Morgan and Forrest were part of Bragg's army, and were free to go on their raids only because Rosecrans failed to keep adequate pressure on Bragg. It was with considerable disgust, therefore, that Grant found his army depleted, and his plans for vigorous conduct of the war disapproved, while Rosecrans sat idle.

Finally, however, after more prodding from the government, Rosecrans set his army in motion from Tullahoma. His was to be the main effort in a campaign to take east Tennessee from the Confederates and to bring its loyal people back under Union protection. This was a concept which had been uppermost in the mind of President Lincoln since the beginning of the war. General Burnside, with the Army of the Ohio—about 15,000 strong—would move through the Cumberland Gap to seize Knoxville, heart of the pro-Union region, while Rosecrans was to secure the southeastern corner of the state by driving Bragg out of Chattanooga. Burnside set out from Lexington on August 16, the same day that Rosecrans, leaving Tullahoma, headed for Chattanooga.

Chattanooga, literally the gateway to the southeastern portion of the Confederacy, had become its most vital strategic point. Here the Tennessee River, after flowing southward through the mountain valleys of east Tennessee, turns west to break through the southern chain of the Appalachians just north of the Georgia-Tennessee border and just east of the point where these states

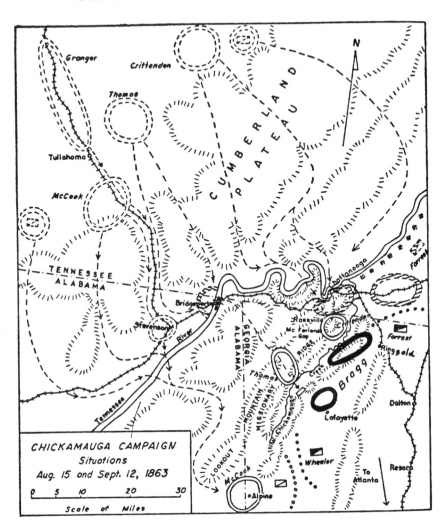

CHICKAMAUGA CAMPAIGN
Situations
Aug. 15 and Sept. 12, 1863

0    5    10        20        30

Scale  of  Miles

meet Alabama. From Chattanooga, northeast through Knoxville, ran the only direct railroad from the West to Virginia. And to the southeast, through Atlanta, ran the Memphis & Charleston R.R., the most important and only direct route from the West to Georgia and the Carolinas.

Once he got his rested army in motion, Rosecrans moved promptly and skillfully. Bypassing the defensive positions which

Bragg had prepared in the mountains to the north and northwest of the city, and moving almost directly south along the railroad from Tullahoma, he reached the Tennessee River and the vital east-west railroad near Stevenson and Bridgeport, Alabama. Turning promptly eastward, he struck rapidly for the Chattanooga–Atlanta railroad in northwestern Georgia, threatening Bragg's line of communications. The Confederates were forced to withdraw from Chattanooga on September 7, and Crittenden's corps of Rosecrans' army occupied the city on the ninth.

President Davis now rushed all possible reinforcements to his old friend Braxton Bragg. Most important of these was Longstreet's corps, sent by railroad from Lee's army in Virginia. When Longstreet's units arrived, Bragg's army would be 70,000 strong—the flower of the Confederacy. The Union Army of the Cumberland, probably equally excellent and well trained, would be outnumbered for the first time in its existence. And worse, Rosecrans, thinking Bragg was fleeing in confusion, was pursuing through the mountains with his army—now about 58,000 men— badly spread out. Locations of the scattered Federal units were well known to the Southerners, through reports in Northern newspapers.

While waiting for Longstreet, Bragg, to the disgust of his senior subordinates, on September 12, ignored an opportunity to strike Crittenden's corps of 15,000 men with about 40,000 veteran Confederates. His failure to attack the isolated Union corps, and to defeat them in detail, was much like that of McClellan before Antietam, exactly a year previously. Unlike McClellan, however, when Bragg finally decided to attack, he did produce a simple, excellent plan, as he had at Stones River.

With his army concentrated along the east side of Chickamauga Creek, some ten miles south of Chattanooga, he planned to turn the left flank of Rosecrans' now gathering army. He would cut him off from the Rossville and McFarland's Gap roads leading back to Chattanooga.

Rosecrans had guessed his opponent's intention; the dust

clouds from the marching Confederate columns indicated a massing beyond the left of the Union army. He began moving into the space between the creek and Missionary Ridge, to prevent the seizure of the two key roads. Chickamauga—"River of Blood" is the translation of the Indian name—was to live, literally, up to its ancient title.

With the arrival of Hood's division of Longstreet's corps early on September 18, Bragg, itching to take the initiative, began moving across the creek. By morning of the next day most of his assaulting troops were on the far side, and Forrest's cavalry, dismounted, on the Confederate right, had clashed with Rosecrans' left. The heavily wooded terrain prevented accurate reconnaissance; none of the Federal commanders yet knew that seven-tenths of Bragg's army was on the west bank. Haphazard, piece-meal development of the battle ensued.

Throughout the nineteenth, Rosecrans built up his position against a succession of heavy attacks. By nightfall, although his left flank had been bent slightly back, he was still firmly anchored to defend the vital Chattanooga roads. By this time his entire army was on the field, engaged or in close support, except for Granger's corps of 6,000 men. This was held in reserve on the Union left, in the vicinity of McAfee's Church on the Ringgold road, about two miles north of the main battle action.

By this time, divisions within the various corps had become so intermingled that command became a nightmare on both sides. Rosecrans arbitrarily assigned Thomas to command his left and McCook to control his right, while Bragg gave the right of his army to Polk and the left to Longstreet, who by this time had come up with most of his corps. This confused jumbling of units would next day have particularly serious effect on the Union fortunes.

Bragg, still striving to turn the Federal left, renewed his attack next day in a series of successive assaults, beginning on his right. Although Polk was slow in starting, Confederate pressure, confined to the northern flank of the battlefield during the morn-

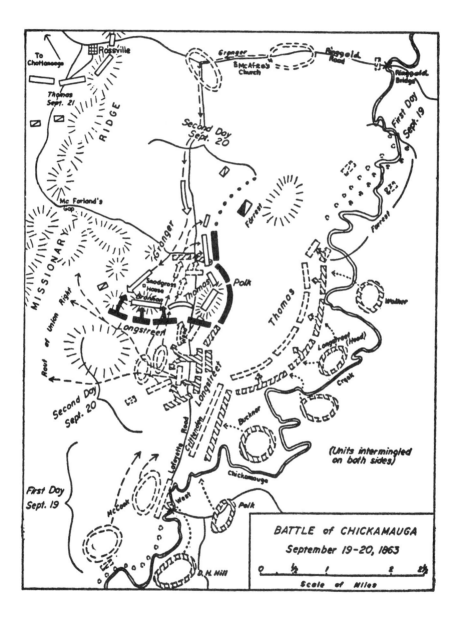

BATTLE of CHICKAMAUGA
September 19-20, 1863

Scale of Miles

ing, was so strong that over-anxious Rosecrans, without McCook's knowledge, began personally to shift divisions from McCook to support Thomas. The last one he moved was Wood's, which he thought lay in reserve behind McCook's front. Actually, Wood was already in the line; put there by McCook to replace a division earlier shifted.

Receiving the army commander's order, Wood, without question, began withdrawing and started north behind the front, leaving a gap in the Federal center.

At this precise moment, Longstreet's corps was moving to attack this very spot. The veterans of the Army of Northern Virginia drove through the convenient opening and erupted, geyser-like, on the troops in movement. Within a few moments the Union right ceased to exist. A stream of fugitives went scurrying back towards Chattanooga and the gaps of Missionary Ridge in their rear. With them they carried Rosecrans and his headquarters.

Thomas was now threatened by a double envelopment, thanks to battle-wise Longstreet's immediate action. The entire battle situation had changed. Bragg's envelopment of Rosecrans' left became a turning of what was now the Federal right, closely gathered astride the Lafayette road.

Bent almost in semicircle around a knob east of the road were five Federal divisions and the disorganized remnants of three more, fending off Bragg's main force. Behind them, one division—Brannan's—anchored on another knob west of the road and facing south, was making gallant but seemingly futile resistance against Longstreet's three divisions of seasoned troops.

And then came Granger! Gordon Granger's orders were to hold his little corps in reserve on the Ringgold road to guard the eastern approaches to Chattanooga. But Granger, good soldier, heard the roar of battle two miles away and marched to the sound of guns. His leading division came down the Lafayette road just as Longstreet hurled five brigades to batter Brannan away from his hold on that western knob; Thomas threw it in to meet the Confederate charge and Granger drove Longstreet back. All afternoon Longstreet tried without success to gain the knob. Bragg had no reserves to help him; his remaining strength was engaged in the still unsuccessful effort to turn Thomas' left.

Thomas, who had ignored Rosecrans' order to retire (sent him as the army commander was himself being driven from the field), was now running short of ammunition; Longstreet's assaults had to be met at the last by the bayonet. It was time, Thomas felt, to go.

One by one, he pulled the divisions east of the Lafayette road back onto the western knob, known as Snodgrass Hill. Here they held till seven o'clock in the evening. Then, and not until then, George Thomas, the "Rock of Chickamauga," withdrew his troops to McFarland's Gap to take up positions along Missionary Ridge. The Union army had suffered a serious defeat, but the way to Chattanooga was still barred to the Confederacy.

But even Thomas' stouthearted resistance would have been in vain had Bragg seized the opportunity granted him by luck and Longstreet. Longstreet and Forrest urged immediate pursuit. They and their men were tired, but they were buoyed up by victory, and by the clear opportunity which still existed to destroy Rosecrans' army—equally tired—as it streamed back to Chattanooga in confusion and defeat. But Bragg had had enough. As he had twice before demonstrated, Bragg's moral strength was never equal to the pressure of a prolonged or intensive strain; he lacked what Napoleon had called "two o'clock in the morning courage." He was still not sure that victory had been as complete as his corps commanders insisted. "What does he fight battles for?" intrepid Forrest asked in disgust. So the Confederates spent the night on the gory battlefield, and the last opportunity for a great Southern strategic victory flickered, then disappeared.

The cost to both sides in casualties was dreadfully high. As might be expected, during their headlong assaults on both days, the Confederates lost far more than the defending Federal troops, while Thomas' valiant rear guard action and Bragg's subsequent moral collapse lost a Southern opportunity to inflict greater losses on the fleeing foe. The Army of the Cumberland lost 1,657 men killed, 9,756 wounded and a staggering 4,757 missing, for a total of 16,179. Bragg's Army of Tennessee had 2,312 killed, 14,674 wounded and 1,486 missing; a total casualty toll of 18,454. The North could not afford such a humiliating defeat, but the South could not afford such losses in return for a victory not fully exploited.

Once more official Washington was thrown into semi-hysteria as the result of a Union disaster. Frantic messages went off to Grant to send all the troops he could spare to reinforce Rosecrans. (Grant, immobilized in bed because of a fall from his horse, had already alerted several divisions, under Sherman, even before the messages reached him.) Two corps of the Army of the Potomac—Howard's XIth and Slocum's XIIth—were hastily marched north from the Rapidan, to be piled into railroad cars at Alexandria, Virginia. "Fighting Joe" Hooker was called back from obscurity to command this 12,000-man expeditionary force, which was then rushed west and south by railroad to augment the decimated Army of the Cumberland. The move—1,192 miles by rail—was completed to Bridgeport, thirty miles from Chattanooga, in six days.

But there they stayed—because Chattanooga now was virtually besieged. Hooker's men could probably have marched into the city, though this is not at all certain. But their arrival would merely have added 12,000 mouths to feed, where more than 30,000 fighting men were already on half rations.

Bragg, having recovered somewhat from his funk of September 20, had eventually pushed his army to the outskirts of Chattanooga. The mountains to the east, south and west of the city had been seized and entrenched by the Confederates. The railroad to Bridgeport had been cut and was held by Southern troops, supported by great batteries of menacing guns dug in on the heights of Lookout Mountain. Similarly, powerful entrenchments and artillery on Missionary Ridge effectively cut any possible communications with Burnside, who had reached Knoxville. Only the muddy, almost impassable mountain road leading north across the Tennessee River from Chattanooga was still in Federal hands. It was soon discovered that the shortest approach over this winding road to the nearest railroad in Federal hands—Bridgeport— was sixty miles, and that this was virtually impassable to wagons. Mules and horses attempting such a route could barely carry enough forage to feed themselves on the road. It was impossible for the Union army to march north from Chattanooga; it could not have been supplied, even if there had been enough supplies in the city to support such a movement. Only individual messengers, or small bodies of armed men could negotiate the difficult mountain track. Rosecrans and his army, it appeared, would soon suffer the same fate that had befallen Pemberton and the garrison of Vicksburg.

The Army of the Ohio, in Knoxville, was hardly better off. Like the road from Bridgeport to Chattanooga, Burnside's supply route through the Cumberland Gap was studded with the corpses of mules and horses, and the wreckage of wagons. It was clear that large armies could not be supplied in autumn over the mud roads of eastern Tennessee.

Gloom and despair in Washington grew heavier. After high hopes and great promise, two Union armies were on the verge of complete destruction. It was a far cry from the jubilation in the capital when, early in July, on the heels of the great victory at Gettysburg, the telegraph had carried Grant's message of the surrender of Vicksburg. But the tired, patient man in the White House evidently remembered both the man and his message. For on October 9–10 Grant, in bed at Vicksburg (his smashed leg still painfully swollen), received a curt message dated October 3, to report to Cairo for further instructions. Rushing upriver by boat, he found (in treasure-hunt fashion), word that he was to go to Louisville. As his train passed through Indianapolis October 17, truculent, bearded War Secretary Stanton boarded it to clear up the mystery. Ulysses S. Grant had been placed in command of all Federal forces between the Mississippi and the Alleghenies, and the President desired that he give his personal attention to the crises at Chattanooga and Knoxville.

Arriving at Louisville on the seventeenth, Grant and Stanton next day received word that Rosecrans was contemplating a desperate and almost certainly disastrous retreat from Chattanooga. Grant, with the approval of Stanton, immediately sent a telegram relieving Rosecrans, and placing Thomas in command of the Army of the Cumberland. Thomas was directed to hold Chattanooga "at all hazards." The new commander of the Army of the Cumberland replied, promptly and characteristically, "We will hold the town until we starve." Grant now hastened to the beleaguered city. Reaching Bridgeport on October 21, he immediately mounted a horse, swollen leg and all, for the sixty-mile detour over the mountains to Chattanooga. Unable to walk without crutches, he had to be carried over some of the worst parts of the road, where the footing was too treacherous for men on horseback. He arrived at Chattanooga on the twenty-third. Then things began to happen.

Before dawn on October 27, a portion of Thomas' army slipped downstream from Chattanooga in pontoons, past Lookout Mountain, where the Confederate positions overlooked the hairpin bend in the river, to surprise the Confederate defenders at Brown's Ferry, on the road to Bridgeport. Simultaneously, Hooker's men struck from the west, to join forces, and the blockade was broken that simply. The pontoons were assembled into a bridge, and a few hours later a long supply train of food-laden wagons, which had accompanied Hooker, rumbled into the city to the cheers of the hungry soldiers waiting there. The men quickly called the new road the "cracker line." In a few days food was abundant, worn-out clothing and equipment had been replaced, and the meager store of ammunition had been replenished. The Army of the Cumberland was ready to fight again.

But though the blockade had been lifted, Bragg's powerful defenses effectively blocked any advance to the south or the east.

And Washington was now clamoring for Grant to do something to relieve Burnside, isolated in the Knoxville region. President Lincoln felt that Confederate reconquest of the loyal populace would be as great a disaster as the loss of Burnside's Army of the Ohio. And it now looked very much as though both of these calamities were likely.

Grant could only reply to the stream of messages from Lincoln, Stanton and Halleck, that he could do nothing to help Burnside until he could drive Bragg from the heights overlooking Chattanooga. Even with Hooker's arrival, his combat force was numerically inferior to Bragg's, who had the additional advantage of the most formidable fortified position which any army occupied during the entire war. Brag considered the position impregnable, and so reported to Richmond. Grant may not have shared this opinion but he refused to attempt any sort of offensive until Sherman—whom he had ordered overland with the 20,000 veterans of the Army of the Tennessee—arrived from Memphis.

Things had been difficult for Bragg in the days immediately following Chickamauga. He had not been well—evidently he suffered from ''nervous stomach''—and his principal subordinates had come close to outright mutiny as a result of their disgust at his timidity after Perryville, after Stones River, and now after Chickamauga. Following the last battle, several of his generals, led by Longstreet and Buckner, had signed a round robin letter to President Davis pleading that Bragg be relieved, on account of his ''ill health.'' Davis personally came down to observe the army in its entrenchments outside of Chattanooga, and held a conference with Bragg and his generals. Despite the obvious dissatisfaction of officers and men, Davis kept his old friend in command, and returned to Richmond.

But as the weeks went by, Bragg's confidence returned—even if his army's did not. So sure was he of the strength of his positions, that, on November 4, he sent Longstreet and 20,000 men north to crush Burnside and reconquer east Tennessee. He still had at least 40,000 men manning the trenches on the heights

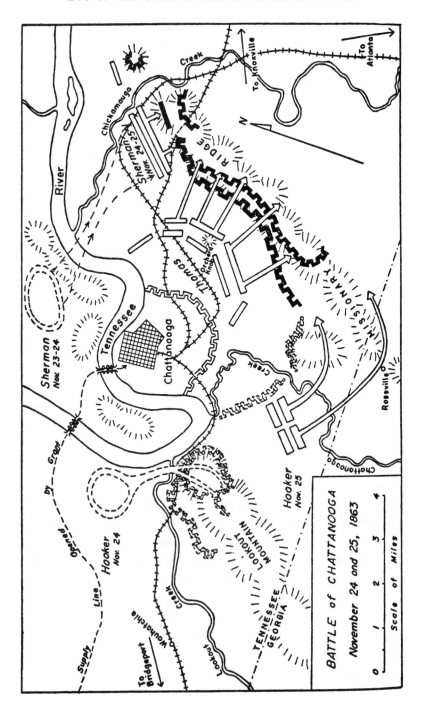

BATTLE of CHATTANOOGA
November 24 and 25, 1863

overlooking Chattanooga, sufficient to repulse more than three times their number of Union attackers. Furthermore, he and Longstreet didn't get along, and so the expedition to Knoxville would not only further the cause of the Confederacy, it would relieve some of the tensions in the Army of Tennessee.

Meanwhile Grant was making all possible preparations to start an offensive as soon as Sherman arrived. The roads were muddy, the supply lines were uncertain, and much of the country was hostile, but Sherman could be relied upon. (And in fact, despite the conditions, Sherman was to complete in twenty-five days a march from Iuka that Buell, after about sixty days of marching in the fine summer weather of 1862, had never finished.)

While waiting, Grant made a personal reconnaissance of every stretch of the front lines, made plans, and even issued orders for an attack, leaving blank only hours and dates, since these depended upon the weather and upon Sherman's arrival.

Grant, who remarks dryly that "the most friendly relations seemed to exist between the pickets of the two armies," recounts several interested and amusing experiences during the four weeks he was waiting at Chattanooga. One of these deserves retelling. Shortly after his arrival Grant visited the pickets of his army at the point where Chattanooga Creek enters the Tennessee River, at the foot of Lookout Mountain. The Confederate pickets were just a few yards beyond, on the south bank of the little stream.

"As I would be under short-range fire and in open country," Grant wrote, "I took nobody with me . . . When I came to the camp of the picket guard of our side, I heard the call, 'Turn out the guard for the commanding general.' I replied, 'Never mind the guard,' and they were dismissed and went back to their tents. Just back of these, and about equally distant from the creek, were the guards of the Confederate pickets. The sentinel on their post called out in like manner, 'Turn out the guard for the commanding general,' and, I believe, added, 'General Grant.' Their line in a moment front-faced to the north, facing me and gave a salute, which I returned.''

Relations along the outpost line were somewhat less friendly, however, on November 23, when Sherman, despite the delays of torrential rain, arrived at Brown's Ferry and crossed the pontoon bridge to a concealed position north of Chattanooga. Grant at once commenced the operations he had so long planned. He now had 61,000 effective combat troops, opposed to Bragg's well-entrenched 40,000.

As a preliminary to a major assault on Bragg's positions, Thomas on the twenty-third drove back the Confederate outposts from the plain between the city, and Missionary Ridge to the east. This action was successful, and the Southerners withdrew about a mile, to the foot of the steep ridge. Grant had no intention of assaulting the main Confederate position here, with its lacework of entrenchments in two defensive lines, the uppermost over five hundred feet above the plain. He merely wanted to obtain more maneuver room, and to attract Bragg's attention and reserves to the center of his line, because the Union battle plan contemplated a double envelopment early on the twenty-fourth.

Hooker, with his two corps from the Army of the Potomac, and one division of Sherman's army, was to clear the Confederates from Lookout Mountain, then cross the valley of Chattanooga Creek and strike the left extremity of the Missionary Ridge fortifications. Sherman, without even a day of rest, crossing the Tennessee River before the dawn, was to strike the right flank of the Missionary Ridge position simultaneously.

Sherman executed a brilliant river-crossing in the dark, and pressed vigorously against the steep hills on the Confederate right. But the Southerners were better prepared than Grant had expected, and General Pat Cleburne, of Hardee's corps, fought stubbornly and valiantly. By their numerical superiority Sherman's soldiers were able to push Cleburne's men back from their more advanced entrenchments, but by nightfall the situation had stabilized without any severe threat to the main position of Bragg's right flank.

Hooker, on the Union right, was more successful. Bragg had weakened his army by sending Longstreet away, and did not have enough men to hold his long line adequately. In order to be sure of retaining the key positions at Missionary Ridge, he could spare only two to three thousand men to garrison the towering rampart of Lookout Mountain, on his left. Hooker's augmented force, about 15,000 strong, swarmed up the precipitous sides of the mountain against relatively light resistance from the spreadout Southerners. As Hooker's men scrambled up into a low-lying mist, romantic Northern newspaper reporters dubbed the action "the Battle Above the Clouds," but it was not much of a battle. The difficulties of the climb created more delay than the outnumbered defenders could impose. By dark, the mountain was securely in Union hands, but Bragg's main position was still as powerful as ever.

In reply to a telegraph message from Grant reporting the results of the fighting of the twenty-third and twenty-fourth, President Lincoln replied: "Well done . . . remember Burnside." To make sure Grant would not forget, Halleck telegraphed: "I congratulate you . . . I fear that Burnside is hard pushed, and that any further delay may prove fatal."

That night Grant issued his orders for the next day. Sherman would again smash at Bragg's right, while Hooker was to descend from Lookout Mountain, cross Chattanooga Creek and strike the Southern left. Thomas and the Army of the Cumberland, under Grant's immediate supervision, would stand fast in the center until the double envelopment was well under way.

Sherman attacked with vigor, and again achieved some success, though the going was far slower than Grant had hoped. But Bragg sent strong reinforcements to his right flank, and by noon Sherman had been stopped completely. Grant in his turn sent a division from Thomas' army to Sherman's assistance but again this reinforcement was matched by Bragg, and by late afternoon it was obvious that the Union left had not seriously dented the Confederate right flank. Sherman, in fact, was hard pressed to hold the precarious positions he had gained.

Hooker's progress was equally disappointing to Grant. There was a delay of four hours in crossing Chattanooga Creek. By late afternoon he had hardly been able to begin skirmishing against the left flank of the Missionary Ridge position.

Grant had not intended to allow Thomas to move forward until Hooker had struck the Confederate left, and Bragg's army had become seriously engaged on both its flanks. It had been his plan that the Army of the Cumberland would merely keep the Confederate center busy enough to prevent Bragg from reinforcing his flanks once these were engaged; he had no intention of attempting a desperate assault against the 500-foot rampart of Missionary Ridge. But it was necessary to do something to relieve the growing Confederate pressure on Sherman, and Hooker's army did not look as though it would be able to do this before nightfall. Grant ordered Thomas to move forward in a limited attack, to engage the Confederate first line at the base of the ridge.

Grant and Thomas stood on a small hill, known as Orchard Knob, close to the center of the line of the Army of the Cumberland. They had practically a grandstand view of the army's spectacular advance, almost 20,000 strong, moving forward in a long blue line, rank after rank, battle flags flying, eagerly responsive to the long-awaited order. Despite heavy fire from the serried Confederate lines, the army swept forward, up the slight slope at the base of the ridge, and into the first line of trenches. In the face of this irresistible advance, the Confederate defenders ran back to the next line, high above.

Now occurred one of the most amazing episodes of the Civil War. There has never been a fully satisfactory explanation of what happened. Without orders, the whole line of the Army of the Cumberland suddenly heaved itself out of the captured trenches and began chasing the Confederates up the hill. It was as though an unspoken thought had suddenly communicated itself to each man in each unit. In some regiments the officers led the advance; in others they vainly tried to halt the unordered assault. It didn't matter. In a long, ragged line, battle flags still in the lead, the army climbed up that steep slope, facing fierce Confederate fire without flinching, apparently with utter disregard of losses.

This was an army with several scores to settle; with the enemy, with themselves, with the other two armies under Grant's command, and with Grant himself. In their last battle they had been humiliatingly defeated. And now, obviously not trusted by Grant, they had been given a minor role while the men of the Army of Tennessee and of the Army of the Potomac had been assigned the major tasks. For almost two days they had fretted at the foot of that hill, waiting for an order which they thought would never come.

Grant watched this movement with mounting alarm. He turned to Thomas and asked who had ordered the attack. Thomas replied that he hadn't. Helpless, cigar gripped firmly between his teeth, Grant watched the unprecedented spectacle of mass psychology.

And from an even better grandstand, half of Bragg's army was also observing. Unable to depress their guns sufficiently, the Southerners could not bring to bear the kind of artillery fire that had stopped so many assaults by both sides during the war. And musket fire didn't seem to be slowing the advancing Federals at all. Now mass psychology began to work on the Confederate side. As they watched the vast panorama spread beneath them, the great lines of troops advancing with apparently unstoppable ardor, their bayonets twinkling in the setting sun, Southern veterans were seized by a panic they had never before experienced. Suddenly the gray-clad soldiers began to jump out of their trenches, to run back over the crest of the ridge, and down on the far side. Bragg and his other officers vainly tried to check this tide of disaster. In a few minutes it was all over, with most of the Confederate army, officers and men, running away in terror, sweeping Bragg and his staff along with them.

General Pat Cleburne now played the role which Thomas had performed over this same ground more than two months before. A valiant, effective rear guard action kept Sheridan's pursuing division from achieving much success before early autumn darkness closed in. And most of the Army of the Cumberland, dancing jubilantly on the heights they had just stormed, were too excited to be effectively reorganized for pursuit.

For all its decisiveness, the number of troops engaged, and the duration of the battle, casualties had not been as heavy as might be expected. So far as the Federal forces were concerned, this was largely due to the care with which Grant had prepared his plans, and his refusal to take unnecessary risks with the lives of his men. The Confederates, of course, had suffered relatively little during their defensive actions, and lost most of their casualties by capture, on the twenty-fourth at Lookout Mountain, and on the twenty-fifth after the rout of the center. Grant lost 753 killed, 4,722 wounded, and 349 missing; a total of 5,824. Bragg's losses were 361 killed, 2,160 wounded, and 4,146 missing; a total of 6,667.

Grant did not feel that he could afford the time or forces necessary for pursuit the next day. The stream of messages from Washington left him no choice but to move immediately to the relief of Burnside at Knoxville. He could not risk sending his army in two directions at once. He had initially ordered the Army of the Cumberland to relieve Burnside. He had now come to the conclusion, however, that for all of his stubbornness on the defense, Thomas had neither the aggressiveness or initiative to handle an urgent independent mission. Once more Grant turned to his old Army of Tennessee and his ever-reliable friend Sherman.

Sherman's men slept on the battlefield. Starting at dawn on November 26, Sherman arrived at Knoxville on December 6, to find that Longstreet had abandoned the siege on the fourth. Burnside and his army were safe; the loyal inhabitants of east Tennessee were securely retained by the Union.

Now Grant could turn his attention to the more important strategic challenge—stepping through the newly-opened gateway to the eastern Confederacy.

# 20

# The Union Navy Tightens the Noose

It is high time we turn our eyes seaward. Along the vast coastline extending from the mouth of Chesapeake Bay around the tip of Florida into the Gulf of Mexico, and on the broad reaches of both the Atlantic and Pacific Oceans, another type of warfare was being waged. It ran its course in boredom and vexation; in long months of weary waiting punctuated now and again by brief but violent action. Its individual effects—with some few exceptions, which we shall note—were lost in the more spectacular action on land, for that is the way of sea power. The cumulative effect was to bar the Southern Confederacy from the foreign resources on which it depended. Without application of sea power the North would indeed have been hard put to win the war.

Until the end came, the South did what it could to change the situation. Its maritime resistance took three forms; privateering, commerce destruction, and an amazing development in armor-clad and submarine vessels, and in submarine mining.

The first phase—privateering—was short lived. A few Union coastal vessels were surprised on the high seas off the coast, causing some panic in Northern shipping circles. But the lightly armed converted merchantmen manned by civilian crews were, of course, no match for the Union Navy vessels gathering off Confederate ports in ever increasing numbers. The Hatteras Inlet expedition of August, 1861, already mentioned, virtually ended Southern privateering by depriving Pamlico Sound to the Confederates.

Commerce destruction by vessels of the Confederate Navy, beginning with the cruise of the CSS *Sumter* (see page 41), was something else again. It would have a far-reaching effect on the United States merchant marine, and will be taken up in detail later. For the moment, we are interested in a series of operations along the Atlantic coast, stemming from the Union blockade.

As 1862 opened, the Federal Navy, with the Army cooperating, went about the business of further clearing the North Carolina sounds—the back-door to Norfolk and Richmond. Flag Officer Louis M. Goldsborough led an amphibious expedition from Hampton Roads down through Hatteras Inlet and north to Roanoke Island, where Confederate batteries and a mosquito fleet controlled the gut between Pamlico and the Albemarle Sounds. With the force went General Burnside and 12,000 Army troops.

A flotilla of eighteen light-draft warships on February 7, cleared the southern craft away and bombarded the Roanoke Island batteries. Burnside's troops, landing on the island unopposed, captured the garrison next day. Federal control of the inland waterways was thus assured. Norfolk was deprived of its major supply of pork, corn and forage; Richmond no longer had any nearby convenient blockade-runner bases. But a final objective—an Army drive towards Raleigh to cut the Richmond-Charleston rail line—went by the board when McClellan recalled Burnside's command for the Peninsular campaign.

Meanwhile, south of Savannah and all the way to Cape Canaveral, Florida, the Unoin naval forces under Rear Admiral

Du Pont had been occupying islands and ports. Under these circumstances the entire Confederate plan for coastal defense had had to be reassessed in late 1861. General Lee, who at that time commanded the coastal area, decided as soon as Port Royal fell to Du Pont, that Southern major defense lines must be withdrawn inland out of Northern naval reach, except for the strongholds of Charleston and Savannah, and Fort Fisher, which protected the Cape Fear entrances to Wilmington, North Carolina. These ports, together with Mobile, Alabama, on the Gulf of Mexico, were now becoming the major termini of the blockade-runners, and therefore objectives for Northern naval action.

The fortifications at these key ports were strengthened. Mines—''torpedoes'' they called them in those days—were laid extensively in the various approach channels. Most of these mines were of the impact type; detonated by percussion caps which exploded when a ship's bottom scraped them. In some cases mines were detonated by electrical—and unreliable—control from shore. Here was the birth of submarine mining; crude and inefficient, perhaps, but brilliant in concept and improvisation. Mines became a major hazard to all Union naval operations against Southern seaports.

Hampered by lack of raw material and technological resources, Confederate iron-clad construction nevertheless went on apace, while resourceful minds were also experimenting with submarine boats; both with astounding results. Meanwhile the blockade-runners and their vital cargoes must be assured safe harbor in Confederate ports.

Blockade-running was becoming big business. Before the war, the governments of England, Holland, France and Spain collected annually a total of $64,000,000 in taxes on imports of Southern tobacco. Southern cotton exports to England in pre-war days amounted each year to $150,000,000. ''King Cotton'' was the basis of livelihood for some five million British subjects in the mill-towns of the Midlands. Cotton could still be purchased in the South for less than ten cents a pound, and each pound delivered overseas netted fifty cents. In Nassau, salt was worth $7.50 a ton; delivered in Richmond, it brought $1,700. Coffee, bought in Nassau at $240 a ton, sold in Richmond for $5,500. And all this time Confederate agents abroad were crying for shoes, clothing, blankets, hats, medicines, lead, artillery and small arms.

Here were all the ingredients for European prosperity. A one-way cargo trip in either direction promised a financial harvest; a round-trip could be a bonanza. It is small wonder, then, that European ingenuity set about devising schemes to pierce the floating curtain of weather-beaten Union warships which barred eager traders from such wealth.

Some idea of the profits to be made in the traffic may be gained when it is realized that the average fast, specially designed blockade-runner could earn $172,000 a month. The expenses, including marine insurance issued in London at a 25 percent premium, would run approximately to $80,000, leaving a net profit of $92,000. Under such conditions an owner could afford the loss of a ship and cargo after two successful voyages.

In England, particularly, merchants and ship-builders combined to make blockade-running a profitable business. Clyde ship-yards began turning out a special type of craft by the score. This was a sharp-lined, lightly sparred vessel of from four to six hundred tons, with low freeboard; usually driven by paddle-wheels of "feathering" type to cut down noise. She could make at least fourteen knots speed. Her funnel or funnels—some had two—could be telescoped down to the rail. Burning anthracite coal of highest grade—exported from Pennsylvania to British ports—she emitted little smoke, and her steam exhausts were blown underwater.

A vessel of this type, painted a dull gray, was difficult to sight even by day. At night, with all lights doused, she slipped ghostlike through the seas, practically invisible to the keenest lookout. Evasion and speed were the blockade-runners' weapons. So it was not long before the specially-constructed vessels began to replace the hodge-podge collection of both steam and sailing craft which first entered the trade.

Southern patriotism played small part in this multi-million dollar business. Confederate government-owned and manned vessels were but a minuscule portion of the blockade-running fleet, most of which flew the British flag.

Like all black-market ventures, blockade-running attracted not only the daring but also the unscrupulous. Oily *entrepreneurs* flourished in the Southern seaports, fattening on the misfortunes of their fellows; individuals of similar ilk up North made no bones about trading with the Confederacy through devious channels.

There was no lack of experienced sailors to man these vessels. Mariners familiar with the coastal waters flocked to win high rewards. A captain got $5,000 per month; a deckhand or fireman $200; wages unheard of in normal merchant marine circles at that time. Among the skippers were comparatively few Americans. A special group consisted of Royal Navy officers, officially on leave, who were averse neither to turning an honest penny nor to the lure of a spot of derring-do.

One can gauge the scope of the traffic by noting that in 1861 the Union Navy captured nearly 150 ships; that by June, 1863, 885 vessels had been bagged; and by 1865, some 1,500 craft in all had been gathered in. Yet during all this period the traffic never lagged, as the clever runners sought and found holes in the necessarily wide-meshed Federal net. In this, of course, they were materially aided from time to time by sorties of Confederate Navy ships, by chance encounters between Southern commerce-destroyers and Union blockaders, and by coastal military operations.

Sleepy little Nassau in Britain's Bahama Islands, becoming the focal point for the new trade, mushroomed into a roaring, ship-filled seaport with preferential treatment granted to the blockade-runners; rebates on port charges and on customs duty. From Nassau the ships plied to Charleston and Wilmington—each an approximate five hundred miles away. Bermuda, too, and Halifax, Nova Scotia, handled a share of this traffic, while a secondary stream flowed from Havana, Cuba, to Mobile on the Gulf, and to Matamoras, Mexico, at the mouth of the Rio Grande, where contraband passed by flatboat to and from Brownsville, Texas. When the Mississippi River fell under Federal control the Havana-Matamoras trade began to dry up. Nassau, however, maintained its activity until the end of the war.

It soon became evident to the Union Navy that the only really effective way to stop blockade-running was to capture the Southern ports. Of these Charleston loomed large in Federal eyes as the most important. In fact, since Charleston was rightly considered as the birthplace of the Confederacy, and hence anathema to every supporter of the Union cause, an undue emphasis was placed upon its capture—somewhat to the detriment of operations against the other important termini of the blockade-running trade.

Equally, the defense of Charleston became a symbol in Southern eyes, and energies were bent upon supporting it and its defending commander, Beauregard. The utmost ingenuity was displayed—an ingenuity which would culminate in one of the most important developments in naval warfare: successful submarine boat attacks against surface warships.

# FORTRESS UNAFRAID

For a long time Admiral Du Pont resisted the pressure being placed on him to attack Charleston. He felt that a run-by, such as Farragut's at New Orleans, or his own attack on Port Royal, was simply impossible. ". . . The harbor," he pointed out, "is a bog, or *cul de sac*, to say nothing of obstructions. . . ." This attitude, it would seem, is the key to what happened when he was finally forced to attack the place.

The harbor mouth did bristle with defenses. On the right hand, as one approached it, lay Sullivan's Island, with an imposing cluster of fortifications built about old Fort Moultrie. To the left, on the northern tip of Morris Island, stood Forts Wagner and Gregg. Dead ahead and a good mile beyond these flanking batteries, lay Fort Sumter in the middle of the channel; renovated and heavily gunned. The Confederates could concentrate the fire of some 100 guns in a three-way cross-fire on any vessel daring the harbor mouth. Inside this array lay two additional layers of batteries, prepared to dispute progress all the way up to the city, four miles beyond.

Confederate General Beauregard, commanding at Charleston, had prepared its defenses with characteristic energy and thoroughness. Mines had been thickly sown in all the channels, and a boom of piles, logs, chains and ropes stretched between Forts Sumter and Moultrie, designed to hold incoming vessels indefinitely under the cross-fire. In addition, two iron-plated rams, CSS *Chicora* and *Palmetto State*, were prepared to fight it out in the bay with any vessel breaking through this barricade.

These two ships rocked Du Pont's flotilla January 31, 1863, when they dashed out under command of Flag Officer Ingraham, in an attempt to rescue a British blockade-runner which had been captured by Union vessels. They surprised and captured one Federal warship and crippled another before they were driven back by four other Union vessels. Du Pont, impressed, called for monitors to reinforce his squadron. He received several in February and tested them on February 28, against Fort McAllister on the Ogeechee River. During this action CSS *Nashville*, elusive commerce-destroyer and blockade-runner, was sunk. Although the ironclads passed their baptism of fire successfully, one of them was seriously damaged by a submarine mine. This confirmed Du Pont in his hesitancy to attack the even more formidable defenses of Charleston. However, with Washington insisting, he reluctantly stood in to the harbor on April 7, with an ironclad squadron of nine ships.

The Union column steamed by Morris Island without a shot being fired. The leading ship, reaching the channel boom at 2:10 P.M., slowed down to avoid fouling it and the line of ironclads

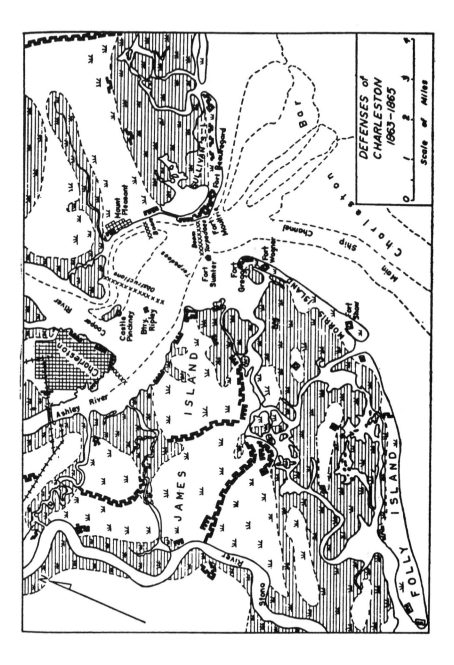

piled up in confusion—sitting ducks for the Confederate gunners, who now opened up from all the forts.

For nearly two hours the flotilla circled and bumped one another, in a crazy melée, and then Du Pont retired to report failure. His ships had been hit 400 times out of 2,200 rounds fired from the forts and had returned but 139 rounds in all the fray. Only one Union seaman was killed, but all the vessels had received severe pounding and one of them foundered that night. Gun turrets were jammed, plates badly broken, bolts sheered off wholesale.

All the while a force of 12,000 Federal troops under old General David Hunter, poised on Folly Island five miles south of Fort Wagner, had remained immobile.

This fiasco added no luster to Union arms. While the Confederacy rejoiced, the North added another bead to its rosary of sorrows. Lincoln, wisely fearing the psychological effect of the repulse, promptly ordered Du Pont to remain inside of Charleston bar. This he did, maintaining the blockade with his wooden ships, while the ironclads were sent to Port Royal for refitting.

In early July Du Pont was relieved by Rear Admiral John A. Dahlgren. General Hunter was also replaced; Major General Quincy Adams Gillmore—brilliant engineer and artilleryman—took over his command. On July 10, the Dahlgren-Gillmore team went into action. For some two months Fort Wagner was incessantly bombarded and attacked in joint efforts to reduce it. Several assaults were repulsed with sanguinary losses. In one of these, on July 18, Colonel Robert Gould Shaw, commanding the 54th Massachusetts Volunteers, the first Negro troops from a free state to be mustered into Federal service, was killed while leading his regiment in a charge on the ramparts.

A final attack started September 5. For forty-two hours USS *New Ironsides* drenched the Confederate works with her 11-inch shells. On the night of September 6, as the Federal troops on shore massed for assault, the garrison evacuated the fort. Landing expeditions were sent in then, to attack Fort Sumter, but were repulsed by gallant, determined defenders, even though the fort itself was reduced to rubble by Union naval guns.

With the occupation of Fort Wagner, Charleston's importance as a blockade-runner's haven diminished. When Beauregard rejected demands for surrender, long-range Union Army guns bombarded the city and waterfront, while the incessant activities of the Federal Navy's ironclads cruising the channels further tightened the blockade. Confederate ingenuity now turned to the submarine boat.

Theodore Stoney, of Charleston, contructed at private expense a peculiar cigar-shaped single-screw vessel, propelled by steam. This quasi-submarine boat floated submerged except for her smokestack and central cockpit two feet high. She was designed to carry before her, on a long, maneuverable spar, a copper-cased torpedo containing some sixty pounds of explosive, fused to detonate on impact. Christened CSS *David*, she went into action October 5, 1863, under command of Lieutenant W. T. Glassell, CSN, with a crew of three other daring souls. Glassell, fearing that his torpedo attack might be considered beyond the pale of lawful war, carried with him one "conentional" weapon—a shotgun.

That evening the lookout on *New Ironsides*, as she lay inside Charleston bar, discovered a low-lying object approaching. His hail was answered by Glassell's shotgun, as the odd-shaped craft made for the ironclad at high speed. Seconds later the torpedo exploded under the Northern flagship's stern, doing extensive damage. The assailing craft disappeared from sight in the geyser of water spouting from the explosion. Federal small-boats searching the vicinity picked up two men; one of them Glassell. The other two men managed to hang on to the *David*, which remained afloat, though her boiler fire had been doused by water pouring down her smokestack. Amazingly, they re-ignited the fire and returned safely to rejoicing Charleston.

Charleston's defenders were not through assailing the Federal squadron blocking the harbor mouth. Down at Mobile in 1863 H. L. Hunley, of the firm of Hunley & McClintock, had designed and constructed a real submarine boat, provided with ballast tanks to govern submergence, and lateral fins to effect diving and resurfacing. The craft was powered by a propeller, hand-cranked by eight men. A ninth man was both skipper and torpedo officer, manipulating the "torpedo," or mine, she dragged after her. Her fatal defect was lack of means to store fresh air.

Named after her inventor, CSS *H. L. Hunley* on her first trial suffocated her entire crew. Nevertheless, she was shipped to General Beauregard for use at Charleston. There, in as many experimental runs she suffocated or drowned three more crews—including the inventor himself—to earn a ghoulish nickname: "The Peripatetic Coffin."

Lieutenant George E. Dixon, 21st Alabama Infantry, now volunteered, with a fifth crew of men as daring as himself, to take the submarine out again and attack USS *Housatonic*, wooden steam frigate, as she lay off Beach Inlet. Beauregard agreed, with the proviso the craft would attack on the surface only, using a spar torpedo like the *David*.

Discovered as he got close to the Federal ship, Dixon drove at her broadside. On board the *Housatonic* the alarm had been given, her cable slipped, and her engines were going full astern. But it was too late. *Hunley's* torpedo struck her on the starboard side, just forward of the mainmast, and exploded. With a great hole torn in her side, *Housatonic* sank in five minutes. Five of her people were killed by the explosion or by drowning; the remainder of the crew took to the rigging and were saved by other Union ships. This, on February 17, 1864, was the first sinking of a surface warship by a submarine boat.

But the "Peripatetic Coffin" lived up to her name. Swamped by the explosion, or dragged down by suction, *H. L.*

*Hunley* and her crew went down with her victim. When the harbor was later cleared of wreckage, both hulks were found; the Confederate submarine still pointing at the *Housatonic*, 100 feet away.

But despite these devoted Southern submariners, the Northern noose had forced the blockade-runners to forsake Charleston for Mobile and Wilmington. The city, however, held the invaders at bay for another year and a half, despite constant pounding from long-range Federal guns. Defiant Charleston and its indomitable commander had become a symbol of Southern determination, gallantry and ingenuity in the face of overwhelming odds.

# GUNBOATS IN THE RAPIDS

During the spring of 1864, while Charleston choked at the end of a Union Navy noose, Admiral Porter's Mississippi River gunboat flotilla engaged in a fantastic fight against both the Confederate Army and the elements of Nature. Federal General Banks took an expedition up the Red River valley in March. It was a joint Army-Navy affair, with Porter and eighteen gunboats—twelve of them armorclads, steaming up the Red River in supposed conjunction with Banks' 30,000 men on land. The objective of the Administration was to put Banks' troops into Texas by an overland route, as a hands-off warning to the Emperor Napoleon III of France, whose bayonets then controlled Mexico. As a secondary objective—also approved by the President—Porter was to escort civilian Northern cotton speculators bound on a prospectively lucrative foray.

At Alexandria, Louisiana, Porter with great difficulty got twelve of his gunboats over the rapids above the city, and the combined force got as far as Natchitoches and Grand Ecore. There Banks struck inland from the river, Shreveport bound. But with the usual Banks facility for getting into trouble, he was ambushed at Sabine Crossing, April 8, by Confederate Generals Richard Taylor and Edmond Kirby Smith and retreated back to Alexandria.

Porter, with a fast-dropping river under his gunboats' keels, and Confederate cavalry snap-shooting at him from the river-banks, got back to Alexandria to find the water over the rapids now but three feet deep, while his ironclads drew seven!

While Banks—perhaps reluctantly—obeyed the blunt or-ders of Grant—now in supreme command—to hold his ground at Alexandria until Porter could get out, troops and sailors delved on a fantastic scheme devised by Colonel Joseph Bailey, 4th Wisconsin Cavalry, an engineer in civil life. Some 3,000 men and 300 wagons labored to make cribs, transport stones and construct a dam. As the water rose, the lighter vessels got out.

Then the pressure washed out a central section of the dam, just as the ironclad *Lexington* was approaching the rapids. Porter hastily ordered the vessel to attempt the run anyway. With a full head of steam, she shot over the crest, rolled, bumped and twisted in the mile-long rapids, then rocked safely into the deep water beyond.

Colonel Bailey and his frantic workers now constructed a series of wing dams from the banks, to compress the channel. Through these flumes, May 13, the remaining six ironclads plunged in succession like a school of porpoises.

Next day Alexandria was evacuated. The Red River cam-paign was over, and the Union Navy could turn its attention to bigger business.

# Presidents and Generals

**B**y the beginning of 1864 the Presidents of the United States and of the Confederate States of America each had separately come to the crossroads of decision. Both men had taken upon their own shoulders the direction of their respective armed forces. Neither Lincoln the civilian nor Davis the soldier had as yet successfully solved his problem.

## MR. LINCOLN'S PROBLEMS

From the standpoint of President Lincoln the first days of July, 1863—with victories at Gettysburg and Vicksburg—seemed to presage an early and successful conclusion to the war which had dragged out for two long years. Then came Meade's failure to pursue Lee, and the Draft Riots in New York. For four red days, from July 13 to 16, a lawless mob had controlled the city and was only quelled by troops rushed up from the Army of the Potomac.

Meade's further indecision as he followed Lee back into Virginia disturbed the President. By mid-September Lee and Meade were facing one another in the old, familiar triangle between the Rapidan and the Rappahannock. All indications were that Longstreet's corps was moving West to reinforce Bragg. This left Lee with some 50,000 men to oppose Meade's 90,000 or more. Yet with all this superiority of force, Meade, to the President's annoyance, instead of taking the offensive queried Halleck for instructions.

Lincoln sat down and put his views on the situation in a letter which is probably the most remarkable military document ever written by a civilian. Its revelation of the operations of a logical, if unmilitary, mind, cause it to deserve the attention of every military man, as well as all students of the Civil War:

*Executive Mansion, Washington*
*September 19, 1863*

Major-General Halleck:

By General Meade's despatch to you of yesterday it appears that he desires your views and those of the government as to whether he shall advance upon the enemy. I am not prepared to order, or even advise, an advance in this case, wherein I know so little of particulars, and wherein he, in the field, thinks the risk is so great, and the promise of advantage so small.

And yet the case presents matters for very serious consideration in another aspect. These two armies confront each other across a small river, substantially midway between the two capitals, each defending its own capital, and menacing the other. General Meade estimates the enemy's infantry in front of him at not less than 40,000. Suppose we add fifty per cent to this for cavalry, artillery, and extra-duty men stretching as far as Richmond, making the whole force of the enemy 60,000.

General Meade, as shown by the returns, has with him, and between him and Washington, of the same classes of well men, over 90,000. Neither can bring the whole of his men into a battle; but each can bring as large a percentage in as the other. For a battle, then, General Meade has three men to General Lee's two. Yet, it having been determined that choosing ground and standing on the defensive gives so great advantage that the three cannot safely attack the two, the three are left simply standing on the defensive also.

If the enemy's 60,000 are sufficient to keep our 90,000 away from Richmond, why, by the same rule, may not 40,000 of ours keep their 60,000 away from Washington, leaving us 50,000 to put to some other use? Having practically come to the mere defensive, it seems to be no economy at all to employ twice as many men for that object as are needed. With no object, certainly, to mislead myself, I can perceive no fault in this statement, unless we admit we are not the equal of the enemy, man for man. I hope you will consider it.

To avoid misunderstanding, let me say that to attempt to fight the enemy slowly back into his intrenchments at Richmond, and then to capture him, is an idea I have been trying to repudiate for quite a year.

My judgment is so clear against it that I would scarcely allow the attempt to be made if the general in command should desire to make it. My last attempt upon Richmond was to get McClellan, when he was nearer there than the enemy was, to run in ahead of him. Since then I have constantly desired the Army of the Potomac to make Lee's army, and not Richmond, its objective point. If our army cannot fall upon the enemy and hurt him where he is, it is plain to me it can gain nothing by attempting to follow him over a succession of intrenched lines into a fortified city.

Yours truly,

A. LINCOLN

But the day the President thus revealed his grasp of strategic fundamentals, events were taking place south of Chattanooga that were to affect the situation in Virginia. The Battle of Chickamauga had begun. By evening of September 20, 1863, Lincoln knew that Rosecrans had been severely defeated, and it soon became evident that the Army of the Cumberland was in a desperate situation, practically besieged in Chattanooga.

Now the President put into action the thoughts expressed in his letter. Meade, inactive in central Virginia, had more men than he needed. The President ordered two corps from Meade's army to Chattanooga. Then he sent Grant to make sure these men were put to good use.

Taking advantage of this reduction in Meade's strength, Lee, on October 9, began crossing the Rapidan south of Cedar Mountain, then marched west and north to turn the right flank of the Union army. As soon as the Southern move was detected, Meade gave immediate orders for a retreat northward, to protect his line of communication. The Southerners marched fast— though not as they had under Jackson and Longstreet—but the Northern army, retiring up the railroad on interior lines, and under good control, was able to move faster.

At Bristoe Station, not far from the old Bull Run battlefields, on October 14, in a brisk action, Lee's leading corps was repulsed. Having lost his opportunity to strike the Union army at a disadvantage, Lee now retired to the Rappahannock-Rapidan triangle. Meade, following him back to Mine Run, abandoned further offensive movement after several sharp but indecisive encounters, and went into winter quarters north of the Rapidan.

During December the President gave much thought to the operations of the coming year. If the war continued to drag on in 1864 as it had in 1863, there was a good chance that the Administration would lose the elections in the fall. There can be no question that Lincoln was more concerned about possible recognition of the Confederacy by a Democratic administration than he was about the personal consequences of such an electoral defeat.

By a process of elimination, two capable and successful Union generals had emerged as the men who would lead the most important armies in the coming year: Grant and Meade. But five months of inconclusive maneuvering had clearly proven that Meade—a competent, workmanlike soldier—was too cautious, too unimaginative, and too respectful of Lee's prowess to do more than continue the stalemate in Virginia. Grant probably could command the Army of the Potomac much more capably. But if he were to be taken from the West, who would command there? Meade's limitations would certainly not permit him to be more successful in the larger theater south and west of the Appalachians.

Another related problem was the need for coordination of the efforts of all of the Union armies. With the minor exception of the dispatch of Hooker to Chattanooga, the Union forces west of the Appalachians and those in Virginia might have been separated by oceans—rather than by a narrow mountain range—for all the effect their respective operations had on each other, or on the opposing Confederate armies.

But having noted the lost opportunities resulting from lack of over-all coordination and direction, the President must have been favorably impressed by the results Grant achieved so quickly in Tennessee, after he was given over-all control of forces west of the Appalachians. Would it not be possible to coordinate on an even larger scale?

Halleck had proven himself as a good administrator, but this still did not provide for really competent military planning by a man who could make military decisions on military grounds— with due regard, of course, for over-all policy to be set by the President and his civilian Secretary of War.

Such thinking was bound to lead Lincoln to a decision with which he had been toying, perhaps only partly consciously, ever since May of 1863. It appeared that there was, after all, one Union general who had the qualities required in a real General-in-Chief; a fitting successor to the position of old General Scott, rather than the glorified clerical status with which Halleck appeared to be content.

Grant was the man! To his hands could safely be entrusted the responsibility for both Eastern and Western theaters. Having reached this decision, probably in December of 1863, the President moved cautiously to set the stage for Grant's appointment in a way that would be most acceptable to the Army, to the politicians, and to the public. Events of the previous three years had made him realize the importance of psychological factors both on a commander, and on the willingness with which his subordinates cooperated with him. Lincoln was aware that false rumors about Grant's supposed drunkenness had appeared in the press, and had been whispered around Washington. He felt it would be harmful to Grant and to the country if these allegations were to become issues subsequent to Grant's appointment as General-in-Chief.

It became known to influential members of Congress that the President favored restoration of the rank of Lieutenant General— previously held only by George Washington and (as a brevet) by Winfield Scott. Once created, the rank would naturally go to the Army's General-in-Chief. Was it intended for Halleck? No, whispered the insiders; it would go to Grant—the hero of Vicksburg and Chattanooga. Introduced in February, the measure to recreate the rank was passed overwhelmingly by both Houses on February twenty-ninth. With this vote of confidence behind him Mr. Lincoln signed the measure into law on March 1, and two days later Grant was ordered to Washington.

Grant, of course, had been aware that the result of this Congressional activity would affect him personally. The whole country knew it. So with more than passing interest he had noted a fantastic cavalry raid taking place in Virginia at this time.

Brigadier General Judson Kilpatrick with 4,000 horses

slipped past Lee's right flank on February 28, bound for Richmond. An advance party of 500, under Colonel Ulric Dahlgren, would circle wide, cross the James and enter the Southern capital from the south. On hearing the tumult of Dahlgren's entry, Kilpatrick would attack from the north and join him in the city. The objective: to free 15,000 Union prisoners of war, spread copies of a recent Presidential amnesty proclamation, create confusion, and generally do as much incidental damage as possible behind the Confederate lines.

It was a hare-brained scheme, even though Richmond was at that time virtually unprotected; Meade permitted it only because so ordered by Washington. Poorly planned and coordinated, it was a dismal failure. Dahlgren never reached the James; his party was ambushed and scattered and he himself was killed. Kilpatrick, in front of Richmond, hung about vainly for a day, then was put to flight by alerted Confederate militia and chased back down to Fort Monroe.

But the worst aspect came from papers allegedly found on Dahlgren's body. Purportedly notes he used in explaining the mission to his men, their gist went far beyond the original objective: in addition to releasing the prisoners, the raiders were "to destroy and burn the hateful city" and to kill "the rebel leader, Davis, and his traitorous [cabinet]."

Publication of these papers enflamed the entire South and caused consternation in the North. Lee, sending photographic copies to Meade, inquired if they properly represented United States Government aims. Meade, after prompt and impartial investigation, in good conscience replied that "neither the United States Government, myself, nor General Kilpatrick authorized, sanctioned, or approved" the alleged objectives "nor any other act not required by military necessity and in accordance with the usages of war."

There now appears to be little doubt that the documents were either forgeries or alterations of the original version jotted down by Dahlgren. Whether or not this was done with the knowledge or connivance of Confederate officialdom is unknown. The validity of the Dahlgren documents is still a subject for violent debate amongst Civil War "buffs." But at the time the papers were of inestimable propaganda value in the South, arousing popular opinion against Northern "barbarians."

Grant, on his way to Washington as the newspapers flared with this sensational affair, had reason to ponder on the value of aimless, fruitless cavalry dashes about the countryside.

On March 9, Grant met the President and received his appointments as Lieutenant General and General-in-Chief. Their conversation revealed to the President that his three-year search for a general was ended. This man knew what to do and how to go about it.

To Grant came assurance of complete responsibility for and complete authority over the armed forces. Lincoln put his assurances later in writing:

"The particulars of your plan I neither know nor seek to know . . . I wish not to obtrude any constraints or restraints upon you . . . If there is anything wanting which is within my power to give, do not fail to let me know it."

By mid-March Grant's plan was ready for implementation. It envisaged a gigantic turning movement, embracing half a continent as maneuver area. Meade's Army of the Potomac would engage Lee's army in unceasing conflict, while the Western Federal armies, under Sherman, would sweep from Chattanooga through the deep South, inflicting, as he wrote Sherman, "all the damage you can against their war resources . . ." All other Union forces, along the seacoast and in the interior, would operate in close coordination with the two main armies.

Here was total war; designed—in combination with the naval blockade—to bring Northern superiority in manpower and productivity fully to bear against an opponent who would be granted no opportunity to rest nor to shift forces from one threatened area to another.

Grant recognized that Lee was the most dangerous adversary. So he would "stay with the Army of the Potomac and operate directly against Lee's army wherever it may be found . . . ," while keeping constantly in touch with the President and the Secretary of War. There was always the telegraph to maintain communications. This decision was all the more easy since Grant hated Washington with its political whirlpools and administrative bogs. Halleck, who loved the job, would continue as chief of staff to attend to the paper work.

Meade had tactfully suggested that Grant might wish a new commander for the Army of the Potomac. Grant had not intended to replace the hero of Gettysburg, and Meade's self-effacing suggestion made Grant respect this competent soldier even more. Relations between the two were always cordial and efficient. If Meade resented the fact that his Army of the Potomac soon became known as "Grant's army," he never showed it.

Two changes, however, Grant made at the outset. With the Kilpatrick-Dahlgren fiasco in mind, and his own reluctant admiration for Confederate Nathan Bedford Forrest's efficient cavalry leadership, he demanded "a thorough leader . . . the best man in the army," to weld his cavalry arm into a working combat organization; disciplined, fast-moving, hard-striking. Philip H. Sheridan was the choice.

Grant's second change was one popular indeed to the combat soldiers of the Army of the Potomac. Out from their billets in the Washington garrison were cleared the "homesteaders"—the heavy artillerymen, the orderlies, the cavalry escorts—who had been living a life of ease far from mud and bullets. Literally in thousands, these "coffee-coolers" found themselves dumped unceremoniously into the muddy Rappahannock cantonments and transformed into fighting men—mostly in the infantry.

War had suddenly become a serious business for every man in United States Army uniform. It would remain such for almost a year.

# MR. DAVIS' PROBLEMS

Unlike Lincoln, Davis was not concerned about matters of overall direction and control. He was confident of his own ability as a one-time professional soldier, as a former Chairman of the Military Affairs Committee of the U.S. Senate, and as a successful U.S. Secretary of War, to supervise and direct the military operations and administration of the Confederacy. What worried him, however, were the shortcomings of his generals, with the significant exception of course, of Robert E. Lee.

Davis shared the universal Confederate admiration for "Marse Robert." If he had the slightest twinges of jealousy of the great general, whose popularity far exceeded his own, the President hid it successfully. But Lee, in Davis' eyes, while "first among equals," was still only one of several department commanders. Nor did Lee by any word or act ever imply that he was even thinking beyond his own responsibilities as Commander of the Army of Northern Virginia. Carefully and sincerely he remained subservient to civilian authority.

What to do about Bragg was something else. The warm personal friendship dating from Buena Vista, in the Mexican War—when the military reputation, and probably the very life of each man had depended on the exceptional heroism and fighting qualities of the other—could never be dissolved. But Davis had been disappointed in his old comrade-in-arms as a general. The first flaw had been Bragg's inexplicable retreat during the successful invasion of Kentucky. Then came the defeat at Murfreesboro and the abandonment of Chattanooga. In the face of most violent criticism Davis had sustained his general at that time and sent him the reinforcements with which he later won at Chickamauga. But Bragg had then lagged outrageously by failing to pursue and reap the fruits of victory.

But the defeat at Missionary Ridge had been too much. The only reason the President had delayed in relieving Bragg—before the general submitted his own resignation from his command on

December 2—had been the problem of a successor. Davis had considered Longstreet briefly, but "Old Pete," an obstinate man who fought well as a corps commander under Lee, tended to be insubordinate of all other authority, including the President himself. He had on more than one occasion had the effrontery—from Davis' point of view—to challenge Presidential decisions on assignments of brigade and division commanders in his I Corps. Certainly any further consideration of Longstreet had been dismissed after he had been unsuccessful as an independent commander against Burnside and Sherman at Knoxville in November and early December. Finally, Longstreet had suggested Joe Johnston as a fit successor to Bragg.

Davis' dislike for Johnston dated from that general's nine-page complaint about having been "illegally" put in fourth place in Confederate general officer rank at the outset, rather than in first place. Since that autumn of 1861 nothing that Johnston did could be praiseworthy to Davis. Capable soldier he might be, but in the President's opinion he was cantankerous, obstinate and conceited. So Davis at first dismissed the possibility of Johnston to succeed Bragg. Parenthetically, one notes that this smouldering animosity between the twain would have a tragic effect on the fortunes of the Confederacy.

Davis had seriously considered shifting Lee to the West to recover Chattanooga and the rest of Tennessee. But he dropped that idea quickly; not only didn't Lee wish to leave his Army of Northern Virginia, but there wasn't another man of sufficient caliber to take his place in that most vital and critical theater of war.

Possibly Beauregard could have handled either of the two major army commands. But the proud, touchy Louisiana general was another of Davis' headaches. The Confederate President considered Beauregard to be a trouble-maker as bad as Johnston, or worse. When Beauregard got close to Richmond he was always bothering people with grandiose strategical ideas that the President considered even less practical than those proposed by Longstreet. He seemed to be well placed as commander of the Department of South Carolina, Georgia and Florida.

Then, too, there was Ewell. But Davis and Lee agreed that this was impossible because of Ewell's poor health since he had lost a leg at Second Manassas.

And that brought Mr. Davis right back where he had started: the selection of a leader to contain the Union threat now menacing the Southland's west-central area.

Reluctantly, pessimistically even, on December 16 Davis appointed Johnston to replace Bragg in command of the Army of Tennessee. Two months later he brought old friend Bragg to Richmond, to be entrusted with "the conduct of the military operations in the armies of the Confederacy." This was as close as Davis had yet come to the appointment of a General-in-Chief; Bragg was really a military advisor and assistant to the President.

The appointment, at first resented and feared by most Confederate senior officers, was a happy one. Bragg, relieved of the responsibility of an army command, developed unexpected tact and consideration. His keen, capable mind and experience enabled him to relieve some—though not enough—of the burdens of detailed military matters which Davis had voluntarily laid on his own shoulders.

Perhaps the most encouraging news of the winter was the report Davis received about the Battle of Olustee, Florida. There a force of 5,200 Confederates, under Brigadier General Joseph Finegan, on February 20, had defeated an invading Northern force of equal strength, under Brigadier General Truman Seymour. And by mid-April Davis had the pleasure of promoting and congratulating Brigadier General R. F. Hoke for capturing the Union naval base at Plymouth; an indication of progress in the planned efforts to eliminate Federal footholds on the North Carolina coast. In Davis' eyes this was further confirmation of his belief regarding the innate superiority of Southern manpower, and the inevitability of Southern victory—if only the troops could be adequately supplied.

The blockade was certainly having a dreadful impact on the supply situation. But the local manufacture of war matériel was progressing relatively satisfactorily, and the agricultural Confederacy was producing enough food. Yet many of the troops were on short rations—particularly in Lee's army. This disturbing situation was a matter of distribution; and of obtaining cooperation from local authorities; particularly from the state governors.

Not the least of Mr. Davis' military problems embraced these eleven governors. Each of them had good reasons for pointing out why not one inch of his own state soil should be surrendered to the Northerners, and why its resources should be husbanded locally. In a nation founded on the principle of States' Rights, no President could have resisted political pressure for scattering regular Confederate forces through all the states. Nor could any form of logic have persuaded the local populations and governors that the state militias should fight in and for all the Confederacy, not just when their own states were invaded.

Davis was unable to overcome this pernicious sectionalism in order to make proper use of the South's interior lines and its railroad network in order to effect such concentration. How utterly frustrating it must have been to him to see how a nation founded on States' Rights contained within it the seeds of its own destruction.

From an over-all standpoint, Davis was an excellent war president. Unfortunately his faults have become better known than his abilities. He permitted himself to become too involved in the details of the War Department and to meddle in minor matters of army administration—to the annoyance of his five successive Secretaries of War, and to the despair of many of his generals. He was stubborn, and he could never permit even the slightest apparent challenge to his authority or dignity to go unpunished. (This was perhaps the most significant difference between Davis and Lincoln.) He was austere and unbending. He cherished grudges and was frequently blind to the faults of his friends.

Yet these were relatively minor human weaknesses, in contrast to his unquestioned capability, his truly extensive knowledge of military affairs, his energy, his will power, his unfailing dauntless spirit in the face of adversity. History has been much kinder to many men who had greater faults and fewer virtues. It is perhaps unfortunate that Davis possessed extensive military experience and knowledge. Otherwise, he might have been more charitable about the shortcomings of inexperienced and less able subordinates. In such case, of course, the excellent early administration of the Confederacy would have suffered, but a more efficient military apparatus probably would have evolved eventually. The President, less involved in petty administrative details, might have been able to concern himself more thoroughly—and with a less exhausted mind—about major policy matters.

In the last analysis, however, Davis could have done nothing about two terrible blows fate dealt him. As a war president he could never avoid being measured against Abraham Lincoln. And as a Confederate leader he would always—and most unfairly—be compared with Robert E. Lee.

# 22

# Meeting of the Giants

At midnight May 3, 1864, the Army of the Potomac, concentrated in the Culpeper triangle between the Rappahannock and Rapidan Rivers, moved southeastward towards Germanna and Ely's Fords over the Rapidan. That army now consisted of Sheridan's cavalry corps and four infantry corps: Hancock's II, Warren V, Sedgwick's VI and Burnside's IX. Its total strength was slightly less than 105,000 officers and men.

Some of these veterans had followed five generals south of the Rappahannock and Rapidan only to meet defeat. This new man, Grant, had made quite a reputation for himself out West. Yet Pope had had the same recommendation. Was there any reason to think that Grant would do any better than the others when he found himself up against the first team—Lee and the Army of Northern Virginia?

In Grant's over-all plan for coordinated operations against the Confederacy, the Army of the Potomac was the pivot of maneuver, around which Sherman and the various smaller Union forces were to operate. This army, under Grant's personal supervision, was to engage Lee's Army of Northern Virginia, fighting it relentlessly until it was destroyed in battle, dispersed, or forced to surrender. Grant decided that the best way to do this would be to go around Lee's right flank and to attempt to cut his communications with Richmond. Whether or not he accomplished this, Grant felt that by turning Lee's right he would eventually force the Southerner either to fight a battle against superior numbers under unfavorable circumstances, or be driven into the mountains, where destruction of his army would be inevitable.

Another reason for turning Lee's right would be to ease the Federal supply situation. It would be impossible to live off the war-torn country of central Virginia; Grant intended to obtain logistical support, with the assistance of the Navy, from various ports or landings in tidewater Virginia. He abandoned his overland line of communications along the Orange & Alexandria R.R.; the army would carry with it, over the Rapidan, ten days' supply of food and ammunition in a train of about 5,000 wagons. Though slowing the advance, this would permit complete freedom of maneuver. He expected that his wagon train would first be replenished from supplies moved by ship to Belle Plain on the Potomac, near Fredericksburg.

When Grant began his advance, Lee's army was still generally in the positions of the Mine Run campaign. Ewell's corps, with its right flank on Mine Run, held the Confederate right; A. P. Hill was on the left, near Orange Courthouse. Longstreet, recently returned from east Tennessee, was in reserve south of Gordonsville. Stuart's cavalry was in the vicinity of Fredericksburg, where forage for the horses was more plentiful. A thin screen of pickets observed the Rappahannock and Rapidan fords between Mine Run and Fredericksburg. Lee's effective combat strength was probably about 61,000; Confederate records for the 1864 campaign are most sketchy and unreliable.

Lee, anticipating the direction and route of march of the

Union army, made no effort to interfere with the Federal river crossing. Uninterested in partial success, or in merely discouraging the Union forces, he realized that he and his men were much more familiar with the area into which the Union army was entering than were Grant or any of his subordinates. This was the Wilderness of Virginia, an area of dense forest and almost impenetrable thicket about ten miles deep, extending along the southern bank of the Rapidan roughly from Chancellorsville and Spotsylvania on the east to beyond Mine Run on the west. In this region, where movement off the few miserable roads was difficult in the extreme, a few determined men could easily stop much greater numbers. Lee had conclusively demonstrated that at Chancellorsville.

Lee chose the Wilderness as a battleground deliberately, seeking, as always, complete victory. If he was surprised by the speed of the Federal advance—the II, V and VI Corps and much of the train were across the river by evening of May 4—he was unconcerned by it. His intention was to beat all of Grant's army, not just part of it. In fact, since Longstreet could not arrive until late on the fifth, or early on the sixth, Lee had instructed Ewell and Hill, the leading corps commanders, to feel out the Federal advance but to avoid bringing on a general engagement "if practicable."

Shortly after dawn of the fifth, Warren and Hancock—whose corps led the two-pronged Union advance—moved southward from their respective bivouacs in the vicinity of Wilderness Tavern and Chancellorsville. Simultaneously, Ewell's corps resumed its eastward march from Locust Grove up the Orange-Fredericksburg Turnpike. By 7:00 A.M. the Confederate advance guard halted about two miles west of Wilderness Tavern, having sighted columns of Federal troops marching southward across the main road. Ewell immediately formed a line of battle across the road, but mindful of his orders to avoid a general engagement, he reported the situation to Lee and awaited instructions.

The Federals soon simplified Ewell's problem. When scouts

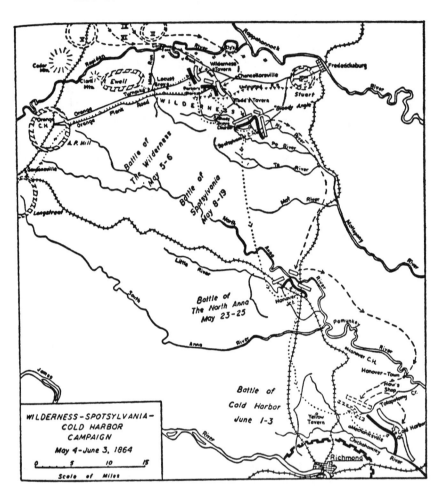

WILDERNESS - SPOTSYLVANIA -
COLD HARBOR
CAMPAIGN
May 4-June 3, 1864

Scale of Miles

reported the Confederate location, Meade ordered Warren to attack, in the belief that this was merely a Southern diversion to
delay the Union army's advance. Warren's attack was initially
successful; Ewell's leading division was put to flight. But the
Northerners, unprepared for a counterattack now delivered by the
full weight of Ewell's two remaining divisions, were soon thrown
back. The Confederates regained their initial positions and both
sides entrenched. Sedgwick's corps came up on Warren's right
about noon, and established a line north of the Turnpike. How-

ever, there was no further major action on Ewell's front during the fifth.

Meanwhile, to the south, A. P. Hill had been advancing up the Orange Plank Road. At Parker's Store his scouts ran into part of Wilson's cavalry division, which had been covering the advance of Warren's corps. Hill, also mindful of Lee's instructions, halted, deployed and reported the situation.

Almost simultaneously the leaders on both sides realized the significance of the action developing along the Plank Road. The Army of the Potomac, astride the Rapidan (Burnside's corps was still on the north bank), was being snubbed in its southerly advance along the axis of the Brock Road. Its right flank was open to attack, and its overwhelming superiority in numbers was unavailing in that tangle of brush where maneuver was practically impossible.

The junction of the Brock and Plank Roads had become a key point. Lee ordered Hill to press forward to seize it, if this could be done without bringing on a general engagement. Grant watched, while Meade ordered Sedgwick, who had been following Warren, to rush his leading division (Getty's) south past Wilderness Tavern to the same objective. Hancock, further south, who had already advanced from Chancellorsville to Todd's Tavern, was ordered north up the Brock Road to assist Getty.

Hill's scouting had convinced him that the crossroads was held in strength. He reported that an advance would probably bring on the engagement Lee was anxious to postpone. Again the Northerners had no qualms about precipitating a full-scale battle. About mid-afternoon Hancock, on orders from Grant—through Meade—moved forward from the crossroads, with Parker's Store his objective. But while waiting for instructions, Hill's men had entrenched. A desperate fight took place in the tangled underbrush on both sides of the Plank Road. It continued until dark, with heavy casualties on both sides, but with no advantage gained by either.

Up to this time the Battle of the Wilderness had consisted

of two entirely separate engagements within one mile of each other. The dense, jungle-like thicket had prevented any effective coordination between the separated elements—Ewell and Warren on the Turnpike in the morning; Hill and Hancock on the Brock Road in the afternoon.

It was a battle between bewildered brigades and regiments and companies, where officers could not see the whole length of their commands; where no one was sure if the men on his right and left were advancing or retreating. Brush fires, ignited by the musketry, smouldered and smoked, still further befogging the contestants. Worse yet, the little, licking flames were roasting helpless wounded men, whose thin screams punctuated lulls in the battle din. In one little clearing between two firing lines, a cluster of wounded lying in the matted vines and creepers was swept by a gush of flame that began exploding the paper cartridges in the men's belts, and Yank and Reb alike flung down their arms to rush out and try to drag the unfortunates to safety.

In late afternoon, Grant had ordered Warren to send his reserve division (Wadsworth's) to assist Hancock. But Wadsworth's men, hacking their way slowly through the underbrush, guided by compass and the sound of firing, did not reach Hancock's right flank until after dark, when both sides had stopped fighting to try to get some sleep in their shallow trenches and rifle pits.

Grant ordered a general attack to commence at 5:00 A.M. on the sixth. Burnside had crossed the Rapidan with three of his divisions before dark on the fifth, and was ordered to fill the gap between Hancock and Warren in time to take part in a coordinated operation. Recognizing that there had been a similar gap in the Confederate line, Grant ordered Burnside to press forward to envelop Hill's left flank and thus split the Confederate army.

Lee had been reasonably satisfied with the results of the battle on the fifth. Longstreet, and Anderson's division of Hill's corps, were expected to arrive around dawn. Lee planned to pass these fresh troops through Hill's two exhausted divisions on the Plank Road, and to envelop the Union left flank.

Sedgwick, Warren and Hancock attacked promptly at 5:00 A.M., as ordered. But Burnside was not in position, and would not reach his assigned starting point until early afternoon. Grant excused the extreme slowness of the IX Corps' advance as being due to the denseness of the underbrush through which it had to advance. This dense thicket was to affect all of the operations during the day, and the fighting consisted of a series of confused and desperate struggles between small groups of men all along the line.

In the north, Ewell's corps had little difficulty in holding its positions astride the Turnpike against the attacks of Sedgwick and Warren. Hancock, however, had better luck in his initial assault, and Hill's troops were thrown back in confusion. Hancock's units pushed slowly after them through the underbrush. As Lee was trying personally to rally his defeated troops, Longstreet's corps swung up the Plank Road, having completed a forty-two-mile march in thirty-six hours.

Lee, who was apparently more perturbed than at any other time in his career, made ready to lead Longstreet's men in counterattack. But the soldiers would have none of it. One of them grabbed his horse's bridle, and led the fuming general back down the road, while his comrades shouted: "General Lee to the rear, General Lee to the rear!" Others made it clear to the general that they would refuse to move forward while he was there.

Reluctantly acceding to their demand, Lee rode off to find Longstreet, and the leading division deployed to attack the unsuspecting Federals, less than one hundred yards to the eastward. Lee found Longstreet just as the attack got started. In the hail of bullets Longstreet pointedly suggested to his commander that if Lee was planning to remain there to direct the I Corps, he, Longstreet, would be happy to go to the rear to a safer spot. Lee apparently was touched, amused and frustrated by the firm solicitude for his safety he had encountered from all ranks of the I Corps. But realizing that no one could conduct a hard-fought tactical battle better than Longstreet, he rode off, confident of success.

Nor was the confidence misplaced. Before noon Hancock's men had been pushed back to their original position, and were in danger of being driven through the crossroad. Grant threw one of Burnside's divisions into the fight, and ordered Sedgwick and Warren to stop their attacks in order to send assistance if necessary.

Longstreet, meanwhile, had sent four brigades along an abandoned and unfinished railroad line to strike Hancock's left flank. The attack, a complete surprise, was very successful. As Hancock's left collapsed, Longstreet ordered an advance all along the front. The Federals were pushed back to the crossroads itself. Thoughts of Chancellorsville, and Jackson's flank attack, flashed through the minds of Northerners and Southerners alike. The parallel was to become even closer.

Following his advancing troops towards the crossroads, Longstreet and several other senior officers were suddenly cut down by heavy fire from their right. It was the enveloping force from his own corps, not realizing how the line had advanced, and unable to see clearly through the thicket. The situation was soon straightened out, but Longstreet was seriously (some thought fatally) wounded, about two miles from the spot where Stonewall Jackson had been wounded by his own men almost exactly one year earlier.

Longstreet, in dreadful pain, ordered the attack to continue before he was taken to the rear. Lee rode up, and Longstreet insisted upon explaining the situation to his shocked commander. Lee now personally assumed command of the right wing, but the momentum had gone from the attack. The Union troops, still holding grimly to the crossroads, repulsed the renewed Confederate assault, and the fighting ended on the Plank Road around 5:00 P.M.

But Lee thought there might be an opportunity for one more blow against the Union right. Riding north to Ewell's headquarters, he discovered, to his great annoyance, that early that morning Ewell had received a report from one of his brigadiers, John B. Gordon, that the Federal right extended only half a mile north of the turnpike, and that it was completely unprotected. Ewell and his senior division commander, Jubal Early, did not believe Gordon. So he had not been permitted to attack.

Though it was now nearly sunset, Lee ordered the attack to take place at once. Gordon, supported by another brigade, complied promptly and proved his point, throwing back Sedgwick's right flank in considerable confusion. Sedgwick promptly established a new line, refusing his right flank, but it is impossible to say how far the Southern advance might have gone had it not been halted by darkness.

The terrible Battle of the Wilderness had come to a close. Grant saw no reason to continue the battle on the seventh, and prepared for his next move. Lee's army, physically and morally exhausted by the two-day conflict, was thankful for the opportunity to rest, and to bury the dead. Both armies' respites were interrupted, however, by efforts to put out the forest fires and to rescue the wounded caught in the flaming underbrush. The Union army had lost 2,246 killed, 12,037 wounded and 3,383 missing; there is no record of Confederate casualties, but these could not have totaled less than 12,000–14,000.

The question in the minds of officers and men on both sides, as the armies held their lines on the seventh, was what would Grant do now?

Under similar circumstances McClellan, Hooker and Meade had acknowledged failure or defeat when fought to a standstill by Lee, had withdrawn to lick their wounds, and waited for Lee to assume the initiative. Most Southerners, and not a few Northerners, expected that the same thing would happen this time. There has not yet been an instance of a Northern advance following a great battle on Virginia soil.

But Lee made a different estimate of the situation. An aggressive Union commander would push southeast down the Brock Road, trying to turn the Confederate right flank, and get to more open country where the Northern numerical superiority could be brought to bear. Obviously, this man Grant was aggressive.

Lee therefore ordered his engineers to cut a road through the thicket, parallel to the Brock Road, that would enable his right flank corps to reach the Shady Grove Church Road to Spotsylvania without having to make a long detour. This would permit Major General Richard H. Anderson—who now commanded Longstreet's corps—to march quickly to the vicinity of Spotsylvania Courthouse and block any Union advance down the Brock Road.

On the seventh various reports reached Lee, corroborating his estimate that the Union army would march southeastward. He ordered Anderson to leave his entrenchments after dark, to give his men some rest in the rear, and then to start for Spotsylvania before 3:00 A.M. Lee also alerted Stuart, who had units of Fitzhugh Lee's cavalry division prepare road blocks by felling trees along the Brock Road.

In his Western campaigns, Grant perhaps had had a bit more than his share of good luck. Now was to come the first of three instances of bad luck which would materially affect the 1864 campaign.

Grant had ordered his own army to start moving down the Brock Road, and parallel roads further east, shortly before midnight. Had Anderson waited until three o'clock to move, Warren's V Corps would have been in Spotsylvania three or four hours before the Confederate I Corps could have arrived, and Lee's communications with Richmond would have been cut, perhaps irretrievably. But as Anderson pulled back after dark, he discovered that his proposed rest area was being consumed by a forest fire. So he decided to march directly to Spotsylvania, and rest there.

As it turned out, the men would get no rest, but thanks to

Lee's foresight, combined with a lucky forest fire and effective delaying tactics by Stuart's cavalry, Anderson reached the Brock Road, two miles west of Spotsylvania, less than five minutes before Warren's advanced guard arrived in musket range of the same spot. The Northern infantry were driving Fitzhugh Lee's cavalry screen down the road when they were suddenly taken under fire by Anderson's skirmishers, hastily thrown across the road. The Battle of Spotsylvania had begun.

As the main bodies of their respective corps came up, Anderson and Warren deployed them on both sides of the Brock Road. Both sides promptly entrenched; now become an automatic tactical practice in both Northern and Southern armies. Whenever possible the trenches were strengthened by chopping down trees, on which earth was thrown and packed down. If necessary, the trenches were quickly widened and deepened during lulls in the fighting.

Anderson was able to send some reinforcements to Fitzhugh Lee, who was trying to eject Wilson's cavalry division from the village of Spotsylvania. Wilson was driven off towards Fredericksburg as Sedgwick came up from the other direction on Warren's left, extending the Union front. Shortly after noon the two Union corps attacked Anderson, and as additional units of the VI Corps came on the field, extending the Federal left, the Confederate position became precarious. But late in the afternoon Ewell arrived, to take up position on Anderson's right. This ended the first day's battle, and both sides fell to work in improving and extending their trenches.

Due to the illness of A. P. Hill, Jubal Early had taken temporary command of the Confederate II Corps. Early had hoped to move via the Brock Road to Spotsylvania, not realizing that this had become the principal artery of Union advance. As he approached Todd's Tavern, shortly after noon on the eighth, he ran into Hancock's corps, which had stopped and entrenched there while the Brock Road was blocked by Warren's and Sedgwick's men. After some skirmishing, Early withdrew, bivouacking his corps near Shady Grove Church. On the ninth, he moved eastward to Spotsylvania along the Shady Grove Church Road, while Hancock continued down the Brock Road.

On the ninth, Burnside moved southeastward to the Fredericksburg-Spotsylvania road, where he turned right, to approach Spotsylvania from the northeast. To meet this threat to his right rear, Lee sent Early to take a position at right angles to Anderson's and Ewell's line. Early, therefore, was facing generally east, from Ewell's right flank to Spotsylvania.

The Confederate line, about four miles long, now took the shape of an inverted V, with Ewell's corps holding the apex. The left flank was on the Po River—here an insignificant stream— and the right was on a minor tributary of the Ny. The battlefield was situated at the eastern extremity of the Wilderness, and though the country was heavily wooded, there were a number of farms and open fields, and the underbrush lacked the jungle-like density of the region the armies had just left.

There was no major action on the ninth. During the morning Sedgwick was killed by a Southern sharpshooter and Major General H. G. Wright assumed command of the VI Corps. Hancock's corps, moving from Todd's Tavern, probed the Confederate left flank late in the day. Early on the tenth Hancock withdrew north of the Po, behind Warren, the Confederate left following in a brief flurry of activity.

Grant had ordered a coordinated attack of Hancock's, Warren's and Wright's corps to be mounted at 5:00 P.M. between the Po and the apex of the Confederate vee. But Warren thought he detected a weakness in Anderson's lines, and was given permission to attack at four o'clock, before either Hancock or Wright was ready. This attack was repulsed and the idea of a general assault that day given up. Colonel Emory Upton, shortly after six o'clock, with two brigades of the VI Corps supported by Mott's division of Hancock's corps, made a carefully prepared assault against the left side of the apex of the vee.

This attack, delivered in a column of short, heavy lines, had great initial success. A considerable stretch of Ewell's line was seized and about 2,000 prisoners captured. But Mott, his division halted by heavy artillery fire from the apex of the Confederate position, never came up. Gordon's (formerly Early's) division of Ewell's corps, in reserve just below the apex, counterattacked Upton. A fierce hand-to-hand struggle took place. To try to relieve the pressure on Upton, Grant ordered Hancock, Warren and Wright to make the general attack previously planned. Launched hastily, this was repulsed at dusk, after suffering heavy losses. Upton had to withdraw from his hard-won position under the cover of darkness. The young colonel, seriously wounded, was rewarded by Grant with an immediate promotion to brigadier general. It was after this fierce struggle that the Confederate soldiers, and later the Northerners, began to call Ewell's salient, at the apex, the "Bloody Angle."

There was little action on the eleventh. Burnside, who had been relatively inactive opposite Early, was moved north, to eliminate the gap between his corps and Hancock's, and to engage in a major assault on the Bloody Angle, ordered by Grant to take place early on the twelfth. Hancock would make the main effort against the tip of the apex, supported by Burnside and Wright. Hancock's troops were formed in several heavy lines, to attack in mass on a very narrow front; a formation similar to that used so successfully in Upton's much smaller attack of the tenth.

The attack was launched just after 4:30 A.M., and smashed through the apex, virtually destroying one of Ewell's divisions, and capturing about four thousand men. Much of the Confederate artillery had been withdrawn during the night in anticipation of another turning movement by Grant, so there must be some doubt whether this violent charge could have been as successful if Confederate infantry had been adequately supported by cannon.

In the excitement and confusion of the struggle, the second and third lines of the attackers became intermingled with the first. They pressed forward, however, to be met by a well-organized and gallantly-led counterattack by Gordon's division, again in reserve behind the apex. Though greatly outnumbered, Gordon and his men, observed by General Lee himself, stopped the advance, then threw it back. Assisted by units rushed up from Anderson's and Early's lines, Gordon actually pushed the Northerners right back to the original entrenchments at the apex.

As he was organizing his counterattack, Gordon saw Lee ride up, and requested the older general to withdraw from danger. When Lee refused, the men took up the cry shouted by Longstreet's men on the sixth: "General Lee to the rear, General Lee to the rear!" Escorted by a volunteer bodyguard, Lee was hustled from immediate danger.

For the remainder of that foggy, rainy day the Bloody Angle more than earned its name, in the most sustained and most desperate hand-to-hand fighting of the war. The Confederates held their original line of entrenchments, with its high parapet of logs and earth. But the Northerners refused to withdraw, and stayed on the opposite side of the parapet. Bayonets, pistols, clubbed muskets, and even rocks were the principal weapons. Every time a man tried to fire his piece over the parapet, he risked the danger of having his arm grabbed from the other side and of being pulled over bodily.

Grant ordered Warren to attack Anderson's entrenchments, to relieve the pressure, but this effort was repulsed. He then planned to move Warren up to join in the attack on the Bloody Angle, but rejected that idea since there were already more Union troops in that small area than could maneuver or properly protect themselves.

Lee, meanwhile, had decided to abandon the Bloody Angle salient; it was now obvious that it could be held only at a fearful cost in Lee's scarcest commodity: manpower. So during the struggle at the apex, Confederate engineers had labored all day to construct a new line of entrenchments across the base of the salient, just east of the Brock Road.

After dark, as though by mutual agreement, both sides withdrew from the scene of slaughter.

There was no important action on the thirteenth, but Grant was preparing for another assault on the fourteenth. During the night Warren and Wright were to slip quietly out of their entrenchments on the west side of the line, march around behind Hancock and Burnside, and envelop the Southern right flank south of Spotsylvania. Plans were carefully made to permit a surprise attack at 4:00 A.M. on Early's exposed right flank.

Grant now had his second stroke of bad luck. A torrential nightlong rain so mired the dark and muddy trails that the head of Warren's corps didn't reach its planned position until 6:00 A.M.; Wright's corps arrived several hours later. It was evening before the units were in place and ready to attack, so the assaults was called off. By late afternoon the Confederates realized what was happening, and during the night Anderson's corps was rushed over to cover Early's right, south of Spotsylvania.

There was little fighting on the fifteenth, sixteenth and seventeenth. On the eighteenth, Grant attempted one more effort against the new Confederate entrenchments below the Bloody Angle. This was now the left flank of the Southern line, the armies having almost completely reversed their initial positions. When the attack was repulsed, Grant determined to start south again, around Lee's right.

Grant had intended to continue the battle on the Spotsylvania line. Confederate casualties, he believed, must be as great as his own. He could afford the loss; Lee could not. So, by the grim arithmetic of attrition an unreinforced Lee must finally give up or make a dangerous withdrawal. On the eleventh Grant had written Halleck to this effect, concluding: "I propose to fight it out on this line, if it takes all summer."

But Lee *was* receiving reinforcements. (As we shall see, two other Union armies which should have kept the Confederates tied down elsewhere, had completely failed in their missions.) So, he might be able to maintain the bloody struggle indefinitely, and Grant had no intention of spending Union lives unless Union objectives could be gained. Consequently he decided to continue southward, in accordance with his original plan, hoping to catch Lee at a disadvantage in the more open terrain nearer to Richmond.

Grant's movement was delayed for one day because of a reconnaissance in force carried out by Ewell on the nineteenth, to find out if the Union right flank had been withdrawn, since Lee now expected another of Grant's leap-frog movements around his right. Ewell was repulsed with considerable loss. This was the last action of the Battle of Spotsylvania.

During the twelve days of intermittent combat the Union army had had 14,267 casualties. There is no record of Southern losses, but they must have lost at least 6,000 captured and another 6,000 in killed and wounded.

While the Battle of Spotsylvania had been going on, Sheridan's cavalry corps had been busy elsewhere. Four days after crossing the Rapidan, Sheridan proposed to Grant that his cavalry corps raid south towards Richmond, draw off Stuart and, if possible, bring on a cavalry engagement.

Grant agreed, so Sheridan started on May 8, with slightly more than 10,000 men, organized in three divisions: Merritt's, Gregg's and Wilson's. This operation has been criticized by some military analysts as merely one more useless cavalry raid that deprived both armies of their needed eyes and ears at a time of critical operations. But Sheridan accomplished all of his objectives. As he had predicted, Stuart followed, and three days later, at Yellow Tavern, on the outskirts of Richmond, a fierce battle took place between the two cavalry commands. Stuart, outnumbered by about 10,000 to 4,500, was defeated, his force was thrown back into the fortifications of Richmond, and he was mortally wounded. This in itself was a fearful blow to Lee and to the South.

Sheridan, realizing that it would be useless to try to storm the now alerted fortifications of the Southern capital, turned eastward, fought his way across the Chickahominy, and reached Butler's supply base at Haxall's Landing, opposite Bermuda Hundred on the thirteenth. (We shall learn later how Butler got there.) Resting men and horses for three days, Sheridan moved out on the seventeenth, and rejoined Grant's army in his positions above the North Anna River on the twenty-fourth.

As to whether or not the raid was useless, Grant—a critic of earlier cavalry raids—was satisfied. "Sheridan . . . ," Grant wrote later, "passed entirely around Lee's army; encountered his cavalry in four engagements and defeated them in all; recaptured 400 Union prisoners and killed and captured many of the enemy; destroyed and used many supplies and munitions of war; destroyed miles of railroad and telegraph, and freed us from annoyance by the cavalry of the enemy for more than two weeks."

Meanwhile, after dark on the twentieth, Grant began moving south again from the Spotsylvania battlefield. An alert Lee took advantage of more direct roads to the south, and reached the railroad at Hanover Junction, just below the North Anna River, early on the twenty-second. The Southerners threw up entrenchments on the south bank of the river, covering the main road and railroad, and awaited the arrival of the Northerners. Union troops reached the river on the twenty-third. For two days Grant probed the Southern defenses, but Lee's position had been too well chosen, and was too well fortified for Grant to attempt a major assault. He decided to continue around Lee's right.

On the twenty-seventh, after a rapid night march, the leading elements of the Army of the Potomac began to cross the Pamunkey River at Hanover Town. It was necessary to delay here for two days, while the remainder of the army and the trains crossed the river. On the twenty-eighth Sheridan's cavalry pushed westward, engaging with entrenched Confederate cavalry near Haw's Shop. Behind this screen Lee was taking new positions south of Totopotomy Creek, a small stream northeast of Mechanicsville, covering the approaches to Richmond.

On the thirtieth and thirty-first the Northern army felt out

Lee's new position, but Grant found it too strong to be assaulted. The night of the thirty-first he shifted his lines southeast to Cold Harbor, again in hopes of being able to turn Lee's right. The Southerners, however, moved with equal promptness. Lee's right was now on the Chickahominy, about three miles from the outermost fortifications defending Richmond. Fighting was sporadic on June 1, as both commanders built up their new lines and the men entrenched. Grant ordered an assault on the second, believing that the Southerners were spread too thin to stop a determined attack. Though he could no longer get between Lee and Richmond, there seemed to be a good chance of splitting Lee's greatly overextended army by a drive to the Chickahominy from Cold Harbor.

General W. F. Smith, with the XVIII Corps from Butler's Army of the James—about 10,000 men—had just joined; he with Hancock and Warren would make the attack at four-thirty. But Hancock's men, making a night march of fifteen miles, were slow in arriving; while Smith protested that he had inadequate ammunition and was too weak to attack. Reputedly, Meade commented angrily: "Why in Hell did he come at all?" Grant, equally annoyed, had to postpone the attack for twenty-four hours.

The situation early on June 2, had probably been as propitious for a Union attack as at any time during the campaign. Lee had less than 40,000 men holding a line about six miles long between the Totopotomy and the Chickahominy. Grant had now been reinforced to more than 100,000, with about 50,000 concentrated on a three-mile front just west of Old Cold Harbor. It is difficult to see how Lee's men, spread out as they were in shallow, unimproved trenches, could have stopped a vigorous attack in that relatively open country.

But twenty-four hours later the situation was considerably different. Lee had set his infantry and engineers to greatly strengthening the trenches. More important, 14,000 relatively fresh troops, all buoyed up by recent successes over Northerners, arrived during the day, and were put into the threatened center of the line. These included two brigades brought by Breckenridge from the Valley, and two of the divisions that had stopped Butler at Drewry's Bluff.

The Northern attack began as scheduled at dawn on the third. But instead of a weak, thinly-held line, the Union troops were facing confident, ready defenders, strongly supported by artillery, with clear fields of fire along the entire front. In a few places, the Union troops reached the Confederate entrenchments, only to be thrown back. But along most of the line the attackers were pinned down by fire within five minutes after leaving their trenches. It was repulse, complete and absolute. Grant, admitting defeat, called off the attacks. The Union attackers lost between 6,000 and 7,000 men in less than an hour; the Confederate defenders suffered fewer than 1,500 casualties.

Though the armies were to remain in their trenches opposite each other for nine more days, the campaign begun in the Wilderness came to its close with Grant's order calling off the attack at Cold Harbor.

What had been the result of those thirty days of practically incessant warfare?

On the map, the Union army had advanced steadily and inexorably sixty miles from the Rapidan River to the outskirts of Richmond. Many Northerners took this to mean that the war was practically over.

Southerners, on the other hand, saw that Lee's army, outnumbered two-to-one, had repulsed Grant in four major battles, had forced the Northerners to withdraw from every position in order to seek a new route of advance, and had finally brought the invasion to a complete halt further from Richmond than McClellan had been, two years earlier.

Neither of these extreme viewpoints was correct. Grant had been unable to cut Lee's line of communications, or to destroy the Southern army in battle. Lee had been unable either to throw

back the invaders—as he had invariably done in previous campaigns—or to inflict on the Northerners losses sufficiently punish-
ing as to discourage their advance.

Grant had failed because he was opposed by a Lee; Lee had
failed because he was opposed by a Grant. There is no comparable
example of two great, evenly matched generals fighting each
other to a standstill in operations marked on each side by wary
caution, brilliant boldness, sound estimates of the opponent's
capabilities and intentions, coupled with sincere respect for the
other's ability.

But when the month ended, the advantage unquestionably
lay with Grant, despite the disappointment and losses suffered at
Cold Harbor. This was inevitable, assuming that there was little
or nothing to choose between the fighting abilities of opposing
commanders and their armies. Superior Northern resources were
bound to make themselves felt in a war of attrition. The picture
is best viewed in terms of losses, and of the effect these had on
the opposing sides.*

Grant lost 54,929 men from the Wilderness to Cold Harbor.
This is approximately 52 per cent of an initial combat strength of
about 105,000 men. Lee lost at least 39,000 men in this same
period, or 59 per cent of his original combat strength of 61,000.
More significant than the casualty figures, but corroborating their
impact on Lee and his army, is the fact that after the Wilderness
no major offensive was undertaken by Lee. He knew that he was
taking more losses than the South could afford, and from that
time on he took all possible efforts to husband the lives of his
men.

*There is considerable debate about the relative strength and loss figures of the two armies
in this campaign, particularly since Southern records are so sketchy. This debate, however,
has arisen from the understandable but—in our opinion, untenable—low estimates which
Southerners have made of Lee's light losses in the Wilderness and at Spotsylvania.
Bearing in mind known losses on certain days, and comparative losses in comparable but
better-recorded conflicts, such as Malvern Hill, Antietam, Chancellorsville, Second Bull
Run and Fredericksburg, the authors—who yield to no one in their admiration of Lee's
tactical generalship and of his defensive genius in this campaign—feel that their estimates
of Southern casualties are minimum figures.

It is significant, incidentally, of the solicitude for their men shared by the opposing generals in this campaign, that for all the desperate fighting that took place, on no single day of the campaign did their losses approach those suffered by both armies at Antietam, or on the second and third days of Gettysburg. The largest day's losses for the Army of the Potomac was about 7,500 killed, wounded and captured, on May 10, at Spotsylvania. The heaviest Southern loss was also at Spotsylvania, on the twelfth—around 6,000 men; at least as many as Northern casualties that same day.

Grant's losses had been severe, but they were magnified at the time by both Northern and Southern press, with the result that his conduct of the campaign is often ignorantly presented as the artless hammering of a bludgeon by a man of little skill, but possessing overwhelming superiority of force and inexhaustible sources of supply. Such a picture cannot be reconciled with the facts. Even Grant's attack at Cold Harbor had as much—or more—chance of success as had Lee's bloody repulse at Gettysburg. But like Lee after Pickett's charge, Grant was man enough to acknowledge a mistake, without trying to justify it.

So it was that in the days of early June, two great generals warily eyed one another, each seeking the earliest opportunity to seize the initiative, and each determined to do everything in his power to make his cause prevail.

# 23

# Not Since Xerxes

After the Cold Harbor repulse, and while completing his plans for operations against Lee, Grant reviewed the situation around the periphery of the Confederacy.

Sherman's situation was not unlike his own. The Western armies had advanced some seventy miles in the first month of the campaign, but were now held up by Johnston, strongly entrenched on high ground north of Marietta, Georgia. As Grant had expected, he need have no worries about Sherman. But it was different elsewhere. Three other small Union armies had failed miserably in their initial efforts.

Least important of these was the Red River expedition, in Louisiana, the details of which we have already noted, and which had been mounted prior to Grant's promotion. His only concern about its failure was the psychological effect, and the unfortunate waste of manpower.

More serious, however, was the dismal performances of political Generals Franz Sigel in the Valley, and Ben Butler on the banks of the James River. Both of these generals had started operations on May 4, in coordination with the Army of the Potomac. Within two weeks both had failed.

Butler had steamed up the James River from Fortress Monroe with an army of 36,000 men, comprised of the X Corps under Major General Quincy A. Gillmore—recently arrived from the Carolina coast, and the XVIII Corps, commanded by Major General William F. Smith. Grant's instructions to Butler had been, in part, as follows:

> Take City Point with as much force as possible. . . . Intrench at once and concentrate all your troops for the field there as rapidly as you can. From City Point directions cannot be given at this time for your further movement. . . . The fact that . . . Richmond is to be your objective point, and that there is to be cooperation between your force and the Army of the Potomoc . . . must be your guide. This indicates the necessity for holding close to the south bank of the James River as you advance.

Butler botched the job. Instead of basing himself at City Point—on the south bank of the Appomattox River—as Grant had directed, Butler on May 5, concentrated above it at Bermuda Hundred, where the meanderings of the James and Appomattox Rivers created a bulging peninsula more than twenty-five square miles in area, beyond an isthmus only three miles wide. After wasting three days building entrenchments across this narrow neck, he curtly rejected the recommendations of his corps commanders to cross the Appomattox and to seize Petersburg from the east, as they felt Grant's orders implied. Instead, moving cautiously southwestward towards Petersburg, he permitted himself to be blocked at narrow Swift Creek by an insignificant

Confederate force. Then, hearing rumors of Southern reinforcements coming from Richmond, he hastily withdrew again to Bermuda Hundred. (See map on page 339.)

The rumor was false, and on the twelfth Butler timidly pushed half his command up towards Drewry's Bluff, below Richmond. By this time all surprise had been lost and President Davis had taken energetic emergency measures for the security of his capital. Instead of capturing Petersburg, and perhaps Richmond itself, Butler's operation had become merely a futile gesture.

By chance, the Federal landing had come at the junction of two Confederate departments. Beauregard, now in command of the Department of North Carolina and Southern Virginia, was responsible for the defense of the region south of the Appomattox and lower James River, including Petersburg. Richmond, in Lee's Department of Northern Virginia, was defended by Major General Robert Ransom.

To rectify this dangerous split responsibility in the face of Butler's threat, Davis had placed all of the region south of Richmond under Beauregard's command, had given him some troops from the Richmond garrison, and had sent for more reinforcements from South Carolina to meet an ever-increasing threat to the Confederate capital. It will be recalled that Sheridan's raiders were probing the northern fortifications around Richmond on the eleventh and twelfth. Beauregard, meanwhile, had sent for Major General Robert F. Hoke, who was then operating against Union forces holding New Berne, North Carolina.

Butler, who had already wasted a precious week, halted and entrenched when he found himself facing the weak Drewry's Bluff defense line. Had he shown any energy on the twelfth this short, thinly-held line would almost certainly have fallen, since it was completely exposed to a turning movement around its western side.

By May 15, Beauregard, energetic and capable, had assembled about 18,000 men north of Drewry's Bluff. He attacked

Butler vigorously at dawn of the sixteenth, pushing the Union right flank back but otherwise not making much impression on the Northern entrenchments. Butler, however, had had enough. He withdrew immediately to the Bermuda Hundred entrenchments. Beauregard followed promptly, and with about 12,000 men spread across the narrow peninsula, was able completely to bottle up Butler's much more numerous force.

During the remainder of May and early June, Butler's only contributions to the campaign were to act as supply point and rest camp for Sheridan's cavalry corps—May 13–17—and to furnish Grant with about 15,000 reinforcements at Cold Harbor. On June 9, he sent General Gillmore with about 4,500 men in an abortive effort to capture Petersburg from the east. The 2,000 Confederate defenders—mostly raw militia—easily repulsed the half-hearted attempt.

Up in the Shenandoah Valley, Sigel, in command of the Department of West Virginia, had also been instructed to advance in coordination with Grant's move into the Wilderness. His mission was to keep the Confederates in southwestern Virginia and the Valley so occupied that they would be unable to send reinforcements to Lee. He was to move southward in two widely-separated columns; one based on West Virginia, the other in the Valley.

The western force, about 10,000 strong, moving in two columns southward from the upper Kanawah River, was to start things off with a raid across the Alleghenies against the Virginia & Tennessee R.R., southwest of Lynchburg. These forces, commanded by Brigadier Generals George Crook and William H. Averell, were most successful in disrupting traffic along the railroad, and in destroying considerable quantities of Confederate supplies. They then returned back across the mountains, according to plan, after clashing with Morgan, to await further instructions from Sigel.

Sigel himself, based on Winchester, was to advance from Cedar Creek. Moving cautiously on May 4, he had reached the vicinity of New Market by the fifteenth. There he was attacked by some 5,000 men under Major General John Breckenridge, who commanded Confederate forces in southwestern Virginia. Sigel, utilizing only 5,000 of his 7,000 men available, was decisively defeated.

Retiring precipitously and in confusion to Cedar Creek, Sigel stayed there, doing nothing. Breckenridge, with 2,500 men, then hastened to Richmond in time to help repel the Union assault at Cold Harbor. Sigel had thus failed utterly in his mission of cooperating with Grant by keeping Southerners occupied in the Valley.

Disappointed though he was with the manner in which these two diversionary operations had been conducted, Grant determined to try to salvage something from both efforts to assist in his next move with the Army of the Potomac.

Now that he could no longer get between Lee and Richmond, Grant decided that he would cut off both Lee's army and the Confederate capital. To do this he would first have to move his army south of the James River and seize the vital railroad junction of Petersburg. Having foreseen this possibility even before Cold Harbor, he had ordered Halleck to send pontoons and bridging equipment to Butler's supply depot on the James. He felt that Union troops in the Valley—now commanded by General David Hunter—could assist him in deceiving and distracting Lee, while the Army of the Potomac was making its dangerous crossing of the James. Hunter, assisted by Breckenridge's departure from the Valley, had been able to move south again, defeating a force of about 5,000 Confederates at Piedmont on June 5. On the sixth he had seized Staunton, where Crook had joined him on the eighth.

Grant now decided to send Sheridan's cavalry raiding westward toward Charlottesville. This in itself would serve as a diversion, and would probably cause Lee to send his cavalry in pursuit—thus keeping them from detecting and interfering with the proposed river crossing. In addition, Grant planned to have Hunter move eastward from Staunton to Charlottesville to meet

Sheridan. Then the combined force, about 24,000 strong, would march eastward along the Virginia Central R.R., destroying tracks, telegraph wires and supplies as they came, to meet Grant somewhere near Petersburg or Richmond.

Sheridan rode off north, then west, on the seventh. Lee, not knowing Sheridan's objective, but aware of the danger to the Virginia Central line, promptly sent Wade Hampton, with his cavalry division and that of Fitzhugh Lee, to try to stop Sheridan somewhere north and east of the railroad. The Southern cavalry-men, starting a day and a half after Sheridan, had a shorter and more direct route. The race was a dead heat, the two forces meeting on the eleventh at Trevilian Station, eight miles southeast of Gordonsville. Both sides claimed victory in the confused two-day battle that ensued, though the Southerners suffered consider-ably greater casualties. In any event, Sheridan gave up his plan of going to Charlottesville, and returned eastward. Otherwise relatively fruitless, the raid did serve its purpose as a diversion, and in attracting the attention of Lee's cavalry as Grant wished.

While Union and Confederate cavalrymen were still milling around Trevilian Station, the Army of the Potomac began to move again. It was one of the best-planned, best-executed operations of military history. Five corps, approximately 15,000 men each, silently left their trenches—many only a stone's throw from the Confederate lines—without the Southerners realizing what was happening.

Marching in four columns, each supplied with pontoon bridge equipment for crossing the Chickahominy, the army headed east, then south, during the hours of darkness of June 12–13. But the westernmost column, Warren's V Corps, headed by Wilson's cavalry division, on crossing the Chickahominy at Long Bridge turned sharp to the right, towards Richmond. By dawn, Wilson's horsemen were advancing westward on a wide front between the Chickahominy and the James, over the old Seven Days' battlefield of 1862, alerting Southern cavalry pickets in the area. The V Corps, close behind, took up a position just south of White Oak Swamp. The remainder of the Army of the Potomac was meanwhile hurrying directly southward, its three columns converging on the James River some ten miles east of the Wilson-Warren demonstration.

Lee, having discovered the departure of the Federals on June 13, and receiving reports of Wilson's and Warren's moves, assumed that Grant was again trying to get around his right flank to Richmond. Shifting rapidly south, Lee's army by evening had taken up positions south of White Oak Swamp, reaching the James near Malvern Hill.

On the fourteenth and again on the fifteenth, Wilson's troopers actively probed along this front. This activity, combined with confused rumors of concentration of most of Grant's army east of Malvern Hill, convinced Lee that Grant was planning to make a powerful push towards Richmond along the north bank of the James. He continued to hold this opinion until late on the seventeenth, discounting other, conflicting, reports as being evidence of more Union diversions, such as Sheridan's raid to Trevilian Station.

Meanwhile, before noon on the fourteenth, Grant's engineers had commenced the construction of a pontoon bridge at Wyanoke Point, just south of Charles City. The James, half a mile or more wide in most of its lower tidewater course, here narrows to about one third of a mile. The bridge was completed before midnight. In eight hours the Union engineers had built what admiring Confederate General Alexander describes as: "The greatest bridge the world has seen since the days of Xerxes." His comment still holds good. More than 100 pontoon boats spanned a river ninety feet deep, and with the strong currents accompanying a four-foot tidal rise and fall. The central span, supported by several anchored schooners, was a draw; gunboats and transports had to pass.

While the bridge was building, the Navy was ferrying the II Corps across the river at Wilcox' Landing, about two miles to the northwest. Earlier in the day W. F. Smith's XVIII Corps,

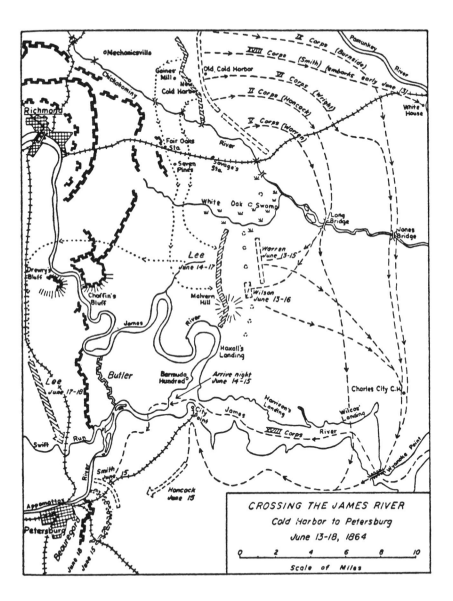

CROSSING THE JAMES RIVER
Cold Harbor to Petersburg
June 13-18, 1864

Scale of Miles

which had embarked on transports at White House at daybreak on the thirteenth, steamed up the river past this scene of feverish activity, to land at Bermuda Hundred—which they had left only two weeks earlier.

All that night, the following day and night, and well into the sixteenth, the rest of the Army of the Potomac poured across the bridge. First came the IX Corps. Behind it marched the V Corps and Wilson's cavalry, who had cleverly abandoned their Malvern Hill demonstration position further north. The VI Corps brought up the rear. By evening of the sixteenth, while Lee was still anticipating a full-scale attack next day by the entire Union army on the north side of the river, the Army of the Potomac was south of the James.

This was an amazing logistical and operational accomplishment. But bad luck would again dog Grant, to prolong the war for ten more months.

While Smith's men were unloading at Bermuda Hundred, Grant himself took a boat there to give orders personally to General Butler. These were clear and unmistakable: Butler was to send Smith's corps, immediately, that very night, to capture Petersburg as quickly as possible. Butler was to reinforce Smith with as many additional troops as could be spared from the entrenchments of the Bermuda Hundred position. Grant informed Butler that he, Grant, would return to the Army of the Potomoc and hurry it forward to support him. He made it clear to Butler that danger was negligible and the opportunity magnificent; all of the Army of the Potomac could reach Petersburg and Bermuda Hundred before a single man of Lee's army could arrive.

Grant then returned to his headquarters, where he directed Meade to move Hancock's corps as rapidly as possible to join Smith at Petersburg. Both generals were satisfied that Hancock could arrive soon after noon the following day—the fifteenth.

In accordance with his instructions, Smith crossed the Appomattox before dawn on the fifteenth and headed westward along the south bank of the river. Petersburg was eight miles away—a four-hour march at most. In addition to his own corps of 10,000 men, Smith had an inexperienced division of colored infantry, 3,700 strong, and a fine division of cavalry—2,400 sabers. He had been informed that the Confederates had only a skeleton force defending Petersburg.

In fact, there was one small brigade of Confederate troops, plus a considerably larger number of raw Virginia militiamen—2,400 men all told. In addition to this insignificant force defending Petersburg, Beauregard had less than 5,000 men in the lines at Bermuda Hundred, facing Butler's remaining 15,000. Another Confederate division—perhaps 5,000 men—was on its way from Drewry's Bluff, but could not reach Petersburg till after midnight.

It was well before noon when Smith's command arrived in front of the eastern defenses of the city. These were formidable indeed, having been carefully prepared long before for possible occupation and use. A series of forts had been constructed on high ground east of the city, connected by breastworks and entrenchments. Fields of fire had been cleared in front, with artificial obstacles placed wherever there were not sufficient felled trees to make an abatis of slashings. Smith could not tell how strongly these works were held.

A reconnaissance in force, by most of his command, would have determined the strength of the defenders. Smith, however, chose to halt, while he made a detailed personal reconnaissance. Not till 7:00 P.M. did he start his attack. It is interesting to note that he ordered the attack to be made by the inexperienced Negro division.

The colored soldiers, eager to prove their worth, dashed forward in a line of skirmishers, on the heels of a well-conducted artillery preparation. Taking moderate casualties, they captured two forts, several guns and some prisoners. Smith now realized that the defenses were lightly held, and by nine o'clock had captured five more forts, holding almost two miles of the fortifications. Had he acted with more energy, this same result could have been accomplished seven hours earlier.

Learning from prisoners that the defenders were expecting reinforcements, Smith, instead of pushing into the nearly defenseless town, decided to wait till morning. About this time Hancock arrived. His corps had been moving up behind Smith's advance since 7:00 P.M. and was now mostly assembled just east of the captured fortifications.

Hancock was an angry and frustrated man when he reached Smith. A series of staff failures had resulted in his not being informed precisely of his mission. After wasting time at City Point to get rations which were not there, it had been late in the afternoon before he had received word that he was to help take Petersburg that day. In addition, he had a faulty map and had become lost several times. To cap everything, he was suffering from an old wound, and felt sick.

Smith now recommended to Hancock that there be no further advance that night, but that the II Corps take over the captured entrenchments and advance in the morning. This suited Hancock, who wanted no more trouble that day. This was done, much to the disgust of the II Corps, which had been collectively looking forward to the prospect of an easy victory. The soldiers, it seemed, sensed the urgency better than did their leaders.

Beauregard now had arrived to take personal direction of the defense of Petersburg. Thanks to his entreaties earlier in the day, Hoke's division was marching down from Drewry's Bluff, though Lee refused to send any of his main army from its entrenchments east of Richmond. Learning that the fortifications had been penetrated, Beauregard ordered Johnson's division down from the Bermuda Hundred lines. Hoke's division arrived shortly after midnight and was put to work with the original garrison, constructing entrenchments just west of those captured by Smith. Johnson's division arrived before daybreak. With these reinforcements, and other odds and ends of units scraped up between Petersburg and Drewry's Bluff, by midmorning Beauregard had nearly 14,000 men holding the new and old fortifications. He had courageously taken the appalling risk of leaving only 1,000 men in the entrenchments facing Butler at Bermuda Hundred.

And now Butler, having lost the shining opportunity to capture Petersburg on the fifteenth, lost it again on the sixteenth. Major General Alfred H. Terry, who had replaced Gillmore in command of the X Corps at Bermuda Hundred, learned during the night that Confederate troops on his front were withdrawing. Attacking vigorously before dawn, he captured the Southern entrenchments, reporting his action to Butler. Butler, with 15,000 men, was now little more than five miles from Petersburg, with only about 1,000 men between him and the Appomattox River. But, fearful of arrival of more Southern troops from Richmond, he did nothing. Sure enough, a day and one-half later. Southern troops did arrive; Pickett's division. After a brief skirmishing against this much smaller force, Butler withdrew to his former lines.

Meanwhile Hancock, still sick, learned that Beauregard had been reinforced. Seeing the new line of entrenchments he was most cautious in ordering his men and Smith's to advance. When Grant came up during the morning to look at the situation, Hancock and Smith both stressed the unexpected strength of the enemy, and the formidable nature of the defenses. Grant, impressed, sent orders to Meade to keep the divisions coming as fast as they could, and told him and Hancock to make a major attack by 6:00 P.M.

The attack took place as directed and Hancock's corps, with that of Smith and part of Burnside's, captured the rest of the original fortifications east of the city, and a considerable portion of the new entrenchments. This, of course, could have been done just as well in the morning. Now, with dusk settling over the field, Hancock called off the attack.

On the seventeenth the Confederates were pushed back all along the line, but no major attack was mounted. Part of the trouble was Hancock's continuing sickness, which finally forced him to turn his corps over to Major General David B. Birney. Later in the day the pressure on Beauregard became greater, and fierce fighting lasted till 11:00 P.M. By this time Beauregard had expended all of his reserves and had practically resigned himself to defeat. His troops were holding only a single line of shallow entrenchments at the eastern edge of the town. But, as on the two previous evenings, the Union attacks halted just as Petersburg was about to fall into their hands.

That night, in response to Beauregard's repeated entreaties, Lee finally began to move part of his army south towards Petersburg. Even then he was not sure that Grant's entire army was south of the James, but it was obvious that Petersburg—and thus his entire army—was in dire danger. Once convinced, he moved with typical speed and energy.

Grant, who had now assumed personal command in front of Petersburg, had ordered a heavy assault early on the eighteenth. But most of Anderson's Confederate I Corps had arrived in Petersburg before dawn, and the attackers were stopped with relatively minor gains. Another and more powerful attack was launched early in the afternoon, but by now Lee and most of A. P. Hill's corps were on the ground. Lee had about 40,000 men defending the town, Grant about 65,000 in the attack. It was the old story of Spotsylvania and Cold Harbor over again. No army in the world could have budged those veterans from an adequately manned line of entrenchments, supported by ample artillery. Grant now knew that he could not take Petersburg by assault.

From the Northern point of view it is difficult to know on whom to pin the major blame for the failure to take Petersburg on the fifteenth. The eminent military analyst Steele makes this comment:

". . . the fault was mainly General Grant's. He forgot, or otherwise failed, either to name the hour for Hancock's start, or to inform Hancock, or his immediate superior, Meade, when Smith was going to start; and Meade even failed to inform

Hancock that there was to be an assault upon Petersburg in which Hancock was expected to take part.''

It has been suggested that the Grant of June 15, 1864, was not the Grant of Champion's Hill or of Chattanooga. Instead of being up in person to oversee the operations of the assaulting troops, Grant had left the job to a crotchety, meticulous-minded engineer—''Baldy'' Smith—and to blundering Ben Butler, who had already once let him down badly. Then, as Steele suggests, he had failed to supervise Meade and Hancock in the move to support Smith.

Such criticism, however, fails to consider the situation as Grant saw it. On the fifteenth and sixteenth his army was engaged in crossing the James River, under the very nose of an undefeated enemy, commanded by one of the greatest generals of history. If Lee had suspected what Grant was doing, and had pushed through Warren's and Wilson's screen, half of the Union army would have been in danger of annihilation on the north bank of the James. Typically, Grant decided to remain most of the time near the scene of greatest danger, limiting himself to two brief visits to the vicinity of City Point and Petersburg. His instructions to Meade should have been enough for that usually competent soldier to have given better orders to Hancock.

Grant had no confidence in Butler, of course, but had not been permitted to relieve that incompetent officer. He had been most explicit, therefore, in ordering Butler to send Smith to seize Petersburg. And here he made his one serious error of judgment in an otherwise faultless operation. He had been warned against Smith by other officers, including Halleck. But Grant had promoted ''Baldy'' for outstanding performance as an engineer at Chattanooga, and was mistakenly confident that Smith would do as well at Petersburg.

It was not for several weeks that Grant discovered how Butler and Smith had failed so miserably on the fifteenth and sixteenth of June. He then endeavored to have Butler dismissed from active service. Lincoln, knowing Butler's political influence in Massachusetts, would not permit this in an election year. And so the frog-faced politician would have one more opportunity to sacrifice young lives on the altar of "political necessity." Smith, a Regular, was relieved, carrying to his deathbed his hatred of Grant, and never having missed an opportunity to attack his old commander with vitriolic tongue and pen.

Meanwhile, Grant had Lee pinned down behind entrenchments. Stretching south and west from Petersburg were the railroads, vital lifelines of Lee's army and the Confederate government. Knowing that Lee realized the importance of these lines as well as he did, Grant foresaw a difficult struggle for them. Further turning movements would be dangerous—his own lines of communications would be exposed—and could only result in temporary blocking of the railroads. He knew he could stand the attrition of active trench warfare better than Lee. And he determined that it would be active and incessant. Grant did not realize, however, the length of time it would require to complete the battle.

# 24

# Raiders and Blockaders

## THE SEA WOLVES

A fantastic campaign of commerce destruction was waged by a handful of Confederate Navy ships on the high seas while the U.S. Navy was engaged in the colossal blockade of the Southland. It cost the United States 250 ocean-going craft destroyed or captured. In addition, more than 700 other vessels were shifted to foreign registry—chiefly British—as increased insurance rates and fear of capture drove Northern shipping firms to sell or transfer their vessels. A round million tons of shipping were thus transferred to British interests alone.

The war-making resources of the North were not one whit affected by this. Foreign trade increased, as did national wartime prosperity. Union exports and foreign imports, carried in vessels flying foreign flags, plied the oceans unmolested. But the United States merchant marine was practically obliterated for eighty years to come.

Great Britain assisted the South tremendously by complacently permitting the very competent Captain James Dunwoody Bullock, CSN, Confederate purchasing agent in London, to build, arm and equip Southern craft. It was an attitude which later, in 1867, would cost Her Majesty's Government $15,500,000, when the so-called "*Alabama* Claims" were adjudicated in Geneva by an international court. The court ruled that England owed this amount to the United States for the damage caused.

Bullock's operations all followed the same general pattern. British shipyards were contacted, plans were presented, and the vessels were purchased by a firm operating in the United Kingdom. Under British register, the completed ships, unarmed, cleared from British ports for West Indian or Portuguese destinations, where they were turned over to Confederate Navy officers. Their armaments, which followed them in British bottoms, were transferred, and the ships then put to sea as full-fledged Confederate warships.

Three ships were specifically involved in the "*Alabama* Claims"—CSS *Florida, Alabama* and *Shenandoah*. *Florida*, a steam corvette commanded first by Captain J. N. Maffitt, CSN, and then by Lieutenant Charles M. Morris, CSN, ravaged the Atlantic coast from August, 1862 to October, 1863. One of her officers, Lieutenant Charles W. Read, CSN, in a prize converted to a warship, actually sailed into Portland harbor on the Maine coast on June 27, 1863, and blew up a Union revenue cutter before he was captured by a local posse. *Florida* herself was captured in Bahia on October 7 in deliberate violation of Brazilian neutrality, by the USS *Wachusett*, commanded by Captain Napoleon Collins, USN.

*Alabama* was a single-screw sloop of war, also British-built and British-armed specifically for the Confederacy. Under daring Captain Raphael Semmes, CSN, of *Sumter* fame (see p. 41), she had ranged the high seas since August, 1862, on a cruise which would write indelibly the name of ship and skipper on history's pages. Semmes first cruised from the Azores to the Grand Banks and down to Brazil. Off Galveston, January 11, 1863, he blew the light-armed USS *Hatteras* out of the water.

He crossed the South Atlantic and rounded the Cape of Good Hope to run up the Indian Ocean to the Straits of Sunda, and into the China Sea. Then, Semmes, retracing his course, returned to the Indian Ocean and after cruising the Bay of Bengal, once again rounded the Cape of Good Hope. He ran clear back to Brazil and finally, turning northeast, dropped anchor in Cherbourg harbor on June 11, 1864. In twenty-three months Semmes had burned fifty-three merchantmen, released nine additional prizes on bond (they carried his prisoners), and destroyed one Federal warship.

While Semmes was trying desperately now to wangle permission from the French government for the overhaul *Alabama* sorely needed after a 75,000 mile cruise, USS *Kearsarge*, alerted by U.S. consular information, steamed into the harbor on June 14, from Flushing, Holland.

Captain John A. Winslow, USN, frustrated by being kept idle in European waters for two years while a war was raging at home, had taken out that frustration on his ship and men by grooming for the combat he hoped some day would occur. Chain cables were festooned along her sides to protect her engines; incessant drill and target practice had brought her gun crews to perfection. She was a taut ship in every sense of that naval phrase.

Winslow's opportunity had come and he wasn't going to risk tangling it in neutrality restrictions. So *Kearsarge*, having spotted *Alabama*, turned on her heel without dropping anchor and hove to outside the three-mile limit to wait.

She didn't have to wait long. Semmes, either made over-confident by his past success, or because he felt sure the French authorities would not let him remain in port indefinitely, took the initiative. With formal, old-style naval courtesy, he challenged Winslow to single-ship duel, in a note sent through the U.S. consul.

On paper the ships were fairly evenly matched, with a slight preponderance of speed and firepower in *Kearsarge*'s favor. But

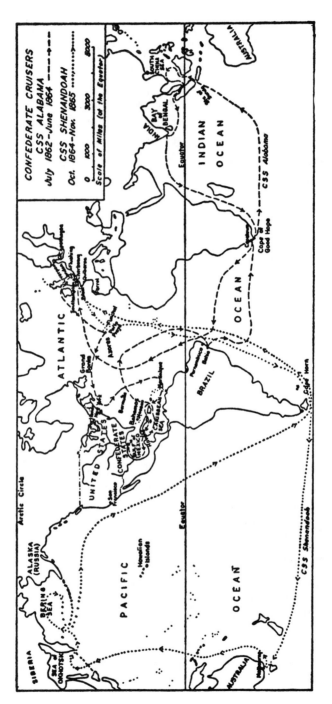

*Alabama* was a tired ship and Semmes' gun crews poorly trained. He had had no powder to waste in gunnery practice, and pot-shots against unarmed merchantmen made poor substitute, as he would soon find out.

By nightfall June 18 Semmes felt he was ready. Allegedly he turned over his chronometers, specie, and the ransom bonds obtained from prizes to the owner of the British steam-yacht *Deerhound*, which was in port. That night a party of ladies and gentlemen was entertained on board, and next morning at 9:30 *Alabama* steamed out to do battle. Escorting her was a French iron-clad—to preserve neutral waters from violation—and behind came *Deerhound*. What with the attending ships and the crowds of townspeople gathered on Cherbourg's heights and bright Sunday morning, the scene had more of the aspects of a regatta than a seafight.

*Kearsarge* moved well out beyond the three-mile limit, then turned to meet her opponent. At 11:10 Semmes opened fire. For sixty minutes the two ships battled in circles about a common center, with *Kearsarge* gradually closing until they were about 500 yards apart. The Federal ship had seven guns to the Confederate's eight, but two of these were 11-inch, while *Alabama*'s largest was a 7-inch piece. Winslow's gunners served their weapons well, punching great holes along *Alabama*'s wooden waterline. By the hour's end *Alabama*'s fires had been extinguished by the water pouring in. Semmes vainly hurried to make sail and escape to neutral waters, but his ship was settling fast, and as the sea lapped his gun-deck, he struck his colors. But through misunderstanding in the confusion of the battle, firing continued on both sides.

Semmes then sent one of his two remaining boats to *Kearsarge* to announce his surrender, and the firing ceased. Winslow, who also had only two serviceable boats left, put these out to pick up survivors. While they were pulling in seventy Confederates, Winslow hailed the nearby *Deerhound* to help in the rescue work. The wallowing *Alabama* now sank, stern first, spilling her survivors into the water. The British yacht hauled on board Captain Semmes and forty-one of his men, then—to Winslow's astonishment and rage—made off for the English coast. Raphael Semmes would remain a free man, to fight again for the Confederacy.

*Alabama's* losses had been forty-odd killed and wounded. Only 3 of *Kearsarge's* crew were wounded, and the Union sloop-of-war was practically undamaged, her chain-cable armor having resisted 28 of *Alabama's* projectiles—28 out of 370 rounds fired. The one shell which might have caused serious injury, a 100-pounder lodging in *Kearsarge's* sternpost, failed to explode.

The *Shenandoah* was one of the last of Bullock's many attempts to keep the Stars and Bars flying on the high seas. A full-rigged ship with auxiliary steam power, her objective was the destruction of the United States whaling industry.

Her cruise was truly amazing. Commander James I. Waddell, CSN, took her in October, 1864, from Funchal in the Madeiras all the way to Melbourne, Australia. Ranging north to the Bering Sea, she then buttered the ocean with flaming hulks. All but five of the thirty-two whalers and merchantmen she took were destroyed; those spared carried her prisoners back to San Francisco under cartel. Ironically enough—Waddell, entering no port, was ignorant of the fact—most of *Shenandoah's* prizes were taken after the war was ended; its last bonfire of eight whalers flared June 28, 1865.

Cruising down the California coast Waddell on August 2, spoke to a British ship and learned hostilities had ceased. Dismounting his guns, he rounded the Horn and crossed the Atlantic to arrive in Liverpool on November 6, and surrendered to British authorities. *Shenandoah* was turned over to the United States after the release of her crew.

Of necessity, our sketch of high-seas operations has carried us far beyond the pace of events at home. We return to the Gulf of Mexico in 1864, and a crusty Northern admiral with a long over-due engagement of great importance to the United States.

# "DAMN THE TORPEDOES!"

Mobile, Alabama, had developed into a Confederate stronghold rivalling Wilmington in importance as a blockade-running terminus. Pugnacious Admiral Farragut, who had wanted to take Mobile as soon as he had captured New Orleans back in 1862, returned to his Gulf Command in 1864 from a long, recuperative leave, determined to do the job. Many things had intervened to thwart his original intention; the clearing of the Mississippi River, the Red River campaign and the world-wide hunt for Confederate sea-raiders. Meanwhile the defenses of Mobile had become formidable, while the presence in the harbor of the ram *Tennessee*, most powerful Confederate warship of them all, brought added complications.

In order to take Mobile, Farragut would need, besides his deep-draft wooden ships to hammer past the forts, monitors to operate against the *Tennessee* and other light-draft Southern ships inside the harbor.

*Tennessee*, built at Selma, more than 200 miles up the Alabama River, and brought down to Mobile after much labor, was 209 feet long and 48 feet in beam. Her wrought iron plates were 6 inches thick, she carried 6 heavy guns, and her light draft permitted maneuver in shallow waters.

Farragut didn't get his monitors until the end of July, when Sherman was driving at Atlanta. Grant, well knowing the value to Sherman's campaign of a diversion at Mobile, was in hearty accord with Farragut's idea. He assigned to him General Gordon Granger and an Army detachment to cooperate in operations against the forts.

Mobile Bay opens to the sea through a three-mile mouth between Mobile Point on the east and Dauphin Island on the west. The deep-draft ship channel hugs Mobile Point, on which sat Fort Morgan, whose sixty-nine guns covered the channel.

A hundred yards west of the fort a triple line of submarine

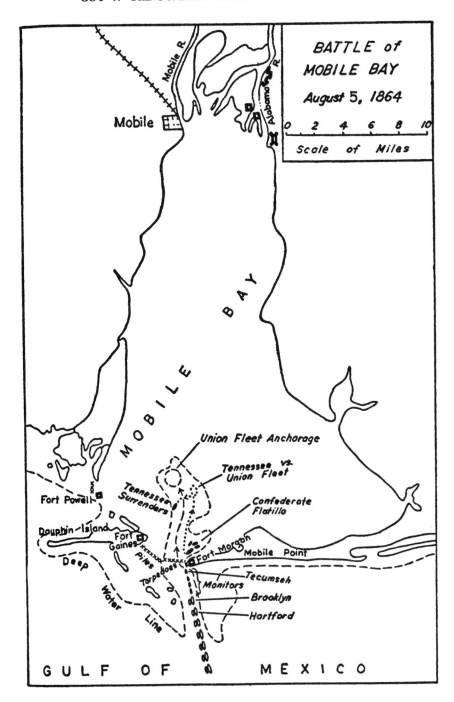

BATTLE of
MOBILE BAY
August 5, 1864

Scale of Miles

mines—180 of them—stretched west, blocking all the remainder of the mile-wide deep-water channel, while in the shallows beyond a line of obstructions reached to Fort Gaines on Dauphin Island. A blue buoy marked the beginning of the mine field; attacking vessels must keep east of this, thus putting them directly under Fort Morgan's guns.

Farragut, who had made personal reconnaissance in a small boat, had the mine field and buoy plainly marked. He could see, also, north of Fort Morgan, the *Tennessee* and three smaller ironclad gunboats prepared to charge on any Union vessel successfully making the runby. Farragut knew that Flag Officer Franklin Buchanan, CSN—"Old Buck" to his former comrades of the U.S. Navy, and the first commander of the *Virginia* (*Merrimack*)—flew his blue command flag on the *Tennessee*.

By early August, General Granger's troops were investing Fort Gaines on Dauphin Island. Farragut decided to attack on August 5. He planned to run by Fort Morgan, drowning it in fire. The monitors, leading, were to draw the fort's fire, then tackle the *Tennessee*. The light Union gunboats were slated to destroy the other Confederate craft. The heavy wooden ships would assist Granger's troops in attacking both forts, before moving up the bay to Mobile itself, thirty miles away.

At daybreak, August 5, 1864, in the lifting fog, the squadron steamed in. First came the monitor division of four ships. The wooden-ship division, fourteen vessels lashed in pairs—one light and one heavy each, for mutual assistance in case of breakdown—followed close. *Brooklyn* and *Octorara* led. Then came the flagship *Hartford* and *Metacomet*.

Farragut had grumpily yielded to his captains' insistence that *Brooklyn*, which could train four guns in forward fire, take the lead place from the flagship. But he climbed into the port main rigging of *Hartford* to direct the fight, and there his fleet captain insisted he permit a length of light rope be lashed about him.

*Tecumseh*, the leading monitor, opened on Fort Morgan at 6:47 A.M., and the cannonade began. Coming in on the peak of the flood tide, the wooden ships overhauled the slower monitors. *Tecumseh*'s skipper, glimpsing the Confederate flotilla waiting beyond, shifted course at the narrowest point in the channel, to close with *Tennessee*. He cut the corner of the mine-field. *Brooklyn*, now close behind, sighted buoys ahead and reversed engines, veering with the tide and blocking the passage of following ships.

In consequence, monitors and wooden ships began to pile up, trying to avoid collision. Eight Union vessels were now receiving crossfire from the fort and the Southern flotilla, reminiscent of Du Pont's pile-up in front of the Charleston forts. At this moment *Tecumseh*—only 200 yards from *Tennessee*, and 500 from *Hartford*—hit a mine and blew up, sinking almost instantaneously.

Here it was that Commander T. A. M. Craven, caught with his pilot in *Tecumseh*'s conning tower, stood aside from the narrow escape hatch. "After you, pilot," called Craven. The pilot, as well as twenty-one other officers and men who scrambled from the ship, reached the water safely; Craven and ninety-two other officers and men went down.

And here it was that Farragut soared to the peak of leadership.

"Damn the torpedoes! Four bells!" he roared.

Veering *Hartford* to the left, he drove into the mine-field, signaling the remainder of the squadron to follow. He'd either make it, or his own ship's death would clear the way for the others.

As *Hartford* churned past the foam of *Tecumseh*'s sinking, she dropped a boat to pick up survivors. Confederate General Richard L. Page, CSA, former ship-mate of Farragut and now commanding Fort Morgan, from his parapet warned all gunners to spare the lifeboat.

But that was the only target spared on either side, as the Union squadron followed their leader. The flagship's crew, exchanging round for round with the fort, felt the scratch and bump of the mines scraping her keel, but not a one exploded. Their primers, corroded by long immersion, would not function.

The entire squadron ran safely by. *Tennessee* now tried to ram *Hartford*, but—under-engined—missed. The three Confederate gunboats, escaping ahead of the Federal column, raked it severely with their stern guns, until Farragut's light ships were cut loose and chased them into shallow water. One was captured; the other two took shelter back behind the fort. The Union squadron now dropped anchor, four miles up the bay, and went to breakfast.

But the fight was far from being over. "Old Buck" Buchanan in his *Tennessee* steamed deliberately up-channel, to take on the entire Federal flotilla. Hastily the Union ships slipped their cables and moved down on him. *Monongahela*, ramming the Confederate, only succeeded in crushing her own bow. *Lackawanna*, ramming at full speed, was followed by *Hartford*, which struck a glancing blow. The slower monitors came waddling in and one of them—*Chickashaw*—hanging close to *Tennessee*'s stern, pounded her for thirty minutes with 11-inch shot.

Ringed by Union vessels, her plates buckled, her smokestack and rudder-chains shot away, many of her guns disabled, wounded *Tennessee* at last wallowed impotently. As four of Farragut's ships approached again to ram, "Old Buck" Buchanan, himself severely wounded, gave up his gallant fight and Mobile Bay was won. Later, all the forts surrendered to joint Army-Navy action, although the city itself remained in Southern hands until the spring of 1865. Farragut's casualties totalled 335, including the *Tecumseh*'s sinking. Confederate casualties were negligible, except for *Tennessee*; she lost twelve men killed and nineteen wounded.

Blockade-running in the Gulf of Mexico had ended.

We pick up now the trail of long-legged Western men, marching inexorably into Georgia with William T. Sherman.

# Marching into Georgia

**Y**ou I propose to move against Johnston's army, to break it up and get into the interior of the enemy's country as far as you can, inflicting all the damage you can against their war resources."

These words, written by Grant one month earlier, were on the mind of William Tecumseh Sherman as he observed his troops move south from their encampments below Chattanooga on May 5, 1864.

Sherman that day unsheathed one of the finest instruments of war the United States has produced; a small group of armies, composed largely of veterans, and commanded by leaders upon whom he could rely, and who were as loyal to him as he was to Grant. The component forces were the Army of the Cumberland, 61,000 strong, commanded by George H. Thomas; the Army of the Tennessee, 24,500 strong, commanded by James B. McPherson; and the Army of the Ohio, 13,500 strong, commanded by

John M. Schofield. They made a fine team, these four West Pointers, and they worked well together.

This was an army ready to march and to fight. Sherman had issued strict orders that officers and men would at all times have five days' rations on their persons or their animals, and he had reduced to a minimum the number of pack animals and wagons that would be used to carry either personal equipment of officers, or unnecessary headquarters or supply equipment. There would be no tents for officers or headquarters, though there were canvas tarpaulins, without poles, to provide some shelter for senior commanders and the operating staffs. Sherman himself set the example, and his staff officers, with mixed pride and chagrin, noted that their mess and other facilities were more austere than those of the average regiment.

Opposing them was an army commanded by another, somewhat older, West Pointer: Joseph E. Johnston. There were some marked differences in his situation and that of Sherman—but there were also similarities. Whereas Sherman had the complete confidence of his superior—Grant—Johnston knew that he was not trusted, was in fact disliked by his superior, President Davis. Sherman's army was austere in the comforts of life permitted it by its commander, but it was rich in the vital matériel required for war-making. Johnston's men had abundant food available from the farms of Georgia, but their weapons were of many types—some good, some poor—and ammunitions supply arrangements could not always provide ammunition in proper proportions to the different weapons, and to the varying rates of expenditures. Equipment was frequently makeshift, and was rarely as good or as ample as that of the Northerners.

But Johnston's army was, for the most part, an army of veterans. The three infantry corps commanders—Hood, Hardee and Polk—were capable, experienced self-reliant men. The cavalry commander—Wheeler—was one of the three or four best cavalry leaders of the war, and far more able than any of the horsemen serving Sherman.

With his 60,000 men Johnston knew that he could not hope to take the initiative in the campaign now starting. But he hoped that Sherman—whom he at first considered to be a bit impetuous—would dash his army against entrenchments, and otherwise provide opportunities for effective counterblows. He knew, furthermore, that if he were to be forced back from his initial position near Dalton, Georgia, the further south he went the longer and more vulnerable would be Sherman's lines of communications, and the more men he would have to use to guard these communications. Meanwhile Johnston would inevitably pick up strength as his supply lines shortened. So canny Joe Johnston could afford to play a waiting game. Whenever he got Sherman out on a limb he would strike.

Johnston's defensive position west of Dalton—twenty-five miles southeast of Chattanooga by railroad—was a strong one, covering Buzzard Roost pass where the railroad wound its way through rugged Rocky Face Ridge. This ridge stretched out to the southward for another twenty-five miles, and part of Wheeler's cavalry covered the few trails that traversed it, none really suitable for the passage of major forces. The remainder of the cavalry protected Johnston's right flank, in a wide arc from the northern rim of the ridge to the Conesauga River. Johnston rightly estimated that Sherman would be reluctant to leave the railroad, and he hoped that the Northerners would try a frontal assault. The only alternative appeared to be a wide turning movement over poor roads to Rome, which would dangerously expose the Union flank and line of communications.

Sherman's estimate of the situation was similar to Johnston's. His plan, however, was bolder—though really less rash—than Johnston expected. Sherman had no intention of smashing his army against the well-nigh impregnable Rocky Face Ridge position. Thomas and Schofield were to advance opposite this position—without assaulting—to hold the Confederates in their entrenchments, while McPherson's army would make a wide

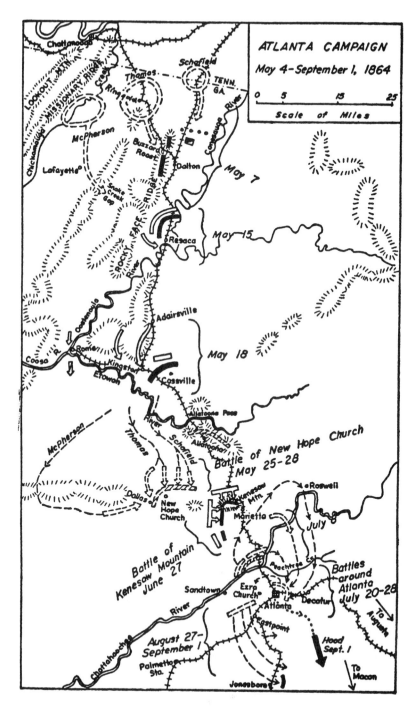

ATLANTA CAMPAIGN
May 4–September 1, 1864

0    5    15    25
Scale   of   Miles

turning movement, down the valley west of the ridge, crossing it, if possible, in order to get behind Johnston at Dalton. If this should prove unfeasible, or if Johnston should withdraw, McPherson would continue southward to Rome, whence he would operate against Johnston's flank or line of communications. To do this he was accompanied by a wagon train with twenty days' supplies, and a herd of beef cattle was with the train.

There was some risk in this division of forces, but Sherman was confident of the fighting and marching qualities of his troops. If Johnston should try to concentrate against McPherson, this would permit Thomas and Schofield to advance to seize the railroad behind the Confederate army, cutting it off from Atlanta, while McPherson had an open line of retreat to the north if he should be faced by superior forces.

By the seventh Thomas and Schofield were entrenched below the main Confederate position. McPherson then proceeded to move southeast, through Lafayette and Villanow. On the ninth he discovered that the narrow trail over Snake Creek Gap, fourteen miles south of the Buzzard Roost railroad pass, had been left undefended. He pressed through with his entire corps, driving back a small detachment of Southern cavalry covering the eastern end of the pass. McPherson then pushed to within a mile and a half of the railroad at Resaca, but finding the place apparently strongly fortified, he withdrew to the vicinity of Snake Creek Gap, entrenched, and reported his situation to Sherman.

On this day both Sherman and Johnston had been ill-served by two of their most reliable subordinates. There is no excuse for Wheeler having left the approaches to Snake Creek Gap uncovered and even unobserved. There was equally no excuse for McPherson's not having made a reconnaissance in force to determine the strength of the defenders of Resaca. He would have discovered one brigade, which could easily have been pushed aside. Johnston, who was completely surprised by this appearance of a Northern army in his rear, would have been cut off from Atlanta, and would have been forced eastward over poor roads.

The errors, however, canceled each other out, and neither of these fine young soldiers would make such mistakes again.

As Sherman shifted the rest of his army behind McPherson through Snake Creek Gap, Johnston retired to Resaca. There was considerable skirmishing north and west of the town on the fourteenth and fifteenth, while Sherman sent a division each of infantry and cavalry to cross the Oostenaula River, to the south, to threaten the railroad in Johnston's rear. On the night of May 15, therefore, Johnston abandoned his untenable position and withdrew to the vicinity of Cassville. Sherman followed promptly, moving on a broad front stretching from Adairsville to Rome.

This region between the Oostenaula and Etowah Rivers was the only open stretch of country between Chattanooga and Atlanta, which was generally rugged and heavily wooded. But the movements of both armies were slowed by almost incessant rains, which turned the roads and fields into quagmires and swamps.

Johnston now hoped to take advantage of the wide frontage of Sherman's army. Just north of Cassville he concentrated Polk's and Hood's corps against Schofield while Hardee took up a delaying position near Kingston to hold off Thomas and McPherson. But Hood, who was supposed to attack Schofield's left flank, discovered a small cavalry force operating on his own right. Thinking this to be much larger than it was, he called off his projected attack, and faced the supposed threat. This delay permitted Sherman to become aware of the Confederate dispositions, and to concentrate between Kingston and Cassville. The opportunity having passed, Johnston withdrew on the eighteenth to a strong position just south of Cassville. He had received reinforcements, bringing his strength to more than 70,000, while Sherman's strength had declined to about 90,000. Johnston decided, therefore, that the combination of a strong defensive position, together with near-equality of forces, would permit him to fight a battle with considerable chance of success. The Southern army made ready for battle.

Sherman pressed after the Confederates, and the nineteenth was a day of heavy skirmishing. That evening Hood and Polk apparently reported to Johnston their concern about Union artillery enfilading the right flank of the position. There is some question about what actually took place between the three generals, because after the war Hood denied making such a report, and Polk, who was killed a few days after the incident, never commented on it. In any event, Johnston apparently felt that two of his corps commanders were not wholeheartedly ready to fight in that position, so he withdrew again, this time to an extremely strong position overlooking the Etowah River where it flows through the mountains to form the Allatoona Pass.

As a young lieutenant Sherman had been stationed for some time in this part of Georgia, and knew the country well. He did not even think of moving against the Allatoona Pass position. Provided with 20 days' rations, his three armies struck directly south toward Dallas in another turning movement around Johnston's left.

Johnston now decided to try to take up a position that would force Sherman to attack him under conditions favorable to the defenders. Retiring quickly down the railroad to Marietta, he marched westward to entrench his army near Dallas and New Hope Church, directly in Sherman's path. On May 25, Hooker's XX Corps, leading the left of Thomas' army, encountered the Southerners near New Hope Church. Not realizing that Johnston's entire army was in front of him, Sherman ordered Hooker to press forward, and a fierce fight took place. The next day the fighting spread, somewhat sporadically, right and left of New Hope Church, as the rest of the Union army came up. For three more days the battle continued, as Sherman probed for weak places in Johnston's line. Finally, after several repulses on the twenty-eighth, he came to the conclusion that the position was too strong for further attacks, and began to maneuver around Johnston's right flank, to cut the Confederates off from the railroad.

To meet this threat Johnston extended his lines to the right.

Both armies continued to sidle eastward, until, by June 6, they were again astride the railroad, with the Confederates entrenched on high ground a few miles north of Marietta. Sherman's troops pushed close to this line, pressing particularly strongly against Johnston's overextended left flank. In the face of this pressure the Confederate general was forced to contract his line, and to withdraw about a mile. His right flank was now entrenched along the crest of Kenesaw Mountain, covering the railroad, while his center and left were refused, parallel to the railroad. His line, therefore, formed a great arc north and west of Marietta.

During the early stages of this maneuvering, on June 14, General Polk was killed by artillery fire while Johnston and other senior officers were observing Federal movements from the crest of one of the hills. Command of his corps was turned over to Major General William W. Loring.

By June 25, Sherman realized that his army had been stretched to the limit in trying to overlap the Confederate position. He concluded, therefore, that the Confederates must be even more extended. After careful reconnaissance of the Southern lines, he and his commanders came to the conclusion that Johnston was relying on the natural strength of the Kenesaw Mountain part of his line to permit him to thin out the defenders there, in order to put more strength on his left, further south. The hill, then, seemed to be the most vulnerable portion of the Confederate position. He decided to attack on the twenty-seventh; McPherson would strike the left of Loring's corps, on Kenesaw Mountain, while Thomas attacked Hardee, on lower ground, in the Confederate center. Schofield would make secondary attacks and demonstrations against Hood, on the left.

Sherman ordered this attack somewhat against his better judgment. But many of his officers and men had been grumbling about so much marching and so little fighting. They felt that the Confederates could be beaten more quickly by a direct assault than by so many wide turning movements. Sherman had considerable respect for the defensive value of trenches, and, as he said,

"As a rule, whichever party attacked first got the worst of it." However, the apparent weakness of Kenesaw Mountain, the over-extension of the entire Southern line, and the aggressive desires of his men all combined to overcome his innate caution.

The attacks took place early on the twenty-seventh, and were repulsed at all points. Sherman lost about 3,000 men in this battle, Johnston only 800. This fight was a valuable object lesson to both armies. Sherman's men never again complained about too much marching.

Sherman now ordered another turning movement around Johnston's left. McPherson's army was pulled out of its trenches on the left of the line, as Sherman ordered the same kind of leap-frog movement that Grant had been making against Lee in Virginia. McPherson was to head for Sandtown, on the Chatta-hoochie River and then, if opportunity offered, to cut eastward for the railroad behind Johnston. Thomas and Schofield, as be-fore, were to keep pressure on Johnston, and follow him aggres-sively as soon as he withdrew from his untenable position.

The movement began on July 2, and Johnston, as Sherman had foreseen, was forced to withdraw. But he had had the fore-sight to construct a powerful entrenched line north of the railroad bridge over the Chattahoochie, to which he retired the evening of July 4. Sherman, expecting to be able to attack the rear of the Confederate army while it was retreating in confusion over the river, was now stopped by what he termed "one of the strongest pieces of field fortifications I ever saw."

Promptly Sherman sent his cavalry north and south of the Confederate bridgehead, to find suitable crossing places over the Chattahoochie. All of these were covered by Southern cavalry, but on the eighth Schofield was able to force a crossing about five miles north of Johnston's fortifications. McPherson was now swung wide north of Schofield, to cross at Roswell, while Thomas maintained pressure against Johnston's position.

Once more, on July 9, the Southern army was forced to abandon its position by a Union turning movement. Johnston now fell back below Peachtree Creek, just north of Atlanta. He felt that the time had at last come when he could strike back successfully against the attackers. Keeping his army concentrated on high ground just north of Atlanta, he planned to attack any exposed portion of the Union army, whenever Sherman should begin to maneuver closer to the city. He noted that McPherson on the Federal left was heading toward Decatur, while Thomas, on the right, was advancing slowly eastward just north of Peachtree Creek. He felt sure, therefore, that he would be able to concentrate greatly superior forces against one of these flanks of the Union army. He prepared his plans for attack.

But Johnston was not to have a chance to carry these out. On July 17, he received a telegram from Richmond which stated in part: ". . . As you have failed to arrest the advance of the enemy to the vicinity of Atlanta, and express no confidence that you can defeat or repel him, you are hereby relieved from the command of the Army and Department of Tennessee, which you will immediately turn over to General Hood."

Johnston promptly complied with this order, and in reporting this to the Secretary of War, commented: "Confident language by a military commander is not usually regarded as evidence of competence."

Johnston was very bitter toward President Davis for having thus relieved him at the end of two and a half months of skillful delaying action against a numerically superior foe, just as he was perfecting plans for an aggressive counterstroke. Though there had been some strain between him and Hood since the Cassville incident, the new commanding general now requested him to give the necessary orders for the following day. Johnston complied, and outlined his plans for striking the Northerners either as they crossed Peachtree Creek, or as they approached Atlanta from the northeast, as now appeared to be their intention.

The evidence is fairly clear that there would have been aggressive Southern action against Sherman shortly after mid-July. The relief of Johnston, and the appointment of Hood confirmed this. John Bell Hood was a naturally aggressive, impetuous soldier, who had proven his gallantry on many a hard-fought field. He had lost the use of an arm at Gettysburg, and had lost a leg at Chickamauga. But these terrible wounds had not in any way diminished his ardor or ambition.

McPherson and Schofield had been classmates of Hood at West Point, and they reported to Sherman that they considered the new Southern commander to be brave, determined and rash, but without great mental capacity. Sherman opined that under the circumstances in which Hood came to command, even the most cautious and most stupid soldier would realize that he was expected by his government to seize the initiative and to strike vigorously and repeatedly at the advancing enemy. Sherman, therefore, warned all of his command to be prepared for hard fighting in the near future.

Meanwhile there had been two major changes in Hood's army. His old corps was now commanded by Benjamin F. Cheatham, while Alexander P. Stewart had succeeded Loring in command of Polk's old corps.

By evening of the nineteenth the Union forces were advancing on Atlanta from north and northeast on a front almost ten miles wide. McPherson's army had reached Decatur, and was moving southwest down the Decatur-Atlanta road and railroad. Two miles to the northwest Schofield was crossing the South Fork of Peachtree Creek. About three miles separated Schofield from the left flank of Thomas' army, which was crossing Peachtree Creek directly north of Atlanta. The advance elements of all three armies were less than five miles from the city.

The gap between Schofield and Thomas had been foreseen by Johnston, and was the opportunity for which he had been waiting. Hood decided to seize it promptly. Sending Cheatham and Wheeler, plus a contingent of Georgia militia, east of the city to demonstrate against Schofield and McPherson, Hood ordered Stewart's and Hardee's corps to attack the left wing of Thomas' army.

Though the specific assault came by surprise, all of the Union troops were alert. The forces engaged on each side were almost equal in size—about 20,000 men each—and the Northerners had little trouble in repulsing the assault. Confederate losses were about 2,500 in about two hours of intensive combat; Union casualties numbered 1,600.

Next day the Union army continued its left wheel, and that evening Hood withdrew from the entrenched line south of Peachtree Creek and back into the fortifications of Atlanta itself. His reason for doing this was to free as many troops as possible for another attack, planned for the twenty-second. Sherman interpreted the withdrawal as presaging an evacuation of Atlanta, and ordered his subordinates to follow close behind the Southerners and into Atlanta if possible. At the same time the cavalry division covering the Union left flank was ordered to move east of Decatur to destroy the railroad approaching Atlanta from that direction.

This order to the cavalry was one of Sherman's most serious mistakes. It meant that the left flank of his army, from the outskirts of Atlanta to Decatur, was completely uncovered. Apparently McPherson and his three corps commanders were unaware of the absence of their normal cavalry flank protection, or else had been so misled by orders to pursue that they neglected the routine precautions that would be expected from such veteran troops and commanders. Whatever the reason, it nearly resulted in disaster.

Because Hood had withdrawn from the Peachtree Creek line only in order to release sufficient force to make a full-scale attack on the Union left on the twenty-second. Hardee's corps—the best troops and most reliable leader of the army—was ordered to make a fifteen-mile night march through Atlanta and wide to the south and east to make this attack. Wheeler's cavalry corps was also to take part.

Two of McPherson's corps (Logan's and Blair's) were in line opposite the southeast corner of the Atlanta fortifications. Dodge's corps, which had been in reserve, was moving up from

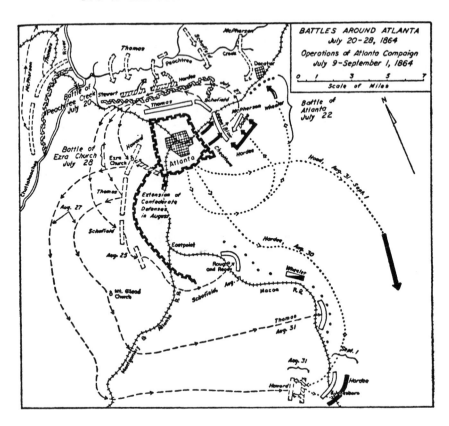

the rear toward the left flank, in anticipation of the forward move in "pursuit." At noon the exposed flank of Blair's division was struck a powerful blow by the left of Hardee's line, which approached in complete surprise through the woods southeast of Atlanta. Blair's left crumbled, and fell back in confusion.

Almost immediately after hitting Blair, Hardee's men struck the left flank of Dodge's long march column; a surprise to both sides. The attack was unexpected, but the Union veterans merely faced left to form a battle line almost immediately. The Southerners had not expected to run into anything like this behind the Union left flank, and the initial assault was thrown back. About the same time Wheeler's troopers swept into Decatur, where one infantry brigade, and a few cavalrymen, were guarding McPherson's trains.

McPherson himself had been talking to Sherman at his temporary headquarters behind Schofield's line, just north of the railroad. The young general promptly jumped on his horse, and followed by his staff galloped toward the sound of the guns. He soon got the picture of what was going on, and sent various officers to give orders to his different commands. He then galloped alone through the woods behind Blair's corps to take personal command at the point of greatest danger. But the situation was more serious than he realized; the Confederates had reached that stretch of woods; McPherson was ambushed, shot from his horse, and killed instantly. The riderless horse galloped back the way he had come, thus informing the army of the loss of its leader.

General Logan, commanding the XV Corps, immediately assumed command, and sent one of his divisions to fill the gap between Blair's shaken left, and Dodge's right. At about this same time Cheatham's corps still further shook the Army of the Tennessee by a sortie from the Atlanta defenses. They penetrated the center of the XV Corps near the railroad, but were repulsed elsewhere. Prompt counterattacks quickly re-established the situation along the railroad.

Sherman, staying at his temporary headquarters just at the northern edge of this confused battle, alerted Schofield and Thomas to be ready to send reinforcements but held off further orders until he could be sure that his old army could not handle its own problems. He also ordered Thomas and Schofield to test the defenses in front of them to see if the concentration of troops on Hood's right had caused him to denude the rest of the fortifications. These exploratory attacks were thrown back by the Southerners, at about the time that it became obvious that the Army of the Tennessee had driven off the attacks of Cheatham, Hardee and Wheeler. Sherman's faith in his old army was justified.

This violent struggle, known as the Battle of Atlanta, had started under the most auspicious circumstances for Hood and his men. But the final results were entirely the opposite of what Hood had hoped for. Once they had recovered from their initial shock, the Northerners had thrown back the Southern attacks with great losses. The exact number of Confederate casualties is not known, but it was about 8,000 men. Northern losses were only 3,722. And Sherman's army, save for the loss of one of its best officers, was better off when the battle ended than when it had begun.

It was now obvious to Sherman that he did not have enough men to completely invest Atlanta. And he had no intention of assaulting the powerful defenses. His only means of bringing Hood out into the open, therefore, would be to cut the railroad lines into Atlanta from the south. To approach these from the northeast would result in extreme danger to his own line of communications. He decided, therefore, to swing his army in a great wheel to his right, to the west side of Atlanta, whence he could better operate against the railroads.

At the same time he sent most of his cavalry in a raid south of Atlanta for the purpose of cutting the railroad seriously enough as to force Hood out to fight for his communications. General Stoneman, with two divisions—about 4,000 troopers—left Decatur on July 27. At the same time General McCook, with about 2,000 men, headed southwest on the other side of Atlanta, down the Chattahoochie, before turning east toward the railroad.

Stoneman had been given permission to raid south toward Macon to liberate some 30,000 Union prisoners held at Andersonville, after he had cut the railroad at Jonesboro. But he became so enthralled with the possibilities of the glory he would gain from such a fear that he hardly bothered with the railroad. He sent only one division to destroy the tracks while he struck directly south for Andersonville with the other. The result was that neither force was adequate for its task. The railroad wasn't cut, and Stoneman, repulsed by militia at Macon, was surrounded and captured. McCook's division didn't fare much better, and was badly defeated by part of Wheeler's cavalry. Sherman, greatly disappointed, decided that the only way to take the railroad was to reach it with the entire army. But for the moment the risk of thus jeopardizing his line of communications deterred him.

Meanwhile the Army of the Tennessee had initiated the movement which would prepare for this. Pulling out from the far left of the Federal line, east of Atlanta, on July 27, it marched behind the other armies to swing to the west of the city. The Army of the Tennessee was now commanded by Howard, who had taken over from Logan after the Battle of Atlanta. The appointment assured the continued teamwork of four commanders who completely understood and trusted one another; Howard was unquestionably a far abler soldier than Logan.

While Logan accepted Sherman's decision loyally and without question, trouble was stirred up by a trouble-maker *par excellence*—Hooker, who stood next behind Sherman and Thomas in seniority. Hooker commanded a corps in Thomas' army with his old aggressive spirit, re-earning his nickname of "Fighting Joe." But he had caused Sherman some trouble during the campaign by "pulling rank" on other officers. Now, incensed that he had not been given command of McPherson's army, Hooker, in high dudgeon, submitted his request to be relieved; a request Thomas forwarded "approved and *heartily* recommended." Sherman immediately assigned General Slocum to command Hooker's corps, and let Hooker go "with a sense of relief."

Logan's corps of Howard's Army of the Tennessee took the brunt of a Confederate attack near Ezra Church on July 28, as it completed its swing to the west. Hood again thought he saw an opportunity to strike a detached portion of Sherman's army, but the Northerners were ready for the attack, behind hasty entrenchments. The Southerners were repulsed with a loss of 4,300 men, while there were only 632 Union casualties. Both Logan and Howard performed well, with Howard particularly impressing his new command by his competence, and by the coolness with which he sauntered down behind the lines, under fire, at the height of the Confederate attack.

Sherman was still preparing for all-out action, regardless of any threat to his communications. Beginning August 2, Schofield and Thomas in turn peeled off from east and north of Atlanta, to circle west and take up positions extending Howard's Ezra Church line, and facing generally southeast.

Schofield, August 5, jabbed at the railroad near Eastpoint. But another argument over relative rank spoiled the effort. For the operation Sherman had temporarily assigned to Schofield's command the corps of Major General J. M. Palmer, ordinarily part of Thomas' army. Palmer, claiming he was senior in rank, refused to accept Schofield's orders. Sherman quickly relieved Palmer, but the Southerners were alerted during the delay, and the operation was a failure.

About this time Wheeler and his cavalry were raiding along the railroad back to Chattanooga. Sherman decided to take advantage of the absence of this intrepid and able cavalryman to suspend his main operation and let his own cavalry make one more effort to cut the railroad south of Atlanta, to force Hood into the open. But Kilpatrick—of Richmond raid fame—accomplished no more this time than he had then. On August 23, the day after he had returned to claim success, Confederate trains were chugging into Atlanta again.

Sherman delayed no longer. Leaving Slocum's XX Corps behind to guard the Chattahoochie bridge at his rear, he swung his armies in a great wheel to the east on the twenty-seventh, with Schofield's army, opposite Eastpoint, on the pivot. First Schofield moved to a position between Eastpoint and Mt. Gilead Church, to cover the advance of the other two, and to protect the armies' trains, carrying fifteen days' rations. Thomas and Howard, in that order from the left, swung wider, south and east of Schofield's protection. Both of these armies hit the Montgomery and Atlanta R.R. on the twenty-eighth, and devoted the next day to destroying a great section of track.

On the thirtieth the wheeling movement continued, meeting much resistance from Wheeler's cavalry. On this day, Hood sent Hardee, with about half his army, to Jonesboro. On the thirty-first Hardee attacked Howard, on the extreme Union right, but was repulsed. At about the same time both Schofield and Thomas reached the Macon R.R. line further north; Hood's line of communications was cut.

That night Hood destroyed the supply and ammunition stores in Atlanta, and evacuated the city, moving east and south. Slocum's corps marched into Atlanta the next morning. Sherman decided to move his entire army into the city, to rest and prepare for further operations. The Atlanta campaign was over.

Grant's scheme of massive envelopment was slowly being unveiled. But around its uneasy perimeter some significant events had occurred and more were to come. So we move now up to the Shenandoah Valley.

# 26

# The Last Days
# in the Valley

While still facing Grant in the Cold Harbor lines in early June, 1864, Lee had discovered another threat. Across the Blue Ridge, Union General David Hunter, picking up the task which Sigel had failed to accomplish, was, as we have seen, inching his way up the Shenandoah Valley— menacing Lynchburg and the Southside R.R. running into Petersburg and Richmond. By June 11, Hunter was at Lexington, where he wantonly burned the buildings of Virginia Military Institute. Shorthanded though he was, Lee determined to clear the Valley and frighten Washington.

Appropriately, Jackson's old II Corps, now commanded by General Jubal Early, was selected for the job. Including a small cavalry brigade, the force numbered 13,000 men.

Gimlet-eyed, rasp-tongued Early wasted no time. His troops piled into Lynchburg by rail and by road and old General Hunter's brief day of glory in the Valley ended. On June 17–18 Hunter, without a fight, retired precipitately westward across the Alleghenies, never actively to re-enter the military picture. The Valley highway to the North was open.

By July 2, Early was in Winchester. The next day Sigel had evacuated Harpers Ferry, and on the sixth the Confederate troops had crossed the Potomac at Shepherdstown to invade Maryland for the third time. On Hagerstown's burghers Early levied $20,000; on Frederick $200,000.

This was a diversion with a vengeance. Official Washington had gone into one of its panics at the first news of Early's advance down the Valley. Grant, obeying frantic appeals, had started the VI and XIX Corps north to protect the capital. One division of the former was already in the Baltimore area, where Union General Lew Wallace was collecting a scratch aggregation of militia and Regulars some 6,000 strong.

Early, starting toward Washington, found Wallace facing him across the Monocacy River on the morning of July 9. In a sharp attack, marked by excellent Confederate artillery work, the veteran invaders crossed the river and drove Wallace off. Union losses were 1,800 against 650 Confederate casualties.

Washington was but forty miles away. Early covered thirty of them next day, driving his gaunt foot-sloggers mercilessly through the torrid July heat and dust. On the eleventh they passed through Silver Spring to halt before the ramparts of Fort Stevens, inside the District line on the Seventh Street road.

Jubal Early faced a hard decision. Before him lay a dazzling prize; the Federal capital, goal of the Confederacy's hopes. Its frowning belt of fortifications, laid out by master engineer George B. McClellan, were impregnable to a force of Early's strength if they were manned by capable troops. But were they?

Behind him Early had left scattered the troops of three Federal commanders—Wallace, Sigel and Hunter. If these troops could be rallied, reorganized and concentrated, he would never get back home. Time was ticking out.

Early had not been ordered to take Washington; in all probability neither he nor Lee had ever expected he could come so far and so fast on what was definitely intended to be a diversion. But if he could take the city, even temporarily, the effect on the war-tired North would be incalculable.

He tried.

Washington's fortifications were manned that morning only by a rag-tag-and-bob-tail assortment of government clerks rushed into uniform, home guards, invalided soldiers and casual detachments. But down at the wharves a fleet of transports was de-gorging Wright's VI Corps from Petersburg—some 15,000 sunburned, sturdy veterans whose appearance sent the scared townsfolk into a tumult of joy. By afternoon, as Early's skirmishers probed the defenses, Wright's troops were taking over. Next day Early tried again, in earnest. This time the Federals, under President Lincoln's eyes, debouched to meet him. They meant business and Early recognized it; these were fighting soldiers. The jig was up.

Breaking contact quickly, the Southern troops retired through Rockville and Poolsville, leaving their 400 wounded behind them. The last of the precious specie wagons, carrying the $220,000 cash booty, got safely across the ford at White's Ferry on July 14, one jump ahead of the pursuing Federals. It rattled through sleepy Leesburg and Jubal Early was on his way to the Shenandoah Valley. Washington could breathe again.

Followed a short period of marching and counter-marching by the VI Corps and the XIX—which had by now also come up to Washington—as well as the troops of Hunter's former command, led by George B. Crook. The objective was to drive Early up and out of the Valley. But contradictory orders from Washington prevented any coordinated effort and Early stayed around Winchester. Finally he pounced on Crook, drove him out of the way, and sent Confederate cavalry back into Pennsylvania on July 30. From Chambersburg the raiders demanded $100,000 in gold; reparation for the burning of Virginia Military Institute. The money being refused them, the town was burned, despite the protestations of some of Early's officers. On the way back the expedition was badly mauled at Moorefield by Averell's Union cavalry.

Grant knew that so long as there was a Confederate army in the Valley the communications of the Army of the Potomac were unsafe. He also knew that as long as Washington's politicians could meddle with nearby defense forces, no concerted effort could be made to drive the Confederates from the Valley. He took characteristic action. Coming up secretly from the Petersburg front, and bypassing Washington, Grant dropped into the local headquarters at Monocacy Junction, and ordered the concentration of all Washington defense forces at Halltown, near Harper's Ferry. Sheridan would command.

Total war was coming. Early was to be destroyed and the resources of the Valley—breadbasket of the Army of Northern Virginia—wiped out. Sheridan was to "eat out Virginia clean and clear . . . so that crows flying over it for the balance of the season will have to carry their own provender." Grant then returned, as secretly as he had come, to his own Petersburg problem.

It was easier said than done, as Sheridan found out when he assumed his new command August 7. In front of him he had a determined, elusive opponent, whose strength was for some time unknown to him. (Actually Early never had more than 20,000 men, but they were good.) And behind him, and on his flanks, Sheridan had the guerrillas. A motley crowd, these guerrillas of Northern Virginia; mostly ragamuffins and cutthroats who throughout the war had robbed and ravished their neighbors with as much glee as they ambushed Federal detachments. Colonel John S. Mosby was an exception; he held a Confederate Army commission and even Grant recognized him as a soldier and an efficient leader in partisan warfare.

For the most part, the guerrillas were as much disdained by Confederate professional soldiers as they were hated by Federal troops. To General Thomas L. Rosser, for instance, the guerrilla was "a nuisance and an evil to the service." General Lee summed them all up in a sentence: "I regard the whole [guerrilla] system as an unmixed evil." And many and bitter, to this day, are the comments of Southern folk in Loudoun County whose forebears suffered from the midnight ravages of these bushwhackers.

But the guerrillas were there, as they were in all the other border states, for that matter; nuisances whose sting was poisonous, and whose operations hindered communications. Parenthetically one must note the presence also of pro-Union guerrillas in all these states, but by 1864 those in Northern Virginia had been eliminated by Mosby.

Sheridan decided to fight fire with fire. He gathered at his headquarters a scout detachment mainly recruited from the 17th Pennsylvania Volunteer Cavalry. "Sheridan's Scouts" were daredevils who rode with a price on their heads, for they wore Confederate uniforms and their mission was infiltration; to garner information and to eliminate guerrillas. They were sometimes shot by Union soldiers as they roamed; a number were executed by Confederate leaders whose commands they had penetrated. But before the campaign was over they had become Sheridan's eyes and ears, and they were apparently an important factor in ridding the Valley of guerrillas.

Sheridan's Army of the Shenandoah was 48,000 strong— 6,400 of them cavalry. It consisted of the VIII Corps—the sadly mishandled and battered troops of Banks, Hunter and Sigel— with George B. Crook now trying to make it a battle-wise unit; Wright's veteran VI Corps—among the best troops in the Army of the Potomac—and Emory's XIX Corps, up from the Louisiana area.

The cavalry, commanded by Brigadier General A. T. A. Torbert, consisted of the divisions of Wesley Merritt, Alfred N. Duffie and James H. Wilson, from the Army of the Potomac; and William W. Averell's division, already in the Valley. Of the artillery—some 100 guns—half were veteran Regular horse artillery.

Early, in the beginning, mustered perhaps 19,000 men; the

II Corps and Breckenridge's troops, already in the Valley. The cavalry was poorly organized, but the twelve batteries of artillery—some 70 guns—were hard-shooting veterans. Now, in early August, with the Valley becoming a major battleground, Lee depleted his Richmond-Petersburg line by reinforcing Early with a division each of infantry and cavalry—welcome additions which swelled his strength to about 25,000.

For a month the opposing forces maneuvered. Sheridan, busy shaking his extemporized army into shape, and feeling the nips of the guerrillas roaming around him, was as yet cautious. His scouts were still neophytes, and he was uncertain of Early's strength. He got part way up the Valley, then retired to Halltown.

"Old Jube," mistaking the Union caution for timidity, became over-confident. Despite the fact that Lee soon had called back the newly-arrived infantry division, Early decided to take the offensive. With less than 19,000 men, he started north, to find that Sheridan was moving, too.

Grant, impatient of the delay, had made another quick, secret trip to Halltown, and Sheridan, perhaps with a burning ear, was coming up the Berryville Road, Winchester-bound.

Just east of Opequon Creek the opposing forces met on September 19. Early at first snubbed the Union attack, but the Federal cavalry overlapped his left flank while Sheridan, streaking across his own front like a sky-rocket, sparked the Federal main effort. Early's line was driven in and after an ineffectual attempt to stand on the outskirts of Winchester he was thrown back all the way to Fisher's Hill, some twelve miles south on the nineteenth.

In this, known as the Battle of Opequon Creek or the Third Battle of Winchester, Confederate losses were 4,600 (1,800 of these prisoners), including Rodes, one of the best division commanders of the Confederate Army, killed while leading a charge. Sheridan's casualties were 5,000.

Sheridan gave his opponent no time to catch his breath. On September 22 he assaulted the Fisher's Hill position. While his infantry demonstrated in a frontal attack, most of his cavalry, riding wide to the westward, turned and drove in on Early's left. The entire Confederate line collapsed and once more Early had to retreat, with the loss of 1,250 men and twelve guns. Meanwhile Wilson's cavalry division had smashed through Front Royal on the Confederate right, and drove Early's cavalry up the Luray Valley. Wilson was unable, however, to reach the New Market Gap in the Massanutten in time to block the retreat of Early's main body.

The pursuit continued all the way to Waynesboro. Then the Federal tide receded, deliberately, while Sheridan systematically devastated the Valley. Barns and stables were destroyed, crops ruined, cattle driven off. The breadbasket of the Army of Northern Virginia became a vale of desolation. Behind the Federal army trailed a pitiful train of refugees who had abandoned their ruined farms. Early's troops followed close, but ineffectually. On Sheridan's flanks and down the line of communications the guerrillas buzzed like angry hornets, cutting off and killing stragglers, waylaying wagon trains, and being themselves killed by Union cavalrymen in numberless little skirmishes—most of these "no quarter" affairs.

By mid-October Sheridan's army, its work of destruction completed, went into position along Cedar Creek, a little more than twenty miles south of Winchester. Sheridan, leaving General Wright in command, went to Washington for a conference as to the future disposition of his troops.

But indomitable Jubal Early, reinforced by the return of the division originally loaned him by Lee, as well as a brigade of cavalry—giving him a total strength of some 18,400 men— still had a shot in his locker. Back in Richmond he was being criticized—popular clamor knows neither rhyme nor reason in such cases—for a really splendid campaign against immense odds. Here in the Valley his troops were starving. So Jubal Early diced once more with Fate—and nearly won, as it turned out.

Just north of Strasbourg, Cedar Creek flows from west to east across the Valley Turnpike to empty into the North Fork of the Shenandoah. The North Fork, flowing through a gorge, unites with the South Fork at Front Royal, eight miles further east.

Sheridan's army, astride the Pike on the north side of Cedar Creek, lay with the VI and XIX Corps on the west side of the highway and the VIII Corps on the east. The position, crowning a line of low hills, was well selected to block any Confederate move down the Pike, but it had one weakness. On the Union left lay a good mile of unprotected open ground extending to the junction of creek and river. The possibility that an attack might come over the cragged, wooded nose of the Massanutten and then through the seemingly impassable gorge below it, had been completely discounted.

That was just what Early had decided to do. The suggestion was John B. Gordon's; made after a careful reconnaissance. The Confederate main effort, three divisions strong, would move in the night over the mountain nose, clamber across the Shenandoah, and by dawn would hit the Union left and rear in surprise assault. Another spearhead would attack straight down the Pike. One of the little cavalry divisions would provide a diversion on the Union right flank, the other—pushing through Front Royal on the Union left—would get far in the rear of the Federals.

All through the night of October 18, Gordon's troops, sometimes in single file, moved over the mountain, then into and through the Shenandoah gorge. Stripped of all impedimenta except arms and ammunition, lest clank of tin cup or rattle of cooking utensil give warning as they scrabbled over the rocks and through dense woods, they made it, unobserved. The foggy dawn found them in battle array on the plain. First warning of the assault was the Rebel yell resounding in the ears of Crook's VIII Corps. Then the Confederate artillery, massed on Hupp's Hill, sprayed the Union front, and the roar of battle spread along the entire line.

The Union VIII Corps stampeded *en masse* (it would not be rallied for forty-eight hours), and its captured artillery was turned immediately on the rest of the Union forces. First the XIX and then the VI Corps in turn began to crumble. By noon, only the latter, after two successive stands, was established in a third delaying position as General Wright tried desperately to hold. The rest of the Federal forces were moving to the rear; the turnpike and the fields on each side crowded with men, wagons and horses surging slowly north towards Winchester.

The Army of the Shenandoah was licked. One further sharp, decisive blow by a Confederate reserve would have ended it all in complete rout. Unfortunately for Early, there was no formed reserve. His starved troops, flushed with victory, fell on the Union camps like a host of locusts. For two precious hours they could not be reorganized. And then it was too late.

"Little Phil" Sheridan, by a brilliant demonstration of personal leadership, had reversed the whole situation.

Sheridan, breakfasting in Winchester that morning, on the way back from Washington, heard the distant sound of the guns. He and his escort, trotting up the Valley, began to meet the first spray of retreating troops. Off like a shot, with his aides and three squads of troopers, the Union commander hammered up the Pike, his flat hat waving in his hand, his bull voice bellowing. The hordes of fugitives saw him as they had seen him and time again in battle, symbolizing victory—man, horse and little swallow-tailed red and white guidon with its two white stars bobbing behind.

In their thousands they turned, now, galvanized by a wave of mass psychology; turned back to the field they had fled. Sheridan reached the VI Corps, rocketed down the line. Booming cheers reverberated from brigade to brigade; tired, angry men caught their second wind. And when Early at long last gathered enough strength to resume his attack the Southern assault was halted in its tracks.

That was but the beginning.

"Jubal Early drive me out of the Valley?" snarled Sheridan to a pessimistic staff officer. "I'll lick him like blazes before night."

He was systematic about it. The stragglers were coming back; shattered units reforming, shamefaced but eager to erase the smear of panic. By four in the afternoon the Union counterattack started. The VI and XIX Corps struck straight ahead. Merritt's cavalry division covered the left and Custer's the right. Early's army crumpled, then collapsed entirely. By dusk the field was cleared, the Southerners driven in complete rout, again all the way to Fisher's Hill. The captured Union cannon were retrieved and twenty-four Confederate guns bagged. Early's casualties were only 2,900 as compared to Sheridan's 5,600-odd, but the toll in Southern officers was severe. An attempt to rally at Fisher's Hill was unavailing; that night Early's remnants were retreating to New Market. The back of Confederate resistance in the Shenandoah Valley had been broken.

But the Northern Administration was taking no chances of another Southern eruption there, so Sheridan's troops stayed through the end of the year. Back to Lee went the battered II Corps in early December, leaving Early at Waynesboro with but 1,000 men and six guns. When the snow went out of the upper Valley, Sheridan sent Custer to deliver the *coup de grace*. On March 2, 1865, he overran this shadow of an army. Early, with but a score of companions, left the field after his troops collapsed, and got back to Petersburg. His reward, for faithfully fulfilling his chief's desires and thus prolonging the war by six months, was to be relieved of command and sent home to await orders which would never come.

# 27

# War Is Cruelty!

For seven weeks after the fall of Atlanta, Hood was more than content to rest his beaten army at Lovejoy's Station, some thirty miles from Atlanta. At the same time Sherman's army, to his horror, seemed to "sink into a condition of idleness." A great number of the men in the regiments who had enlisted in the late summer and fall of 1861 claimed discharges, or re-enlistment furloughs. The Administration, in facilitating the return home of these men, hoped they would demonstrate their gratitude by voting properly in the November election. At the same time political leaders in uniform— like corps commanders Blair and Logan—were given leave to go home to take part in the Presidential campaign as it approached its climax. Thus, as Sherman wrote, "with victory and success came also many causes of disintegration."

Though Sherman deplored the effect of electioneering activity on his army, he was too astute not to realize that for all of their vital military significance, his victories would have an even greater political impact on the outcome of the war. On June 7, President Lincoln had been nominated for re-election by the National Union Convention (Republicans and a scattering of pro-Administration Democrats) at Baltimore. To symbolize the bi-partisan nature of the support his administration was receiving in its prosecution of the war, the Convention nominated Tennessee Democrat Andrew Johnson for Vice President.

The Democratic Party held its convention at Chicago later in the summer, and a coalition of Copperheads and rabid anti-Lincoln Democrats were able to capitalize on the growing discouragement of the Northern people. Grant, after taking terrible losses from the Wilderness to Cold Harbor, was locked in a stalemate with Lee at Petersburg. At that time Sherman seemed to be having little better success against canny Joe Johnston in Georgia. Banks had been ignominiously defeated on the Red River, and Union efforts along the seacoast periphery of the Confederacy had apparently been unproductive.

Boldly the Democrats built a platform whose key plank was an assertion that the war was a failure, making clear their intention, if they won the election, of quickly reaching a negotiated peace with the Confederacy. On August 29, they nominated General George B. McClellan as their candidate for President. Though McClellan refused to endorse the key plank of the platform—failure of the war effort—he was unable or unwilling to disavow it publicly. Rightly or wrongly, then, he became identified as an advocate of Southern independence.

As September began, Lincoln was ready to concede the election to McClellan. He was convinced that the war-weary Northern people would not support his firm intention to continue the war until the Union was re-established. Then came the galvanizing news that the stalemate had been broken in Georgia. On September 3 Lincoln conveyed to Sherman and his army "the national thanks . . . for the distinguished ability and perseverance displayed in the campaign in Georgia which, under divine favor, has resulted in the capture of Atlanta."

The Democrats could now hardly persuade the people that the war was a failure. Even so, the election was hard-fought. Though Lincoln won with 212 electoral votes to 21 for McClellan, the closeness of the popular vote—2,216,067 to 1,808,725—was evidence that the decision would possibly have been different without Sherman's great victory.

Sherman and Hood, meanwhile, had begun to keep each other occupied in Georgia. At first their renewal of the conflict was limited mainly to the pen rather than the sword.

The Union general had decided that he would convert Atlanta into a purely military base. Distressed by the diversion of strength and effort which had been required to protect, govern and supply other captured Southern cities, such as Memphis, Vicksburg, Nashville and New Orleans, Sherman was determined this would not happen in Atlanta. All private citizens were ordered to leave the city. Those who wanted to could go north, under protection of Union forces; others would be given safe conduct to points within the jurisdiction of the Confederacy. But none would be permitted to remain as an embarrassment to further military activity by Sherman's army.

There was an immediate outcry against this "barbarism." In reply to a petition from the mayor and leading citizens of Atlanta, Sherman revealed much of his philosophy concerning the nature of war in general, and that of this conflict in particular:

"I . . . shall not revoke my orders, because they were not designed to meet the humanities of the case, but to prepare for the future struggles in which millions of good people outside of Atlanta have a deep interest. We must have peace, not only at Atlanta, but in all America. . . . We must stop the war that now desolates our once happy and favored country. . . .

"You cannot qualify war in harsher terms than I will. War is cruelty, and you cannot refine it; and those who brought war into our country deserve all the curses and maledictions a people can pour out. . . .

"Now that war comes home to you . . . you deprecate its

horrors. I want peace and believe it can only be reached through union and war, and I will ever conduct war with a view to perfect and early success.

"But, my dear sirs, when peace does come, you may call on me for anything. Then will I share with you the last cracker, and watch with you to shield your homes and families against danger from every quarter."

This document was written while Sherman was in the midst of an acrimonious exchange of letters with Hood on the same subject. On September 7, Sherman proposed a local truce at a point midway between the two armies to facilitate the evacuation of non-combatants from Atlanta. In his reply on the ninth, Hood accepted Sherman's proposals for a truce, since, as he said, "I do not consider that I have any alternative in this matter." He then concluded his letter in the following words:

"And now, sir, permit me to say that the unprecedented measure you propose transcends, in studied and ingenious cruelty, all acts ever before brought to my attention in the dark history of war. In the name of God and humanity, I protest, believing that you will find that you are expelling from their homes and firesides the wives and children of a brave people."

If Grant had received such a letter he would have shrugged, and gone quietly about his business. But to Sherman this was an epistolary challenge that could not be ignored. Hood, as well, was ready for the contest of words and wits. A few more letters passed between the two commanders, and at the close of the correspondence it was evident that each was satisfied that he had worsted his opponent in rhetoric and logic. Meanwhile, their officers and men at the exchange point were fraternizing in the most cordial fashion, and "parted good friends" when all of the civilians from Atlanta had passed through.

Meanwhile both generals were pondering what should be the next move in Georgia. Sherman, guided by Grant's original concept of carrying the war into the heartland of the Confederacy, was toying with the idea of marching into central Georgia, and even on to the seacoast near Charleston or Savannah, if Union beachheads in the Carolinas could be expanded sufficiently to provide him with a base. Hood, on the other hand, was dreaming of cancelling Southern reverses in the West by a successful invasion of Tennessee and Kentucky. As the weeks passed, and Sherman's army rested in Atlanta, the 400 miles of Union communications seemed ever more tantalizing to the bold Southerner.

On September 21, Hood moved from Lovejoy's Station to Palmetto, southwest of Atlanta, where he was visited by Jefferson Davis. On October 1, with the encouragement and blessing of the Confederate President, Hood started northwest across the Chattahoochie to threaten Sherman's line of communications with Chattanooga. At the same time Forrest moved north from Mississippi to join Wheeler, who had for several weeks been raiding successfully in central Tennessee.

Sherman in counter-stroke paid the most sincere possible tribute to the ability of two great Confederate cavalrymen by ordering his most trusted subordinate—General Thomas—back to Chattanooga and Nashville to handle the grave threat to his base area. He commented on this action in a telegram to Halleck:

"Forrest's . . . cavalry will travel a hundred miles where ours will ten. I have sent two divisions up to Chattanooga and one to Rome, and General Thomas started today to drive Forrest out of Tennessee. . . . I can whip [Hood's] infantry, but his cavalry is to be feared."

On October 3, Sherman, leaving one corps to hold Atlanta, moved northwest to try to force Hood into a battle. Next day he received information leading him to believe that Hood would try to seize Allatoona. He sent a message, relayed by heliograph over the heads of the Southerners, directing Brigadier General John M. Corse, commanding the division just sent to Rome, to come to the assistance of the Allatoona garrison. At the same time he marched toward that town with the rest of his army as rapidly as possible.

Hood had, in fact, sent a corps to cut the railroad and telegraph lines south of Allatoona, and one division of this corps—
about 6,000 men—tried to capture the town early on the fifth.
But Corse, who had just arrived in response to Sherman's orders,
rejected the demand for surrender, and made ready to defend the
town with about 1,900 men.

At this time Sherman reached Kenesaw Mountain, almost
20 miles away, from which he could see the movements of his
own and Hood's troops. He received a heliograph message reporting the arrival of Corse in the threatened town, and in response
sent his famous message: "Hold the fort; I am coming."

While Sherman was watching, the Confederates attacked.
For several hours the issue was in doubt. Though Corse was
seriously wounded, he remained in command, and by mid-afternoon the Confederates acknowledged failure, and marched rapidly westward to avoid Sherman's advance.

For another ten days the armies continued to traverse—but
in the opposite direction—the same region over which they had
maneuvered and fought from May to August. Finally, after capturing Dalton, and having reached Johnston's old position at
Rocky Face Ridge, twenty miles from Chattanooga, Hood on
October 15, turned southwest. Marching down the Coosa Valley
he reached Gadsden, Alabama, on the twenty-second, while Sherman, at the same time, was about thirty miles to the northeast at
Gaylesville.

Some time before this Sherman had come to the conclusion
that he could not possibly hope to catch Hood's fast-moving,
lightly encumbered army, particularly since its withdrawal was
now screened by Wheeler's magnificent troopers. It had become
obvious to the Union general that he had been out-maneuvered
by Hood. Sherman was, in effect, chasing a will-o-the-wisp,
and was doing nothing to further Grant's strategy of constant,
unrelenting pressure on the Confederacy.

As early as October 9 Sherman sent a telegram to Grant
suggesting that he could best carry out the strategic concept by

abandoning his line of communications with Chattanooga and the North, and taking his entire army eastward from Atlanta to Savannah, on the Atlantic seacoast, where he could make contact with the Union Navy.

Though this was consistent with Grant's ultimate intentions, and reminiscent of his own actions in the Vicksburg campaign, Sherman's bold suggestion evidently made the Union General-in-Chief gasp. His initial reaction was negative. In the first place he did not approve of the idea of leaving Hood free to operate as he pleased in Georgia, Alabama, and Tennessee. Secondly, there was no suitable Union base near Savannah to which Sherman could move in the event of trouble; this could mean disaster. But Grant must have read and reread the key sentences of Sherman's persistent messages.

"It will be a physical impossibility to protect the roads, now that Hood, Forrest, Wheeler, and the whole batch of devils, are turned loose without home or habitation . . . ," he telegraphed on the ninth. "Until we can repopulate Georgia, it is useless for us to occupy it; but the utter destruction of its roads, houses, and people, will cripple their military resources. By attempting to hold the roads, we will lose a thousand men each month, and will gain no result. I can make this march, and make Georgia howl!"

Next day Sherman added the following arguments:

"Hood is now . . . bound west. . . . Had I not better execute [my] plan . . . and leave General Thomas with the troops now in Tennessee, to defend the state? He will have an ample force. . . ."

"We cannot now remain on the defensive. . . ." Sherman telegraphed on the eleventh. "I would infinitely prefer to . . . move through Georgia, smashing things to the sea. Hood may turn into Tennessee and Kentucky, but I believe he will be forced to follow me. Instead of being on the defensive, I will be on the offensive. Instead of my guessing at what he means to do, he will have to guess at my plans. . . ."

These were arguments which Grant's aggressive nature

could not deny, and largely offset his two major objections. His initial approval, which Sherman received on October 21, was a bit reluctant, however. Grant wavered somewhat, as he received the news of Hood's continued northwestward movement to the banks of the Tennessee River near Decatur and Florence. But, after further deliberation, and despite the grave fears of President Lincoln, on November 2 he endorsed Sherman's plan completely and enthusiastically:

"With the force . . . you have left with General Thomas, he must be able to take care of Hood and destroy him. I do not see that you can withdraw from where you are to follow Hood, without giving up all we have gained in territory. I say, then, go on as you propose."

Jubilant Sherman now completed his arrangements for the coming march. All wounded and sick men were sent back to Chattanooga, as were all non-combatants remaining with the army near Atlanta. Great quantities of equipment—everything that could not be carried by a fast-moving army—were also sent back. By evening of the 14th all that remained in Atlanta were 68,000 veteran troops, fit, ready and eager for action; 65 guns, 2,500 wagons loaded with ammunition and a few days' supply of food, and 600 ambulances. Everything else had been moved north; the railroad and telegraph line to Chattanooga had been destroyed, and the engineers were in the process of wrecking the train yards, machine shops and industrial facilities in Atlanta itself.

On the 15th, with the last strand of wire communication ripped away, Sherman and his army disappeared from Northern ken. For more than a month the people of the Union would worry, the rest of the world wonder. Foreign military leaders predicted that Sherman and his army would be swallowed up and destroyed in the heart of the Confederacy. These predictions were shrilly echoed by Northern prophets of doom, reading the first accounts of Sherman's movements in optimistic Southern newspaper reports. Anxious President Lincoln was somewhat comforted by the calm attitude of his General-in-Chief, and is later reported to have reassured other worriers in these words: ''Grant says they are safe with such a general, and that if they cannot get out where they want to, they can crawl back by the hole they went in at.''

# "WHOLE BATCH OF DEVILS"

Charged by Sherman with the defense of Tennessee, George H. Thomas at Nashville in October surveyed his troubled situation. Hood, he knew, might be expected to invade the state, but there were other potential threats.

Thomas was spared further annoyance from John Morgan, the brilliant Confederate Cavalry raider, who for the last six months had been rampaging in northeast Tennessee and southwest Virginia. Morgan had been killed in action September 4.

For three years the meteoric Morgan had been a thorn in the Federal side, usually playing the part of a lone wolf—independent of the major Southern commands. At Hartsville, Tennessee, December 7, 1862, he had captured a Union brigade, much superior in strength to his own command. In 1863 he ran into bad luck while trying to distract Rosecrans' attention from Bragg's planned withdrawal from Tullahoma to Chattanooga. Exceeding his instructions, Morgan crossed the Ohio River, riding daringly into southern Indiana and Ohio. Northern Regular and militia forces closed in on him and after a desperate chase Morgan was forced to surrender on July 26, just west of the Ohio-Pennsylvania border.

But a P.O.W. cage couldn't hold Morgan. He escaped from Columbus, Ohio, regained the Confederate lines and by April, 1864 was commanding all Southern forces in northwest Tennessee and southwest Virginia. After repelling a Union cavalry raid from West Virginia, Morgan in June rode through the mountains with 2,000 men all the way to Lexington, setting central Kentucky in uproar. At Cinthiana he overwhelmed a Federal cavalry force as large as his own. He was surprised and defeated next day— June 12—by Brigadier Stephen G. Burbridge who had been chasing him. After a hard fight, Morgan lost half his strength of 1,500 men. By September, Morgan was in the field again. While raiding along the railroad towards Knoxville, his advance was met by Union Brigadier General Alvan C. Gillem at Greenville, Tennessee, and Morgan was killed in the clash.

If Thomas now no longer had Morgan to fear, he was forced to cast his eyes west of the Mississippi River, where the indestructible Sterling Price was operating. After the Iuka-Corinth campaign Price had been campaigning in Arkansas against Union General Steele, with varying fortunes.

On September 1, he crossed the Arkansas River, about midway between the Federal positions at Little Rock and Fort Smith. Turning northeastward with 13,000 veteran troops and twenty guns, he headed directly for St. Louis. The speed of his approach caused consternation. Rosecrans, then commanding the Department of Missouri, called for reinforcements, and was given the veteran corps of General A. J. Smith, then enroute up the Mississippi from the Red River expedition to join Thomas' army.

Price arrived outside the defenses of St. Louis early in October. Rosecrans, however, with the addition of Smith's troops, repulsed his attacks, and so Price turned westward along the south bank of the Missouri River, heading towards the state capital at Jefferson City. Hastily assembled defenders held him off long enough to permit pursuing troops from St. Louis—under Generals Smith and Pleasanton—to arrive in the vicinity. So Price continued northwestward towards Kansas City and Fort Leavenworth, conscripting on the way all able-bodied young Missourians who had remained at home.

Union Major General Samuel R. Curtis, commanding the Department of Kansas, now began to collect forces east of Kansas City. To delay Price he sent Major General James G. Blunt to Lexington, Missouri. On October 20, after a brisk fight, Price drove Blunt from Lexington toward Independence. Curtis joined Blunt at Independence on the twenty-first, and the battle was renewed by the aggressive Price on the twenty-second. Just as

Price was forcing the Union troops over the state line into Kansas, near Westport, he was struck in the rear by Pleasanton's cavalry, which had been following from Jefferson City. Price's troops were badly shaken, but he was able to rally and reorganize them in time to meet the attacks of the combined Union forces on the twenty-third.

For several hours the battle raged, but by evening the veteran Southerners were forced to give way. Harried by Curtis, Pleasanton, and A. J. Smith, Price retreated into Arkansas, thus bringing to a conclusion the last major operation of the war west of the Mississippi.

But within the vast triangle Memphis-Louisville-Chattanooga, in Thomas' own bailiwick, the most dangerous threat to Union installations and communications between the Mississippi and the Appalachians still rode unchecked—Nathan Bedford Forrest. We must examine Forrest, to appreciate Thomas' problem, and the reason why Sherman had put Thomas where he now was.

# FUSTEST WITH THE MOSTEST

Midway between the regions where Morgan and Price were operating in 1864, General Nathan Bedford Forrest was continuing the workmanlike activity which had already earned him grudging praise from Northerners like Grant and Sherman. Forrest's fame as a cavalryman already rested as solidly upon his performance as a subordinate commander in a mixed force as upon his raiding ability.

It has been reputed that Forrest described his own theory of war in the words: "Git thar fustest with the mostest." It is doubtful if self-educated Forrest spoke so ungrammatically in his mature years; but if this colorful statement was apocryphal, nonetheless it typified the method of operation of a magnificent soldier.

His escape from Ft. Donelson had been the one bright spot

in that dismal Confederate disaster. His mounted charge on the second day at Shiloh had halted the Union pursuit of the retreating Southern army. His raids in northwestern Tennessee late in 1862, and early 1863, had been a principal factor in Grant's decision to abandon the overland approach to Vicksburg. More than anything else, it was Forrest's raids on Rosecrans' communications which had slowed the Union advance in the Murfreesboro, Tullahoma and Chickamauga campaigns. At the Battle of Chickamauga, Forrest's cavalry corps was on Bragg's right flank, its mounted action and determined fighting on foot both contributing greatly to the Confederate victory.

Forrest's greatest year was probably 1864, and he began it with a spectacular success. Early in February Sherman had marched with 20,000 men from Vicksburg to Meridian, Mississippi, for the purpose of destroying the important north-south and east-west railroads that joined in that town. A cavalry column of 7,000 men under Brigadier General W. Sooy Smith was to start east from Memphis about the same time with the mission of sweeping down the railroad in eastern Mississippi to join Sherman at Meridian. Sherman, knowing that Forrest was based in northern Mississippi, had instructed Smith to "attack any force of cavalry you may meet and follow them south." Sherman then proposed to move eastward from Meridian with the combined force, tearing up the railroad, and capturing and destroying the important Confederate arsenal at Selma, Alabama.

Smith started on February 11. On the twentieth, he came upon part of Forrest's force in a strong position amongst swamps and rivers about thirty miles south of Okolona. Later it was discovered that at the time Forrest probably had less than 1,000 men, but Smith decided not to attack. Instead, next day he withdrew toward Okolona, apparently hoping to lure the Confederate leader into open country more suitable for battle.

This was an invitation. Forrest was not loath to accept. Being joined by additional troops, Forrest pressed quickly after Smith with about 3,000 men. Early on the 22nd Smith prepared for battle, then—evidently bluffed by Forrest's truculent attitude—again ordered a withdrawal. Forrest caught up with the retreating Northerners at Okolona, and began a running fight that lasted all day, with the Union troops becoming demoralized as darkness approached. About this time Smith decided to make a stand, but Forrest pressed rapidly against the hastily-formed line, threatening the exposed flanks of the much more numerous Union force. To allow more time to organize his position, and to steady his jittery men, Smith ordered a regiment to make a mounted charge. The dismounted Southern troopers, however, soon halted the charge with a steady, accurate fire, and the attackers retreated in considerable confusion. This seemed to take all of the remaining fight out of Smith, who now ordered a general retirement, which culminated in a disordered flight to Memphis. In three days of fighting, Forrest inflicted about 400 casualties on his more numerous, better equipped foe, losing about 150 of his own men.

Sherman, meanwhile, had been waiting at Meridian for the arrival of Smith. When the cavalry failed to join, he abandoned the more ambitious project against Selma, and returned to Vicksburg, keenly disappointed. Forrest with less than 3,000 men had frustrated the operations of some 27,000 Northerners, and in so doing had completely defeated a force more than twice as large as his own. It was, according to one of his enemies, "the most glorious achievement of his career."

The tough Southerner, however, wasted no time resting on his laurels. He was soon raiding northward again, reaching Paducah, Kentucky, on the Ohio River. On the return he became involved in the most controversial incident of his military career: the so-called "Massacre" at Fort Pillow, April 12, 1864.

Fort Pillow, an earthwork on the Mississippi River about forty miles north of Memphis, had been in Union hands since its capture in the spring of 1862. Two years later, far removed from the active regions of the war, it was garrisoned by about 560 Union soldiers, half of them Negroes. Suddenly the surprised Northerners found themselves invested by Forrest's command.

His demand for surrender being rejected, Forrest's dismounted troopers stormed the ramparts, overwhelming the defenders, despite support from nearby Federal gunboats on the river. In the fight the Northerners suffered about 400 casualties, more than half of whom were killed. Losses among the Negro troops were particularly heavy.

Union survivors later asserted that the Southern troops deliberately shot down many of the colored soldiers after they had laid down their arms. Forrest, in his first report, apparently indicated his satisfaction at the heavy loss of life among the Negro troops. His final report, however, goes to considerable lengths to establish the fact that the losses were the result of the effectiveness of the attack, and the demoralization among the defenders, many of whom were drowned in trying to escape.

It has never been proven that any Federal troops, white or colored, were slaughtered after the survivors formally surrendered. It is doubtful that Forrest would have ordered, permitted or condoned the massacre of which his men have been accused.

A month after the Fort Pillow incident, Sherman, well on his way toward Atlanta and knowing the danger which Forrest posed to the long line of communications, sent General Sturgis from Memphis with some 3,400 cavalry, 2,000 infantry, and twelve guns to defeat Forrest. The Federals came in contact with Forrest's troops at Brice's Cross Roads, in north central Mississippi, on June 10. Forrest had but slightly more than 3,000 men. He immediately seized the initiative, however, and pressed his skirmish lines repeatedly against the Federal troops who had hastily deployed in a partially wooded farm area. As usual, he sought the Federal flanks, found them, and attacked vigorously. Accurate artillery fire was coordinated with the movements of the dismounted Southern troopers. The fight raged for several hours, and then as his men pressed vigorously against the Northern line, Forrest sent a small detachment to strike the Union rear. The Northern troops became demoralized, and fled in confusion, abandoning ten guns, and their entire supply train of 250 wagons loaded with food and ammunition. Northern losses in killed and wounded were 617, with another 1,623 men captured by Forrest, who lost 500 men in the hard-fought engagement.

A second Union expedition from Memphis to destroy the Confederate raider had better luck. General A. J. Smith with 14,000 men, its main element the corps just brought North from the ill-fated Red River expedition, pushed over to Tupelo. There Forrest and Lieutenant General S. D. Lee, with some 10,000 men, attacked Smith, July 14, but were thrown back. Time after time, throughout the day, the Confederates returned to the attack, but it was unavailing. Smith, however, withdrew next day. Tupelo, sometimes claimed as a Union victory, was in reality a drawn battle. In this hard-fought action Union losses were 674, Confederate, more than 1,300.

Evidence that Forrest had not suffered severely from the engagement at Tupelo, is the fact that he was soon again raiding northward into Tennessee, as Sherman had feared he would. At dawn of August 21, Forrest actually dashed into the city of Memphis itself, almost capturing the departmental commander, Major General C. C. Washburn. Washburn escaped in his night clothes, but Forrest rode off with his uniform. Shortly after this Forrest returned the captured clothing under a flag of truce. Not to be outdone in courtesy, the Union general sent the Southerner a new Confederate uniform, made by Forrest's old tailor in Memphis.

Aside from this exploit, Forrest caused little damage on this raid, and was soon forced to withdraw by a concentration of Federal troops in western Tennessee. After the fall of Atlanta he again raided northward, as we know, joining Wheeler in creating uproar along Sherman's line of communications in central Tennessee.

Toward the end of October Forrest moved south to join Hood, in preparation for the proposed invasion of Tennessee. Appearing suddenly on the north bank of the Tennessee, he attacked unsuspecting Federal naval forces plying the river west of Chattanooga. In a series of artillery and small arms engagements, he captured one gunboat and five supply transports, while seriously damaging three other gunboats and a number of transports. For a few days Confederate cavalrymen actually manned the captured craft, but were happy to return to their horses after some gallant but unsuccessful engagements with the aroused Union Navy. This was one of the most amazing exploits in the annals of land warfare. Sherman wrote later that this was "a feat of arms which, I confess, excited my admiration."

Immediately after this unusual incident, Forrest and his men displayed that versatility and flexibility which enabled him to contribute to the Southern cause so much more effectively than any other Confederate cavalryman. From swashbuckling, independent raider, he suddenly transformed himself into a loyal, self-effacing subordinate; his cavalry corps became the eyes and ears of Hood's army, as it prepared to mount the last major Confederate offensive.

# FRANKLIN AND NASHVILLE

During early November, Hood rested his army in the vicinity of Florence and Tuscumbia, astride the Tennessee River in northern Alabama, building up strength, and amassing supplies for the coming invasion of Tennessee. With the arrival of Forrest, he had about 54,000 men. The Confederate Army began to move northward on November 19, one day before Hood received an urgent message from Beauregard to start the planned invasion in hopes that this would stop, or at least offset, Sherman's march through Georgia from Atlanta.

Grant and Sherman had both expected that Thomas would gather forces to meet Hood in southern Tennessee, leaving garrisons only in a few of the larger cities. Thomas, at Nashville, preferred, however, not to call in the outlying garrisons, and was awaiting the arrival of A. J. Smith's veteran corps, now enroute to Nashville from Missouri.

Meanwhile Major General James H. Wilson, sent by Grant to assist Thomas, was working with might and main to extemporize a fighting cavalry corps out of raw recruits and green remounts. Sparring for time, Thomas directed General John McA. Schofield, with two corps totalling about 34,000 men, to delay Hood's advance while he—Thomas—concentrated additional troops at Nashville.

Schofield attempted to withdraw slowly from the vicinity of Pulaski in southern Tennessee, but soon found that the aggressive Forrest, leading the Confederate advance, was moving to seize Columbia, on the south bank of the Duck River. This was a grave threat to Schofield's line of communications with Nashville. The Union general fell back rapidly, barely in time to keep the Southern cavalryman from taking Columbia on the twenty-fourth. Hood deployed in front of the Union defenses of Columbia, and on the twenty-seventh, began preparations to turn Schofield's flank by crossing the river east of the town. Schofield, again fearing for his communications, withdrew across the river, destroying the bridges.

But Forrest was already on the move, crossing the river east of Columbia, getting between Wilson's cavalry corps and the rest of Schofield's army, then driving northward to seize the railroad at Thompson's Station, cutting the Union line of communications. For nearly two days Schofield's situation was precarious, as he marched north toward Franklin. Forrest was behind him and the right of his marching column was completely exposed to Hood's army pressing northward towards Spring Hill.

But Hood failed to seize the wonderful opportunity presented him on the twenty-ninth, when he had two corps within sight and artillery range of the road at Spring Hill, as Schofield's army was approaching from the south. By hard fighting, and marching all night of November 29, the Union troops were able to push Forrest aside, and to escape under the very noses of the Southern infantry at Spring Hill. Realizing too late the opportunity he had missed, and apparently trying to pin the blame for his own error on

General Cheatham, one of his corps commanders, Hood now rushed after the retreating Federals. But Schofield had already placed his troops in the previously prepared defenses of Franklin, awaiting the Southern advance. Wilson had rejoined, and now protected the Union left, north of the Harpeth River.

Arriving in front of Franklin late in the afternoon of November 30, Hood attacked at once with two-thirds of his army. It was a stubbornly contested struggle. Hood's men advanced with old-time determination and gallantry, and Cleburne's division actually penetrated the defenses. But the result of an attack against veteran troops strongly entrenched was almost a foregone conclusion. Cleburne was killed, and the attackers thrown back with heavy losses. Meanwhile, east of the town, Wilson held the line of the Harpeth, preventing Forrest from again getting behind the Union army.

Not until 9:00 P.M., four hours after dark, did Hood call off the attack. His losses had been appalling: 6,300 casualties out of 38,000 men engaged, while Schofield had lost 2,300 out of 32,000.

But Schofield knew that Hood had at least 16,000 more men marching to join him, and was fearful that Forrest's more numerous and more experienced cavalry would get the best of Wilson. So that night he withdrew from Franklin, marching northward to Nashville, where his leading elements arrived before noon. He had most capably performed his mission; the successful defense of Franklin, in particular, seriously weakened Hood's fighting strength, and took the heart out of the Southern infantry.

But this did not deter Hood. The authorities in Washington were appalled by the sudden appearance, on December 2, of a Confederate army in northern Tennessee, at the gates of the state capital. The alarm deepened as Thomas, with a numerically superior army, sat inside the defenses of Nashville waiting, so he said, to provide remounts for his cavalry. Grant sent a telegram ordering Thomas to move out at once to fight Hood in front of Nashville. Then, as Thomas was belatedly about to follow this

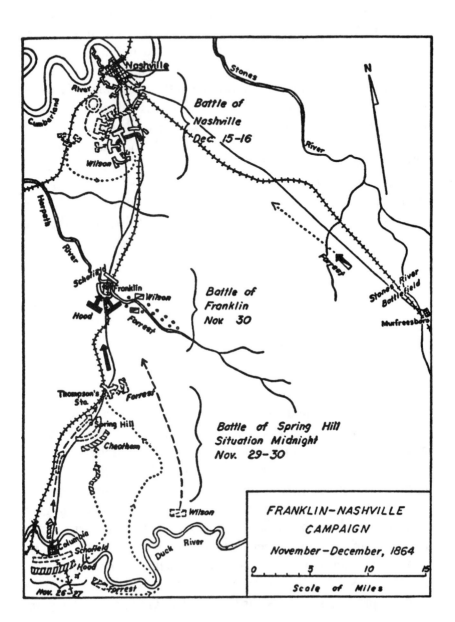

Battle of
Nashville
Dec. 15-16

Battle of
Franklin
Nov. 30

Battle of Spring Hill
Situation Midnight
Nov. 29-30

FRANKLIN-NASHVILLE
CAMPAIGN
November-December, 1864

Scale of Miles

order, a sleet and snow storm made movement impossible. He so reported to Washington.

To impatient individuals not on the spot, this explanation appeared to be simply another excuse for procrastination. On December 13, Grant ordered General Logan, XV Corps commander, then on leave in Washington to proceed to Nashville to replace Thomas. On December 15, Grant himself left Petersburg to take a train to Nashville to assume personal command against Hood. But when he arrived at Washington, on the sixteenth, he received a message from Thomas which caused him to leave the "Rock of Chickamauga" undisturbed in his command. Thomas reported that he had successfully attacked Hood on the fifteenth, and was confident of a complete victory that very day.

And complete victory it was—the most decisive of the war. Thomas had ever been slow to act; his was not the nature nor mentality to fight aggressive, offensive war in the manner of men like Lee, Grant, Jackson, or Sherman. But neither was he one who ever became stampeded. His plans were well matured, his troops were ready, supplies were plentiful and available, when he struck on the fifteenth, the day after the ice thawed. A hammer blow by the bulk of his army shattered Hood's left flank, while one division made a spirited demonstration against the Southern right, and a skeleton force in the defenses of Nashville neutralized the rest of the Southern army.

Hood had made a grave mistake in maintaining his exposed position in northern Tennessee, isolated from any assistance, and in the face of a numerically superior foe. More serious, he had sent Forrest, with most of his cavalry corps, and with some supporting infantry, to threaten Murfreesboro. Thus he was without his most able subordinate; his exposed left flank had inadequate cavalry protection, and he lacked reserves to re-establish the situation.

Nevertheless, though badly shaken, and driven two miles from its entrenchments, the Southern army was still intact at nightfall. Hood determined to try to continue the fight next day, hoping that Forrest would arrive in time to help prevent disaster.

But Thomas pressed vigorously, enveloping both Southern flanks on the sixteenth, and in the afternoon sending Wilson swinging around behind the Confederate left rear. By mid-afternoon the Confederate line was crumbling everywhere, and before dark the once proud army had become a fleeing rabble; the first time this had happened to a major army on either side since First Bull Run.

It is high time now that we return to Sherman, marching to the sea.

# A CHRISTMAS GIFT

Sherman's four corps had swept forward into central Georgia in parallel columns, on a front varying in width from fifteen to twenty-five miles. The right wing, consisting of the XV and XVII Corps, was commanded by Major General O. O. Howard; the left wing, XIV and XX Corps, was directed by Major General H. W. Slocum.

Sherman's orders were quite explicit, but permitted considerable latitude in their execution by wing and corps commanders. Rate of march was to be about fifteen miles a day, thus allowing plenty of time for foraging, and for the destruction of railroads and other public property along the projected line of march— Atlanta-Milledgeville-Savannah. The army was to live off the country; obtaining food and replacement animals for cavalry, artillery and wagons from the countryside, "discriminating, however, between the rich, who are usually hostile, and the poor and industrious, usually neutral or friendly." Unless they actively interfered with the advance, noncombatants were to be unmolested, and private property—other than supplies and animals needed by the army—was to be respected. Negroes "who are able bodied and can be of service" could be taken along, but subordinate commanders were not to allow themselves to be encumbered with swarms of Negro refugees.

For the most part these orders were strictly adhered to, as the army moved smoothly and efficiently across Georgia. There were exceptions, and the foragers interpreted their instructions freely. A belt of countryside 300 miles long and 50 miles broad was swept clean of food and supplies; more than 200 miles of railroad were "utterly destroyed" as were such public properties as the arsenal at Milledgevile. Despite the violent protestations and accusations in the Southern press, few if any noncombatants were physically harmed. They were generally treated with respect, courtesy—and firmness.

There was no effective opposition to the advance. Hood sent Wheeler—with perhaps 3,000 cavalry—to do what he could to interfere. A like number of Georgia militia, under General G. W. Smith (whom we last saw at the Battle of Fair Oaks) also operated against the army's flanks. The militia accomplished nothing; Wheeler was able to kill or capture a number of the more adventurous Union foragers, but failed to delay the march of the main army for even a few hours.

Over-all command of the effort to stop Sherman was now assumed by General Beauregard, who had recently been transferred from Petersburg to command of the Military Division of the West. The Department of South Carolina, Georgia and Florida, commanded by Lieutenant General W. J. Hardee, was not a part of Beauregard's Military Division of the West, but the hero of Bull Run had been empowered to take authority in an emergency, and upon his arrival Hardee referred to him all major matters for decision.

Beauregard and Hardee met in Macon late in November to determine what action could be taken to stop or slow Sherman. It soon became evident to both that nothing could be done in central Georgia. Hardee therefore hastened to Savannah, which seemed to be Sherman's objective point, to try to organize the defense of that place, while Beauregard returned to his former headquarters of Charleston to try to gather up additional forces to support Hardee, and to prepare to contest a subsequent Union movement into the Carolinas.

So it was that when Sherman's leading elements reached the vicinity of Savannah, on December 9, they found the town well fortified and held by Hardee with a force of about 15,000 men. The Union general decided that he would not try to assault or besiege the city until he had established a base and was assured of a reliable supply line. He expected to make contact with Union naval forces in Ossabaw Sound, at the mouth of the Ogeechee River, some fifteen miles southeast of Savannah. He discovered, however, that the river mouth was protected by small but formidable Fort McAllister, where the Confederate raider *Nashville* had been sunk by USS *Montauk* early in 1863. Sherman promptly dispatched a division of the XV Corps across the Ogeechee River against the fort, which was taken by assault just before dusk on December 13, under the approving eyes of Sherman and Howard, who remained on the north bank of the river.

Sherman at once established communications with the naval forces on Ossabaw Sound, and sent messages reporting his arrival to Grant and President Lincoln. He then set about the investment of Savannah. Hardee, however, was too good a soldier to allow himself to be trapped in a besieged city. With the approval of Beauregard, he had decided to evacuate Savannah before his line of communications with Charleston should be cut. As Union troops began pushing across the Savannah River in considerable strength above the city on the nineteenth and twentieth, Hardee and his garrison marched out across an improvised pontoon bridge before dawn on the twenty-first. That same morning Sherman occupied the city, and dispatched his famous message to President Lincoln which—going by warship to Fort Monroe, and thence by telegraph—was received by the President on Christmas Eve:

"I beg to present you as a Christmas gift the City of Savannah with one hundred and fifty heavy guns and plenty of ammunition, also about 25,000 bales of cotton."

Thus ended "The March to the Sea," one of the most dramatic episodes of American history, and a striking example of total war, efficiently conducted.

For more than a month the Northern Government and people had lost all contact with Sherman, their only information being that which could be gleaned from Southern newspapers. When, therefore, word was received of Sherman's arrival before Savannah, and, soon after, of his capture of the city, the North indulged in the greatest rejoicing of the war.

Though there had been no battles fought, this devastating movement of a great army through the heart of the Confederacy plunged the South into a gloom from which it would never emerge. As a consequence, Sherman—quite unfairly—became to Southerners the chief symbol of Northern oppression. Because he had made frightfully clear to them, as to the rejoicing North, that the sun of the Confederacy was inevitably setting.

# 28

# Stalemate and the Closed Gate

**G**rim and unromantic was the struggle between Petersburg and Richmond; a siege that was not a siege. Relentless trench warfare, the like of which the world had never seen before nor would see again for fifty years to come, was intermingled with sorties, irruptions and bitterly-contested fringe maneuvers.

On June 19, the day after Grant called off further assaults on Petersburg, Lee's army of 55,000 men was manning a line of entrenchments more than 25 miles long. It extended from White Oak Swamp, east of Richmond, across the James below Chaffin's and Drewry's Bluffs, down past Bermuda Hundred to the Appomattox, and then along the eastern edge of Petersburg to the Jerusalem Plank Road.

Lee realized that the army was extended to its limit, and that he could assemble no force for maneuvering without seriously endangering security along the line. Yet he knew that it would be fatal merely to sit behind those entrenchments. The army, and the Confederate capital it was protecting, depended for existence upon food coming from the south and southwest. This fact would be as important to Grant as it was to him, so Lee was determined to keep open the vital supply routes, and at the same time take advantage of any opportunity that appeared, to wrest the initiative from the Northerners. To do these things he would need men, and so he would have to risk manning the trenches with scanty forces. He was as determined as ever that his army must not be besieged.

Both armies were showing the effects of the terrible fighting since Grant crossed the Rapidan into the Wilderness. Both had replaced their losses, and Lee even had been able to risk sending Early to the Valley without substantially modifying the relative combat strength of the two armies. But the replacements, on each side, could not measure up to the quality of the men who had been killed, disabled or captured.

Grant realized this fact, which was to affect the conduct of his operations near Petersburg. He had some 90,000 effectives in the combined Armies of the Potomac and of the James (a number soon to be substantially reduced by detachments to Washington and the Valley). His attacks would be fewer, but he had no intention of relaxing his pressure against the South, or of giving Lee any opportunity to rest his army.

The Union commander, of course, had had his eyes on the railroad lines when he had moved his army across the James towards Petersburg. There were three of these still in Southern possession. The Richmond & Danville R.R., the main link with the remainder of the Southern states, passed thirty-five miles west of Petersburg. The Virginia & Tennessee ran from Staunton in the Shenandoah Valley through Charlottesville and Lynchburg and thence into Tennessee; a branch of this line—which tapped the agricultural resources of the Valley and Western Virginia— ran east from Lynchburg, meeting the Richmond & Danville at Burke's Station, and thence fed into Richmond through Peters- burg over the Southside R.R. Finally, the Wilmington & Weldon

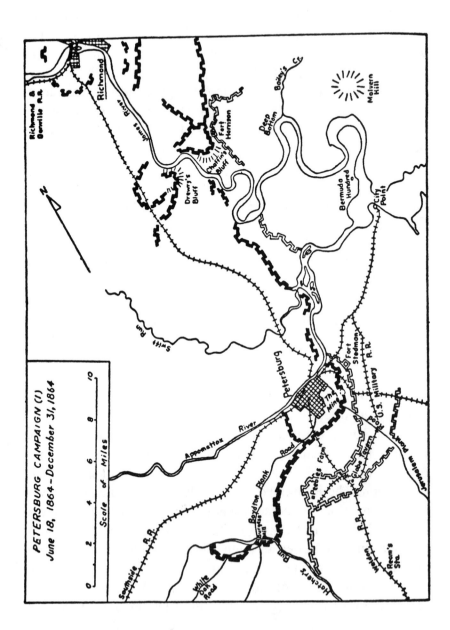

PETERSBURG CAMPAIGN (I)
June 18, 1864–December 31, 1864

ran north through Petersburg to link Richmond with Wilmington, the one remaining seaport still open to blockade runners.

Grant lost no time in attempting to cut the railroads. Birney's II and Wright's VI Corps moved to extend the Union lines west of the Jerusalem Plank Road, and at the same time J. H. Wilson, with his own and August V. Kautz's cavalry divisions, swung south and west of them to break up the railroad junction at Burke's Station (Burkesville), fourteen miles west of Petersburg. If successful, this combined movement would have cut all three of the rail lines at the same time.

But Birney and Wright, losing contact with one another as they probed in dense woods towards the Weldon R.R. on June 22, were hit by A. P. Hill—sent to meet the threat—and thrown back with a loss of 1,700 men. Wilson, with 5,500 sabers, crossed the Weldon line that same day, heading for the Southside.

Harassed from the beginning by Confederate cavalry, the Union force was finally stopped by Wade Hampton and Fitzhugh Lee's troopers, reinforced by two infantry brigades. Wilson turned back after a 100-mile long foray, during which some 60 miles of track were torn up. Narrowly escaping capture at Ream's Station, Wilson got away with the loss of 1,500 men, some guns and his train. He had caused more damage than had been done on any comparable raid of the war, but Confederate engineers soon had the rail lines back in operation. So the net result of this first attempt against the Petersburg-Richmond supply lines was merely an extension of the Union lines one mile west of the Jerusalem Plank Road.

When Grant in July had had to send the VI Corps back to Washington to repel Early's threat to the capital, it prevented him, temporarily, from continuing his probings south of Petersburg. Meanwhile the commander of a Pennsylvania regiment, Lieutenant Colonel Henry Pleasants, had proposed an intriguing scheme to Burnside, whose IX Corps held the trenches each of Petersburg. Pleasants had been a mining engineer in civil life, and most of his men were coal miners. These mining men felt sure they could blast a gap in the Confederate defenses. The idea was to dig a typical mine shaft, or tunnel, under the nearby hostile fortifications, then to explode mine and defenses with a great charge of gunpowder. The idea appealed to Burnside, who quickly obtained the approval of Meade and Grant.

Digging began on June 25, and progressed quite rapidly. It was not long before the Southerners got wind of the mining operation. (The most carefully guarded secrets on both sides always seemed to appear in the newspapers.) Two counter-mines were sunk by the Confederates, but they failed to discover any trace of the Union tunnel. Finding that the air in their shafts got stale after a short distance from the entrance, and convinced that it would be impossible to dig a mine tunnel more than 400 feet without ventilating shafts, the Southerners soon decided that either they had been hoaxed, or that the mining operations had been a failure; it was almost 500 feet between the front lines at their nearest point.

However, Pleasants and his men had devised a novel method to get fresh air to the men working at the tunnel face. An air shaft was put just behind the Union front lines, and at the bottom of this was a furnace. The hot air rising from the furnace created a draft, pulling stale air from the tunnel, while a wooden pipe within the main gallery brought in fresh air to replace that drawn up by the furnace flue. The total distance from the entrance to the magazine galleries under the Confederate line was almost 600 feet; it was about 500 feet from the ventilating shaft to the magazines.

Though Meade was somewhat dubious of success, Grant had been greatly intrigued by the mining operation, and felt that it had great possibilities. He developed a plan to make the most of the opportunity which the blast would create. In order to reduce the strength of the Confederate forces defending Petersburg, he planned a diversion north of the James late in July. He sent the II Corps—which Hancock again commanded—and three cavalry divisions under Sheridan, across the James opposite Bermuda

Hundred near Deep Bottom. To meet this threat Lee responded as Grant had hoped, sending four infantry divisions and two of cavalry to protect the eastern approaches to Richmond. This left but three Confederate infantry divisions and one cavalry division south of the Appomattox on July 29. In accordance with Grant's plan, Hancock and Sheridan hurried back south of the James that night, to take part in the general attack scheduled to take place after the mine exploded, at 3:30 A.M. on the thirtieth.

Burnside's corps, of course, was to lead the attack. He had been told to push the assault with all possible vigor as soon as the mine exploded. He was directed to remove all obstacles from in front of the Union trenches and to make arrangements to get the troops quickly over the parapets and on their way over the ground between the two lines. His objective was a cemetery on the top of an undefended hill at the edge of town, about 500 yards behind the mined entrenchments. The IX Corps would be followed by elements of the XVII and V Corps, while other units kept the defenders busy along the entire line.

The day before the attack was scheduled, Meade discovered that Burnside planned to have the assault spearheaded by a colored division, with his three white divisions following behind. Meade objected strenuously to this. The colored division, though numerically the largest in Burnside's corps, had had practically no combat experience. Furthermore, it might be interpreted as a callous employment of the inexperienced Negro troops as cannon-fodder. When Burnside protested that the colored division had been specifically prepared for the job, Meade referred the matter to Grant, who decided against it.

By this time it was past noon on the twenty-ninth. Burnside, instead of picking the best of his three white divisions, had the division commanders draw lots. By chance, the draw was won— or lost—by the least experienced commander, Brigadier General James H. Ledlie, with the weakest division in the corps. Ledlie, furthermore, had been known to get drunk during combat.

Ledlie made no effort to see that his troops were adequately informed of their part in the assault, and gave only the vaguest of instructions to his subordinates. If Burnside told him, or the other division commanders, to make the preparations for getting out of the trenches, there is no record of the fact.

A faulty fuse delayed the mine explosion for more than an hour. At 4:45 A.M. four tons of gunpowder blasted a crater in the Confederate position about 150 feet long, ninety feet wide and thirty feet deep. Earth, trees, cannon and men were hurled in all directions. Some of the debris came close to the Union front lines and Ledlie's men, not properly prepared, started to scamper to the rear. (Those Southerners who could were also scampering in the opposite direction as fast as they could go.)

It took about ten minutes to get the troops reformed. Then it was discovered that despite Meade's stringent instructions, there were no steps, or planks, or any other means to get the men out of their eight-foot deep trenches and over the parapet. Man by man they had to scramble up, while a few inventive soldiers cut steps with bayonets or thrust bayonets into the side of the trench to make shaky ladders.

Then, as men dribbled across the open space between the lines, stopping to help occasional Southerners half-buried in the loose earth, they headed directly for the crater and gathered, awe-stricken, around its lip. Soon a swarm of men, in no semblance of military order, were bunched at the crater's edge, while a few adventurous souls wandered into the abandoned trenches on either side of it, looking for loot.

Burnside was observing all this from an artillery position just behind the Union lines. Apparently he saw nothing wrong with what was going on, because for the first half-hour after the explosion he issued no orders concerning this failure to follow the plan of attack. But perhaps the most incredible aspect of the corps commander's lack of leadership was the fact that he had no idea of where the assault division commander was or what he was doing, and evidently was unconcerned.

As to Ledlie, he had come to the conclusion that he wished

to avoid all possible participation in the operation. If Grant and Meade wanted his men to be cannon-fodder instead of the Negroes, that was all right. But he had no intention of risking his own life. Well prior to the time scheduled for the blast, he had gone into a bomb-proof with another general officer, and by this time the twain were merrily drunk on medical rum. Since many commentators have said that the Negro division should have been allowed to lead the way, and that the attack failed because Burnside had been forced to change his plans, it is interesting to note that Ledlie's companion in the bomb-proof was none other than Brigadier General Edward Ferraro, commander of the colored division.

If Burnside seemed unconcerned by lack of results more than half an hour after the explosion, Grant and Meade, a few hundred yards directly behind him, were becoming alarmed. Pressed by telegraph messages, Burnside now sent the rest of his corps after Ledlie's division. But when they reached the mass of men in and around the crater, these units, too, became mingled. No progress at all had been made toward the objective when the Southerners began to recover from the initial shock.

A little over an hour after the explosion General Lee was informed and immediately ordered the division of Major General William Mahone to shift eastward from the right of the line. Mahone, moving promptly, took energetic action.

Now rifle and cannon fire began falling on the men in and around the crater. Union troops who had wandered into the trenches were soon driven out, to join the mass of humanity seeking refuge in the crater. This, now, was pummelled with mortar fire, while Confederate troops from higher ground shot at the mob within. Soon the hot July sun was beating down on the mass of frightened men crowding amongst their dead and dying comrades. About this time the Negro division—minus its commanding general—moved to the attack. Most of them joined the white soldiers already overcrowding the crater.

By 9:30 it was obvious to Grant that the attack had failed.

Ordering other units to try to keep the Confederates busy else-where along the line, he instructed Burnside to withdraw. Incredi-bly, that general seemed to think there was still some chance of success, and delayed. Finally, about noon, the withdrawal began. Many of the retreating troops were cut down by murderous Con-federate fire, and many of the men still alive in the crater preferred to surrender rather than attempt to get back across that open space.

The so-called Battle of the Crater, or of the Mine, was one of the great fiascos of the war. As a debacle it can only be compared with Fredericksburg—where also Burnside had been responsible for disaster. There were approximately 4,000 casual-ties among the 20,000 Union troops involved. The Confederates lost about 1,200 out of 11,000.

There is an aftermath to this story of shocking inefficiency. Burnside was removed from command, and resigned from the Army the next April. Ledlie was permitted to resign. But Ferraro not only remained in command of the Negro division he had so shockingly betrayed, but four months later was awarded a major general's brevet "for meritorious service in the present campaign before Richmond and Petersburg." Both Ledlie and Ferraro were political appointees from New York.

It was about this time that Early's continued activities in the Valley and north of the Potomac again required Grant's personal attention for a short time, as we know. Then, fearing that Lee would take further advantage of the reduced strength of the Union army, and its lowered morale after the Crater disaster, by sending more troops to the Valley, Grant decided to threaten the Rich-mond defenses from the east. He immediately sent Hancock's II Corps, Birney's X Corps and a cavalry division across the James near Deep Bottom.

But the Confederates holding a line along Bailey's Creek were able to hold on until Lee could rush help from Petersburg. Hancock and Birney were unable to make any headway. Since they were holding three Confederate infantry divisions and two cavalry divisions north of the James at Deep Bottom, Grant ordered them to continue to demonstrate, while he readied another movement against the Weldon R.R.

Grant now had but two corps facing the Petersburg defenses: the IX Corps (now commanded by Major General John G. Parke) and Warren's V Corps. But the Union entrenchments were now every bit as strong as those of the defenders. So Parke's corps was extended to hold the entire line from the Appomattox to Jerusalem Plank Road, while Warren drove westward on August 18, rounding the southern end of the Union works to overrun the Weldon rail line at Globe Tavern.

Confederate reaction was immediate. Troops were pulled from the James River sector and A. P. Hill with three divisions almost recaptured Globe Tavern. After three days of bitter fighting and two desperate attempts to dislodge this Union clutch on the vital supply line, Hill was forced to give up the attempt. Both sides had rushed reinforcements from the Richmond sector. Union losses were 4,500 against the Confederate toll of 1,600.

The Weldon R.R. was securely in Union hands; Grant's grip was tightening.

To compensate for the cutting of the Weldon rail line at Globe Tavern, Confederate wagon trains began to shuttle supplies between Petersburg and a new rail head some three miles to the south, not far from Ream's Station. Grant sent Hancock, with two divisions and some cavalry, south along the rail line to destroy it for a ten-mile stretch; imposing a thirty-mile roundabout haul for anything coming to the railroad below.

Again Lee reacted immediately. On August 25, Wade Hampton, with a mixed force of infantry and cavalry, surprised Hancock at Ream's Station. In a savage engagement Hancock rallied, beat off the Confederates and completed the job of destruction. Southern losses were 720; Union losses were more than 2,000, mostly made prisoner in the first surprise attack.

Neither Grant nor Lee felt able to take the initiative for the next month. Due to a combination of casualties, disease, discharges and the reinforcements they had sent to their respective subordinates in the Valley, their armies had both dwindled to their lowest strength of the year. Grant had 59,000 men; Lee between 35,000 and 40,000. By late September, however, Union strength had been built up to about 75,000, and though Lee's army had also grown proportionately, Union forces could be and would be strengthened.

As Lee at this time wrote Confederate War Secretary Seddon: "Without some increase in strength, I cannot see how we can escape the natural military consequence of the enemy's numerical superiority."

By late September Grant felt able to resume his pressure. He was ready for another of his one-two punches. While Warren and Parke, opposite Petersburg, demonstrated against the defenses near the Jerusalem Plank Road and the Weldon rail line, the X and XVIII Corps were thrown against the Confederate fortifications at Chaffin's Bluff in the Richmond sector, overrunning Fort Harrison. Lee, fearing lest the entire Richmond line collapse, pulled reinforcements from Petersburg and counterattacked—unsuccessfully—on the 30th. Fort Harrison remained in Union hands.

Taking advantage of Lee's withdrawal of troops from Petersburg, Grant that same day ordered Warren to move against the advanced entrenchments which the Confederates had constructed southwest of Petersburg to protect the approaches to the Southside rail line. Warren succeeded in capturing these outworks at Peeble's Farm, but found the main defensive line too strong to be taken. This advance brought the Union entrenchments about two and a half miles west of the Weldon line and only three miles from the Southside.

During the next two months two important changes occurred in Confederate command arrangements. Beauregard, who had been chafing in a subordinate role in a static position, was sent to command the newly created Military Division of the West, comprising the forces between the Alleghenies and the Mississippi—Hood's and Taylor's armies. A. P. Hill was placed in command of all Confederate forces in Petersburg. Longstreet, who had recovered from his Wilderness wound, was put in charge of all of the defenses of Richmond north of the Appomattox and the James.

Late in October Grant decided to make one more effort to capture the Southside R.R., before the winter season made the roads impassable for large troop movements. Once again he used the whip-saw tactics that had been relatively successful in August and September. While Butler commenced a demonstration east of Richmond, near the old Peninsular Campaign battlefields, Meade sent three army corps—Hancock's II, Warren's V and Parke's IX, 43,000 men in all—to envelop the Southern line opposite Peeble's Farm, then to strike northwest across Hatcher's Run and the Boydton Plank Road to the railroad.

Hill, with 20,000 men, moved quickly to meet the threat to the Southside R.R. Parke had been stopped by the existing entrenchments east of Hatcher's Run and Warren, in the middle, had been delayed in trying to cross the Run to get behind these entrenchments. Hill struck Hancock, who had reached the Boydton Plank Road, halting the Union advance at Burgess' Mill. As soon as it became obvious to Grant that he had failed to surprise the Confederates, he withdrew his troops to their entrenchments. Hill's prompt, aggressive and bold action had frustrated another Union plan.

Longstreet, up at Richmond, had reacted with comparable vigor. In a short, sharp fight along the railroad, just east of the old Fair Oaks battlefield, he repulsed Butler with losses of more than 1,100 men, while suffering very few casualties himself.

These reactions of Longstreet and Hill to Grant's double-offensive must have reminded Lee of the glorious days of 1862 and 1863. Once again the Army of Northern Virginia had shown its prowess in the open field.

Except for an expedition by Warren in early December, which destroyed the rest of the Weldon R.R. almost to the North Carolina border, winter weather now prohibited further mobile operations. The daily artillery duel between the opposing works became the one major evidence of hostilities.

In Richmond and Petersburg, that winter, the plight of both military and civilian populations grew steadily worse. Shortage of food, the growing hopelessness of the Southern cause, and a general war-weariness weighed on everyone.

On the Northern side of the earthworks there was nothing to see except the chugging little locomotives of the Military R.R., a twenty-one-mile long line paralleling the trench system, and which provided ample food and munitions to the Federal besiegers. Here was another ''first'' in war; the specific harnessing of the railroad to logistical support. The railroad linked every inch of the front lines to the enormous base Grant had constructed at City Point.

The soldiers did not lack for outside news, since the Northern newspapers came in every day, while in the constant interchange of gossip and goodies between the opposing pickets—when they were not firing on one another—Southern newspapers and news drifted in.

Both sides found time to wonder, in October, about the fantastic Confederate raid on St. Albans, Vermont; some twenty-odd Southern soldiers in civilian clothing, led by Lieutenant Bennett H. Young, infiltrated the little Vermont village from Canada, held up three banks, and made off with $75,000 in cash.

At his headquarters at City point during the winter of 1864–1865, Grant never allowed the vicissitudes of the war—at Petersburg or elsewhere—to obscure his concept of constant, unremitting pressure around the circumference of the Confederacy. Yet, with all this firmness of purpose, his remarkably practical and flexible mind was constantly adapting itself, and the means available, to all changes in a series of dynamic situations.

Wilmington, North Carolina, Grant felt, should be seized as soon as possible—not only to close the last remaining Southern port open to blockade runners, but to provide a base from which Sherman's army or other Union forces could operate in the Carolinas. A preliminary to the occupation of Wilmington would be the capture of powerful Fort Fisher, at the entrance to the Cape Fear River.

# FORT FISHER

The importance of Fort Fisher to the Confederate cause may be gauged by Lee's personal message to its commander, Colonel William Lamb, that the fort must be held at all costs, or else the Army of Northern Virginia could no longer be supplied.

There were several Confederate fortifications protecting the two shoal-infested entrances to the Cape Fear River estuary, defying the Northern blockading squadrons, whose deep-draft vessels were forced to cruise well to seaward of the long, treacherous shoals. The key to this defensive complex was Fort Fisher, overlooking the northern entrance from the tip of Federal Point. Fisher was perhaps the strongest fortification constructed by either side in the war. With fifty powerful guns, garrisoned by 1,500 men, the fort had been designed to withstand the heaviest possible bombardment. All its landward approaches were protected by palisades, *chevaux de frise* and land mines.

With approaches for large warships limited to one or two narrow channels, it had been long realized by the Union Navy that the Cape Fear River defenses were invulnerable to naval effort alone. But the Army high command, occupied with other important projects, had shown no interest in the half-hearted Navy suggestion for a joint expedition. And so Wilmington prospered as the Confederacy's most important, and now, only remaining haven for blockade runners.

But after Farragut's victory at Mobile Bay, the Navy Department brought the problem to Grant, who was well aware of the importance of Wilmington as a supply base for Lee's army. He immediately responded that troops would be forthcoming if a really energetic Navy officer were appointed to command the

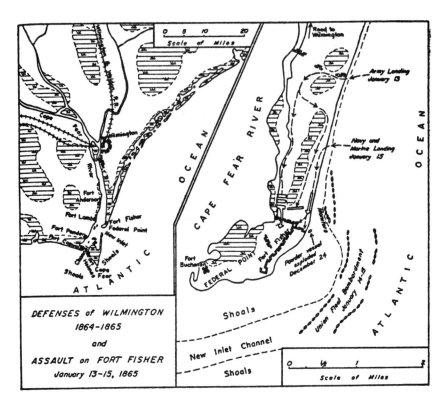

DEFENSES of WILMINGTON
1864-1865
and
ASSAULT on FORT FISHER
January 13-15, 1865

expedition. Farragut, first chosen, had to decline because of ill health. Grant approved enthusiastically when Porter, his old, dependable comrade-in-arms of Vicksburg, was selected.

Porter, equally pleased at the opportunity to leave the frustrations of the Gulf and the Red River, felt that the first step toward capturing Fort Fisher would be to secure his bases along the Albemarle and Pamlico Sounds on the North Carolina coast.

In April, 1864, the Confederates had recaptured Plymouth, where the Roanoke River empties into Albemarle Sound, in a well-planned joint operation. Such an action along the periphery of the Union beachhead would not have been significant, save for one thing. The chief cause of the Confederate victory was a powerful, shallow-draft gunboat—the *Albemarle*—which had been constructed with marvelous ingenuity in a cornfield beside the Roanoke River. In the surprise attack on Plymouth this well-designed ironclad had sunk one Union gunboat and had driven another down the Sound, before turning her guns landward to help force the surrender of the Union fort.

During the months since this fight *Albemarle*, still based at Plymouth, had defeated a squadron of eight Union gunboats and had established unquestioned domination of the western end of the Sound. No shallow-draft Union vessel had the power to cope with the Confederate ironclad, and no large warship could get close enough to fight her.

Porter felt that he could not leave this menace unchecked when he sailed against Fort Fisher with his fleet. He therefore approved a plan to destroy the *Albemarle*, suggested by Lieutenant William B. Cushing, USN. Cushing, already well-known for his dare-devil exploits, was provided with a small, fast, specially-built launch, bearing a powerful torpedo lashed to a long spar over the bow.

On the night of October 27, 1864, Cushing, with a picked crew of volunteers stealthily approached *Albemarle*, then, at full speed, actually slid the light launch over a boom of logs protecting the moored ironclad. Under devastating fire from *Albemarle* and from the shore, Cushing personally detonated the torpedo, sinking both *Albemarle* and his own vessel. Wounded, Cushing and one of his men escaped by swimming through the chilly water; the remainder of the crew were all killed or captured.

With *Albemarle* destroyed, Porter could now take away most of the Union vessels in the Sounds in order to carry out his planned joint expedition against Fort Fisher. But the admiral's troubles were just beginning.

Grant had selected for the Army contingent a division of Butler's Army of the James, then relatively inactive in the Bermuda Hundred lines.

Grant had not intended to entrust to Butler the important Fort Fisher mission. He had wished to relieve the frog-faced general from command of the Army of the James after his dismal performances in May and June near Petersburg. But Butler controlled too many votes in Massachusetts for the Adminstration to be willing to risk the loss of that key state in the 1864 Presidential election. And so, though the election was over and won, Butler still held his command in December. Instead of handing over the Fort Fisher task to an able subordinate, as Grant had expected, Butler took personal command, hoping that a success would shore up his sagging military reputation. He concocted a plan for destroying the fort without fighting; by exploding a gunpowder-laden vessel under its walls. Grant was extremely sceptical, but Porter seemed to think the scheme worth trying. So, after informing the President of his doubts, Grant let the expedition go as planned.

Butler's failure was as complete as Grant had feared and expected. On December 23, after several delays due to poor planning, the powder-boat was exploded under the walls with practically no effect. The garrison of the fort merely thought that their own artillery fire had resulted in blowing up a boiler on one of the attacking gunboats.

Porter's squadron then stood in and kept up a heavy fire for an hour and a quarter, completely silencing the fort. Butler, expected to land under cover of this fire, did nothing, to Porter's disgust. Christmas Day the bombardment was resumed, and this time Butler put ashore 2,000 of his 6,500 men. The troops advanced, almost unopposed, to within 100 yards of the fort, then Butler decided that insufficient damage had been done to the stronghold, and without a word to Porter, hurriedly re-embarked—so hurriedly, in fact that 600 men were left on the beach for the Navy to rescue, while the Army transports were steaming back to Fort Monroe. This was a deliberate violation of Grant's instructions that Butler should establish a beachhead, even if the fort could not be captured immediately.

Porter's justified recriminations rocked Washington. Grant, equally furious, sacked Butler (the elections being over, Lincoln made no objection) and then sent Porter this message: "Hold on, if you please, a few days longer, and I'll send you more troops, with a different general.''

He did. The original expeditionary force, now reinforced to 8,000 men, returned to Porter on January 8, 1865. In command was capable Major General Alfred H. Terry. Complete cooperation became the order of the day.

With the support of the fleet, Terry, on January 13, landed his troops on the peninsula north of the fort and about five miles away. Establishing an entrenched base, he promptly began an efficient, deliberate approach against the fortifications.

Having been alerted to danger by Butler's mismanaged effort, Confederate General Bragg, who now commanded in North Carolina, had increased the garrison to 2,500 men. They were well supplied, determined and confident. But they were unprepared for the fury and accuracy of the gunfire from Porter's fleet of sixty warships. In a day and a half of intense bombardment the Navy destroyed most of the defending guns facing eastward, towards the sea, and all save one covering the north face, which Terry's men were now approaching.

On the afternoon of the fifteenth, in a very carefully planned and well coordinated action, the assault began, while the naval gunfire lifted to targets inside the walls—probably the first attempt in history to apply the principle of the rolling barrage. As Terry's men struck the north face, a mixed Navy-Marine force of 2,000 men attacked the fortifications facing seaward. The bluejackets, armed only with cutlasses and revolvers, were repulsed after extremely bitter hand-to-hand fighting, in which both sides displayed the greatest gallantry. But Terry's men, aided by this diversion, overwhelmed the defenders on their front, and broke into the fort. A confused struggle continued for several hours, as the defenders fell back, step by step, fighting desperately and furiously.

Finally, late that night, having been driven to a small outwork on a sand pit at the very tip of the peninsula, Colonel Lamb and 2,000 brave Confederate soldiers surrendered. Reports of

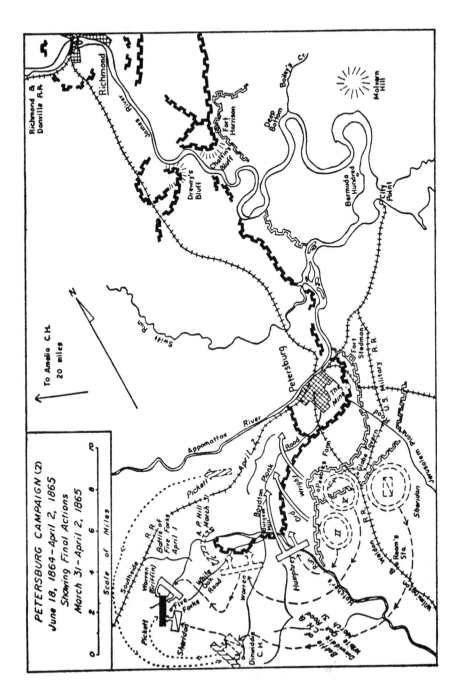

PETERSBURG CAMPAIGN (2)
June 18, 1864 – April 2, 1865
Showing Final Actions
March 31 – April 2, 1865

Confederate casualties are conflicting, but they were between 500 and 700, killed and wounded. Terry lost 955 and Porter 386.

One or two nights later, two blockade runners slipped through the Union fleet, and having gotten inside the river, signaled their arrival to the fort. Terry, with the assistance of a freed slave, gave the expected replies, and the vessels came in closer and their officers came ashore. Not till then did they discover that Fort Fisher was in Union hands, and the Confederacy irretrievably cut off from the outside world.

In an effort to recoup the Fort Fisher disaster, or at least to save Wilmington from capture, Bragg personally took the field for the first time since his defeat at Chattanooga. Though many Southerners thought he had failed to take adequate measures for the security of the fort, he had done his best with the means available; sending 1,000 reinforcements, and placing his one regular division in reserve between Fort Fisher and Wilmington. There was little more he could do now, save to attempt to prevent Terry from moving inland.

Bragg, with the able assistance of General Hoke and his division, was initially successful in limiting the Northern beachhead. But even before the fall of Fort Fisher, Grant had had the foresight to send for Schofield and a corps of Thomas' army to hasten eastward to assist in gaining control of North Carolina. When Schofield arrived a few weeks later, bringing with him about 20,000 men, the fate of Wilmington was sealed. Schofield, who commanded both his own and Terry's troops, captured the city on February 22. He now prepared to join forces with Sherman, already in the heart of North Carolina.

# The Sands
# Run Out

## THROUGH THE CAROLINAS

Five days before the fall of Fort Fisher, Sherman's army had begun moving north from Savannah into South Carolina. Incessant rain slowed down progress, and the resultant floods would have stopped most other armies. But these veterans had business in South Carolina, and would not be deterred by inclement weather.

Every one of the 60,000 men in Sherman's army felt that South Carolina had been responsible for starting the war, and consequently each felt a personal grudge against that state and its inhabitants. Marching through Georgia had been business, but there had been no rancor against the populace. This was different. Sensing this feeling in his army, Sherman had written before he left Savannah:

The whole army is burning with an insatiable desire to wreak vengeance upon South Carolina. I almost tremble at her fate, but feel that she deserves all that seems in store for her.

Frantic orders now came from Richmond, ordering most of the remnants of Hood's army to rush back across Georgia to try to stop the slow, steady advance of this vengeful Northern army into the Carolinas. By the end of January there were about 40,000 Southern soldiers in the field in South Carolina in front of Sherman, with perhaps half as many more gathering under Bragg in North Carolina to oppose Schofield's anticipated advance from Wilmington and New Bern. A large number of these men, of course, were militiamen, with relatively little combat experience. Worse yet, the command situation was extremely confused. Not only was there little coordination between the two senior commanders, Bragg and Beauregard, but they in turn seemed to be unable to exert firm, cohesive control over their subordinates. Wade Hampton, who had been sent south from Lee's army to help defend his native South Carolina, was nominally under Beauregard, as was Hardee. Actually, there was little cooperation between their forces. Similarly, in North Carolina, Hoke was operating against Schofield with considerable independence from his departmental commander, Bragg.

Thus, as Sherman marched northward into South Carolina, his enemies seemed to be unable to determine whether his objective was Augusta or Charleston. Thus, when he marched between these two cities, after feinting at both, Sherman found negligible opposition to his seizure of Columbia, capital of South Carolina, on February 17. Before abandoning Columbia, its few defenders, under Wade Hampton, burned the cotton stored there to prevent it from falling into Federal hands.

That night most of Columbia was destroyed in a great fire, which had been whipped into a fury by a high wind. Because of the known attitude of the Union army toward the state, most Southerners have insisted that the fire was started by Federal troops—perhaps acting under orders from Sherman. There is no question that some soldiers had found liquor in the city, and a few bands of drunken men had wandered around the town in the afternoon and early evening, terrorizing the inhabitants. It is possible that these men may have started the fire. More likely, however, is Sherman's version; namely, that the wind had spread the fire from the cotton left burning by Hampton's men. Sherman called out his troops to attempt to halt the blaze, and next day he turned over a considerable quantity of food and other supplies to the mayor of the city to alleviate the suffering caused by the fire.

The day Sherman's troops marched into Columbia, Hardee evacuated Charleston, which was promptly occupied by Union forces holding Morris Island, at the entrance to the harbor. But though the Stars and Stripes once more flew over Fort Sumter, the South was not yet ready to concede the loss of the war which had started there.

On February 3, President Davis, responding to the frenzied clamor in Richmond, had appointed Lee General-in-Chief of the Confederate Army—a step he should have taken, of course, long before. On the twenty-third Lee exercised his new power to rectify the chaotic command situation in the Carolinas. Joseph E. Johnston, who had been left without employment since he was relieved of command at Atlanta in July, was assigned to command all the Confederate forces in the Carolinas. No better choice could have been made and it was a tribute to Johnston, as well as to such difficult personalities as Beauregard and Bragg, that the disparate Southern forces scattered around the Carolinas were quickly brought under Johnston's firm control. Incompleteness of Confederate records precludes any accurate strength figures, but the total force in North Carolina commanded by Johnston in March and April of 1865 was probably about 45,000 men. About half of these were quickly assembled in the central part of the state to contest Sherman's advance, while Bragg, with most of the remainder, was delaying the advance of Schofield's forces upon Goldsboro from Wilmington and New Bern.

Sherman's army, though slowed by the continuous rain, entered Fayetteville on March 11, after a cavalry skirmish on the outskirts. Sherman now established contact with Schofield and ordered him to press on and join him at Goldsboro.

While at Fayetteville, Sherman learned of the change in the Confederate command in the Carolinas. As he wrote later: "I then knew that my special antagonist, General Joseph E. Johnston, was back, with part of his old army; that he would not be misled by feints and false reports, and would somehow compel me to exercise more caution than I had hitherto done."

Estimating Johnston's available forces as about 37,000, but knowing they were still widely scattered, Sherman decided to push on to Goldsboro as rapidly as possible, to prevent Confederate concentration there. On March 15, he again cut his communications with the seacoast and marched rapidly northward.

But Johnston saw the situation with equal clarity. His only hope was to defeat Sherman before the Union army could reach Goldsboro, where it would be reinforced by Schofield, and regain communications with bases at Wilmington and New Bern. Aware that Sherman had been marching with his four corps abreast, on a broad front, Johnston's plan was to concentrate the strongest possible force against one flank of the Union army and thus defeat Sherman in detail. He put the plan into operation with speed, skill and resolution.

Bragg was ordered to join the main army southwest of Goldsboro, while Hardee was assigned the mission of delaying Sherman's advance until Bragg arrived. Hardee performed his task with his usual efficiency, in the so-called Battle of Averysboro, on the sixteenth. Sherman's left wing was forced to halt, deploy, and then to attack successive delaying positions held by the Southerners. By the eighteenth Johnston had assembled a considerable portion of his command near Bentonville, just northwest of Sherman's left wing. These, with Hardee's men, who were marching up from Averysboro, gave Johnston about 27,000 men. He decided that the time had come to strike. Sherman did not dream that Johnston would be able to concentrate so rapidly, and so the Union advance on the nineteenth was made with no thought of an approach to battle.

Johnston had hoped to be able to strike the Federal left wing while "in column on the march," but Hardee being delayed, this was impossible. The Southerners therefore took up a defensive position in front of the line of march of the Union XIV Corps, on Sherman's left, intending to counterattack when Hardee arrived.

The Union troops, when confronted by skirmishers, deployed to brush aside what they assumed to be another Confederate delaying position. To their surprise, however, they were repulsed, and fell back in considerable disorder from Johnston's entrenchments. But the Confederate counterattack was not pushed with the speed or the aggressiveness that Johnston had intended.

Hardee arrived when expected, but Bragg (acting loyally as a corps commander, despite his rank as a full general) had failed to realize the extent of the success his troops had gained in repulsing the Federal morning attack. Consequently, Slocum, commanding the Union left wing, was given time to rally the XIV Corps and to bring up the XX Corps. Nevertheless, the Southern attack, when it came shortly after noon, was able to drive the Union troops from the first of two lines of hasty entrenchments, and Slocum's left was seriously shaken. The Union troops withdrew to new positions, which they were able to hold until dark, only with difficulty.

Sherman, meanwhile, had received word of the battle, and hastened to the scene with the right wing of his army, arriving on Johnston's left flank early on the twentieth. The Confederate general now realized that he was faced by Sherman's united army, and that he had no hope of defeating it in detail. He believed, however, that he might still inflict serious casualties if the Northerners were to try to assault his entrenchments.

Sherman, unwilling to risk a general battle when his supply wagons were almost out of food, and evidently not appreciating that he had more than double Johnston's force, contented himself with exploratory probes against the Confederate position. On the twenty-first, in the face of increasing pressure on his flanks, Johnston decided to withdraw.

Johnston had failed in his objective, but he and his subordinates had covered themselves with glory in a splendid failure. Northern casualties were 1,646; Confederate losses are not known exactly, but they were probably about twice as great. Most of the losses on both sides occurred during the fierce fighting of the nineteenth.

Sherman now realized that he had lost an opportunity to crush Johnston. Apparently somewhat annoyed at himself, he continued his march to Goldsboro, which he reached on the twenty-third, just as Schofield was arriving. This concluded the march of some 425 miles from Savannah. Considering the weather, the time of the year, and the nature of the opposition encountered near the end, this march had been a splendid accomplishment, and much more difficult than the better known march through Georgia. Because of the bad weather and the atrocious condition of the roads, Sherman now determined to rest his army for about three weeks, expecting that the campaigning would be easier about mid-April. At that time he planned to continue the northward advance, expecting to join Grant near Petersburg to overwhelm the united forces of Johnston and Lee.

# STARS OVER ALABAMA

After Farragut's victory in the Battle of Mobile Bay, and the subsequent Federal capture of Fort Morgan, there had been little activity near the port of Mobile. The city itself remained in Confederate possession. But in mid-January of 1865, in accordance with his overall plan for destroying Confederate strength in Alabama, Grant ordered General Canby, commanding in New Orleans, to capture Mobile as soon as possible. The city was then to become a base for further operations against Selma and Montgomery, in central Alabama, in coordination with a force to be sent from Tennessee by General Thomas.

Not till mid-March did Canby get started—much to Grant's annoyance—and it was not until March 27, that he actually began operations against the city. Once he arrived, however, he moved with vigor and efficiency. With some 45,000 men, opposed by 10,000 defenders, he quickly seized several outlying forts and began to invest the city. On April 8, a well-prepared assault was mounted, covered by siege artillery and the fire of a number of gunboats in the bay. A portion of the lines was seized before dark, and that night the Confederate defenders evacuated the city.

Canby now discovered that there was no need for him to carry out the remainder of his mission: an advance on Selma and Montgomery. Another general had gained the glory that could have been his had he followed Grant's orders more promptly.

Typically, Thomas had been a long time getting ready to send his expedition southward from Tennessee into Alabama. But equally typical, this force, when it left, was fully equipped and well prepared in every way for the task at hand. Thomas had selected—aided by some broad hints from Grant—an "energetic leader"—quite different from himself in every way except thoroughness and courage. This was young Brevet Major General James H. Wilson, the engineer who Grant had converted into a successful cavalryman in the Wilderness-Petersburg campaigns, and whose cavalry had played a decisive part in defeating Hood at Nashville.

On March 18, Wilson's corps of 13,500 men crossed the Tennessee River at Eastport, Alabama. Three days were spent in getting pack horses, 300 supply wagons, eight artillery pieces and a light pontoon train across the river, and readying his command for what would turn out to be one of the most remarkable cavalry campaigns in history. Speed was to be of the essence. Each trooper carried 5 days' rations for himself, grain for his horse, 100 rounds of ammunition, and 2 horseshoes. Fifty days of food and forage were carried in the wagons.

Early on the twenty-second the expedition moved southeastward into central Alabama, in three parallel columns. Living off the country, Wilson marched seventy miles in the first three days, before running into opposition near Jasper, on March 25. Pushing aside this resistance, Wilson pressed south to Elyton—where Birmingham now sprawls—and struck directly south for Selma.

The only organized Confederate force available to oppose this invasion was Forrest's depleted cavalry corps. By the end of March, Forrest had been able to gather less than 3,000 men with whom to try to halt the fast-moving Northerners. Wilson quickly brushed the Confederates aside from their delaying positions at Montevallo and at Six Mile Creek.

On April 1, Forrest took up a strong position at Ebenezer Church, about twenty-five miles north of Selma. Deploying his forces rapidly, Wilson assaulted the Confederates, and Forrest's badly outnumbered men were soon forced to withdraw. But by this action Forrest had delayed Wilson for about a day, permitting more of his distant units to arrive at Selma to help defend this vital arsenal. Forrest now had about 7,000 men. Less than half of these were part of his veteran cavalry corps; the remainder were local militia with little training and even less combat experience. But even untrained men had shown they could be effective when fighting behind defensive works, and Forrest had the advantage of an arc of bastioned earthworks, six to eight feet in height, completely ringing the city on the north bank of the Alabama River. In front of this wall lay a ditch five feet deep and about fifteen feet wide.

By afternoon of April 2, Wilson's troops appeared before the city's defenses. While his columns closed up, and the troopers dismounted and deployed in front of the fortifications, Wilson made a hasty reconnaissance. He decided to attack at once. His eight light artillery pieces opened fire, a division of his dismounted cavalrymen dashed across a fire-swept clearing in front of the earthworks. They piled into the ditch and, clambering on one another's shoulders, flowed up over the parapet. The astonished Confederates, not expecting an attack until the next morning, were completely surprised by this audacious frontal assault; their fire was wild, and the Union soldiers suffered few casualties.

No sooner had the leading division fought its way into the defenses, driving the Southerners back in hand-to-hand conflict, than another division dashed across the clearing to join the attack. Forrest now knew he could not hold the town. His exhausted, ill-fed men were demoralized, Wilson's troopers unstoppable. Salvaging as many of his men as possible, the tough Confederate rode off, hoping to be able to fight again another day.

But this time it was not to be. For a week Wilson rested his men, while destroying the foundries, ammunition depots and stores that had made Slema so important to the Confederacy. Then, on April 10, he crossed the Alabama River and moved east towards Montgomery and then on to Georgia.

In the next ten days, marching practically unopposed at a rate of about twenty-five miles a day, Wilson and his men swept on through Montgomery, Columbus and West Point in succession, destroying railroads, supplies and everything which might be useful to Confederate troops. On April 20 he seized Macon. Next day, as he was about to resume his march, Wilson received a message from Sherman directing him to suspend hostilities until negotiations for Confederate surrender were completed.

Wilson's exploit—no mere cavalry raid but a mounted expedition in the truest sense of the word—was a signpost pointing to the armored *blitzkrieg* of the future. Grant and Thomas could agree that they had chosen ''an energetic leader'' for the expedition into Alabama.

# A PARLEY AND A GAMBLE FAIL

Inside the Richmond-Petersburg lines as 1865 opened, privation pinched hard. All European supply ceased with the fall of Fort Fisher at Wilmington. True, sufficient food still trickled in from the south to prevent outright starvation, but everyone was hungry. The desertion rate in Lee's army increased alarmingly. His strength, grown to about 70,000 in late December, slowly declined during January and February to little more than 60,000.

Boredom was the major complaint of the Northern army. There was no place to go, nothing to do. But food was plentiful, delivered by the little railroad practically to the back door of each company mess.

But on January 31, both sides had something tangible to whet their interest. Under cover of a flag of truce and a bugler blowing a parley, three Confederate peace commissioners, headed by Vice President Alexander H. Stephens, passed through the Federal lines to confer with President Lincoln on board a warship in Hampton Roads.

At Petersburg, cheers from both Blue and Gray greeted the commissioners as their carriage rolled through the lines. A Southern picket shouted for three cheers for the Yankee army. The thunder had not died away before the Union men were cheering the Confederates. As a final touch, the Federals noted a group of Southern ladies, finely decked out, standing on the Confederate parapet to wish their commissioners Godspeed. Someone called for and got three rousing cheers for the ladies of Petersburg, and a flutter of handkerchiefs returned the salute. For the moment, it seemed the war was just about to end on the spot.

But the ladies left, the cheering died, and three days later the commissioners returned in anti-climax. Lincoln had told them they could write their own terms, provided they agreed to rejoin an indissoluble Union and abolish slavery. But Davis' emissaries had been empowered to discuss only peace terms between two independent nations. The conference ended in impasse four hours after it began. So the guns at Petersburg took up their old refrain.

On February 5, Grant sent a cavalry division and some infantry elements around the Confederate left flank once more, to cut the Boydton Plank Road. Rumors had come in of its use for wagon traffic between the beleaguered city and Hicksford, now the northern end of the Weldon railroad. The raid was successful. It was discovered, however, that the road was practically unused. Since Grant did not want to further complicate his own supply situation over muddy roads, he withdrew the most advanced units from the Boydton Plank Road, but did extend his permanent lines to Hatcher's Run. Once again the thin cord of Confederate defense would have to be stretched—far beyond Lee's manpower capability.

It was during this minor Battle of Hatcher's Run that President Davis, in somewhat reluctant compliance with an act of the Confederate Congress, appointed Lee to be General-in-Chief of the Confederate armed forces. The law had been so written as to permit the new General-in-Chief to assume almost dictatorial powers. One is reminded of the Continental Congress handing similar powers to George Washington in the last dark days of 1776. Whether he wanted to or not, Lee now had to concern himself with the overall military situation of the Confederacy, while retaining his personal command of the Army of Northern Virginia.

Lee made some decisions that he knew were not always pleasing to President Davis. Most notable was his recall of Joe Johnston to command in the Carolinas. Lee, however, was as punctilious as ever in seeking the President's approval of all major decisions. Davis, grateful for this, invariably approved the general's recommendations and gave him the full support of the Government.

The South also had a new Secretary of War. James Seddon, who had received much criticism, resigned and in his place General John Breckenridge was appointed. Breckenridge would retain this post till the collapse of the Confederacy, thus climaxing a remarkable public career which had included a term as Vice President of the United States, nearly successful candidacy for President—against Lincoln—in 1860, and distinguished service as one of the ablest "political" generals of the war.

The desperate nature of the military situation was of course apparent to Lee. He saw only one dim possibility of success. If he and Johnston could unite their armies to defeat Sherman, and then turn on Grant and beat him, perhaps much of the lost territory could be recovered, and the war prolonged. Despite the results of the 1864 election, Lee still hoped, with some justification, that further Union defeats and an indefinite prolongation of the war might result in a negotiated peace granting Confederate independence.

In order to be able to join Johnston, of course, Richmond and Petersburg would have to be abandoned. More serious, militarily, was the problem of evacuating these cities, moving around the left flank of the Army of the Potomac, and getting into the Carolinas without interference from Grant. Lee felt that a powerful blow against Grant's right would cause him to shift troops from his far-flung left flank, thus making it easier for the Southerners to get away. It is noteworthy that Douglas S. Freeman, Lee's biographer, reluctantly writes as follows of Lee's "curious disregard" of Grant's aggressive nature:

> Perhaps it is indicative not only of the desperation but also the distorted military thought of the Confederates, after a winter of hunger and strain, that in planning this they should ignore the certainty of an immediate counter-stroke by Grant.

On the other hand, Lee's determination to seize the initiative before Grant, if possible, shows that he still realized that battles can be won only by vigorous, energetic action; and that a rash move had infinitely greater chances of success than no move at all.

Speed was of the essence; desertions were rapidly weakening the Confederate strength, and starvation, too, was near. Meanwhile—and this too is indicative of Lee's desperation—he wrote Grant (with President Davis' permission) on March 2, proposing an interview for the purpose of negotiating peace terms. Grant at once declined; such negotiations were the province of President Lincoln.

Lee now had about 45,000 men south of the Appomattox River; Gordon's II Corps and A. P. Hill's III Corps. Longstreet's I Corps and a few miscellaneous units—about 15,000 men in all—held the Bermuda Hundred entrenchments and the Richmond fortifications. The total length of the Confederate lines was more than thirty-seven miles.

The Army of the Potomac, holding the lines south of the Appomattox, was now about 70,000 strong. Parke's IX Corps held the old entrenchments east of Petersburg, down to a point midway between Jerusalem Plank Road and the Weldon rail line. Warren's V Corps held from there to the vicinity of Peeble's Farm. Humphrey's II Corps (Hancock was away, raising a new corps near Washington) held the left out to Hatcher's Run.

There were another 35,000 Union troops in the Army of the James, holding Bermuda Hundred and the lines opposite Richmond above Deep Bottom. This army was now commanded by a competent soldier—Edward O. Ord. Most of its strength was available as an additional reserve, ready to be moved either south or north as Grant might direct.

Lee was more or less familiar with the condition and location of the Union units. Like Grant, he was fearful that his opponent might move before he was ready. So he decided to seize the initiative by making his attack late in March, assuming that Grant would not be ready to move until mid-April when the roads were reasonably dry.

With Hill frequently sick, and Longstreet not yet fully recovered from his wounds, Lee was placing ever more reliance on able, courageous, young Gordon. Gordon was to plan and conduct the attack which was to precede the Confederate army's move to North Carolina.

The objective was to smash the Union lines east of Petersburg, just north of where the mine had been exploded the summer previous. The most formidable obstacle in this part of the line was a large earthwork called Fort Stedman, only 200 yards from the Confederate lines. Gordon planned to seize Fort Stedman by surprise early in the morning of March 25, to roll up the Union lines in both directions, then to seize the Military Railroad. Gordon's corps was reinforced; he had practically half of the Confederate army available to him for the operation.

If all went well, Grant's attention would be distracted and Lee would be able to slide out of the southwestern sector of the Union investment.

It was a desperate plan, and its ultimate objective—loosening of Grant's grip on Petersburg—was probably impossible of attainment. Yet it is doubtful if any other operation would have had as much chance of success, or if it could have been better conducted. Fort Stedman was captured by a surprise assault at 4:30 A.M., before dawn. But the Confederates were dealing with veteran troops. The penetration was quickly limited by Parke, Union commander in the area, who rushed reinforcements to the threatened point and then counterattacked. Meanwhile, further west, Warren probed against the weakened Confederate defenses southwest of the town. Less than four hours after the attack was launched, the Confederates had been thrown back into their lines, and both Parke and Warren had succeeded in capturing several advanced posts. The Confederate situation was a little worse than it had been before the attack was begun.

Next day Sheridan's horse from the Valley came jangling into the Union lines; behind them strode Wright's VI Corps. Ulysses S. Grant decided his time had come.

"I now feel like ending the matter," he told Sheridan, as he discussed his plans for a final, overwhelming blow against the Southside R.R. and Lee's right flank. Humphrey's II Corps and Warren's V Corps would swing west of the Confederate lines at Hatcher's Run; their former positions in the trenches south of Petersburg being taken by Wright's VI Corps and Ord's Army of the James. Ord had just slipped south of the Appomattox with about 20,000 men, leaving only skeleton forces to hold the Bermuda Hundred and Deep Bottom lines. Meanwhile Sheridan's cavalry corps would move westward to Dinwiddie Courthouse, and then strike northwest to cut the railroad. Further movements of the cavalry would be governed by Grant's orders issued as the situation developed.

Despite recent heavy rains and extremely muddy roads, the movement began on March 29. Lee at once recognized the danger not only to the positions in Richmond and Petersburg, but also to his planned movement to join Johnston. He reacted with typical vigor. He would attack, even though this still further reduced the strength in his thinly-held fortifications.

While A. P. Hill delayed the advance of Warren and Humphrey south of White Oak Road, Lee sent Pickett with two divisions and Fitzhugh Lee's cavalry—about 11,000 men in all—circling well to the west to strike the left flank of the advancing Federal columns. On the thirty-first the Confederates attacked. A. P. Hill drove around Warren's left flank and though eventually repulsed, he succeeded in halting the Union infantry advance.

At the same time Pickett struck Sheridan's cavalry northwest of Dinwiddie Courthouse. The fighting was hard and furious, but Sheridan would not give way, even though he was faced by a force considerably larger than his own, and consisting mostly of veteran infantry. Sheridan, immediately realizing that Pickett was isolated from the rest of the Confederate army, appealed to Grant for an infantry corps with which to overwhelm Pickett next day.

Grant promptly complied. Warren's V Corps was detached from the Army of the Potomac to Sheridan's command and ordered to join him that very night. Simultaneously Sheridan sent Warren orders to attack Pickett's left rear at dawn, April 1. But Pickett received word of the approach of Union infantry behind him and pulled back during the night at Five Forks. Here he entrenched, obedient to Lee's telegraphed instructions to ''hold Five Forks at all hazards.''

It is strange, under these circumstances, that after establishing his Five Forks position Pickett had accepted the invitation of Tom Rosser, of Fitzhugh Lee's cavalry, to join him and Fitzhugh in an impromptu shadbake well back of the line.

Sheridan, in hot pursuit, ordered Warren to hit Pickett's left flank at Five Forks, while he himself pinned the Southerners down with his cavalrymen, fighting on foot. But Warren's troops, groggy from thirty-six hours of marching and fighting, were slow to come up; two divisions lost their way. When Adelbert Ames' division and Joshua Chamberlain's brigade—hurrying to the sound of the guns—did arrive in late afternoon they found Sheridan—enraged at the delay—directing a fire fight against Pickett's front.

At once Sheridan led a furious combined charge against Pickett's left, his troopers and the infantrymen following him as he leaped his charger over the Confederate breastworks. Pickett rushed back from his shadbake to find his defense unravelled and his troops melting away in panic. More than 3,200 were taken prisoner. The Union loss was 634 killed and wounded; there is no record of Confederate casualties.

When it was over, Sheridan was off again, aiming north for the vital Southside rail line. But before he went he vented his rage on Warren, relieving him of command on the spot for what he considered to have been intolerable delay. Grant later approved Sheridan's action; Warren had always been slow as a corps commander and Grant, on several occasions, had been on the point of relieving him. But it was a sad climax to the career of the man who had saved the Round Tops at Gettysburg.

Receiving the report of Sheridan's overwhelming victory at Five Forks, Grant ordered a general assault against Petersburg at dawn the following morning.

At 4:30 A.M., April 2, Wright struck northward from the vicinity of Peeble's Farm and broke through the main Confederate line. Shortly after this Humphrey and Ord attacked and also broke through. Trying vainly to rally his men near the Southside rail

line, A. P. Hill was killed, shortly after six o'clock. Meanwhile
Sheridan, with his cavalry and the V Corps (now commanded
by Major General Charles Griffin) headed northward across the
railroad a few miles further west, in pursuit of Pickett. Only
Gordon's lines, at Petersburg itself, held firm.

It was now obvious to Lee that Sunday morning that Petersburg and Richmond could no longer be defended. He determined
to carry out his plans of joining Johnston, though the already
slender chances of success had now almost disappeared. To give
time for the movement of his troops near Richmond, and to permit
the evacuation of the Confederate Government, he would have
to hold Petersburg till nightfall, and would also have to delay
Sheridan's advance. With a sure hand that had not lost its cunning
in the face of disaster, he gave the necessary orders and sent a
message to President Davis, who received it in church and left
dramatically in the middle of services.

Longstreet was rushed down to hold the gap between Gordon's sector and the Appomattox River, west of Petersburg. Anderson was sent with three brigades to cover the reorganization
of Pickett's command, and to start marching westward towards
Amelia Courthouse, which was to be the rendezvous point, and
where Lee had directed supplies to be collected. Fitzhugh Lee
was to delay Sheridan; at least until Anderson was able to slip
past between the Southside line and the Appomattox.

Grimly, skillfully, almost miraculously, Lee and his able
assistants got the last ounce of fighting out of their brave veterans.
The Union advance was slowed; stopped in some places. It was
only temporary, but it was enough to permit the orderly evacuation of the Richmond and Petersburg lines. When Longstreet and
Gordon marched out that night across the Appomattox River,
taking parallel roads to Amelia Courthouse, the "siege" of Petersburg had ended.

The curtain was going up on the final act of America's
greatest drama.

# Appomattox and Aftermath

**I**t was April 3, 1865. In central North Carolina Johnston and Sherman were resting, eyeing each other warily; down in Alabama Wilson's men were burying the dead at Selma, while Forrest and a devoted remnant of his command tarried at nearby Plantersville. But the real climax of the war was approaching, in southern Virginia.

Incredibly, the Army of Northern Virginia had rallied from its worst defeat. Brilliantly, Lee had executed a withdrawal from the broken Richmond-Petersburg lines and after an all-night march in abominable weather his weary columns were converging westward towards Amelia Courthouse. Despite the heavy losses incurred south and west of Petersburg in the preceding days, Lee still had approximately 40,000 men available for combat. Wet, dejected and hungry though they were, the flame of fighting spirit still flickered in the sodden ranks, kept burning there by sheer personal leadership.

Paralleling the Confederate retreat and slightly to the south, the Army of the Potomac was also plodding westward. Grant had not tarried to celebrate the capture of Petersburg and Richmond. With Sheridan's cavalry corps in the lead, like hounds in full cry after a wounded stag, the Union troops were hurrying in pursuit.

President Davis and the principal officials of the Confederate Government had fled by railroad from Richmond on April 2, protected by Lee's magnificent delaying action; a temporary capital was established at Danville. On the fourth President Lincoln visited Richmond, arriving unescorted and unannounced. He was soon joined on his sight-seeing tour by Major General Godfrey Weitzel, whose corps occupied the city. Just before the President left to return to Washington, Weitzel asked if he had any instructions on how to treat the conquered Southerners. Lincoln declined to give any orders other than through Grant, but he left Weitzel with this suggestion:

"If I were in your place I'd let 'em up easy, let 'em up easy."

There was no let-up, however, a few miles to the west. Lee's columns had been delayed on the roads by the exhaustion of the men and the difficulties of getting heavily loaded wagon trains over muddy roads. Then Longstreet's corps reached Amelia Courthouse on the fourth, only to discover that rations which Lee had ordered sent from Danville had not arrived. The remainder of the army came up during the night and early next day, but instead of being able to press southwestward along the railroad to Danville, as he had planned, Lee had to delay for twenty-four hours while food and forage were collected from the nearby countryside.

Lee's plan, desperate, but perhaps not impossible, had been to march rapidly south along the railroad to join Johnston south of Danville, and then crush Sherman with the combined armies. It was, of course, highly doubtful that he could have eluded Grant's pursuit, or, assuming a battle could have been fought before Grant's arrival, could have defeated Sherman's splendid army even with Johnston's assistance. But the slender chances of

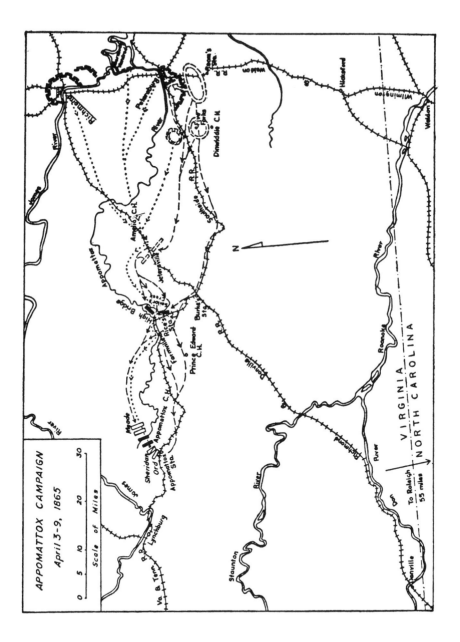

a temporary success were dashed by the day's delay at Amelia Courthouse.

Grant had guessed Lee's intentions as soon as the Confederates had evacuated Petersburg and Richmond. He had resolved not merely to follow Lee in pursuit, but rather to get ahead of the Confederates as rapidly as possible. Though this necessitated keeping the troops marching almost incessantly, night and day, over miserable roads, the Union soldiers responded willingly. The end of the war was in sight. Thus it was that, even though many of the men had been without food for more than a day, Sheridan's cavalry, closely followed by the V, II and VI Corps, reached the railroad at Jetersville on the fifth, and took up positions blocking Lee's intended route of advance.

Grant himself was further south, with Ord's Army of the James and the IX Corps, approaching the railroad at Burke's Station. When he learned from Sheridan of the situation near Amelia Courthouse, he rode most of the night to join Meade at Jetersville to order an attack before Lee could escape.

The indomitable Southerner had already discovered that his line of retreat had been blocked. He had started southward late that afternoon, but now he ordered his army to turn westward towards Farmville. By a night march he would again try to get in front of the Northerners, going around them by way of Prince Edward Courthouse, or if necessary he would go on to Lynchburg before turning south. At dawn, therefore, the advancing Union troops saw only the Confederate rear guards, disappearing to the west.

While the Union II and V Corps pushed rapidly after the Southerners, Sheridan's cavalry and the VI Corps marched directly towards Farmville, in hope of again cutting off the line of retreat. Ord's column, which Grant now rejoined, also headed for Farmville.

By a rapid night march Longstreet's corps had reached Rice's Station, where it could cover the crossing of the Appomattox River at High Bridge, east of Farmville. But Lee's other three corps—Anderson's, Ewell's and Gordon's—were slowed down by their wagon trains. Gordon's—the rear guard—was soon being pressed by the Union II Corps. Meanwhile Sheridan's cavalry, marching by parallel roads a few miles to the south, was harassing the slow-moving Confederates. So the Confederate retreat was still further delayed by a series of running fights along the entire flank and in the rear.

The three cavalry divisions—Crook, Custer and Devens in turn—came sweeping in one at a time, playing a deadly game of leap-frog. As each leading element dismounted, to fight on foot and delay the Confederate column, the remainder pressed ahead, to repeat the process.

In the afternoon Anderson and Ewell took up defensive positions east of Rice's Station, along the general line of Sailor's (Sayler's) Creek, in an effort to halt the Union pursuit long enough to permit the trains and artillery to get across the Appomattox near High Bridge. Although it is doubtful if they could have taken any other course of action, under the circumstances the halt was fatal. Sheridan's cavalry and horse artillery dashed behind the Southern positions, while the VI Corps pressed the defenders from the front. Without artillery, surrounded, and taking heavy punishment, Ewell, just before dark, surrendered his entire corps—then barely 4,000 strong—while more than one-third of Anderson's 6,000 were also forced to surrender.

Lee had been with Longstreet near High Bridge. Turning back upon hearing the noise of battle, he reached the high ground west of Sailor's Creek at dusk, to discover the disaster which had overtaken more than one quarter of his remaining army. Realizing he could do nothing to undo the catastrophe, the Confederate commander ordered Longstreet to march back to High Bridge. There, during the night, Gordon rejoined, having been able to slip past the northern edge of the Sailor's Creek battlefield, but only after losing some 2,000 men as prisoners.

The loss of 8,000 men captured on the sixth, plus constant attrition from desertion by hopeless, hungry soldiers, had brought

Lee's remaining strength to less than 30,000 men. Desperate though the situation was, he determined to press westward toward Lynchburg. He had ordered rations to be collected at Farmville, and this time the orders were carried out. The half-starved soldiers were able to get a good meal, and were provided with additional rations to put in their knapsacks, or their pockets. The march was quickly resumed, the immediate objective being Appomattox Courthouse, where more supplies were ordered to be ready for the retreating army.

But again the pursuing Northern troops were on their heels. Four miles west of Farmville Lee put his small army in defensive line of battle, sending the trains on ahead. As the leading elements of the Army of the Potomac deployed for battle, he quickly withdrew, leaving only a small force to continue to delay the Union advance. One can only wonder at and admire the calm efficiency with which Lee continued to conduct the operation, despite the crushing disasters of the previous week.

But there was comparable skill and efficiency in the Union movements. Sheridan, fully understanding the significance of Grant's strategy, realized that Appomattox was Lee's objective and determined to arrive before the Southerners. Both forces marched as fast as the exhausted condition of the men would permit. Sheridan's cavalrymen arrived at Appomattox Station late on the eighth, just as Lee's advanced guard approached Appomattox Courthouse, two miles to the northeast. At the station the Union troopers seized four trainloads of supplies sent there from Lynchburg for Lee.

As his army collected near Appomattox Courthouse that night, Lee realized that the end was near. Under a flag of truce, Grant had sent him a message on the seventh, pointing out "the hopelessness of further resistance," and urging him to surrender to avoid "further effusion of blood." Lee had replied that same day that he did not consider the situation hopeless, but that he would like to know what Grant's terms would be if he were to consider surrender. Grant had responded on the eighth that he would be satisfied if the surrendering army were disqualified from "taking up arms against the Government of the United States until properly exchanged." Lee, still playing for time, had in turn suggested a meeting on the ninth for the purpose of discussing peace between the respective nations.

Regardless of the response Grant might make to this suggestion, Lee determined that evening that he would make one more effort. The Union troops at Appomattox Station had been identified as Sheridan's cavalry. Lee was certain that no Union infantry could possibly have yet arrived that far west. Fitzhugh Lee's cavalry and Gordon's infantry were ordered to attack at dawn. If they were able to push Sheridan aside, Lee would still try to reach Danville, via Lynchburg. He told both Fitzhugh Lee and Gordon, however, that they were to break off the engagement if Federal infantry were encountered in any force. With the Union II and VI Corps pressing close behind him, the Confederate commander knew that in such case he would have to surrender.

Gordon and Fitzhugh Lee attacked as ordered, early on the ninth. The dismounted Union troopers to their front fought stubbornly, but lacked the staying power necessary to halt the combined infantry-cavalry drive of the veterans of the Army of Northern Virginia. Then, as they appeared to be on the point of breaking through, the Southeners made a chilling discovery: masses of blue-clad infantry were deploying over the rolling fields east of Appomattox Station. Fitzhugh Lee and Gordon halted their troops and reported the situation to Lee.

The newcomers were the XXIV Corps of Ord's Army of the James—closely followed by the V Corps. They had marched all night, save for a three-hour rest after midnight, but now all thought of exhaustion was forgotten by the eager troops. This, they knew, was the end.

Ord, urged on by the exuberant Sheridan, ordered a counterattack. But just as the Federal troops began to move forward, a

Southern officer rode up under a white flag, requesting a cessation of hostilities until General Lee could meet with General Grant and confer on terms.

For Grant and Lee had exchanged two more messages that morning. Grant, properly refusing Lee's earlier suggestion for a mid-morning meeting to discuss peace terms, since this was a Government matter beyond his authority, again urged Lee to surrender. Lee, of course, now that Union infantry had been discovered to his front, had no recourse but to request an interview to discuss specific terms. When his messenger could not find Grant immediately, Lee had sent flags of truce to both Sheridan and Meade requesting a suspension of hostilities pending the expected negotiations.

During the tense lull, youthful, vainglorious cavalry division commander Custer, also under a flag of truce, came galloping into the Confederate lines to demand boorishly of Gordon and Longstreet in turn an "immediate and unconditional surrender." Treated with cold disdain by Gordon, the brash young Union general was then shaken by Longstreet's contemptuous tongue-lashing at this "violation of the decencies of military procedure." Custer took himself off; it is doubtful if he ever forgot this public humiliation for the remaining eleven years of his life.

Grant, who had been riding across country to join Sheridan, hurried to the front as soon as he received Lee's message. Early that afternoon the two great leaders met at the house of Mr. Wilmer McLean, at Appomattox Courthouse. Dignified Lee, wearing his best uniform and a dress sword, gave no evidence of his inner thoughts. Grant, calm as usual, but anxious to spare the feelings of his illustrious foe, apologized for his appearance in mud-stained field attire, then led the conversation to earlier, happier days in the "old" Army.

Then, after Lee politely reminded him of the purpose of the meeting, Grant wrote out the surrender terms: All officers and men of the Army of Northern Virginia were to give their paroles not to fight again until properly exchanged, and would be allowed to return home undisturbed, so long as they kept their parole; all weapons and army property were to be turned over to the Union, but officers could keep their side arms, private baggage and horses.

Lee, obviously touched by the generosity of these terms, said: "This will have a very happy effect upon my army." After a pause, he mentioned to Grant that the enlisted cavalry and artillery soldiers also owned their own horses. Grant promptly replied that he believed this would be the last battle of the war, and though he did not change the written terms, said he would give instructions that "all the men who claim to own a horse or mule [could] take the animals home with them to work their little farms."

For the second time Lee displayed his feelings. "This will have the best possible effect upon the men," he replied gratefully. "It will be very gratifying and will do much toward conciliating our people." Grant's terms for the surrender, and Lee's letter of acceptance, were then copied by staff officers and signed by the generals. After some more polite conversation, Lee left, exchanging salutes with Grant as he rode off to the sad, bitter task of telling his loyal men that the war was ended for the Army of Northern Virginia. At about this time Union quartermasters, at Grant's direction, began moving welcome wagon-loads of rations into the famished Confederate lines.

Three days later the Army marched out of its cantonments to lay down its arms. Drawn up to receive it were two brigades of the Army of the Potomac, commanded by Brigadier General Joshua L. Chamberlain. The Stars and Stripes waved on the right of the Federal line; beside it the flag of the 1st Division of the V Corps.

At the head of the Confederate column plodding through the mud—the incessant rains of the last few days had stopped, but the terrain was still abominably mired—rode John B. Gordon, in command of the II Corps. Behind him marched the Stonewall Brigade, followed by the remainder of the proud Army; their ranks so thin and few that the succession of regimental battle flags gave the appearance of being massed.

The Southern column lapped the flank of the Federal troops. A single Union bugle blared an order. Dejected Gordon raised his head on hearing the familiar slap and rattle as the blue-coated regiments shifted their arms to the marching salute. His back straightened, his saber came up and then down in smart precision. As Chamberlain's blade flickered to return the salute, Gordon's voice rang down his own ranks.

"Carry arms!"

Bent heads lifted, sloping muskets snapped from straightened shoulders to the marching salute. And thus the Army of Northern Virginia passed, in silence broken only by the splat-splat-splat of marching feet in mud.

". . . Not a sound of trumpet more, nor roll of drum," wrote Chamberlain later; "not a cheer nor word nor whisper of vain-glorying . . . but an awed silence rather, and breathtaking, as if it were the passing of the dead."

The column wheeled into successive lines, halted, and arms were stacked. Upon the muskets the color sergeants laid for the last time their tenderly rolled battle flags. Then, like mourners hurrying half-dazed from the grave, the men of the Army of Northern Virginia marched away. Their last parade had ended.

Officially, of course, Lee's surrender affected only the forces of his army present for duty at Appomattox—28,356 officers and men. The practical effect, however, was to serve as a signal of the war's end to all other Confederate troops still under arms. The formalities of negotiation and surrender were punctiliously observed by both sides.

On April 5, Grant had sent a message to Sherman, informing him of Lee's apparent intention to make for Danville, and directing him to push against Johnston. Sherman had complied promptly. Starting his advance on the tenth, he received word of Lee's surrender on the twelfth. Johnston had also received this word, on the thirteenth, and wrote a message to Sherman—who had occupied Raleigh that day—requesting a truce with a view to negotiating surrender or peace terms.

Sherman agreed, and the two old antagonists met on the seventeenth. Just before the meeting Sherman had learned of the assassination of President Lincoln on the fourteenth. Johnston was also shocked at the news, which perhaps engendered in both of them an undue eagerness to hasten peace throughout the land. Quite unwisely, they broadened their negotiations to include the other armies of the Confederacy still in the field, as well as broad and lenient terms for a convention which both sincere generals hoped would become the basis for peace throughout the South.

The armistice and convention, signed April 18, were summarily rejected by the Federal Government. Secretary of War Stanton, embittered by the assassination of the President, practically accused Sherman of treason, and ordered Grant to take over personal command of Sherman's armies. Grant, refusing to do this, soon calmed ruffled feelings. He went personally to Raleigh to help his old friend offer new terms to Johnston, identical to those accepted by Lee. Johnston, naturally, accepted and surrendered for a second time on the twenty-sixth. There were 37,047 men in the Confederate army surrendered at Greensboro. An additional 8,000 had left the ranks since the earlier armistice of the eighteenth.

Further south and west, General Richard Taylor on May 4 surrendered all remaining forces in Mississippi and Alabama to General Canby. West of the Mississippi, Kirby Smith surrendered on May 26. President Davis had already been captured by Wilson's men at Irwinsville, Georgia, just north of the Florida border, on May 10. On the twenty-ninth, President Andrew Johnson issued a proclamation of amnesty to all persons who had taken part in the rebellion, save for senior civilian and military officials of the Confederacy.

The Civil War had officially ended.

# Envoi

**O**ne of the most remarkable things about the Civil War is the suddenness with which the hostilities ceased. There had only been six weeks between Lee's surrender and President Johnson's proclamation ending the war. Northern military leaders, familiar with the usual course of civil strife in European history, had expected that irreconcilable Confederate officers would lead their men into mountains or wilderness, and continue guerrilla resistance indefinitely. Sherman, in fact, at the time his liberal surrender terms to Johnston were disapproved, wrote bitterly: "Now . . . instead of dealing with six or seven States, we will have to deal with numberless bands of desperadoes, headed by such men as Mosby, Forrest . . . and others, who know not and care not for danger and its consequences."

The extent to which Sherman misjudged some of his former enemies can best be estimated from Forrest's farewell circular to his men, issued on May 9, 1865. In part it read as follows:

Soldiers: . . . The cause for which you have so long and manfully struggled, and for which you have braved dangers, endured privations and sufferings, and made so many sacrifices, is today hopeless. . . . Reason dictates and humanity demands that no more blood be shed. . . . It is your duty and mine to lay down our arms, submit to the "powers that be," and to aid in restoring peace and establishing law and order throughout the land. The terms upon which you were surrendered . . . manifest a spirit of magnamity and liberality on the part of the Federal authorities which should be met on our part by a faithful compliance with all the stipulations and conditions therein expressed. . . .

Civil War, such as you have just passed through, naturally engenders feelings of animosity, hatred, and revenge. It is our duty to divest ourselves of all such feelings, and, so far as it is in our power to do so, to cultivate friendly feelings towards those with whom we have so long contested and heretofore so widely but honestly differed . . . You have been good soldiers, you can be good citizens. Obey the laws, preserve your honor, and the government to which you have surrendered can afford to be and will be magnamimous.

These, apparently, were the sentiments of most leading Confederates. A few, like cavalryman Jo Shelby, preferred to escape to neutral countries rather than to surrender. But when, shortly after Johnston's surrender, President Davis suggested to a small group of officers that continued resistance was possible, they respectfully, sadly—and firmly—disagreed.

It is perhaps unrealistic to suggest that the bitter years of Reconstruction, and its lingering aftermath, could have been avoided if soldiers rather than politicians had made the arrangements for readmittance of the Southern states to the Union. But the evidence indicates that the men of war, who had so bitterly opposed one another in deadly combat, had gained a better understanding of peace and justice than had more sheltered politicians.

Be that as it may, the mutual respect displayed for each other by the soldiers of both sides at the close of the war is an impressive tribute to American fighting men, and has become a treasured American military tradition.

Ulysses S. Grant, in 1868, accepting the nomination for the Presidency, spoke for both the Blue and the Gray, and indeed for all time, when he uttered the valedictory of the Civil War:

"Let us have peace."

# Appendix:
# Arms and Uniforms

## SMALL ARMS

In composite, the basic infantry firearm of both sides was a muzzle-loader weighing, with its bayonet, about ten pounds. It fired a lead bullet which weighed approximately one ounce, and whose effectiveness in aimed fire was limited to about 100 yards, although in theory its extreme range might be up to 1,000 yards were it fired from a rifled musket, and half that distance from a smooth-bore.

This bullet, which mushroomed on impact, inflicted atrocious wounds; in particular, its bone-shattering effect usually made amputation of an injured member essential if life were to be saved. As a variant to the single bullet, what was known as the "buck and ball" load was also used in smooth-bores; one bullet and three buckshot—a lethal charge at short ranges. The ammunition was made up in paper cartridges. To load, the soldier first bit off the end of the cartridge, then poured the powder down the muzzle of his piece. The bullet was then inserted and rammed home. With the flint-lock, a sprinkle of powder was first put in the pan; with the percussion lock, a fulminite of mercury cap was placed on the nipple.

When the war began in 1861 some 500,000 firearms lay in government storage. Of these, 35,000 were the Springfield rifle musket, Model 1855, caliber .58, using the famous Minié conical bullet. The remainder of the arms consisted in the main of older Springfields, Model 1842, caliber .69, altered from flint to percussion locks. There were also some so-called "Yager" or "Mississippi" rifles, caliber .54 (relics of the Mexican War and frontier days), as well as antique flint locks. Around 135,000 of these arms, mostly of the older types, were stored in arsenals in Southern states and fell into Confederate hands immediately.

This initial supply of small arms was, of course, too small for the needs of either side. Accordingly, both at once sought the foreign market. Until private firms here and the one remaining government factory—the Springfield Arsenal—could go into full production of the .58 caliber Springfield, the North purchased abroad thousands of more or less obsolete and generally unsatisfactory weapons. The South, which possessed neither munitions nor arms manufactories, purchased at the onset a relatively small quantity of British Enfield muskets, caliber .577—quite similar to the newer Springfield. Later, the Tredeger Iron Works at Richmond became the Southland's principal ordnance factory; its meager equipment was gotten from the machinery captured at Harper's Ferry when that Federal arsenal fell into Confederate hands.

The Union cavalry was armed in the beginning with a Sharps single-shot breech-loading carbine, caliber .52. But, by 1864, it was equipped with the Spencer seven-shot repeating carbine, caliber .52 (its rim-fire metal cartridges fed through a tube in the butt). The resulting volume of fire gave birth to the bitter Southern quip that the Union cavalry "loaded up in the morning and fired all day." The Southern cavalry was at first equipped with a heterogeneous collection of shot-guns, sporting rifles and such other firearms as could be collected or captured. The saber, considered to be an essential cavalry weapon, was in theory normal equipment for both sides, but in fact was in very short supply in the South. On both sides, revolvers were carried by officers, and by cavalrymen; weapons not uncommon during that period. Most of these were Colts; either the so-called ''Army'' .44 or the ''Navy'' .36. A quantity of Remington .44's was also in use.

To put it briefly, more different kinds of firearms were used than in any other conflict in history. The Union Army recognized by 1863 seventy-nine different models of rifles and muskets, twenty-three types of carbines and musketoons and nineteen models of pistols and revolvers. The Confederacy recognized about as many—some of them quite different from the Federal equipment.

# ARTILLERY

Northern field artillery consisted mostly of bronze Napoleons (smooth-bore 12-pounders) and the much superior Parrott cast-iron 3-inch (10-pounder) rifle; both of them muzzle-loading. The Parrott gun became the standard field artillery piece of the Union forces as the war progressed. There was also a sprinkling of heavier guns, the Parrott 4.2-inch (30-pounder) predominating.

Most Confederate field artillery pieces were of earlier models; smooth-bore 6-pounder guns and 12-pounder howitzers. Much Union artillery matériel was captured by the South during the first two years of war, and a small quantity of medium and heavy British ordnance—Whitworth, Armstrong and Blakely rifles—was procured from abroad. However, nothing like the homogeneity of the Union artillery matériel could ever be attained; to the end, the Southern artillery, well-served as it was, was a hodge-podge of guns and horowitzers of varying calibers. To procure ammunition for this conglomeration became a nightmare both for gunners and ordnance officers.

For siege artillery, and in the defense of permanent fortifications, the Union forces used cannon ranging from old-fashioned 24-pounders to 15-inch Columbiads, as well as 12-inch rifles and 15-inch mortars; muzzle-loaders all. Probably the largest piece of ordnance used by either side was the huge Federal mortar "Dictator," which took part in the siege of Petersburg. Weighing 17,120 pounds, it was transported on a railway truck. It threw a 220-pound, 13-inch caliber shell for over two and one-half miles. Confederate heavy artillery consisted of pieces seized or captured in Federal installations, and ranged from 24-pounder smooth-bores to 11-inch rifled Dahlgren naval guns.

Naval artillery on the Northern side was composed of 24-pounder smooth-bores mounted in some of the older Federal vessels, and the much more powerful and—for those days—modern, Dahlgren 9- and 11-inch rifled guns. The Confederate raiders constructed abroad mounted British naval ordnance; other Southern vessels were fitted out with a conglomeration of matériel captured in Federal installations.

Ordnance supply and maintenance was not difficult for the Union insofar as artillery and gunpowder were concerned. Factories and skilled personnel to operate them existed. In addition to the Springfield Government arsenal in Massachusetts, the West Point Foundry at Cold Spring, New York—a private firm, turned out prodigious quantities of cannon. The long-established Du Pont Powder Works became the principal purveyor of gunpowder and high explosives.

The problem was much more difficult in the South, handicapped by the lack of skilled munitions workers and the dearth of raw material. However, by dint of much ingenuity, arsenals, foundries and munitions plants were set up, in addition to the existing Tredeger Iron Works. These other principal installations were at Charleston, Selma and Fayetteville. A powder manufactory was established at Augusta. By importation of skilled technicians from British establishments the growth and output of these munitions plants were considerably accelerated.

The professional military influence, on both sides, in this production phase is interesting. In the North were West Pointers Robert P. Parrott, inventor and producer of the Parrott gun at Cold Spring; Thomas J. Rodman, inventor of the Rodman gun and of improved gunpowder manufacture, who commanded the Watertown Arsenal; and the Navy's John A. Dahlgren, inventor of the gun bearing his name. The patriarch of the Du Pont clan—powder manufacturers since pre-Revolutionary days—was West Pointer Henry Du Pont. Down South the key men were West Pointers Joseph R. Anderson, who had for twenty years headed the Tredeger Iron Works; Josiah Gorgas, the Confederate Army's chief of ordnance; and George W. Rains, who built and operated the Augusta powder plant. (This Rains should not be confused with Gabriel J. Rains, the submarine mine and booby-trap man.)

# UNIFORMS

Officially, the Union uniform color was blue and that of the Confederacy gray. But the expression "Blue and Gray" is somewhat of a misnomer. In the beginning the citizen soldiery of both North and South went to war clad in a multiplicity of finery the like of which was never seen before or since. The three-month militia of the North came down to Washington in a kaleidoscopic color scheme. The "silk-stocking" 7th (National Guards) and the 8th (Washington Grays) New York, as well as the 2d Wisconsin, wore West Point gray. The 39th New York arrived all plumed in Italian *bersaglieri* uniform, and was complete with *vivandieres*—ladies perhaps no better than they should have been; this outfit called itself the Garibaldi Guards. Kilt and sporran marked the 79th (Highlanders) New York.

The following first wave of Volunteers was equally garish in appearance. Showiest of all were the zouaves, apeing the French units of that name who had recently won fame in North Africa. Red fezzes; short, embroidered blue jackets; baggy red trousers and white gaiters dazzled the eye, as did the mincing little double-time step and fancy manual of arms, when the "zouzous" from New York, Brooklyn, Chicago and other localities came to town.

The Regulars, of course, wore Army blue, as did the majority of later Volunteer units. Some of them put on extra frills. For instance, the 2d, 6th and 7th Wisconsin and 19th Indiana Volunteers, who would soon win the name of the "Iron Brigade," had doffed their regulation kepis (forage caps) for broad-brimmed black felt hats, and they wore white gaiters.

South of the Potomac, this brave and fantastic array had its counterpart. The 1st (Tigers) and 7th (Pelicans) Louisiana were zouaves, too. And the Richmond Grays, the Richmond Light Infantry Blues, the Charleston Light Infantry, all hotsy-totsy socialites in the volunteer militia, were among the scores of gaudy-uniformed citizen-soldier outfits who rallied to the Stars and Bars. Their finery made sharp counterpoint to the more prosaic butternut gray in which the Confederacy garbed most of its original volunteers.

But after the war got well started, and all the freshness and innocence and all the valor of ignorance had begun to wash off, away went most of the fancy uniforms on both sides. Away, too, insofar as the Federal soldier was concerned, went all the excess paraphernalia a loving government continued to press upon him to clutter up his movement—overcoat, knapsack and other geegaws. A simple dark blue blouse—shell-jacket for the mounted man—and light blue trousers stuffed into his heavy gray socks were his outer garments. The gray shirt and the blouse above it were open at the neck. On his head was either the bell-crowned forage cap, or a broad-brimmed black felt hat; Western troops favored the hat.

The soldier's hand weapon, canteen and cartridge-box were essentials. One blanket or his overcoat—whichever he had not thrown away—was rolled in a rubber blanket and slung over his shoulder. In the roll, or in his pockets, or in the haversack he sometimes wore, were a change of socks and underwear and—perhaps—part of his current ration. (It was much easier usually to eat the entire ration at once rather than to lug it along.)

Far different was the lot of the Confederate soldier when the tinsel had rubbed off, the finery thrown away, and his impecunious War Department just couldn't provide uniform clothing or even full rations. Actually, the average Confederate soldier was lucky to have garments of any sort—regardless of color—to cover his nakedness; he was doubly fortunate if he possessed a good pair of shoes to keep his feet off the ground. Not infrequently, he wore the uniform and equipment of his Federal opponent, complete to the last detail of insignia and official ''U.S.'' cachet. When he did so, it was proudly and unashamedly. These were spoils of war, captured in battle, and he had no compunctions about doffing his rags in exchange. Not without reason did the Confederates, for instance, dub Union General Banks ''Mr. Commissary Banks,'' because of the quantities of uniforms, arms and rations captured from Banks' troops.

# Selected
# Bibliography

Alexander, E. P., *Military Memoirs of a Confederate*. New York: Scribner, 1907.

Ammen, D., *The Navy in the Civil War—The Atlantic Coast*. New York: Scribner, 1883.

*Army Lineage Book—The Infantry*. Department of the Army, Washington: Government Printing Office, 1953.

Ballard, Colin R., *The Military Genius of Abraham Lincoln*. London: Milford, 1926.

*Battles and Leaders of the Civil War*, 2 vols. New York: The Century Co., 1887.

Birkhimer, William E., *Historical Sketch of the Organization, Administration, Matériel and Tactics of the Artillery, United States Army*. Washington: Chapman, 1884.

Catton, Bruce, *Glory Road*. New York: Doubleday, 1952.

———, *A Stillness at Appomattox*. New York: Doubleday, 1954.

———, *Mr. Lincoln's Army*. New York: Doubleday, 1949.

———, *This Hallowed Ground*. New York: Doubleday, 1956.

Commager, Henry S., *The Blue and the Gray*, 2 vols. Indianapolis: Bobbs-Merrill, 1950.

Dana, Charles A., *Recollections of the Civil War*. New York: Appleton, 1899.

Davis, Jefferson, *The Rise and Fall of the Confederate Government*, 2 vols. New York: Yoseloff, 1958. New edition of work originally published by Appleton, New York, 1881.

Downey, Fairfax, *The Guns at Gettysburg*. New York: David McKay, 1958.

Dupuy, R. Ernest, *Compact History of the United States Army*. New York: Hawthorn, 1956.

————, *Men of West Point*. New York: Sloane, 1951.

———— and Trevor N. Dupuy, *Military Heritage of America*. New York: McGraw-Hill, 1956.

———— and ————, *Brave Men and Great Captains*. New York: Harper, 1959.

Esposito, Vincent J., *Atlas to Accompany Steele's American Campaigns*. Dept. of Military Art and Engineering, West Point: U.S. Military Academy, 1953.

Freeman, Douglas S., *Lee's Lieutenants—A Study in Command*, 3 vols. New York: Scribner's, 1942–1944.

————, *R. E. Lee, A Biography*, 4 vols. New York: Scribner, 1934–37.

Fuller, Claude E., *The Rifled Musket*. Harrisburg: Stackpole, 1958.

Fuller, J. F. C., *The Generalship of Ulysses S. Grant*. New York: Dodd, Mead, 1929.

————, *Grant and Lee, A Study in Personality and Generalship*. London: Eyre & Spottiswoode, 1933.

————, *Decisive Battles of the U.S.A.* New York: Dodd, Mead, 1942.

Furnas, J. C., ''Patrolling the Middle Passage,'' *American Heritage*, October, 1958.

Ganoe, William A., *History of the United States Army*. New York: Appleton-Century-Crofts, 1942.

Grant, Ulysses S., *Personal Memoirs of U.S. Grant*. New York: Century, 1895.

Henderson, G. F. R., *Stonewall Jackson*. London: Longmans (Various editions since 1890).

———, *The Civil War, A Soldier's View* (ed. by Ed. J. Luvaas), Chicago, 1958.

Humphreys, Andrew A., *The Virginia Campaigns of '64 and '65*. New York: Scribner, 1937.

Johnston, J. E., *Narrative of Military Operations*. New York: Appleton, 1874.

Knox, Dudley W., *A History of the United States Navy*. New York: Putnam, 1936.

Leech, Margaret, *Reveile In Washington, 1860–1865*. New York: Harper, 1941.

Lewis, Berkley R., *Notes on Ammunition of the American Civil War*. American Ordnance Association, Washington, 1959.

Lewis, Lloyd, *Sherman—Fighting Prophet*. New York: Harcourt, Brace, 1932.

Livermore, Thomas L., *Numbers and Losses in the Civil War in America, 1861–1865*. Bloomington: Indiana University Press, 1957. (First published in 1900.)

Mahan, Alfred Thayer, *The Navy in the Civil War—The Gulf and Inland Waters*. New York: Scribner, 1883.

McCartney, Clarence E., *Mr. Lincoln's Admirals*. New York: Funk & Wagnalls, 1956.

Miers, Earl S., *The Web of Victory*. New York: Knopf, 1955.

Milton, George Fort, *Abraham Lincoln and the Fifth Column*. New York: Vanguard, 1942.

Peterson, Harold L., *Notes on Ordnance of the American Civil War*. American Ordnance Association, Washington, 1959.

Phisterer, Frederick, *Statistical Record of the Armies of the United States*. New York: Scribner, 1883.

Robinson, William M., *The Confederate Privateers*. New Haven: Yale University Press, 1928.

Ropes, John Codman, and William R. Livermore, *The Story of the Civil War*, 4 vols. New York: Putnam, 1894–1913.

Scharf, J. T., *History of the Confederate Navy*. New York: Rogers & Sherwood, 1887.

Sheridan, Philip H., *Personal Memoirs of P. H. Sheridan*, 2 vols. New York: Webster, 1888.

Sherman, W. T., *Personal Memoirs of Gen. W. T. Sherman*, 2 vols. New York: Appleton, 1875.

Smith, Gustavus W., *Confederate War Papers*. New York: Atlantic Publishing & Engraving Co., 1884.

Soley, J. R., *The Navy in the Civil War—The Blockade and the Cruisers*. New York: Scribner, 1883.

Spaulding, Oliver L., *The United States Army in War and Peace*. New York: Putnam, 1937.

Steele, Matthew F., *American Campaigns*. Government Printing Office, Washington, 1901. Several subsequent editions by Infantry Journal and Combat Forces Press.

Upton, Emory, *Military Policy of the United States*. Washington: Government Printing Office, 1904.

*War of the Rebellion; Official Records of the Union and Confederate Armies*. (130 vols. with Atlas). Washington: Government Printing Office, 1882–1900.

*War of the Rebellion; Official Records of the Union and Confederate Navies*, 30 vols. Washington: Government Printing Office, 1894–1922.

West, Richard S., Jr., *Mr. Lincoln's Navy*. New York: Longmans, Green, 1957.

Williams, Kenneth P., *Lincoln Finds a General*, 4 vols. New York: Macmillan, 1949–1956.

Williams, T. Harry, *Lincoln and His Generals*. New York: Knopf, 1952.

Wood, W. Birbeck, and J. E. Edmonds, *A History of the Civil War in the United States, 1861–1865*. New York: Putnam, 1905.

Wyeth, John A., *That Devil Forrest*. New York: Harper, 1959. Reprint of work originally published in 1899.

# Index